JOHN PAUL II AND WORLD POLITICS:
Twenty Years of Search for a New Approach
1978-1998

Canon Law Monograph Series is an international series of monographs dealing with canon law in the largest sense. It offers a forum for recognized scholars to present the fruits of their research to an international audience. The volumes selected for publication in the series are expected to express some of today's reflection on canon law, on church law and on church and state relationships.

Series Editor: Prof. dr. R. Torfs, Faculty of Canon Law, Katholieke Universiteit Leuven.

Address of the Publisher:
PEETERS
Bondgenotenlaan 153
B-3000 Leuven
BELGIUM

Address of the Series Editor:
Prof. dr. R. Torfs
Katholieke Universiteit Leuven
Faculty of Canon Law
Tiensestraat 41
B-3000 Leuven
BELGIUM
email: <Fac.Canon@law.kuleuven.ac.be>

JOHN PAUL II AND WORLD POLITICS
Twenty Years of Search for a New Approach
1978-1998

UGO COLOMBO SACCO

PEETERS
1999

Cover illustration: Algemeen Rijksarchief, Brussel. Allegorie van het kerkelijk recht, uit het Liber Privilegiorum (ca. 1450), Brussel, Algemeen Rijksarchief, Fonds Oude Universiteit Leuven, n. 3, Fol. 2r.

© 1999, Peeters, Bondgenotenlaan 153, B-3000 Leuven (Belgium)

ISBN 90-429-0684-7
D. 1998/0602/302

CONTENTS

FOREWORD

Lately much has been written on the social doctrine of the Catholic Church, in particular on the social doctrine of the popes, beginning with Leo XIII's famous encyclical letter *Rerum novarum*. There have also been many monographic studies on different aspects of the Church's social doctrine of the popes. Ugo Colombo Sacco in his **John Paul II and World Politics: Twenty Years of Search for a New Approach** gives us a systematic view of the social doctrine of the Church on World Politics.

Ugo Colombo Sacco has very good credentials for such a research. He is a diplomat who closely observes the guiding principles and the fundamental ideas which animate world politics. He began his career in the Italian Foreign Service in 1981, being posted in various embassies, serving in international organizations and holding different responsabilities at Farnesina, the Italian Foreign Office. In 1997, Colombo Sacco was a lecturer on "The Initiatives of the Holy See for the Progressive Development of International Law", by the Faculty of Law, International Law Institute, University of Milano, Italy. Last year, he gave a further set of lectures on "The Involvement of the Papal See in International Affairs", by the Faculty of Canon Law, Catholic University of Leuven.

The author shows the evolution of the Holy See's approach in international politics from a *closed* approach in which theory and activity were mainly directed towards the defense of the rights of the Catholic Church to an *open* one in which its goal is the promotion and the setting up of a worldwide civilization of human rights, the rights of each individual human person from conception to natural death and the rights also of peoples and nations to their freedom and identity. There is also in the Church's social doctrine a clear transition from a defensive attitude, which viewed with suspicion if not with hostility the secularized and in general non-catholic world, to a positive attitude of dialogue and collaboration with all institutions, organizations, religions and individuals in order to build up a new world political order based on the defense of the dignity of the human person and promotion of human rights, on subsidiarity and solidarity.

The author explains briefly the historical background of this epochal transition and describes at length the thinking and the activities of John Paul II.

We might say that John Paul II's social doctrine is based on a prophetic humanism. The Pope evidently sees himself and the Church as missioned and committed to be the advocate of authentic humanity. He is conscious of speaking to a world that is in the throes of a crisis -a crisis of dehumanization. Like a prophet he is not afraid to come out in the defense of the human dignity of every man and woman. The central and unifying task of John Paul II is to rediscover and promote this inviolable dignity in its personal, communal, social, cultural, economic and political aspects.

We owe the author a deep sense of gratitude for giving us an organic and synthetic view of John Paul II's thought and action and we hope and wish that his study will be of great help in the building of a new international order.

Giuseppe PITTAU, S.J.

PREFACE

The English edition of this book is published at a time when its author, the diplomat, Mr. Ugo Colombo Sacco, resides in Brussels.

Brussels is not only the capital city of Belgium, it is also the capital of the European Union and, in that regard, it can be considered a symbol of the ongoing internationalisation of politics, war and peace, human rights but also of life as a whole, with the little things making it either beautiful or burdensome. This evolution is clearly visible at many places and in many fields, for instance, among scholars dealing with the legal relationships between Church and State. The creation of the European Consortium for Church and State Research, with its headquarters in Milan, in 1989, is testimony to the growing need for a truly international approach to formerly rather nationally-oriented problems.

This trend towards more international contacts and an often more global approach should not be perceived as a direct way to grey uniformity, to a society without thoroughly loved local character, without specific flavour. Yet the intervention of the Holy See in international politics has led to some common achievements: the common element *par excellence* then cannot be situated either in the content of ideas or in the way they are still given shape but in the absolute necessity of quality which indeed is always required, whatever local customs or traditions are cherished, kept alive or stimulated.

Pope John Paul II gives an excellent example of such an international quality-oriented approach, which, nonetheless, never abandons local characteristics: no heartless internationalism in the Roman approach.

In the meantime, John Paul II remains one of the only powerful voices in the world able to challenge in a credible way the complete and ultimate victory of free market economics over all other philosophical, political and economic systems.

While John Paul II shows that even in our profit-oriented society one can be both intelligent and sensitive at the same time, he goes slightly against trends which implicitly dominate our society, where the sensible and the sensitive tend to be conflicting notions. He also can be described as being very up-to-date and accurate in his style of communication. His message is well elaborated and duly formulated. And it goes hand in hand with the personal, concrete steps undertaken by the pope in international politics.

In other words, the style of communication stimulates a very valuable but, then again, quite demanding approach of international political and ethical standards, and it offers more than the unbearable consolation of some distant utopia far away in the darkness of the night.

To that extent, the book that Mr. Colombo Sacco has written with so much care offers us hope in many regards. Firstly, it makes the ideas of John Paul II on world politics available to many readers in a concise way. Secondly, it illustrates that the internationalisation of politics does not go hand in hand with a loss of identity for a people. On the contrary, internationally recognised quality standards help precisely to safeguard that identity. Thirdly, the book demonstrates that controversial ideas can be successful when they are communicated in a credible way. Fourthly, a publication like this reassures people: there is not a direct link between intelligence and the search for profit and financial benefits. Another way is possible when one can be both sensitive and sensible. And finally, ideas are more than just ideas. By writing this book Mr. Colombo Sacco, himself a diplomat, already offers an important contribution towards the practical application of the ideas and practices of John Paul II.

Rik Torfs
Dean
Faculty of Canon Law
Katholieke Universiteit Leuven

INTRODUCTION

The transformation in the twentieth century of the Holy See's views towards the international sociopolitical world has been broad. Its main stages have been the promotion, by the Second Vatican Council, of dialogue with the secularized contemporary age, and the powerful resumption, by John Paul II, of the project of re-Christianizing society, the State, and the international community.

The full reinsertion of the Holy See in important international affairs can be ascribed to Pope John XXIII. From the second half of 1961 on, his pastoral inspiration became increasingly focused on international issues. The Berlin crisis and, the following year, the Cuba crisis led the Papal See to express its opinions to all people without regard to religious faith; this change was noticed by Khrushchev himself. Significantly, the papal radio message of 11 September 1962 mentioned the Second Vatican Council as a contribution towards "healing the scars of the two world wars". The main symbol of this change was the audience granted on 7 March 1963 to *Izvestia* editor Alexis Adzubei and his wife Rada, who was Khrushchev's daughter.

The formal completion of the process of internationalizing the Vatican's presence, started by John XXIII, took place on 4 October 1965 with Paul VI's visit to the United Nations.

It marked the decline of a period in which the pastoral universalistic propensity was identified – if not in theory, at least in practice – with Western culture, with which the history of the Church had always been closely connected. The Papal See was opening up to welcome all that was good outside its original traditional sphere, to gradually take on worldwide responsibilities for justice and peace among nations.

The appointment on 16 October 1978 of John Paul II, the first non-Italian Pope in more than five hundred years, spurred a significant process of internationalization within the Church's central government and of full use of the international legal means available to the Papal See: the number of papal nunciatures increased from 89 to more than 140; about fifteen concordats and agreements were entered into; papal peace missions were sent to different countries.

Beyond reactivating the traditional forms of international activity carried out by the Holy See, the Pope – through his (presently about 200) trips abroad and a careful use of the mass media – started the transformation of Peter's successor into a universal public figure committed to a "new evangelization" whose contents include promoting the adoption of Christian ethical paradigms in the relations among states.

After the collapse of Communism, the international activity of John Paul II started a new page in the history of the Papacy, one that gives clear preference to the poor countries of the world and that has increased the gap between the stance of the Holy See and that of the remaining world power on many points relating to justice and peace among the peoples of the earth.

Another important change has been the energy with which John Paul II has worked to have the Catholic Church take the lead in inter-faith cooperation for the settling of international disputes. Hence the unprecedented presence, in this century, of the religious factor in the relations among states.

But the development at the base of the renewed international involvement of the Holy See is the special faith and impetus which John Paul II has given to the elaboration of pontifical teaching in the political, economic, and social fields. In his encyclicals and in the New Catholic Catechism, the present Pope has determinedly updated the *Social Doctrine of the Church*, anchoring it in, and making it a constituent part of, Christian theology, and shifting its emphasis from the deductive to the inductive method. At the same time, he has realistically expressed awareness that the Church's social message "will find its credibility more in the proof of works than in its internal consistency and logic" (see, among other things, the encyclical *Centesimus Annus*).

The *Social Doctrine of the Church* (which was elaborated in 1891 in the encyclical *Rerum Novarum* by Leo XIII) had progressively run aground – thus contributing to the concomitant success of materialist ideologies – on the difficulty of establishing universal ethical guidelines that were capable of becoming part of contemporary secularized reality, but that at the same time retained their transcendent character.

The collapse of socialist anthropology and the disappointments caused to the lay world by the economic view of progress, were taken by John Paul II as a sign of the times that strengthened in him the awareness that the Church, as repository of the ultimate truth, can and should make efforts to elaborate teachings capable of ethically guiding and orienting international political action in order to achieve a world fit for human beings.

The present study aims to analyze in detail the nature of the teachings of the Holy See regarding international affairs and its future prospects, and the ways in which those teachings have evolved during the present papacy.

---

* Statements of fact and opinion appearing in the study are the exclusive responsibility of the author and do not express any official position.

1. THE DIRECT PREDECESSORS
(PIUS XII, JOHN XXIII, PAUL VI, JOHN PAUL I)

Pius XII

Born in Rome in 1876, Eugenio Pacelli was appointed Pope in 1939 with the name Pius XII[1], and held office until 1958. During his papacy, the following events occurred: the worst war in world history, the first stage of the Cold War, the short-lived thaw of 1953–1956, and the Suez crisis.

The Pope's experience in diplomatic issues was certainly excellent. Pacelli entered the Vatican Secretariat of State when he was only 25, early in a century when the Pope's diplomatic representations in the world were still few: Austria, France, Portugal, and Spain (first-class nunciatures); Bavaria and Belgium (second-class nunciatures); Argentina, Brazil and the Netherlands (internuncio offices); Colombia, Peru and Santo Domingo (apostolic delegations). During his ascent, which reached its peak in 1930 when he became Secretary of State, Pacelli witnessed significant developments: the intensification of the Holy See's activity in Latin America; the action of Pope Benedict XV[2] for peace during World War I; the elaboration of new guidelines for diplomatic behavior, which had been made necessary by the dissolution of the Austro-Hungarian empire and by the Russian revolution; the signature of the Lateran Pacts with Italy on 11 February 1929.

When he became Pope, he distinguished his pastoral mission internationally both through initiatives to restore peace in the world and through the total condemnation of communism as a materialistic and atheistic doctrine.

Another important decision, which highlighted for the world the universal character of the Church, was to increase the number of foreign cardinals in the Sacred College[3], including some coming from Eastern

---

[1] N. Padellaro, *Pio XII*, Rome, 1949; C. Patelli, *Pio XII*, Bologna, 1949; D. Tardini, *Pio XII*, Rome, 1960; I. Giordani, *Pio XII: Un grande Papa*, Turin, 1961; M. Olmi, *Pio XII*, Milan, 1983; R. Serrou, *Pie XII, le pape-roi*, Paris, 1992; A. Spinosa, *Pio XII: L'ultimo Papa*, Milan, 1992.

[2] G. Goyau, *Papauté et chrétienté sous Benoit XV*, Paris, 1922; G. B. Migliori, *Benedetto XV*, Milan, 1932; W. H. Peters, *The Life of Benedict XV*, Milwaukee, 1959.

[3] The Sacred College has been the entity responsible for appointing Popes since 1176.

Europe: 37 non-Italian cardinals compared with 18 Italian cardinals. In 1943 Pius XII expressed tolerance for non-Catholic Christians[4], and this also was interpreted as a positive sign of openness. Another relevant step was the replacement of colonial bishops with native church officials. At the same time, diplomatic relations were established with some countries that were entering the international community: Lebanon, Egypt, India, Indonesia, the Philippines, Pakistan, Iran, Syria, Ethiopia.

However, despite the above-mentioned developments, at the end of Pius XII's papacy, the internal life of the Church and its relations with the outside world entered a critical stage. The main reason for it was the enduring withdrawal of the Church in voluntary isolation from contemporary society, which had evolved, from the nineteenth century on, according to cultural forms alien to Catholicism[5]. The serious reduction in the Christian presence on the planet was fingered as a foreseeable consequence of this isolation.

John XXIII

In 1958 Angelo Roncalli succeeded Pope Pacelli with the name of John XXIII[6]. It was the name of an antipope, Baldassarre Cossa, who had been deposed by the Council of Constance of 1415. The assumption was made that, in choosing to succeed John XXII (Jacques Deuze, Avignonese Pope from 1316 to 1334), Roncalli wanted to indicate that the ghosts of the Church's past should not hinder its progress[7].

Born at Sotto il Monte (near Bergamo) in 1881, he had been ordained priest in 1904.

After his experience as a military chaplain during World War I, he had carried out a very intense diplomatic activity: Apostolic Visitor in

---

[4] In the encyclical letter *Mystici Corporis*.

[5] L. Salvatorelli, *Chiesa e Stato dalla Rivoluzione francese ad oggi*, Florence, 1955; E. Jarry and F. Pierini, *La Chiesa e le rivoluzioni dei secoli XIX-XX*. Catania, 1968; S. Tramontin, *La Chiesa nel mondo moderno*, Turin, 1979; N. Bobbio, *Profilo ideologico del Novecento italiano*, Turin, 1986; G. Verucci, *La Chiesa nella società contemporanea: Dal primo dopoguerra al Concilio Vaticano II*, Rome-Bari, 1988.

[6] X. Rynne, *La révolution de Jean XXIII*, Paris, 1963; E. Y. Hales, *La rivoluzione di papa Giovanni*, Milan, 1968; G. Zizola, *L'utopia di papa Giovanni*, Assisi, 1973; P. Johnson, *Pope John XXIII*, London, 1975; P. Hebblethwaite, *John XXIII Pope of the Council*, London, 1984; G. Verucci, *La Chiesa nella società contemporanea: Dal primo dopoguerra al Concilio Vaticano II*, Rome-Bari, 1988; A. Riccardi, "Da Giovanni XXIII a Paolo VI", *Chiesa e Papato nel mondo contemporaneo*, Rome-Bari, 1990.

[7] Jean D'Hospital, "Jean XXIII: le pape du concile", *Le Monde* (June, 5th 1963).

Bulgaria in the 1920s; Apostolic Delegate in Turkey and Greece in the following decade; Apostolic Nuncio in France (1944–1953); Vatican Observer at UNESCO (1946–1953).

He was then appointed cardinal and patriarch of Venice and became Pope at the age of 77, holding office until June 1963.

It was a short papacy during which international peace was often seriously endangered; the main events were: the Cuban missile crisis, the building of the Berlin wall, and the Sino-Soviet split.

John XXIII considered it his pastoral duty to indicate the only realistic way out from the crisis afflicting the Church: to end its withdrawal from the rest of the world by opening up to non-believers and to positive relations with even the communist world.

Once the objective had been identified, it was necessary to provide the tools to achieve it. The Pope believed that a consultation extending to the whole Church hierarchy could be helpful; therefore, on 25 January 1959 he announced the future convening of the Second Vatican Council (the twenty-first Ecumenical Council of the Roman Catholic Church)[8], which he himself described as a contribution towards healing the scars of the two world wars[9].

Pius XII had already outlined the idea of convening an Ecumenical Council[10], but had set the project aside, probably fearing that it could trigger, within the Church and its relations with the world, a change that would be too quick and therefore uncontrollable, that would seriously jeopardize the unity of the faithful.

The reasons advanced by John XXIII for this convocation represented an innovation with respect to the tradition of the previous Councils, which were mainly the result of disciplinary needs within the Church, or of the condemnation of heretical movements[11].

Roncalli followed very carefully the evolution of the international situation during his short but very intense papacy. His personal initiatives

---

[8] The Council began its work on 11 October 1962.

[9] R. Laurentin, *Bilancio del Concilio*, Milan, 1968; Y.-M. Congar, *Diario del Concilio*, Turin, 1964; E. Schillebeeckx, *La Chiesa, l'uomo moderno e il Vaticano II*, Rome, 1966; H. Fesquet, *Diario del Concilio. Tutto il Concilio giorno per giorno*, Milan, 1966.

[10] Caprile, G. "Pio XII e un nuovo progetto di concilio ecumenico", in the journal *La Civiltà Cattolica*, Rome, 1966.

[11] As an example, it is sufficient to recall that the First Vatican Council, which was convened by Pius IX in 1869, though actually dominated by the issue of papal infallibility, was apparently conceived also as a means to further develop the condemnation of a long series of contemporary opinions associated with rationalism, liberalism, and materialism.

were many, sometimes daring, and were a counterpoint to the main international events of the time.

John XXIII's innovative thinking on international issues was first significantly expressed in the encyclical *Mater et Magistra* of 15 May 1961, which highlighted the central problem of underdevelopment in many former colonial countries and invited industrialized countries to act in order to help poor countries to overcome their problems, while at the same time respecting their independence.

After the building of the Berlin wall and the U.S. announcement that nuclear tests would be resumed, in September of the same year John XXIII made a plea for peace to Christians and non-believers against the use of nuclear weapons. In November, Russian Prime Minister Khrushchev sent, for the first time ever, a message of good wishes to the Pope for his birthday.

Almost one year later, John XXIII made an urgent plea for peace, trying to limit the serious repercussions of the American announcement regarding Soviet activity in Cuba for the deployment of missiles capable of reaching U.S. territory.

The year 1963 began with the end of the Cuban crisis and the expression of Soviet willingness to accept three inspections per year in order to halt nuclear tests.

The Pope began a significant new page by welcoming, in March, *Izvestia* editor Alexis Adzubei, accompanied by his wife Rada, Khrushchev's daughter.

On 5 April, the "hot line" between Moscow and Washington was set up.

With the encyclical *Pacem in Terris* – issued on 11 April 1963, less than two months before his death – Roncalli pointed out to the world the two main conclusions of his pastoral thinking: that the error should never be confused with the person who makes it; and that false philosophical doctrines should never be considered to be at the same level as historical movements which, even if inspired by them, try to improve the economic, social, cultural and political situation of human beings. In fact, while said doctrines crystallize into unchangeable principles, movements evolve and can express reasonable demands consistent with justice and truth.

The statements of the Pope, widely publicized by the media, gave the world the image of a Holy See which, by putting itself at the service of international peace and justice, had positioned itself as a neutral party vis-à-vis the East-West blocs.

Before passing away, John XXIII wrote in his diary the following enlightening words that explain the new meaning he wanted to give to papal actions: "Now more than ever, and surely more than in past centuries, we want to serve man as such and not only Catholics; we want to protect, first of all, human rights – and not only those of the Catholic Church. Present circumstances, the needs that emerged in the last 50 years, a deeper doctrinal analysis confronted us with new realities … It is not the Gospel that is changing: we are starting to understand it better …[12]"

Paul VI

Giovanni Battista Montini, who took on the name Paul VI[13], succeeded Roncalli and held office until 1978. He was the first Pope since the seventeenth century to take the name of St. Paul, the Apostle of the Gentiles who set for himself the main task of expanding the boundaries of the Church, while also respecting local differences[14]. His papacy was faced, at the international level, with a series of complex and important international developments: the resumption of the Vietnam war in 1964; the Soviet intervention in Prague in 1968 and the nuclear weapon non-proliferation treaty signed in that same year by the U.S. and the USSR; the Russian-Chinese clashes along the Ussuri river; the Six-Day War and the Yom Kippur War; the Chinese-American reconciliation; the signing of the SALT agreements in 1973 and the beginning of the big oil crisis that same year; the fall of Saigon in 1975; the solemn confirmation of the European territorial status quo on the occasion of the Helsinki Conference.

Born in 1897 and ordained priest in 1920, for about 30 years he worked within the Vatican State Secretariat, with a brief parenthesis at the Nunciature in Poland, and from 1937 to 1954 he was Under-Secretary of State for Internal Affairs. He became Archbishop of Milan, where he stood out for his open attitude towards social reforms, and became cardinal in 1958.

---

[12] L. Capovilla, *Giovanni XXIII: Quindici letture*, Rome, 1970.

[13] A. Santamaria, *Un papa riformista e conservatore*, Rome, 1967; C. Falconi, *La svolta di Paolo VI*, Rome, 1968; J. T. Andrews, ed., *Paul VI: Critical Appraisals*, New York, 1970; G. Verucci, Ibid.; A. Riccardi, Ibid.; P. Fantò, *Una diplomazia per la Chiesa nel mondo*, Rome, 1990.

[14] H. Fesquet, "Paul VI: réforme et transition", in the French newspaper *Le Monde* (August, 8th 1978).

Paul VI also believed it necessary to uphold the principle of opening the Church to the contemporary world. However, from the beginning of his papacy, he tried to prevent this opening from jeopardizing
the innermost nature of the Church, as it had evolved over the centuries. Therefore, he carefully stressed that the reform requested by the
Council could neither have as its object the essential conception of the
Church or its basic structures (reducing their size and scope to their
initial minimal proportions), nor could it result in a profane view of
life[15].

At the beginning of Paul VI's papacy the Second Vatican Council
resumed its work.

Before lowering the drawbridge to the contemporary world, as
John XXIII wished, it significantly devoted its activities to reforming the
internal life of the Church.

The main result of the work was a new self-awareness of the Church,
conceived[16] as the People of God[17], imbued with the breath of life coming from Christ; as a means of salvation, performing an evangelizing
mission; and, finally, as a hierarchically organized society.

In this view, the laity acquired a new role. It became "the common
priesthood of the faithful", next to the traditional "ministerial or
hierarchical priesthood" of the clergy. In other words, the aspects of
spiritual communion became predominant over the legal-hierarchical
ones, which had characterized the previous representation of the
Church.

The Council then moved to reform the Church's relations with the
outside world[18].

The Council Fathers arrived at the conclusion that the Church had
to be present in the community of peoples. To this end, the Church was
encouraged to reorganize itself so that it could fulfill its current duties of
searching for and achieving the common good. In this framework, the
hope was stressed that an international legal-political system would be
set up which could effectively protect human rights.

The strong interest by the Council in international problems was also
reflected in the expression of the desire that a universal Church organism be created to encourage the Catholic community to promote the

---

[15] Encyclical letter *Ecclesiam Suam*, August 1964.
[16] Council dogmatic constitution *Lumen Gentium*.
[17] Or "Mystical Body of Christ".
[18] Pastoral constitution *Gaudium et Spes*.

development of poor regions and social justice among nations. To this end, Paul VI set up the papal commission *Iustitia et Pax*.[19]

When dealing with the dependence of the underdeveloped countries on the rich ones, the Council highlighted the need for justice and dialogue, but seemed to partially tone down the plea by John XXIII for the Church to be first of all the Church of the poor[20].

Similarly, the Council Fathers expressed themselves less strongly than John XXIII's encyclical letters on problems of peace and war[21]. Perhaps also because of the new climate of international détente within which the Council's labors took place, the stockpiling of any sort of new scientific weapons for deterrence purposes was no longer explicitly condemned, but it was stressed that their use might cause huge and indiscriminate destruction "that, therefore, would exceed the limits of legitimate defense"; in such a case, it would represent "a crime against God and mankind". Likewise, they did not restate the ban on nuclear weapons or the overcoming of the "just war", both included in John XXIII's encyclical letter *Pacem in Terris*. Lastly, other problems, like the independence wars of colonial countries, were not discussed.

In his final Council speech[22], Paul VI affirmed that the Council had raised again the theocentric and theological notion of man and universe, stressing the need for the Church to "know, approach, understand, serve, evangelize the surrounding society and to grasp it, almost chase it in its quick and continuing change".

The period of youth protests of the '60s posed a new challenge to the Church. The student protests, which infiltrated even some of the institutions of Catholic universities, helped to spur anxiety and heated debate within different ecclesiastical minority groups. By appealing to the new Council position of opening up the Church to the world, these groups preached a Christianity that was mainly understood as a social and human experience. In their praxis, the transcendent link between man and God seemed to have a secondary position. Some sectors even supported the Church's urgent adoption of a democratic method of government.

---

[19] It was experimentally created through the motu proprio *Catholicam Christi Ecclesiam* of 6 January 1967. The pope himself reorganized it in a stable and definitive way through the motu proprio *Iustitiam et Pacem* of 10 December 1976.

[20] See the previously cited constitution *Gaudium et Spes*.

[21] Ibid.

[22] December, 7th 1965.

The Pope warned[23] that the "teaching of the Council" should not be isolated "from the Church's doctrinal heritage", and that it was necessary "to clearly understand how that teaching fits and is consistent with it and how it provides testimony, development, explanation, application to that heritage. Then, the legislative doctrinal 'innovations' of the Council also appear in their correct dimension".

For the post-Council period, Paul VI pointed to the task of "knowing, studying, applying" the Council documents. Replying to those who questioned his authority as heir of the Prince of the Apostles, Paul VI further explained that the collegiality among the Churches which emerged from the Council better highlighted the Pope's arbitration and his mediator role.

In 1967 Paul VI focused on the problem of cooperation among populations and the aid to the poorest.[24]

The promotion of development, from not only an economic but also an ethical-cultural viewpoint, was indicated as the way to protect peace in the world. Denouncing the negative aspects of neocolonialism and a certain type of colonialism, and the serious economic imbalances within the international community, Paul VI declared the right of newly independent populations to be free from hunger, disease, and illiteracy. Solidarity and justice were identified as a specific duty of rich peoples, who were to give up part of their wealth to meet the needs of underdeveloped countries. As a contribution toward rectifying international economic injustices, Montini also pressed for the establishment of a world fund, whose financial resources were to be deducted from portions of military expenses.

To build international justice, he pointed out to particular peoples the path of urgent reforms, avoiding both total collectivization and extreme forms of liberal and free-trade economics.

Violent and revolutionary methods were, however, firmly declared to be unlawful.

The above-mentioned guidelines suitably reflected the new ethical aspirations of the international community. Very significantly, they were largely confirmed – except for the more specifically religious components – by subsequent papers by the United Nations relating to: the international strategy for the second decade of development activities (1970), the establishment of a new international economic order, and the statement of economic rights and duties of states (1974).

---

[23] January, 2nd 1966.
[24] Encyclical letter *Populorum Progressio.*

The deep interest Paul VI expressed in important issues of contemporary world life affected also the activities of the bishops' regional Conferences, especially those in the third world, which began to elaborate a uniform position of the church on international issues in their respective geographical areas.

From this viewpoint, the most important were: the Medellín Latin-American Episcopal Conference (1968), the Pan-African Symposium of Bishops (1969), and the Conference of Asian Bishops (1970).

On the occasion of the 1969 Synod, the bishops from underdeveloped countries made a key contribution to the successful containment of those groups which denied the supremacy of the pontifical teaching.

They feared, in fact, that reducing the Pope's authority would mean placing the poor churches under the control of the rich ones.

The Synod was a milestone also for another reason: it marked the beginning of the decline of the Western church leadership, which had started the council reforms, in favor of the church of the Earth's South, which was more active in reforming the Church's relations with the outside world.

To achieve the greatest possible dissemination of the Christian ethical message, Paul VI had a happy intuition: to begin a series of personal trips abroad. It was a courageous and new idea: the most recent trips of a Pope outside Rome dated back to the forced exile of Pius VII in France and Pius VI's trip to Austria in 1782!

The means of putting this idea into practice was daring too: Paul VI, in fact, broke with the tradition of following etiquette adopted by the Popes of the Papal States. In his trips he followed a style which highlighted above all the pastoral character of his visits, without denying the "sovereignty" of the pontiff.

The first foreign destination was Palestine. The Pope showed, thus, to the world his desire to strengthen ties among the religions of the Bible, with the further aim of carrying out joint action to promote international peace and justice. The subsequent destinations were: the Holy Places and India in 1964; the United Nations in New York in 1965; Colombia in 1968; Uganda in 1969; Australia and the Philippines in 1970.

In particular, the speech the Pope gave to the General Assembly of the United Nations aroused worldwide interest. On that occasion, he started a new page in the history of Vatican diplomacy. Addressing the representatives of all peoples, including those belonging to other religions and to Marxist political beliefs, Paul VI declared that his authority in the field of international ethical behavior derived from the historical "experience of mankind" of his Church, and that it was the expression of a constant concern for the problems of the world.

In order to achieve a more pervasive international dissemination of the positions of the Holy See, the Pope decided to strengthen the institutional structures of the Vatican's diplomacy: the Papal Representations[25].

Montini had already expressed his opinion on the Holy See's diplomacy in 1951, when he stated that "...if civil diplomacy aims at the unification of the world and the supremacy of reason over force, and at the increase in the welfare of individual countries within the harmony of an ever wider international organization, it finds in the church diplomacy a kind of summit it can gainfully look at, not so much for the ability church diplomacy can display or for the results it can achieve – they might both fail – but rather for the ideal order it springs from and gets inspiration from, the universal brotherhood of men".

Paul VI aimed at clearing up all the doubts that had been raised, even from church sources, as to the maintenance of Papal Representations in contemporary times. These opinions held that papal diplomacy seemed to be a system of supports that made the good of the Church dependent on having ties with powers that had become secular, alien to, and sometimes enemies of the Church. They also pointed out the risk of showing to the world a Church organized in a similar way as the political powers. In reference to the rejection by the Council of such extremist theses, Montini stated that papal representatives were a necessary means of hierarchical communion and unity with local churches. In order to strengthen the role of the papal representative as collaborator of the Pope in solving serious problems relating to peace, justice, development, and the fulfillment of mankind's great hopes, Paul VI affirmed that this convergence of State and Church was based on the fact that both institutions – while being perfect, autonomous, and independent societies – were at the service of man, who was their common subject. From this observation Montini drew the conclusion that it was necessary to have a dialogue in order to understand each other, to cooperate, to avoid disagreements, and to contribute jointly to peace and progress. According to Paul VI, the understanding between Church and State should translate into a balanced realization of the following objectives: to guarantee

[25] Apostolic epistle issued motu proprio *Sollicitudo Omnium Ecclesiarum* (January, 24th 1969).

the freedom of the Church (to preach the faith; to teach its *social doctrine*; to carry out its mission among men without any obstacle; to issue its moral judgment on the activities of individuals and society, and on political activity, in order to promote fundamental human rights and the salvation of souls); to reassure the State as to the peaceful and useful purposes of the Church, which aims at promoting justice and love in the relations among nations and within them; to provide the support of spiritual energies to the authorities of the State, so they can work for the common good of society.

Consistent with this approach, Montini's papacy decided to intensify the presence of the Holy See in multilateral diplomacy. Permanent missions were opened in New York (1964) and Geneva (1967), and the decision was made to have a full-fledged participation in the Helsinki Conference for peace and security in Europe.

In the same vein, the Pope decided to increase the bilateral diplomatic relations of the Holy See, establishing them with many Muslim countries and countries with a substantial Muslim component, thus clearly highlighting the willingness to have a dialogue with the non-Catholic world. Among those countries were: Iraq (1966), Cameroon (1966), Uganda (1966), Central African Republic (1967), Gabon (1967), Kuwait (1968), Ivory Coast (1970), Benin (1971), Niger (1971), Algeria (1972), Tunisia (1972), Bangladesh (1973), Upper Volta (1973), Ghana (1975), Nigeria (1975), Morocco (1976). Over the same period the Apostolic See laid the groundwork for diplomatic relations with Buddhist countries such as Thailand and Sri Lanka, which were later established. Finally, communication channels were developed with the USSR and with Central and Eastern European countries (among other things, the Pope met four times with Soviet Foreign Minister Andrei Gromyko), searching for – as Cardinal Villot succinctly put it – a *"modus non moriendi"* rather than a *"modus vivendi"*: as a result, the *Churches of silence* in the Iron Curtain countries experienced an easing of pressure by local authorities, and those governments became more aware of the considerable commitment of the post-Council Catholic Church to defending peace in the most troubled areas of the Earth.

Paul VI also paid attention to a series of interconnected issues (coordinating the Churches' aid to the poorest populations; looking for a better allocation of resources and means of action in favor of development; achieving maximum efficiency in rescue operations in cases of disaster) that led the Holy See to undertake independent concrete action in favor of the underdeveloped world. For this purpose he set up the Pontifical Council *Cor Unum* (15 July 1971).

However, ten years after the conclusion of the Council, Paul VI noticed the internal divisions that had appeared within the Church in the post-Council phase, which had started a period of inquiry and strong questioning among different currents of ecclesiastic thinking. Knowing that the unity of the Church could be achieved through a new reaching out to the world, the Pope reaffirmed, in *Evangelii Nuntiandi*, the supremacy of evangelization throughout the Church, presenting it as a peaceful contribution to the liberation of mankind. This pastoral option, which adopted a strongly religious perspective, pushed to the background the "political" commitment of the Church and the Catholic *social doctrine* itself. The Church presented itself more as an evangelist, expert in mankind, rather than as a ruler of society.

In August 1978, at the end of Montini's papacy, the prestige of papal diplomacy was well highlighted by the 87 accredited diplomatic missions to the Holy See.

John Paul I

Paul VI's successor, Albino Luciani (whose papacy lasted only 33 days), chose the name of John Paul I, an unprecedented double name in the history of the papacy, which was a clear sign of his will to enhance and deepen the heritage of John XXIII and Paul VI. In his first meeting with the Diplomatic Corps (31 August 1978), after explaining, along the lines followed by Paul VI, the aims of the Holy See's participation in the international activities of governments and international organizations, and after stressing the pastoral aspect of such participation, he ended his speech with a sentence that made a strong impression on the attending observers: "Your countries are trying to build a modern society with often ingenious and generous efforts that receive our sympathy and encouragement as long as they comply with the moral laws written by the Creator in the hearts of men." After its re-entry into the world and the renewal of its international prestige, the Church felt it could frankly assert its ethical authority both in the field of international relations and within states.

2. THE INTERNATIONAL PRESENCE
OF JOHN PAUL II

The Pope from the East

In October 1978, for the first time after five centuries of Italian Popes[1], a foreigner coming from Poland, the most Catholic country of the so-called second world[2], was appointed Sovereign Pontiff.

Karol Wojtyla had carried out his pastoral activity mainly in his home country.

He was born in Wadowice, in Krakow province, on 18 May 1920, and had been ordained in 1946. After studying theology in Rome and at Krakow University he had been assigned the Chair of Ethics at Lublin University. After being consecrated bishop, he carried out his pastoral function in Krakow and went to Rome to participate in the whole cycle of works of the Second Vatican Council, where he contributed to the drafting of the Dogmatic Constitution *Gaudium et Spes* relating to the renewal of relations among the Church, the contemporary world, and the international community. In 1964 he became Archbishop; three years later he was appointed Cardinal.

Thus, the new Pope's religious vision had matured in a local Church which had built its authority and prestige on the uncompromising defense of the rights and needs of believers vis-à-vis civil authorities. The reasons for the proud activism of the Polish clergy were briefly illustrated by Wojtyla in the following statement made on 18 October 1977: "History and culture in Poland were born with Christianity. It is thanks to this that we have a national character. By protecting this heritage, which enabled us to survive, we maintain our national identity and our trust in the future."

In the previous twenty years the habit had spread to call the Eastern Catholic communities "the Churches of silence", to emphasize their oppression and isolation by communist regimes. The news that Wojtyla

---

[1] The last foreign pope had been Adriano Florensz, born in Utrecht, who ruled from 31 August 1522 to 14 September 1523 with the name Adriano VI.

[2] Kloczowski, ed., *Storia del Cristianesimo in Polonia*, Bologna, 1980; B. Cywinski, *Il secolo della difficile prova: Storia contemporanea della Chiesa nell'Europa centro-orientale*, Bologna, 1983; J. Życinski, "L'Eglise de Pologne: point de vue d'un évêque", in the journal *Etudes*, Paris (October 1994).

had been appointed Pope was broadcast without any comment by the Polish television at the opening of the evening news[3], in contrast with the very wide echo of the media in all of the non-communist world, and it meant for those communities the prospect of regaining a voice and rekindling the hope of gradually gaining more breathing room within their respective societies.

At the level of international relations, the mere presence in Rome, capital of Christianity, of a Polish Pope undermined the cold division between the two blocs, putting in question the way East and West looked at each other, which was based on the logic of power and Manicheism.

Faced with the novelty of a Pope from the East, eloquently expressed by the astonishment of the crowd in St. Peter's Square and by the feeble applause out of politeness with which it welcomed the announcement, some media expressed the opinion – later belied by the facts – that, by choosing Karol Wojtyla, the Church wanted to sacrifice its responsibilities towards the third world in favor of the problem of relations with communism.

On 20 October 1978, the diplomatic corps accredited to the Holy See went with great interest to the Vatican to hear the message with which the Pope from the East would express his thoughts on the Church's future actions within the community of states.

John Paul II said that the history of his home country had taught him to respect the specific values and traditions of each nation as well as each nation's rights among other peoples. The constant expression of this attitude would be a guiding principle of his papacy, where all populations would receive the same concern, with special attention to those who "know affliction", that is – as attending diplomats interpreted this sentence – to the Eastern European and the poorest countries of the world.

The Pope also explained that the network of diplomatic relations that would be developed and interwoven by the Holy See would not necessarily express approval for this or that political regime, but rather the will to sustain a dialogue, together with concrete help to human causes and a specific contribution to justice and peace at the level of relations among peoples.

---

[3] The entire investiture ceremony of the new pope was broadcast live by the Polish TV. After initial indecision, local authorities were, in fact, forced to yield to popular enthusiasm.

John Paul II closed his speech by emphasizing that this activism did not imply that the Holy See would abandon its pastoral role: preparing human beings for eternal salvation remained its main duty, but in its activities it could not neglect in any way the concrete good and progress of the peoples on this earth. From this perspective, the Apostolic See committed itself to collaborate in the teaching of moral meaning, through the action of Christians and "men of good will".

Following the example set in 1965 by Paul VI, Karol Wojtyla visited the UN General Assembly less than one year after being appointed, as if to prove his strong interest in the life of the international community.

John Paul II's speech focused on the priority protection of human rights: even in a situation of domestic and international peace – the Pope said – their violation represents a form of war against man. Another guiding principle of the Holy See's future diplomatic action was, thereby, announced to the world.

The debut of John Paul II on the international scene, because of the novelty of a strong Pope from the East and the worldwide scope of his vision of human and state problems, drew considerable attention from the media.

The judgments on the new Pope expressed by the most famous journalists of the time, basically coincided in crediting him with a Messianic and charismatic dimension.

In fact, as time went by, Karol Wojtyla was called: the bearer of a message which goes beyond religion; the leader of a moral crusade against any repression of religious and political freedoms; the symbol of a Church which is less involved in Italian domestic problems and less linked to the traditional schemes of the Curia, and hence able to play a stronger role for the protection of peace and human rights; the beginning of a process of making the Church less provincial.

There were also, however, editorials in which the fear re-emerged that the cardinals, by appointing a Polish Pope, had made a leap in the dark, running the risk of unleashing human, political, and religious forces they did not control.

The Itinerant Papacy

In the past 20 years, John Paul II has applied very intensely Montini's belief in the usefulness of a direct physical presence of the Sovereign Pontiff abroad. In fact, he has visited so far almost 200 countries and some of the most important international organizations[4]. Wojtyla can be said to have actually transformed the papacy into a semi-itinerant institution, marking his pontificate with a will for a universal presence.

It has been a gradual process. In the first years, in fact, commentators still believed they could read, between the lines, travel priorities connected to deadlines of the Church's internal life (such as, for instance, participation in regional episcopal conferences) and to visiting countries whose population was mainly catholic. Later it became clear that, along with these trips, there was an increasing number of others which aimed at starting exploratory dialogues to be extended to the whole planet[5].

The analysis of the speeches given abroad by John Paul II makes it possible to identify some evolutionary threads with respect to his predecessors' thinking. Among them is the strikingly rare use of the word "State". In fact, Karol Wojtyla places the relations between the Church and the International Community in a dimension which goes beyond the traditional institutions of power, namely the states, to aim directly at a dialogue with peoples, nations, and individuals. In this framework, the Pope considers the role of lay diplomacy more in terms of representation of peoples than of government administration[6].

John Paul II constantly stresses that the transcendent dimension linking man to God requires the international community to shape its life according to binding ethical rules. Only in this way, the Pope maintains, is it possible to preserve the peaceful and just coexistence of the peoples of the earth and, ultimately, the dignity of man, who was created by God in His own image.

The teachings of the Holy Father aimed at making the evangelical message part of international reality have become, as Poulat has maintained, a means of thinking about political matters in a religious way in order to make religious matters politically valid.

John Paul II has explained articulately his ideas on the motivations and purposes of the Church's missionary mandate within the relations among peoples[7].

The Pope's analysis starts from a twofold observation. Firstly, in the last twenty-five years the populations who don't know Christ and the

---

[4] UN, UNESCO, FAO, the European Courts in Strasbourg, etc.

[5] A. C. de Montclos, *Les voyages de Jean-Paul II: Dimensions sociales et politiques*, Paris, 1989.

[6] This notion emerged, among other things, in the speech the Pope addressed to the seven new Ambassadors accredited to the Holy See on 25 March 1995. In this speech the Pope dwelt upon the ultimate purposes of diplomatic activity.

[7] Encyclical letter *Redemptoris Missio*, 1991.

Gospel have numerically doubled[8], and they are increasing despite the fact that the Church has now been established in all continents and that the majority of believers live in extra-European areas. Secondly, in both the ancient and the recent Christian populations, there are groups of baptized people who have lost their faith[9].

John Paul II believes that the situation described above requires a renewed apostolate action whose paradigm goes back to the proselytizing activity of primitive Christianity. In this respect, Karol Wojtyla reminds us that the Apostle Paul, once in Athens, goes to the Areopagus – which represented the center of culture of the Athenian people, and "can be considered today as a symbol of the new milieus were the Gospel has to be preached" – where he announces the word of God using a suitable and comprehensible language in that milieu. "Among the modern Areopagi", the Pope says, "there is that of international relations", where the Church has to be attentively involved[10].

With the above-mentioned observations John Paul II has widened the contents of Montini's intuition according to which the best reply to the divisions within Christianity is a firm and strong re-launching of evangelization[11]. In Karol Wojtyla's opinion, the Holy See has to have a persevering voice within the international community so that the peoples of the world may achieve a solidarity which translates at the moral level into an increased interdependence among states, and so that world leaders promote a development which effectively preserves the dignity and progress of the individual.

The Affirmation of an International Social Doctrine

Another important programmatic thread in the present pontificate is the re-proposing of the doctrinal qualification of the Church's teaching

---

[8] For a brief analysis of the Pope's ideas on the position of those who, guiltlessly, do not know Christianity, see John Paul II, "Salvation for those who do not visibly belong to the Church", catechesis at the General Audience of 31 May 1995.

[9] To refer to the activity required to face the problems posed by these people, the phrase *"new evangelization"* was coined.

[10] See: the speech given by the Pope on 9 January 1995 to the Diplomatic Corps accredited to the Holy See, a speech that dealt with the importance of the Church in the community of nations; and the catechesis to the General Audience of 21 June 1995 on the issue of the mission of the Church in relation to the world, where Karol Wojtyla clarifies that it is not possible, in any case, to ask the Church to allow its resources to be either exclusively or primarily absorbed by the mundane world.

[11] For a significant reflection on the times and moments for evangelization, see: John Paul II, "The Mystery of Evangelization", catechesis at the General Audience of 26 April 1995.

as it regards not only the internal social life of different peoples but also their mutual relations within the international community[12, 13].

John Paul II, who taught Church social doctrine in Krakow, indicated this orientation early on in his pontificate, on the occasion of his trip to Mexico in 1979. In the last twenty years he has strengthened it by fostering wide consultations within the Church. The lay world has also been actively involved in them, in order to study the new international situations and thus to arrive at an ethical-religious interpretation which can provide doctrinal guidance to Catholics, to members of other religions, and to "men of good will".

It is a significant development. In fact, the expression "social doctrine of the Church" had basically disappeared from the lexicon of the Second Vatican Council Fathers[14] because of the doubts as to its validity at an historical moment when the Church was committing itself to opening up a dialogue with the contemporary world. A clear echo of it can be perceived in re-reading the following reflections by Paul VI: "Faced with situations so multifaceted, it is difficult for Us to express one single opinion and propose universally valid solutions. On the other hand, that is not Our desire, nor Our task. It is up to Christian communities ... to discern ... what options and commitments to undertake"[15].

John Paul II has maintained, instead, that the challenge regarding the possibility of a social doctrine of the Church, extended also to the complex issues of relations among peoples, can and should be accepted.

Some lay commentators wondered whether this expresses the desire to re-introduce a more clerical conception of international social organization. Because of their insistent frequency, the repeated warnings by the Pope against religious totalitarianisms of any kind make this doubt appear tendentious and misleading.

John Paul II has concretely set forth the doctrinal guidelines of his pontificate for international society through the publication of three

---

[12] A. F. Utz, *La doctrine sociale de l'Eglise à travers les siècles*, Paris-Basel-Rome, 1970; Roger Heckel, "L'emploi de l'expression 'Doctrine sociale de l'Eglise'", leaflet no. 1 of "*L'enseignement social de Jean Paul II*", Commission Pontificale "Iustitia et Pax", 1981; "La dottrina sociale della Chiesa oggi", editorial in the journal *La Civiltà Cattolica*, Rome,1988.

[13] 21

[14] It was reintroduced only in the pastoral constitution *Gaudium et Spes*, after a specific intervention of the Council Secretariat.

[15] Apostolic epistle *Octogesima Adveniens*.

encyclical letters: *Labor Excercens* (14 September 1981)[16]; *Sollicitudo Rei Socialis* (30 December 1987)[17]; *Centesimus Annus* (1 May 1991)[18].

The first one deals with the complex subject of labor, analyzing it not only as a domestic problem for individual populations but also within the wider framework of international relations. The analysis the Pope carried out is rich in content, as it does not confine itself to discussing economic aspects but extends also to political and cultural aspects, which are increasingly topical today.

The second updates the teachings of Paul VI pertaining to the promotion of development, placing them in the perspective of the inter-dependence of all states. It is a considerable step forward in the social doctrine of the Church: to the notion of development, in fact, are attributed complex social, cultural, moral, and spiritual meanings based on the present interrelation of the various peoples worldwide. The Encyclical passes a severe judgment on the list of international priorities of rich countries, which it qualifies as basically incorrect. In reminding readers that the Church desires to be the means of unity for the whole of mankind, Karol Wojtyla also indicated some particular approaches for substantial reforms of the international, commercial, monetary, and financial systems, and firmly stressed the need to offer poor countries the capacity for self-development[19].

The third, which some people called the "post-communism encyclical", is the first apostolic text that deals with the international framework as it emerged after the end of the confrontation of the two blocs, and it tries to identify new exigencies and desirable orientations. A kind of rec-onciliation of the Church with the Western world emerges from this encyclical: in fact, John Paul II does not condemn capitalism but only its misuse, and he considers it legitimate if it adopts humane features, serving the cause of both ethical and material world development.

---

[16] "Scoprire i nuovi significati del lavoro umano: L'enciclica sociale di Giovanni Paolo II", editorial in the journal *La Civiltà Cattolica*, Rome, 1981.

[17] "La Chiesa e il problema dello sviluppo: Dalla Populorum progressio alla Sollici-tudo rei socialis", editorial in the journal *La Civiltà Cattolica*, Rome, 1988.

[18] "La Centesimus annus, attualizzazione della Rerum Novarum", editorial in the journal *La Civiltà Cattolica*, Rome,1991.

[19] P. Laurent, "Per un'etica dei mercati finanziari", in the journal *La Civiltà Cattolica*, Rome, 1991; W. Kessler, "Les riches deviennent de plus en plus riches... Des rideaux de fer à l'Etat social international ou la recherche d'un ordre économique mondial plus juste", in the journal *Concilium*, 1992; "Dalla parte dei poveri e degli oppressi – La pre-senza della Chiesa nel mondo di oggi", editorial in the journal *La Civiltà Cattolica*, Rome, 1992.

In the encyclical, Karol Wojtyla interprets the struggle which led to the famous changes in 1989 as "a warning to those who, in the name of political realism, want to ban law and morals from the political arena". The Holy Father says he feels spurred, by the revolutionary impact of this bloodless struggle, to intensify his activity to disseminate as widely as possible ethical paradigms in the economic, political, and cultural relations among states.

During his pontificate, Karol Wojtyla repeatedly has dwelt upon the nature and purposes of the social doctrine of the Church. The latter, in the Pope's own effective words, "is not a 'third way' between laissez-faire capitalism and Marxist collectivism, nor a possible alternative to other less radically conflicting solutions: ... it represents a category in its own right. It is not even an ideology, but the accurate expression of careful thinking about complex realities of human existence, in society and in the international framework, in the light of faith and ecclesiastic tradition. Its main aim is to interpret these situations ... in order to guide ... Christian behavior. It, therefore, belongs ... to the field ... of moral theology. The teaching and dissemination of social doctrine are part of the Church's evangelizing mission ...Denouncing evils and injustices ... also is part of carrying out the ministry of evangelization in the social field. But it should be made clear that preaching is always more important than denouncing, and the latter cannot do without the former, which gives it the true solidity and the strength of the highest motivation"[20]. "Today more than ever the Church is aware that its social message will become credible through the testimony of works, more than through its internal consistency and logic ... the practical and, in a certain sense, experimental dimension of this doctrine should be remembered"[21]. In the effort to identify the solution to the principal international problems, John Paul II makes an appeal for the cooperation of non-believers and members of other religions, consistently with the indications provided by the Vatican Council.

According to the Pope, the important changes mankind is witnessing pose new challenges for the doctrine of the Church. These differ according to whether one belongs to the thriving societies of the North – which, however, hide many miseries – or to those of the South – which are not succeeding in emerging from the abyss of increasing underdevelopment – or, lastly, to those of Eastern and Central Europe – which recently rid

---

[20] The cited passages are taken from the encyclical letter *Sollicitudo Rei Socialis*.
[21] This statement appears in the encyclical letter *Centesimus Annus*.

themselves of Marxist regimes and are looking for new paths for their future. The novelty and vastness of the changed world atmosphere opens up "many opportunities to promote the cause of justice and solidarity", and the traditional social precepts have to be "adapted, without betraying their authentic meaning or internal consistency, to different cultures as well as to new situations".

On 1 January 1994, John Paul II set up, in the Vatican, the *Pontifical Academy of Social Sciences*[22], with the aim of helping the Church "to have its say" vis-à-vis the economic, social, and political "gigantic challenges" worldwide. The new institution has a universal and interdisciplinary character, and its members include leading jurists, economists, sociologists, and historians, both lay and from the Catholic and other religions.

Already in 1936, Pius XI had founded the *Pontifical Academy of Sciences*[23] to guarantee freedom and promote pure scientific research all over the world as a necessary basis for scientific progress. This was a sign of the Holy See's attention to contemporary needs. The new body created by Karol Wojtyla completes this awareness and represents a clear signal of the Pope's determination to begin a reflection at the universal level that would place the commitment of the Church to a more equitable and fraternal world, within a suitable economic, sociological, and political understanding of international reality.

The Increasing Role of Bishops from All Continents

In his work of fine-tuning the international social doctrine of the Church, John Paul II has resorted also to the increasingly helpful and stimulating contribution of the bishops at the national, sub-regional, regional, and continental levels[24]. In fact, they are the only ones who

---

[22] It was created with motu proprio and will work in close contact with the Pontifical Council *Iustitia et Pax*.

[23] It stems, through several historical events which have widened and updated its purposes, from the *Pontifical Academy of the New Lincei*, set up by Pius IX in 1847 following the footsteps of the *Linceorum Academia* founded in Rome in 1603 by Federico Cesi, Anastasio De Filiis, Giovanni Heck and Francesco Stelluti. The Pontifical Academy of Sciences reports directly to the Pope and has 80 Pontifical Academics proposed by the Academy Staff, which chooses them among the most distinguished scholars of mathematical and experimental sciences from all over the world: it is the only supranational Academy of sciences in the world.

[24] John Paul II specifically dwelt on the importance of local churches during the General Audience of 14 June 1995.

can assist him in his desire to attain a realistic evaluation of the very different situations of the peoples of the Earth, and of their mutual relations[25]. The collective dimension of the episcopate was specifically encouraged by Karol Wojtyla[26]. It resulted in a greater appreciation of the work of important groups such as: the Council of European Episcopal Conferences (CCEE), the Latin-American Episcopal Council (CELAM); the Symposium of Episcopal Conferences of Africa and Madagascar (SCEAM), and the Federation of Asian Episcopal Conferences. Continental and regional synods, among which are the recent ones of European and African bishops, have also gained considerable importance.

Before his papacy, what was the level of attention paid by episcopates to international economic and political life?

As late as 1931, the *World Collection of Episcopal Documents*[27] recorded in its index only two references to the word *economy*, both connected to family savings[28].

It was only in 1952 that an analysis of the religious implications of a given international economic system was introduced in an episcopal text: the document of that year in which the Australian episcopate addressed social justice issues[29].

A further change occurred in 1967 with the above-mentioned Second Conference of Latin American Bishops in Medellín, after which the elaboration of common guidelines for bishops of huge geographical

---

[25] E. Poulat, in "L'epistemologie des documents episcopaux", a speech at the International Colloquium on "The Teaching of the Bishops of the Five Continents" in Freiburg (1–3 April 1993), highlights these differences using of the following comparison between the number of occurrences of the most frequent words in the episcopal documents of this century in the United States and in Africa:

United States: family (21); social welfare, human rights (17); rich-poor inequality (16); State/statism, work, economic system (15); poor/poverty, economic development (13); strikes, popular development, education/training (12) ...

Africa: education (81), family (7); human rights (70); work (61); corruption (53); social peace (52); ethical values (4); power, health (43); agriculture, welfare (38); popular development (37) ...

[26] See, among other things, John Paul II's letter of 16 April 1995 to Cardinal López Rodríguez on the occasion of the fortieth anniversary of the foundation of the Latin-American Episcopal Council.

[27] Published by the *Union de Malines* (Belgium).

[28] E. Poulat, cited speech at the Colloquium in Freiburg.

[29] E. Poulat, cited speech. For a summary description of the development, from the beginning of the century up to 1992, of the stands taken by Australian bishops regarding the social doctrine of the Church, see: Costigan, M. E. "Ethics and economics in the teaching of the bishops of Oceania", speech at the mentioned Colloquium in Freiburg.

areas was assisted by the increasing involvement of lay experts in the drafting of the documents adopted, and was characterized by a more critical analysis and a greater authority. This conference was followed by the important works of the Third CELAM Conference on "The Evangelization of Latin America Now and in the Future", which was held in Puebla de Los Angeles, Mexico, in 1979.

As an example, mention should be made, first of all, of the pastoral letter on disarmament issued in May 1983 by the U.S. bishops[30], which, among other things, asked for: immediate and verifiable bilateral agreements to stop the testing, production, and deployment of new nuclear weapons systems; considerable cuts in the arsenals of both superpowers; a quick completion of negotiations in view of a treaty to ban nuclear experiments; new efforts to prevent the proliferation of nuclear weapons; and ad hoc policies for the promotion of human rights, in particular those of disadvantaged people. Three years later, the U.S. episcopate circulated a new letter completely devoted to American and international economic issues[31]. It was the result of systematic consultation, unusual at that time also at the Vatican level, with hundreds of qualified people and American and third world economists, by an editorial committee of 5 bishops assisted by a group of experts[32]. In this letter, the bishops declare they feel "obliged to teach through examples how Christians can undertake concrete analyses and give specific judgments on economic issues", and state that the Church's teachings "cannot remain at the level of suggestive general statements". Through a comprehensive presentation, the document indicates the need for an increase in international economic democracy and for a new economic order in the relations among states.

Along the path of concrete commitment indicated by American bishops, many other initiatives have followed, among which the following examples can be mentioned: the stand of the Australian episcopate on peace (1985); the fourth CELAM Conference, held in Santo Domingo (1992), on "new evangelization, human promotion, Christian culture";

---

[30] "The Challenge for Peace: God's Promise and Our Response". For a review of the norms of conduct, proposed by the American bishops, concerning the principal international problems, see: L. Sabourin, "L'Amerique du Nord", speech at the mentioned Colloquium of Freiburg.

[31] "Economic Justice for All: Social Teaching and the U.S. Economy", adopted in November.

[32] See the foreword by J.-P. Calvez, to "Justice économique pour tous, l'enseignement social catholique et l'économie américaine", Lettre pastorale des éveques des États-Unis, Paris, 1988.

the opinions of Asian bishops on the development of the region without fostering materialism; the ideas proposed during the eighth symposium of European bishops (1993); the concepts which emerged on the occasion of the Special Assembly for Africa of the synod of bishops[33]; etc.

To confirm the conclusions reached by the bishops as to the Church in Africa and its evangelizing mission towards the year 2000, the Holy Father issued the important apostolic exhortation *Ecclesia in Africa* on 14 September 1995, in which he dwells on the continent's sociopolitical problems also from an international perspective. In it, Karol Wojtyla analyses subjects such as: the issue of foreign debt, refugees and people in exile, civil wars, the building of national unity, good governance in public affairs, and the condition of women.

The core value attached by John Paul II to the maintenance of a deep church community and a true collegiality linking bishops together and to the Holy See, was reiterated by the Pope in his speech of 15 September 1995 to the FABC delegates on the occasion of the twenty-fifth anniversary of its foundation. In his impromptu speech at the end of the meeting with the FABC delegates, Wojtyla expressed his desire to be remembered as the "synod Pope", interested in encouraging the search for continental and global ways to express the collegiate nature of the church.

From the huge amount of documents produced by episcopacies during John Paul II's papacy, a greater sensibility emerges to the need for intervening also in the rules of the international economic game, which are no longer considered – as they were often in the past – as a reality that pre-exists the decisions of economic actors, as if the rules were a law of nature. For both episcopal and papal teaching, it is no longer sufficient to insist only on ethical economic behavior: it is also necessary to act at the level of the mechanisms and institutions that produce structural distortions and inequalities. The appeal for ethically inspired individual behavior is, indeed, no longer sufficient by itself to bring about the desired effects.

---

[33] Synod of Africa's bishops, "Christ est vivant: nous vivrons!", concluding message made public on 6 May 1994, in which, among other things, mention is made of the problems of refugees, of the poor of the continent, of tribal and inter-ethnic conflict, the need for a transition to truly democratic regimes, and the role of the media.

International Relations Become Part of Catechism for the First Time

In December 1992, John Paul II presented what he has called the most mature and complete fruit of the Council's teaching: the new Catechism of the Catholic Church[34].

The Holy Father explained its contents to the 145 diplomats accredited to the Holy See, stating that "it is a gift deeply rooted in the past because it is presented as a synthesis and a new version of a two-thousand-year-old heritage ... it is a gift for the present of the Church. The link with that which is essential and venerable in the past of the Church enables it to carry out its mission in the world of today ... it is a gift ... that the church addresses to the future, open toward the third millennium ... it may become a valid and fruitful tool for further knowledge and authentic spiritual and moral renewal ... Confronted with such a text, no one should feel alien, excluded, or distant ...".

John Paul II has explained[35], significantly, that "this catechism is not aimed at replacing local catechisms duly approved by Church authorities ... It is aimed at encouraging and helping the drafting of new local catechisms that take into account different situations and cultures while carefully maintaining the unity of faith and fidelity to Catholic doctrine"[36].

For the first time in the history of the catechesis texts[37], the new Catechism devotes several paragraphs to subjects such as: human rights and the rights of cultures, as well as international solidarity[38]; the rights of all populations to religious freedom[39]; the protection of migrants and refugees, as well as the condemnation of totalitarian views of the

---

[34] For a summary appraisal of the structure of the new Catechism, requested by the 1985 Special Synod of Bishops and which took five years of collective episcopal work, see G. Colzani, "Il catechismo della Chiesa Cattolica" in the journal *Il Mulino*, Bologna, 1993.

[35] In the apostolic constitution *Fidei Depositum*.

[36] These clarifications are in line with the constant attention the Pope has paid to the reconciliation of the Christian message with the traditions and culture of different populations.

[37] See: the *Didaché* in use at end of the first century; St. Augustine's *De Catechizandis Rudibus*; St. Thomas Aquinas's brief opuscula on the four fundamental issues of the catechesis: Creed, Lord's Prayer, Commandments, and Sacraments; the *Cathechismus ex Decreto Concilii Tridentini ad Parochos*; the *Catechismo di Pio X*; the *Catechismo per la Diocesi di Germania* of 1955, translated into 25 languages; and the various catechisms produced by the various Episcopal Conferences after the Council, with the approval of the Holy See.

[38] See part three, section one, chapter two of the new Catechism.

[39] Ibid., part three, section two, chapter one.

international community[40]; the promotion of international peace through justice, the criteria of moral legitimacy of a "just" war, the identification of moral rules to be followed during armed conflicts, the arms race, the manufacturing of and international trade in weapons[41]; the universal destination of the earth's resources in the economic activities of the community of nations, the respect for the world's ecology[42]; the financial and commercial relations among nations, support for the development of the third world, the reform of international economic and financial institutions[43]; the duties of international mass media to provide adequate information[44].

Thus, the new catechism confirms this papacy's plans to invest the Holy See with the role of a worldwide ethical reservoir[45] of unprecedented dimensions, in view of the content and universality of the population it addresses. St. Peter's See, convinced that "if there is no ultimate truth guiding and orienting political actions, then ideas and beliefs can easily be made into instruments of power"[46], puts itself forward as an ethical beacon at the service of the post-Cold-War international society.

---

[40] Ibid., chapter two.
[41] Ibid.
[42] Ibid.
[43] Ibid.
[44] Ibid.
[45] G. Zizola, "La politica estera di Papa Woytila", in the journal *Views*, 1992; Zizola, G. "Sulla morale la Chiesa sfida il mondo: dopo il crollo del comunismo la politica internazionale della Santa Sede è volta a rilanciare i valori umani", in the daily newspaper *Il Sole-24 Ore*, 1993.
[46] Encyclical letter *Centesimus Annus*

3. GUIDELINES FOR GOVERNMENTS

3.1. *The Creation of a Worldwide Civilization of Human Rights*

The Most Significant Positions of the Popes from the Fifteenth to the Seventeenth Century

In the centuries immediately preceding the eighteenth-century Enlightenment, there were three Pontiffs who, although their teachings were often disregarded by the church hierarchy[1], can be considered as the precursors of John Paul II's action to promote the human dignity of the world's peoples.

The first one is Eugenius IV[2], who, in his Papal bull *Dudum Nostras* of 13 January 1435, summoned "temporal princes, lords, captains of armies and soldiers, barons and knights, communities and, in general, all Christians of whatever class and condition" to refrain from treating the natives of the Canary Islands as slaves. Whoever would commit such a "serious offense against the divine majesty" would be excommunicated at once, if he did not immediately free the slaves and give them back all of their possessions.

Almost one century later, Paul III[3] expressed with a similar resoluteness his opinion about the rights of Native Americans, with his bull *Veritas Ipsa*.

It reads: "... We herewith decide and declare in virtue of Our Apostolic Authority that it is forbidden to deprive of their freedom and possessions" the inhabitants of the West and South Indies "and any other peoples whom the Christians will come to know in the future, even if without faith. We declare and decide, on the contrary, that they can freely and lawfully use and enjoy their freedom and their possessions and purchase them; that they cannot be reduced to slavery, that Indians and other peoples must be invited to embrace the ... faith of Christ through the preaching of the God's word and through the example of a good life.[4]"

---

[1] The prohibitions of the Pope were, in fact, frequently counterbalanced by other documents of equal authority, which gave the kings and their emissaries full power of rule and ownership over the land and peoples they could conquer and subdue. See C.-J. Pinto de Oliveira, "Le discours social de l'Eglise: Apport des Eglises particuliéres", lecture at the mentioned Freiburg Colloquium.

[2] Gabriele Condulmer, Venetian, Pope from 11 March 1431 to 23 February 1447.

[3] Alessandro Farnese, Roman, Pope from 3 November 1534 until 10 November 1549.

[4] The papal bull was published on 2 June 1537.

On 22 April 1639, Urban VIII[5] reiterated in the bull *Commissum Nobis*, directed to the Collector of Portugal, the obligation of forbidding everyone to sell the inhabitants of the West and South Indies, to reduce them to slavery, and to deprive them of their wives, children, and properties. In threatening to excommunicate those who would persist in the above violations, he declared void "any general or particular decrees issued by the Apostolic See or by the general councils, by provincial councils or by synods, as well as any laws adopted by towns or by any religious or secular jurisdiction ... that are in contrast" to the provisions of this bull.

The Process of Opening Up to "New Freedoms"

The eighteenth-century declarations of human rights[6], and the nineteenth-century constitutions referring to them, had to face difficulties, reservations, and sometimes even condemnation by the Church[7], until late in the nineteenth century, and on some issues until very late in the twentieth century. These cautious attitudes, often due to feelings of reaction against agnosticism and totalitarian laicism, and in some cases marked by an attitude of hostile rejection, appeared in several papal documents[8].

The state of mind in which – after some uncertainties due to the gradualness with which the anti-religious attitude of the French Revolution was expressed – the Pope of the time, Pius VI[9], received the first French Declaration of the Rights of Man, appears very clearly in the letter he

---

[5] Maffeo Barberini, Florentine, Pope from 29 September 1623 to 29 July 1644.

[6] The 1776 American Declaration of Independence; the 1785 Statute of Religious Freedom of the State of Virginia; the Bill of Rights appended to the 1789 American Constitution; the 1791 French Declaration of the Rights of Man.

[7] L. Sciout, *Histoire de la constitution civile du clergé*, Paris, 1872; A. Latreille, *L'Eglise catholique et la révolution française*, Paris, 1970; B. Plongeron, "L'Eglise et les déclaration des droits de l'homme au XVIII siécle", in the journal *Nouvelle Revue Thèologique*, 1979; M. Rosa, "Tradition and Renewal in the Christian Churches", in *Modern Europe - The Decay of the Ancient Régime*, Milan, 1987; M. Vovelle, *La révolution contre l'Eglise*, Paris, 1988; Ch. Fauré, *Les déclarations des droits de l'homme de 1789*, Paris, 1988; "L'Eglise et la Révolution française", colloquium organized by the Catholic Institute of Toulouse, 1989.

[8] Among others, the following: apostolic letter *Quod Aliquantum* (10 March 1791) and encyclical letter *Adeo Nota* (23 April 1791) by Pius VI; apostolic letter *Post Tam Diuturnitas* (29 April 1814) by Pius VII; encyclical letter *Mirari Vos* (15 August 1832) by Gregory XVI; encyclicals *Noscitis et Nobiscum* (8 December 1849) and *Quanta Cura* (8 December 1864) by Pius IX.

[9] Giannangelo Braschi, born in Cesena, Pope from 22 February 1775 to 29 August 1779.

wrote to Cardinal Rochefoucauld[10]. In it, he defines as "a monstrous and chimerical right ... contrary to the rights of the Supreme Creator to whom we owe our existence" the one guaranteeing human beings the liberty of thinking, declaring, writing and even printing with impunity "whatever the most unbridled imagination can suggest about religion". However, from a historical retrospective, it is worth noting the – albeit extremely vague – statement by the same Pope that he "did not intend to propose again the restoration of the previous French regime"[11].

An initial moderate change in the attitude of the Church occurred with Leo XIII[12]. He began a circumspect selection of the Christian ideas present in "the new freedoms" announced by the constitutions of modern States[13]. Leo XIII, while insistently re-affirming the spiritual supremacy of the Church, evoked – albeit from a perspective which expressed in several points a rejection of the modern world – the right of citizens to participate in political life, thus acknowledging the legitimate independence of the State from ecclesiastical authority in the management of some sectors of civil life.

The most progressive positions taken by Pope Pecci, expressing a specific sensibility to contemporary liberal requests linked to the industrial revolution and to the rise of the proletariat, can be found in his interventions in defense of labor rights. In fact, the Pope defined as legitimate the following claims[14]: for a job, a fair wage, due rest, the defense of working women and children, for the right of association, for the dignity of the human person ennobled by Christian character.

However, the Church still had a long way to go, especially in the acknowledgment of civil rights, in order to open up to the new ideas preached by contemporary culture about human rights. In this context, the following thoughts, published by Pius X[15] at the beginning of the twentieth century, are enlightening: "Human society, as God established it, is made up of unequal elements ... to make them all equal is

---

[10] Cited in J. Joblin, "The Church and human rights: historical overview and future outlook", International Talks organized by the Pontifical Council for Peace and Justice, Rome, 1988.

[11] Cited apostolic letter *Quod Aliquantum*.

[12] Gioacchino Pecci, born in Carpineto (Anagni), Pope from 3 March 1878 to 20 July 1903.

[13] Encyclical *Libertas* of 1889.

[14] Encyclical *Rerum Novarum*.

[15] Giuseppe Sarto, born in Riese (Treviso), Pope from 9 August 1903 to 20 August 1914.

impossible and from it the destruction of society itself would ensue ...
Equality ... lies only in that all men trace their origin to God the
Creator ... in human society ... it is by the order of God that there are
the masters and the subjects, the rich and the poor, the learned and the
unlearned, the noble and the plebeian, who, united by a bound of love,
help each other to achieve their ultimate purpose in Heaven; and here
on Earth, their material and moral well-being.[16]"

With Pius XI[17], the teaching of the Church progressed significantly
and was characterized by a strong and courageous defense of the "freedom of conscience", of the natural rights of man and family against the
Fascist[18], Nazi[19], Soviet-Communist[20], and 1917–37 Mexican[21] totalitarian regimes, as well as against the state and political monopoly in the
education of youth[22].

Pius XII abandoned the paternalistic view of the role of the State, to
promote a legal-constitutional concept where the citizen becomes the
real political subject. Faced with the disasters of the Second World War,
Pius XII especially highlighted the human being as subject, object, and
foundation of the reconstruction of both the international community
and the national ones. The Pope joined the promoters of an international body common to all states for the maintenance of a peace appropriate to the dignity of human beings and to equality among men and
nations[23].

In 1948, the General Assembly of the new-born United Nations
Organization adopted the Universal Declaration of Human Rights.

With John XXIII and Paul VI, and through the council changes associated to them, the defense of human rights was progressively linked to
the need for social, political, and economic structural changes both
within the states and in their mutual relations, especially with regard to
the de-colonization process.

---

[16] Syllabus issued with the motu proprio of 18 April 1903, which was accepted at
the time as the authentic interpretation of Leo XIII's thinking, as opposed to the progressive and political interpretation of it given by the Christian Democratic movement
led by Father Romolo Murri.

[17] Achille Ratti, born in Desio (Milan), Pope from 12 February 1922 to 10 February
1939.

[18] *Non abbiamo bisogno.*

[19] *Mit Brennender Sorge.*

[20] *Divini Redemptoris.*

[21] *Nos es muy conocida.*

[22] *Divini Illius Magistri.*

[23] These positions were especially proclaimed during the Christmas radio messages
of 1941, 1942, 1944, and 1945.

The Church extended its action from the protection of the rights of its members to the defense of the rights of all humans on the basis of their common nature as beings made in the image of God[24].

With the Second Vatican Council, for the first time in history, the three main trends of modern political thought concerning the defense of human rights – Liberalism, Socialism, and Social Christianity – converged[25]. The various traditions joined to create a single great design in the defense of man, for the three main goods: life, freedom, social security.

The new enhanced and evolutionary valuation of human rights by the Church was made clear by the following words of Paul VI[26]: "A code of rights that the Church recognizes for man as such could be drafted, and still it would be difficult to define the extent of the rights belonging to man thanks to his elevation to the supernatural order, since he is part of Christ."

This is a point of view which, by sanctifying man as the "image of God", presented itself as the only effective bulwark against the actors on the international and national scene who tend to turn man from subject into object, riding roughshod over his rights or altering them in the name of ideologies that can be exploited for political purposes.

In the context of proclaiming God's message, aimed at respecting the genuine freedom of men by inviting them to freely comply with the Gospel, the Council Fathers stressed that the contemporary movement in defense of human rights "has to be protected against any false autonomy. We are all tempted, in fact, to think that our personal rights are fully saved only when we are freed from any rule of the Divine Law. But along this path the dignity of the human person is lost, rather than being saved"[27].

Consistent with this assumption, the Second Vatican Council stated that the respect for religious freedom was the foundation of the international promotion of all other human rights[28]. Montini's papacy insisted that in the view of the Church the right to religious freedom is not

---

[24] Council constitutions *Dignitatis Humanae Personae* and *Gaudium et Spes*.

[25] N. Bobbio, "I diritti dell'uomo oggi", speech delivered at the Accademia Nazionale dei Lincei, 1991.

[26] Included in a speech delivered in 1969.

[27] *Gaudium et Spes* constitution.

[28] Paul VI said this in the speech delivered at the General Assembly of the United Nations on 4 October 1965. For an in-depth analysis, see: P. Monni, *U.N.U.: quale libertà? Trent'anni di dibattito sulla libertà religiosa*, Rome, 1979.

based on a subjective inclination of man, but on his own nature. Thus, the right to immunity from any coercion exists also for those who do not meet the Christian duty of searching for truth and adhering to it, and their behavior, as long as the public order based on justice is respected, cannot be impeded.

During the papacies of John XXIII and Paul VI, the theological-doctrinal acquisitions of the Second Vatican Council in the field of human rights had a practical repercussion on the new, dynamic presence of the Holy See in international fora dealing with the promotion of human rights.

The initiative of the Apostolic See in this area was organized in a wide network of proposals and initiatives whose track has been followed by the current teaching of John Paul II and which included the following[29]:

a) exhortations to effectively implement the international instruments in force protecting human rights[30];
b) specific indications for the progressive development of international regulations[31];
c) specific requirements for a more effective protection of human beings against any kind of racial discrimination[32];

---

[29] Pontifical Commission Iustitia et Pax, "The Church and Human Rights", working document no. 1, 1976.

[30] Among them, in particular:
- the two International Pacts concerning economic, social, and cultural rights, and civil and political rights, with the corresponding facultative protocol (adopted by the UN General Assembly with Res. 2200 (XXI) of 1966);
- the International Convention on the Elimination of Racial Discrimination (21 December 1965);
- the UNESCO Convention on Discrimination in the Field of Teaching (14 December 1960); and
- the procedure contemplated by Resolution 1503 (XLVIII), approved in 1970 by the UN Economic and Social Council, which authorized the Subcommittee for the Fight against Discriminatory Measures and for the Protection of Minorities to set up a working group to analyze, on the basis of specific eligibility criteria, reports of violations of human rights.

[31] On the following topics:
- the elimination of any form of religious intolerance;
- the right to political asylum;
- the freedom of information;
- the protection of the freedom of association and peaceful assembly;
- the due protection of the freedom and the welfare of the family;
- the protection of children in the social environment and in the labor world.

[32] By requesting, in particular:
- specialized studies on such issues;
- new forms of action and intervention in order to eradicate racism.

d) promotion of the rights of women[33] (in this context, mention should be made of the Letter to Women by John Paul II, dated 29 June 1995);

e) exhortations and suggestions for the adoption of innovative legal instruments to adequately protect the rights of human beings as members of ethnic, religious and linguistic minorities;

f) stressing the need to personalize human rights to a greater extent[34];

g) appeals in favor of a more effective legal and social protection of certain rights, in particular of those that, if not recognized, most seriously damage the dignity of man[35];

h) pleadings for the implementation of new legal means, both on regional and international levels, to strengthen the enforceability of the protection of human rights[36].

---

[33] Calling on states to ratify to the greatest extent possible the Convention on the Political Rights of Women;
- promoting the enforcement of the Declaration on the Elimination of Discrimination Towards Women;
- protecting the role of woman as mother, as protector of the household and the sources of life, and as the first educator of humankind;
- promoting a better social status for married and working women and a more appropriate acknowledgment of their rights, above all the right to protect their own children in the event of legal separation or widowhood;
- inviting the states to adopt action plans based on concrete initiatives at the national level to protect women's rights.

[34] By studying how to extend and apply human rights also to the specific needs of some categories of people who are in particular situations, such as the elderly, the sick, and the disabled.

[35] That is, in addition to the above-mentioned right to religious freedom:
- the right to birth, to life, and to necessary nutrition;
- the right to culture and education;
- the rights of foreign workers;
- the right to a dignified job, both in sharing the management of the company and in remuneration.

[36] Promoting the idea of establishing a universal Court or Tribunal for human rights with final jurisdiction in this matter;
- disseminating the idea of creating an Office of a High Commissioner for Human Rights at the UN, giving it a supranational character but taking into account the domestic independence of every state and respecting, at the same time, some specific international juridical principles that have been accepted and progressively codified by the United Nations, principles which the governments should never arbitrarily fail to observe;
- fostering the proposal of establishing tribunals or regional courts and regional committees for human rights, as bodies better suited for understanding and solving local or regional problems of human rights, following the example of the European and Pan-American Commissions;
- suggesting, in order to monitor the observance and enforcement of human rights, the creation, at the international level, of legal procedures like those contemplated by the

John Paul II, the "Crusader of Human Rights"

About one year before Karol Wojtyla became pope, the President of the United States, Jimmy Carter, sent Andrei Sakharov a letter which marked the beginning of a campaign in favor of the respect of human rights viewed as an integral part of U.S. foreign policy.

Towards the end of the '80s, the promotion of the protection of human rights had become a central issue in international affairs, frequently discussed in the Russian-American summits.

When the Berlin Wall collapsed in November 1989 and the subsequent upheavals took place, some human rights activists took power in the Eastern countries where they had been imprisoned for their militant activity[37].

What position did Wojtyla's teaching assume in the setting of the historical situation summarized above?

He wanted to confirm the choices made by his direct predecessors[38], while also bringing new orientations to deepen and enrich the heritage received. This heritage he embraced in the conviction that human rights can really become universal if developed countries are able to make a moral quantum leap that would make it possible to change the structures that cause many people to live in extreme marginalization.

The Pope's vision of human rights was deeply affected by the bloodless 1989 collapse of the socialist conception of man. John Paul interpreted this event as a confirmation of the analysis made by the Church according to which the political and philosophical concepts reducing man to a mere cogwheel of the social machine intrinsically carry the seeds of their own evanescence.

According to Wojtyla, the way in which the Soviet regimes collapsed has proved both the viability of the peaceful demand for social and political rights and the validity of the new orientation of the Church

---

European Commission for Human Rights and the periodic and permanent monitoring carried out by the International Organization of Labor;
- offering the participation and moral support of the Holy See, whenever possible and when circumstances make it necessary, to UN protests against the violation of human rights.

[37] In this regard, the fate of some of the members of the Charter of 77 in the former Czechoslovakia is eloquent.

[38] Achieving meaningful results both in the United Nations (see the 1981 Declaration on Religious Freedom) and during the CSCE process (see the results therein obtained on the same topic through the 1989 Helsinki Declaration and the Vienna Agreement).

towards the strengthening of democratic and pluralistic forms of government all over the world.

Similarly, the repression of individual freedom made by the advanced capitalist societies, which tend to consider the human being as a mere consumer of goods and services, has had a strong impact on the Slavic Pope. From this negative experience comes the Pope's firm belief in the limits of the market, whose logic does not take into account some extremely important human rights and needs: "economic freedom is only a part of human freedom ... capitalism should be accepted insofar as it promotes private propriety and the market, but not when it denies a legal context that puts economic freedom at the service of human freedom ..."[39].

John Paul II maintains that the failure of communist totalitarianism also translates into a prospective rapprochement between the Church and the international labor movement. Both must set out to bring industrialization to the third world within the legal framework of the Welfare State as it has been implemented – albeit with continuing deficiencies – in the few countries of the "first world".

Moreover, he deems it appropriate to reflect also on the "new developments in the technological, economic, and political conditions which, according to several experts, will affect labor and production at least as much as last century's industrial revolution did", and he also points out, to international organizations among others, that it is urgent and necessary "to discover the new meaning of human work and to formulate, likewise, the new tasks"[40].

John Paul II includes, among the crucial components of the current world crisis, absenteeism and psychological disaffection towards daily work, together with the most oppressive forms of international economic neo-colonialism. A consequence of this is the loss of the traditional meaning of human work as a fundamental value of civil coexistence. To reverse this situation, the pontiff advocates "a reorganization and re-evaluation

[39] The above mentioned valuations have been more deeply expounded by John Paul II in his encyclical *Centesimus Annus*. Moreover, the statements made in this document were the subject of a round table organized at the World Bank (Paris, October 1991) during which, along with the positive humanistic approach of the Holy See and its realistic appreciation of the better adaptability of the democratic and capitalist systems, the need was stressed for this papal teaching to develop more thoroughly the relationship between human rights and demographic problems, as well as the right of women to safeguard their own professional aspirations along with the ones concerning their maternal role.

[40] Encyclical *Sollicitudo Rei Socialis*.

of the structures of modern economy and work distribution"[41], without which real risks exist that man and his habitat will die. According to John Paul II[42], the new civilization of labor will have to be based on a widespread international awareness that "the first foundation of the value of work is man himself[43]" and that it is necessary to avoid the mistake made by collectivism and neo-capitalism of treating the human being "as a tool rather than on the basis of the true dignity of his work, that is, as subject and author[44]". This principle of the priority of human work over capital and property implies an updating of the approach to the issue of workers' rights by the relevant international bodies. In fact, workers, besides being threatened – as in the past – by their *direct employer*, are now also oppressed by the *indirect* one. This term was used by John Paul II to mean the current web of interacting factors and responsibilities, at the national and international level, that determine the whole social and economic system or ensue therefrom.

The response to the challenge, states the Pope, must be the implementation of "global planning" in order to fight the plague of unemployment and the denial of the subjective character of human work.

The fact that Karol Wojtyla avoids the analysis of any contingent situations and any conclusions of pastoral character has bewildered some commentators, who have judged the current papal teaching as a step back from John XXIII[45] and Paul VI[46]. However, it must be remembered that the choice of a theological and anthropological level is to be understood as the reflection of his will to incorporate his message into the most varied sociopolitical contexts of the world.

Continuing on the topic of human rights, John Paul II's teaching is characterized by the fact that since the beginning of his papacy the right to life has been increasingly extended to the quality of life[47], intended as the fullness of being and not just one of possession. Besides promoting at the international level the right to an unpolluted natural environment, whose counterpart is the duty of safeguarding the universal and diachronic destination of creation, the pontiff introduces the need for

---

[41] Ibid.
[42] "Scoprire i nuovi significati del lavoro umano: L'enciclica sociale di Giovanni Paolo II", editorial in the journal *La Civiltà Cattolica*, 1981.
[43] Ibid.
[44] Ibid.
[45] Encyclical letter *Mater et Magistra*.
[46] Encyclical letter *Octagesima Adveniens*.
[47] N. Bobbio, cited speech.

international protection of the human ecology, of the all-inclusive right to complete human development.

Another important evolutionary aspect is the engagement of John Paul II in the defense of some new-generation rights[48]: those linked to the protection of human life, freedom, and safety, against the dangers created by technological progress. Among the various activities of the Holy See, it is worth noting the one concerning the right to the integrity of one's own genetic heritage, which goes well beyond that to physical integrity[49].

The latter has also been significantly analyzed in the apostolic teaching from the point of view of eugenic racism[50], which could result from some techniques of artificial procreation using in vitro insemination and from genetic manipulation, and which would try to produce human beings selected by race or some other criterion. Even though these worries are for now only hypothetical, the Holy See deems it necessary to establish some insuperable limits to the techniques and to avoid the proliferation of abuses which would occur should the birth of human beings belonging to a certain social or ethnic group be prevented through abortion and sterilization campaigns.

The right to life is linked to another evolutionary aspect of the doctrinal views of John Paul II: the problem of birth control and its relation with the so-called demographic boom.

At the celebration of the twentieth anniversary of the encyclical *Humanae Vitae* of Paul VI (November 1988), the Pope confirmed Montini's definition of contraception as "an intrinsically illicit act". However, some remarkable differences can be observed between the approaches of the two popes. Paul VI seems to confine himself mostly to the purposes of marriage and to view the virtue of chastity as the most directly violated by the use of contraceptives. The present Pope prefers a wider point of view, considering contraception as the violation of a principle of faith, and therefore as an act which opposes God as source of any life and the Church as interpreter of truth.

According to Karol Wojtyla, any definition of birth control that affirms an absolute right to abortion, without regulations or conditions, is therefore inadmissible.

---

[48] Ibid.

[49] Ibid.

[50] Document "La Chiesa di fronte al razzismo: per una società fraterna" (3 November 1988).

On 11 February 1994, John Paul II created[51] a new organism: The Pontifical Academy for Life[52]. Its main objective is to promote and protect human life from its conception until its natural conclusion. In particular, the Pope has assigned to it the following tasks: "to study, inform, and train in the main issues of biomedicine and law, especially in their direct relation with Christian ethics and the guidelines of the Teaching of the Church". The first text written by the Board of Directors of this new body, significantly, invites the advanced industrialized countries to grant economic aid rather than to foster birth control policies that employ any means, including those detrimental to human life and dignity.

On 30 March 1995, John Paul II published a new encyclical, *Evangelium Vitae*, in which he firmly condemns the present trivialization of death, and calls for a worldwide, general mobilization against the spreading of euthanasia and abortion.

John Paul II has also encouraged international thinking and action on the issue of refugees and people in exile (currently 36 million overall) and their rights[53]. The aim is to foster international solidarity to mitigate not only the effects of the problem, but also, especially, its causes – basically linked to serious violations of human rights, inducing millions of people to abandon their houses and their native countries.

Karol Wojtyla highlights[54] the need to review the definition of refugee given in the Geneva Convention of 1951 and in the Protocol of 1967, so as to include, besides people persecuted because of their race, religion, and membership in social and political groups, also the victims of armed conflicts, mistaken economic policies, and natural disasters. Moreover, it is pointed out that humanitarian reasons require that millions of people who are displaced within their own countries receive a treatment similar to that of refugees.

Finally, he stresses that although some periods of economic recession can justify the imposition of some restrictions in hosting these people, the respect of the fundamental right to asylum for people

---

[51] Motu proprio *Vitae Mysterium*.

[52] The Board of Directors is made up of five members and supported by thirty advisors, subdivided as follows: 22 from Europe, 7 from America, 4 from Asia, 1 from Africa and 1 from Oceania.

[53] See his letter of 25 June 1982 to the High Commissioner of the United Nations for Refugees.

[54] Document prepared by the Pontifical Councils *Cor Unum* and *Pastoral for migrants and itinerants* submitted at the round table held (9–10 March 1993) at U.N. headquarters by the Holy See and the "Path to Peace" Foundation.

whose life is seriously threatened in their own countries can never be denied. Moreover, the burden of assistance to refugees which is currently shouldered by neighboring countries should be taken on by the international community in an equitable manner in the future. Finally, if the relevant governmental offices decide not to accept people asking for asylum, stating that they are not real refugees, they will have to be sure that elsewhere a secure and free existence is guaranteed for them.

John Paul II strongly expressed his opinion, in his Message of 25 July 1995 on the occasion of the Day of Migrants and Refugees, regarding the need for developing international cooperation to cope with the problem of illegal immigrants.

The determination of the Pope to promote a worldwide civilization of human rights also led him, after the collapse of the Communist regimes, to confront the crux of what an attentive observer of the activities of the Holy See has called "the collision course of the instrumental rationality of the North, with its economic system, and the religious potential of the South, with its project of Islamizing society[55]". In order to increase his possibilities of dialogue, with the intention, among other things, of obtaining statutes of religious freedom in Islamic or mainly Islamic countries, intended as barriers to religious totalitarianism[56], John Paul II has fully supported the process of diplomatic approaches started by Paul VI. As a result, about 40 embassies and 30 nunciatures of those countries have been accredited at the Holy See.

The ongoing contacts regarding conventions or concordats on religious freedom to be signed between the Holy See and the Muslim States and the Eastern European countries, are processes to be followed very attentively by those who want to see the perspectives for concrete growth of the public ethic dimension of the Church in the world, possibilities which were opened up by John Paul II through the inclusion of human rights in the Church's catechesis.

A very interesting sign of evolution has been the pope's decision to increase as much as possible the cooperation between different religions, both Christian and non Christian, to support human rights and international peace. From this point of view, another important symbol was the First World Day of Prayer for Peace, celebrated in Assisi on

[55] G. Zizola, "La politica estera di Papa Wojtyla", in the Journal *Views*, 1992.
[56] Ibid.

27 October 1986, during the International Year of Peace declared by
the United Nations. In it, 124 delegates participated, grouped as follows: 62 of non-Christian religions; 50 of Christian non-Catholic
churches, and the rest from the Catholic Church. During the meeting,
each participant prayed in his/her own way, respecting all the other
religions. Since then, Assisi Day has become a point of reference and
inspiration for all the initiatives of the Church, including those at the
international level, to strengthen peaceful relations between countries.
Under John Paul II, the representatives of other religions are encouraged to maintain a "dialogue of life", i.e., a cooperation which, without debating about religion, translates into an exchange of valuations
and possibly of joint initiatives for the protection of international
peace and justice. The first significant moment of this rapprochement
is the use of purely religious language in the pilgrimage to Assisi on
10 January 1993, with Eastern Orthodox, Jews, and Muslims joining
in a plea for peace and respect for human rights in Bosnia Herzegovina. John Paul II's intentions to progressively promote ecumenism[57]
and inter-faith dialogue[58], so that they can play an effective role in
international relations, are clear. In order to fully carry out his apostolic mission of safeguarding human dignity, whenever it is infringed
upon, John Paul II seems to indicate new areas for the future substitu-
tion of governmental diplomacy with joint non-governmental initiatives of various religions, with the aim of exerting ethical pressure and
international mediation whenever the official protagonists do not
act[59].

---

[57] For an in-depth analysis, see, among other things, the 1993 new edition of the
Directory for the Application of Principles and Rules on Ecumenism; the apostolic letter
Orientale Lumen of 2 May 1995; the encyclical letter *Unum Sint* of May 25 1995 on
the ecumenical involvement; the joint declaration by John Paul II and the ecumenical
Patriarch Bartholomew I, adopted on 29 June 1995; the speech given by the Holy
Father on April 30 1995 for the 450th anniversary of the Council of Trent; the catechesis to the General Audience of 2 August 1995 on the commitment of theologians to
ecumenism.
[58] See, among the various speeches by Karol Wojtyla dealing with the need for
such a dialogue, the following: contribution delivered on 21 January 1995 in front of
the leaders of other religious creeds in Colombo; speech to the Bishops of Japan in *ad
Limine* visit on 3 December 1995; speech given on 28 August 1995 to the Bishops of
India in *ad Limine* visit; the speech given on 26 August 1995 to some priests of the
Order of Friars Minor, in which it is stressed that the dialogue with Muslims dates
back to St. Francis.
[59] Caracciolo L. ed., "Le Città di Dio. Il mondo secondo il Vaticano", special issue
of the journal *Limes*, Rome, 1993.

3.2. The Protection of the Rights of Peoples and Nations

The Irreconcilable Historical Conflict between the Right to Self-determination and the Right to Territorial Integrity

The right of peoples to self-determination has been included in contemporary international law with the articles 1 and 55 of the *Charter of
the United Nations*, and with subsequent developments linked to the
declaration of 14 December 1960 that grants independence to colonial
countries and peoples, and to the 1970 declaration on the principles of
international law.

The antinomy between the right of peoples to self-determination and
the right to political unity and territorial integrity cannot be solved
from a theoretical point of view[60]. In the praxis of the United Nations
the former right has, in fact, prevailed over the latter within the de-colonization process, which has been supported by the Church, especially
in the encyclical *Populorum Progressio*.

In other situations, not linked to de-colonization, the second right
has prevailed at the UN (in the case of Biafra, for instance).

The tradition of the Holy See treats states and governments as direct
counterparts at the international level, but at the same time, it considers
that they have significance insofar as they express the views of their people, in whose values and ethical-religious life the Church is particularly
interested. In his message at the Helsinki Conference on 25 July 1975,
Paul VI said: "When we talk about states, we always refer to the people
who are their living reality, their raison d'être and the reason for their
actions … the Holy See is not foreign to any people; on the contrary, it
considers itself part of them, since it shares in the good of each one; this
is even more so when a people is persecuted and denied representation
in the international sphere."

The Approach of John Paul II

Several commentators, in their analysis of the current papal teaching,
have reported that John Paul II has taken to the extreme the traditional
distinction between State, government, and politics, on the one hand,
and society and nation on the other – almost underestimating the first
in favor of the second. They draw attention to the new direct relation

---

[60] H. Thierry, "Le droits des peuples à disposer d'eux-memes", in *Droit International
Public*, Paris, 1975.

the Pope has established with the peoples in his itinerant apostolic mission; to some eloquent passages of the social encyclicals and the Catechism; to the support the Holy See has given to the "springtime of the peoples" in Central-Eastern Europe; and to the precursor role of the Holy See in acknowledging the Slovene and Croatian Republics.

In our opinion, such a radical judgment – even though it is accurate to attribute to John Paul II a stronger sensibility toward the desires of oppressed populations than his predecessors' – seems too harsh. In fact, the Holy See has expressed its opinion on some significant occasions (following its assessments, at the time, regarding the Habsburg Empire) also against the breaking up of multinational states. Such was the case during the initial stage of the upheavals aimed at the dissolution of the USSR and Czechoslovakia. A significant example of attention to claims for unity is the following declaration made by the Pope on the occasion of the Mass at the *Basilica Superiore* of Assisi (10 January 1993): "… each nation has the right to self-determination as a community. This right can be realized through actual political sovereignty, or through a federation or confederation with other nations. Was it possible to save one of these two modes in the case of the former Yugoslavian nations? It is difficult to exclude such a possibility …"

Almost one year later, in a letter to the Italian bishops[61], Karol Wojtyla, clearly responding to the Northern League's ideas of a federalist transformation of Italy, eloquently wrote: "… the heritage of unity, even beyond its specific political configuration, which was developed during the nineteenth century, is deeply rooted in the conscience of Italians who, thanks to language, historical events, and a common faith and culture, have always felt themselves to be part of a single people. This unity is measured not in years, but in centuries of history[62]."

John Paul II has also strongly condemned "exacerbated nationalisms[63]", using vehement words whose last historical precedent goes back to Pius XI, when he censured the totalitarian models of his era[64].

---

[61] Dated 6 January 1994.

[62] For a more thorough analysis of the Pope's opinion on the international role of Italy, see: Impagliazzo, M."Perché il papa polacco vuole salvare l'unità d'Italia", in the issue "A che serve l'Italia: Perché siamo una nazione" of the magazine *Limes*, Rome, 1994.

[63] Speech delivered on 15 January 1994 to the Diplomatic Corps at the Holy See. On that occasion it clearly emerged that in Karol Wojtyla's view, self-determination is only a starting point towards the opening to international cooperation, and it should never lead to a politics of isolationism and exclusion of the other peoples of the world.

[64] On 20 May 1995, arriving in Prague for the first time after the 1993 events in which the Czech and Slovak nations became independent form each other, the Pope

The conclusion can be drawn that John Paul II's view of the "new peoples" is not dogmatic. It can be adjusted to specific situations, to the judgment of local episcopates, to the assessments of dioceses.

The evaluation of the cases in which priority should be given to the disruptive principle of full independent political self-determination or to the more conservative one of setting up federate or confederate bonds, is still very delicate. In fact, one needs to be very aware that – as Cardinal Silvestrini has admitted – the appeal to freedom can sometimes translate into a means of making coexistence very difficult, with serious risks for international peace.

3.3. The Defense of Peace and the "Just War"

The Holy See and the Transition from Classical to Total War

During the first three hundred years after Christ, his followers deemed it right not to participate in any war activity[65].

In the fourth century, emperor Theodosius I reversed this state of affairs[66]. The Christians, in fact, had to participate in the defense of the (Christian) Roman Empire, which was considered as an instrument of the divine design. Military service was even made compulsory for them, on pain of excommunication, and pagans were forbidden to enter the Imperial army.

From the fall of the Western Roman Empire (AD 476) until the Protestant Reform (AD 1519), the international community, which had become *Respublica Christiana*, took inspiration from two principles: papal hierarchic supremacy, and the unity of Christian populations against peoples of different faith[67].

In this long historical period, the Church:

- acted as a barrier against the violence of war, humanizing the practice of war with instruments such as "God's truces", assistance to prisoners, and the promotion of different forms of protection of the defenseless civil population; and

pointed out those events as a clear demonstration of how fundamental self-determination needs can be met in mutual respect and peace.

[65] G. Marra, "Tendenze nel mondo cattolico sul tema della pace e della guerra", conference held at the Centro Alti Studi per la Difesa, Rome, 1992.

[66] Edict of Thessalonica of AD 380, and its sequels.

[67] G. Cansacchi, *I principii informatori delle relazioni internazionali*, Turin, 1972.

• promoted the re-conquest of the Holy Places and the setting up of armed alliances against the aggressions by pagans, especially the Turks.

Saint Thomas elaborated the notion of *just war*, specifying for it the following three characteristics: it is conducted under the control of a legitimate political authority, in order to avoid the risk of proliferation of arbitrary violence; it has a fair cause, such as the restoration of order or the punishment of the guilty; it has an honest intention (that is, to combat evil or to promote the good).

In the sixteenth, seventeenth, and eighteenth centuries, with the proliferation of absolute states and through the sanguinary period of religious wars, the political interests between the states prevailed over those of religious character.

The fall of the Papal States in 1870 brought about, with the full separation of papal authority from temporal jurisdiction, a renewed increase in the spiritual ascendancy of the Holy See, which translated, among other things, into a vigorous opposition to the horrors of war.

During the Second World War, in particular, awareness grew – having started with the 1914–1918 conflict – that the moral categories applied until then in evaluating war events had become inadequate.

The tens of millions of casualties and the invention of nuclear weapons led Pius XII to denounce, with no possibility of appeal, the following:

• the war of aggression in its twofold character as both a tool for settling international conflicts and a tool for achieving national aspirations;
• the recourse, even in a legitimate war of self-defense, to arms of total destruction or those which escape human control.

Pius XII's condemnation was mainly based on the difficulty of accepting that "modern war" can, in certain cases, still be considered – as an outdated application of the scholastic theological doctrine of "just war" would suggest – an adequate means of asserting one's own rights.

Thoroughly examining this difficulty, John XXIII came to abandon, with the encyclical *Pacem in Terris* (1963), the distinction between just and unjust wars, rejecting any recourse to arms, considering such recourse unsuitable for settling conflicts and restoring justice, because of the excessively destructive power of arms. In the conditions of that time, the Pope stressed the very real risk that the instruments of war would trigger off an inexorable escalation of violence.

The Second Vatican Council, though in line with tradition, perceived the need for redesigning the traditional Christian doctrine so as to take into account the ethical problems posed by the use of thermonuclear, bacteriological, and chemical weapons. In fact, the pastoral constitution *Gaudium et Spes* denounces "any act of war that indiscriminately aims at the destruction of whole cities or wide areas, and their inhabitants", as well as the arms race, also considering its negative repercussions for the development of the third world.

The Proposals of John Paul II to Prevent and Reduce the Disasters of War

Karol Wojtyla has deeply transformed the classical doctrine that admitted the lawfulness of wars of defense, not because he moved away from it at the conceptual level, but because of his new total consistency with this doctrine, which considers the war of defense as a last resort that requires the previous exhaustion of all diplomatic means available, so that the war does not become a false and dangerous shortcut, presaging more serious violence, not only at the local level but also worldwide.

The Pope's views are conceptually traditional but new in their radical implementation, of which the most evident example occurred during the Gulf War, on which the Pope publicly expressed his opinion 56 times.

The Pope's views can be summarized as follows[68]:

- the supremacy of peace has to be pursued as a very precious good, if not the most precious good for mankind: it is not sufficient to condemn war in general; intense diplomatic activities are required to protect peace, together with a strong international commitment to the education of younger generations;
- today it is difficult to justify the recourse to war for the purpose of restoring international law, since it could lead to "an expedition of no return";
- thus conceived and invoked, peace should not be mistaken for a pacifism that unrealistically forgets that "war is an ancient slavery";
- wars of defense can remain, unfortunately, the last resort, whenever it is necessary to restore the violated right in a situation of injustice. For this reason, John Paul II has strongly re-affirmed the biblical notion of *opus iustitiae pax*: peace is not the mere absence of war and cannot be reduced to guaranteeing a balance of opposing forces; it is first of all the result of justice and respect for human rights, and cannot be divided into its political, military, economic, and social components;

---

[68] G. Marra, cited conference.

- room is explicitly left for the hypothesis of a restricted recourse to violence for just causes, provided that the means be proportionate to the ends, and that the consequences of military actions exclude, as much as possible, the damage to human beings and civilization (for example, actions of international police, and insurrections against tyrants).

It is worth noting that the Pope seems to adopt a softer position with regard to nuclear weapons than the general condemnation expressed by the Second Vatican Council. In fact, John Paul II, in his letter of 11 June 1982 to the Special Session on Disarmament of the Assembly of the United Nations, makes a difference between their use as a deterrent, and other uses. Deterrence is indicated as a morally acceptable transitory path to build peace on stronger and less dangerous bases[69].

The new Catechism of the Catholic Church, in the context of the discussion of the fifth commandment, systematically examines the above-mentioned doctrinal points[70].

It states, furthermore, that there is a moral law to be observed during armed conflicts, which is specified as follows: the mere fact that a war is being fought does not mean that everything is allowed between the parties in conflict; that civilians, soldiers and prisoners must be treated humanely; that any action clearly contrary to the rights of peoples and to their universal principles, as well as any provision imposing such an action, is a crime; that the extermination of a population, a nation, or an ethnic minority is a crime; that it is morally mandatory to refuse to obey any order commanding genocide. It reaffirms the rejection, mentioned in the constitution *Gaudium et Spes*, of any act of war that indiscriminately aims at destroying whole cities or wide areas and their inhabitants, and it highlights the great risks present in the use of nuclear, biological, and chemical weapons.

After expressing disapproval of the arms race, the Catechism affirms the right and duty of the states to regulate the international arms trade because of its implications for the well-being of nations.

In 1994 John Paul II also promoted a structured ethical evaluation of the international transfer of and trade in conventional weapons and their systems[71].

---

[69] On 8 May 1995, the Holy Father addressed again the subject of armed conflicts in his message on the occasion of the fiftieth anniversary of the end of World War II in Europe.

[70] G. Marra, Ibidem

[71] Pontifical Council for Justice and Peace, "The International arms trade: An ethical meditation", Vatican City, 1994.

In the message he delivered on 8 December 1994 on the occasion of the World Day for Peace, the Pope significantly pointed out the role of women as teachers of peace in the relationships between people and between generations, and in cultural, social, and political life, in particular during conflict or war.

3.4. The Duty of Humanitarian Intervention

On 6 August 1992, Secretary of State Cardinal Angelo Sodano, talking with journalists about the situation in Bosnia Herzegovina, declared: "... it is a sin of omission to remain silent and not to make every possible effort – using the means that the international organizations can offer – to stop the aggression toward defenseless populations", and invoked the right and duty of humanitarian intervention[72] "in order to disarm someone who wants to kill ... not so as to favor war, but to prevent it". The representative of the Pope at the CSCE, in a CSCE meeting in Prague (17 September 1992) about the war in Bosnia, clarified that: "the point is ... to make belligerents understand that the fate of the populations does not depend exclusively on their will".

On 5 December 1992, John Paul II, in his speech at the International Conference on Nutrition at the FAO headquarters in Rome, put the above-mentioned considerations specific to Bosnia on a more general level: "Wars among nations and domestic conflicts must not condemn defenseless civilians to starvation for selfish or partisan reasons. In such cases, food and medical aid must be granted and any obstacle removed, including those which are justified through arbitrarily resorting to the principle of non-interference in a country's domestic affairs. The conscience of mankind, now supported by the provisions of

---

[72] See, among others: G. Concetti, Il diritto di intervento umanitario, Vigodarzere (Padua), 1993; V. Buonomo, "La comunità internazionale e la pace: Una lettura a trent'anni dalla Pacem in terris", in the journal La Società, no. 4, 1993; declarations of the U.S. Bishops on 17 November 1993, "The harvest of justice is sown in peace", in the journal La Documentation Catholique, no. 2088, Paris, 1994; Christine de Montclos, "Le Saint-Siége et l'ingerence humanitaire", in the journal Etudes, Paris, May 1994; R. Etchegaray, (President of the Pontifical Council for Justice and Peace), "Ingerenza umanitaria: diritto dei popoli", interview published in the journal Il regno - attualità, 18/1994, which points out how the concept of humanitarian intervention, postulated some years before in France, represents an answer to the "increasing worries of humanitarian organizations faced with hindrances to their assistance activities, particularly those activities in favor of the victims of domestic conflicts".

humanitarian international law, requests that humanitarian intervention be mandatory in situations which seriously jeopardize the survival of entire populations and ethnic groups."

This thought was later more thoroughly expressed on the occasion of his meeting with the Diplomatic Corps (January 16, 1993): "There are interests which transcend the states: they are the interests of human beings, their rights. Now as in the past, man and his needs are ... threatened ... despite the more or less binding texts of international law, so much so that a new concept has taken hold in recent months, the concept of humanitarian intervention ... The principles of the sovereignty of states and of non-interference in their domestic affairs – which still maintain their full value – must not be a cover for torture and manslaughter. This is, in fact, the point. To be sure, jurists will have to study this new reality further and to define its boundaries ..."

The above-quoted thoughts of Karol Wojtyla have a precursor in the views of John XXIII, who hoped that the United Nations "will increasingly adapt [its structures and means] to the vastness and nobility of its tasks; and that the day will come when each single human being will find in [the UN] an effective protection of the rights which directly ensue from their dignity as persons[73]".

On the duty of humanitarian intervention – which, because of its novelty, is not expressly dealt with in the new Catechism of the Catholic Church – different approaches are being outlined. Some people try to reduce it to a kind of relief aid that excludes any intervention of armed forces; others, depending on the situation, associate the humanitarian aid with gradual initiatives which can result in armed intervention under the aegis of the UN.

However, John Paul II is firmly convinced that "the authority of law and the moral strength of the most important international institutions are the foundations on which rests the right of intervention to protect the populations held hostage by the murderous folly of the advocates of war[74]". Moreover, an armed intervention by the international community for humanitarian reasons is to be considered legitimate only when it meets the criteria sanctioned by the new Catechism of the Catholic Church on the subject of resorting to force for legitimate self-defense[75].

---

[73] Encyclical *Pacem in Terris*.
[74] Message to the Secretary General of the United Nations, Boutros Boutros-Ghali, on 1 March 1993.
[75] R. Etchegaray, cited interview.

3.5. Cooperation for Development

Brief historical background

Towards the end of the nineteenth century, Pope Leo XIII expressed in his encyclical *Rerum Novarum* a conception of the problems of development and underdevelopment that was basically limited to the domestic framework of individual states, which were considered as units without connection to each other. This view reflected the still embryonic status of global interdependence and cooperation between nations[76].

During Pius XII's papacy, the international situation had changed because of the presence of a number of new countries characterized by underdeveloped economies.

Toward the middle of the century, the Bretton Woods agreements, which aimed to liberalize international trade and begin a new expansive phase in the world economy, gave rise to the hope that the pockets of poverty in the planet could be progressively reduced.

On the contrary, in the years of his Teaching, John XXIII had to face the problem of the persisting economic backwardness of various countries: with his encyclical *Mater et Magistra* he included in the concept of development the consideration of factors lying beyond regional boundaries and national frontiers. Roncalli expressed sensitivity to this issue in the following memorable statement: "Probably the main problem of the modern era is that of the relationship between economically developed political communities and the economically developing ones: the former have a high standard of living, the latter live in situations of deprivation or great deprivation[77]". This perception is enriched by a prior assessment. According to John XXIII, in fact, development must be considered as an original process, marked by the system of values of each single country. It cannot be limited to the achievement of a level of well-being reached elsewhere[78]. During John XXIII's papacy, aside from the persistent gap between North and South, some significant doubts emerged as to the validity of the adopted model of development. They were based on the observation of social and economic tensions which were still rife among some developed countries of the North.

---

[76] M. Giuliano, *La cooperazione degli Stati e il commercio internazionale*, Milan, 1978; by the same author, *Cooperazione allo sviluppo e diritto internazionale*, Milan, 1985.

[77] Encyclical *Mater et Magistra*.

[78] Ibid. See also J. Y. Calvez, *Economia, uomo e società: L'insegnamento sociale della Chiesa*, Rome, 1991.

The teachings of the Second Vatican Council followed Pope Roncalli's opinions and were more thoroughly analyzed by Paul VI, who said: "Today, the most remarkable thing, of which everyone must be aware, is that the social issue has acquired global dimensions ... Starving peoples today call on the carpet the wealthy peoples, in a dramatic way. The Church is startled in the face of this cry of anguish and calls everyone to respond with love to his brothers' appeal[79]."

With Montini, the notions of development and underdevelopment became ethically and culturally wider, further motivating and justifying the intervention of the Church[80].

In fact, Paul VI even affirmed the moral obligation of the states to take into account, by adopting specific solidarity measures, the interdependence relationship between their behaviors: development became – according to the Pope – "the new name of peace", and war and the arms race were indicated as the first enemy of a full development of the peoples. During the late '60s, Montini insistently stressed the need for the States and the Secretariats of the main international organizations to set out on "decidedly new paths[81]" in order to promote new international legal norms concerning the right to development. Paul VI clearly understood, also, that a new problem was arising: the interrelationship between development and environmental protection. In 1972, he invited the states to look not only for a fair balance in prosperity among peoples but also for a global environmental balance[82].

Toward the mid '70s, the United Nations started an ambitious project of partial redistribution of international economic power that was called the *New International Economic Order*[83].

Paul VI encouraged the Church to study the project, pointing out that if the individual economic claims included in it were not particularly new, their synthesis was new and interesting (even if not perfect or free of contradictions)[84].

---

[79] Encyclical *Populorum Progressio*.

[80] "La Chiesa e il problema dello sviluppo: Dalla Populorum progressio alla Sollicitudo rei socialis", editorial in the journal *La Civiltà Cattolica*, 1988.

[81] Speech delivered on 10 June 1969 at the International Labor Organization in Geneva.

[82] Pontifical message delivered on 5 June at the UN Conference on the Environment.

[83] Described in the Declaration of Principles and in the Action Program adopted by the VI Special Session of the United Nations (April–May 1974).

[84] Pontifical Council for Justice and Peace, *Le droit au développement: Textes conciliaires et pontificaux (1960–1990)*, ed. Filibeck, G. 1991.

What was then called *Pontifical Commission Iustitia et Pax* prepared a number of serious critical considerations in order to extend the prospects that were opening up within the United Nations.

To begin with, it stated that the formula of a New International Economic Order had to be "interpreted as an aspect of the implementation of a fully human order". In other words, it rejected the notion that "the economic effort is to be intended as the exclusive objective, even if temporarily, in the false hope that later on – much later – it will be possible to create an art of human living": "the economy must be humanized from the beginning of the activities of economic stimulus".

It also pointed out that in the approach suggested in the *New International Economic Order*, there was a real danger of underestimating the domestic changes that, in poor and rich countries alike, were needed as a basis and pre-requisite of this Order. Moreover, it indicated the need to prevent international debates from becoming a game played by diplomats and specialists with no connections to their respective peoples.

It also pointed out that "the dimension and complexity of modern problems create a de facto global solidarity for which diplomatic relations, even if increased and varied, do not provide sufficient support. It is indispensable, thus, to have at the same time the growth of an organic political expression of the human family as such".

Paul VI deemed it appropriate to specify that "the Church has neither the means nor the intention of proposing a New International Economic Order which could be arbitrarily defined as 'Christian'". It is up to the Christian lay world, within a "legitimate pluralism", to offer and experiment with concrete solutions.

The Intervention Activities of John Paul II

Once appointed Pope, Karol Wojtyla confirmed the great insights of Paul VI, though he insisted particularly on the need to try to overcome, in the development negotiations, "any static position stemming from a specific ideology ... we cannot allow the restrictions of ideological prejudices to oppose our concept of man ... and imprison us[85]".

In this way, John Paul II indicated that, in the North-South dialogue, the Holy See had no intention of intervening as a member of one of the

---

[85] Message delivered on 25 August 1980 to the Special Session which opened the third decade of the United Nations for Development.

parties, but in favor of what the two groups and the various ideologies have in common, i.e., human beings[86].

The initial phase of Karol Wojtyla's pastoral teaching on the issue of development coincided with the most serious international economic crisis since the end of the War. A slump in the industrialized world (characterized by its unusual length and by the simultaneous presence of stagnation and inflation), was accompanied by a very high deficit – about 200 billion dollars in six years – in the trade balance of non oil-producing underdeveloped countries struck by the increase in the price of this commodity[87].

In 1987, twenty years after Montini's *Populorum Progressio*, John Paul II observed that the religious, human, economic, and technical development initiatives "have been able to achieve some results ... but, in general, it cannot be denied that the current situation of the world, with regards to development ... has become much worse".

The conclusions that the Holy See currently draws from this bitter assessment[88] point to the dissemination of a notion of development focused on the respect for human rights; the respect for the identity of each people, with its historical and cultural characteristics; and the respect for nature, whose domination by man should respect the universal destination of all goods[89], and protect future generations. Thus, Karol Wojtyla has set in motion a systematic effort of worldwide cultural persuasion aimed at making the increased interdependence among states acquire a moral dimension of solidarity[90].

Aside from the above educational activity, John Paul II intended to promote development by indicating to the Christian lay population and to "any man of good will" the parallel urgency of reforms concerning the following four issues:

• The "international trade system". The Pope observes that it "frequently discriminates in favor of the products of incipient industries

[86] M. Flory, "Le Saint-Siége dans le dialogue Nord-Sud", in *Le Saint-Siége dans les relations internationales* ", J.-B. d'Onorio, ed., Paris, 1989.

[87] G. Mathieu, "La crise économique: quatre caractéristiques", in the French newspaper *Le Monde* (May, 15th 1980).

[88] W. Kessler, "Les riches deviennent de plus riches... Des rideaux de fer à l'Etat social international ou Le recherche d'un ordre économique mondial plus juste", in the journal *Concilium*, 1992.

[89] Pontifical Commission for Justice and Peace, *La Destinazione Universale dei Beni: A Proposito della Conferenza sul Diritto del Mare*, ed. R. Heckel, 1979.

[90] M. Flory, *Ibidem*

of developing countries, while it discourages the producers of raw materials. Moreover, there is a sort of international division of labor in which the low-cost products of some countries that lack effective labor laws or are too weak to enforce them, are sold in other parts of the world with considerable gains for the companies engaged in this kind of production, which knows no frontiers".

- The "global monetary and financial system[91]", which "is characterized by the excessive fluctuation of exchange and interest rates, to the detriment of the balance of payments and the debt of the poor". As for the latter, it should be remembered that John Paul II intends to denounce the transformation of loans to the third world[92] from "a prime instrument for contributing to development ... into a counter-productive mechanism ... [that leads to] increasing underdevelopment ... because debtor countries, in order to pay off the debt, are obliged to export capital that is necessary to increase or even maintain their standard of living, and because, for the same reason, they cannot obtain any new equally indispensable loans".

- "Technologies and their transfer", which "are today one of the main issues of international exchange, and one of the grave harms deriving from it". In this connection, the Pope denounces the "not rare" cases of "developing countries which are denied necessary technologies or are given useless ones".

- International organizations. The Pope stressed that "many people have the impression that these international organizations are in a period of their life when the functioning mechanisms, the operating costs, and their effectiveness require a careful re-examination and possibly corrections. Clearly, it will not be possible to carry out such a delicate process without everybody's cooperation. It requires overcoming political rivalries and renouncing any intention of exploiting the organizations that have common good as their only raison d'être. The existing institutions and organizations have acted well in favor of people. However, mankind, facing a new and more difficult phase of true development, needs today a greater level of international organization, at the service of societies, economies, and cultures of the entire world".

---

[91] P. Laurent, "Per un'etica dei mercati finanziari", in *La Civiltà Cattolica*, Rome, 1991.

[92] A. Fonseca, "Debito internazionale e principi etici: A proposito del documento della Pontificia Commissione Iustitia et Pax", in the journal *La Civiltà Cattolica*, 1987; P. Laurent, "A che punto è l'indebitamento internazionale?", in the journal *La Civiltà Cattolica*, 1993.

During the late '80s, John Paul II's activity in favor of development was expressed in his speeches during his journeys to various continents, where the themes and thoughts he presented to international organizations were reformulated according to local requirements and circumstances.

This approach has allowed Wojtyla to instill the main themes of his Teaching directly into the hearts and minds of publics whose opinions have been thus far marginalized.

The first repercussions of the new approach began to come to light also during the visits of the Pope to the Northern countries. The 1993 meeting in Denver, Colorado, is very significant in this regard, and a journalist wrote that: "the young and old 'Latinos' who gathered" to applaud him "feel they are the real protagonists, the Pope's people ... and ... when the President of the United States listens to the Pope, it's them he is listening to, people who are usually at the margins of the American dream[93]".

After the 1989 events in Eastern Europe, the Papacy had to face a new development problem: the one raised by "the Springtime of the Eastern peoples". In the Encyclical *Centesimus Annus* (1 May 1991), John Paul II indicated the need to "support in their present difficulties the former Communist countries through the solidarity effort of other nations: obviously they must be the first builders of their own development; but they must be given a reasonable opportunity to achieve it, and this cannot happen without the help of other countries ... especially those of Europe, which have shared the same history and bear the responsibility for it."

The Pope pointed out, however, that "this need ... must not lead to a slowing down of the efforts to help and support the third world countries, which often suffer from much more serious conditions of need and poverty". Moreover, from the perspective of the papal teaching, the end of the East-West conflict makes huge resources available for development. These "may become much more abundant if reliable procedures for settling conflicts are established as an alternative to war, and if, as a consequence, the principle of control and reduction of armaments is disseminated also in the third world, by adopting appropriate measures against the arms trade".

---

[93] F. Colombo, "Il giovane popolo di Wojtyla", in the Italian newspaper *La Stampa* (August, 14th 1993). The Denver meeting leads us to highlight another important initiative by John Paul II: the convening, every two years, of meetings of the youth of the world who desire to visibly express "the idea and reality of the people of God".

In 1993, the Pope – on the occasion of the presentation of credentials by U.S. Ambassador Flynn – significantly indicated to the American nation that he expects a considerable cooperation for spreading a new sense of collective ethics in the promotion of development, an increased support to more democratic forms of government, and the setting up of effective structures for an equitable solution to the economic differences between nations and different ethnic groups[94].

In the last years, in an unprecedented way in the history of the Church, the actions of the Holy See on the subject of development of nations are increasingly involving both religious and lay people – also non-Christians – in the identification, at an operational level, of new ethical approaches for financial markets, public debt, and, in general, economic international relations. The increasingly frequent meetings and seminars on these issues are evidence of this orientation[95].

---

[94] Similar significant messages to take on responsibilities were sent by John Paul II on 12 June 1995 during the credentials ceremony for the new German Ambassador and the ceremony held on 17 June 1995 for the new British Ambassador.

[95] See, among other things, Pontifical Council for Justice and Peace, *World Develop ment and Economic Institutions*, Vatican City, 1994.

4. AN ETHICAL BEACON AT THE SERVICE OF THE INTERNATIONAL COMMUNITY OF THE THIRD MILLENNIUM

4.1. The New International Authority of the Holy See

In the mid-1990s, the difficulties that John Paul II had to face in carrying out his mission among the peoples of the earth were numerous[1]: the enduring incomprehension of the secular world toward the impossibility for the Church, at the risk of losing its identity, of revising some difficult dogmas of the Divine Revelation; the difficulty of keeping the attention of important world mass media, continuously searching for something new; the incessant process of de-Christianization of the Western world; the indiscriminate penetration of materialistic and consumeristic values in the countries that have recently gotten rid of the Communist yoke[2]; the unsatisfactory evolution of Church-State-Society relations in his own home country; the aggressiveness of Muslim Shiite fundamentalism, etc.

However, Karol Wojtyla's energies, despite his age, are far from being exhausted, and he is well aware of having succeeded in creating for the Holy See a specific role as ethical conscience of the international community, intervening with suggestions and indications which have a direct impact on how international relations are conducted.

"If the Lord has called you, you must lead the Church into the Third Millennium" – this is what Polish Cardinal Wyszinki told Karol Wojtyla when the latter became Pope[3], an invitation that has become the key for interpreting the whole papacy[4]. In fact, since 1978, John Paul II has considered the preparation for the 2000th anniversary of Christ's birth as the occasion to meditate, without indulging in any new millennialism,

---

[1] See A. Vircondelet, *Jean-Paul II: Biographie*, Paris, 1994.

[2] See, for instance, the concepts expressed by John Paul II in his meeting on 1 July 1995 with the Slovak bishops, where he stressed that the time has come for a new evangelization aimed at fighting the mere acceptance of the materialism raging in many Western societies.

[3] Thus quoted by John Paul II during the Angelus on 29 May 1994.

[4] Apostolic letter *Tertio Millennio Adveniente* of 17 November 1994, on the organization of the Jubilee of the year 2000. The special meaning the Pope attributed to this event has been clearly shown during the past seventeen years in the encyclical letters *Redemptor Hominis* (4 March 1979) and *Dominum et Vivificantem* (18 May 1986).

on the tasks and responsibilities of the Church, including those vis-à-vis larger human communities such as nations and international organizations. The urgency of seeing where Christianity is going and how it is getting there, has been strengthened in this end of the century by several anniversaries[5]: the thousandth of the baptism of Russia, in 1988; the 500th of the beginning of the evangelization of the American continent, in 1992; the 700th of the evangelization of China, in 1994; the 1650th of the episcopal consecration of the first bishop of the Ethiopians; the 1500th of the baptism of Clovis, king of the Franks, in 1996; the 1400th of the arrival of Saint Augustine in Canterbury, the beginning of the evangelization of the Anglo-Saxon world, in 1997; the 400th of the first martyrs in Japan, in 1997.

The energy with which Peter's successor has led the Catholic Church (891 million of followers in 1988, accounting for 17.6% of the world population) in the "modern Areopagus of the relations among states" has been strengthened, among other things, by the following factors that have increased the Pope's authority.

The first one is the support of the Third World Episcopal Conferences for Peter's supremacy. This allows the Pope to firmly carry out his teaching, thus succeeding in impressing upon his Church a basically unitary ethical vision of international relations. John Paul II has thus succeeded in the difficult task – in a historical period of increasing requests for the democratization of Church life – of fostering the papal recourse to intensive consultations with the world's episcopacy, at the same time preserving the protection of the right-duty to make the decisions, according to Christ's precise mandate to the Prince of the Apostles.

The second factor that has reinforced the internal prestige of the Papal See can be identified in the statistical data on the life of the Church, published in 1987, concerning the first decade of rule of the current Pope. They show that the number of ordinations is increasing again – though slowly – all over the world, and that the balance between new ordinations, and death and defections of priests is now almost positive. The number of seminarians has increased by a third over the same decade, even if now such expansion has come to a stop. Finally, during the same period, statistics show a progressive rise in the number of lay movements (to which the Second Vatican Council has given high dignity within the Church) that increasingly contribute to

---

[5] Cited apostolic letter *Tertio Millennio Adveniente*.

the evangelization process by supporting the clergy and making up for its limited increase[6].

The positive balance of these data – as compared with the gloomy period of the late 1970s – is undoubtedly encouraging the Christian world to support the Pope's choices and guidance. Obviously, the Pope is aware of the statistical projections according to which, by the year 2000, Muslims will be numerically more than Catholics for the first time in history. In this regard, however, John Paul II believes that the question as to which religion "has a future" or "is undergoing a system-atic process of decomposition and decline[7]" cannot be answered by quantifying faith with statistics. It has to be faced by meditating on it from the perspective of the Gospel, which "is not a promise of easy suc-cess", where Christ declares: "Fear not, little flock, for it is your Father's good pleasure to give you the kingdom" (Luke 12:32).

The third factor that makes John Paul II's message more credible is his wholehearted engagement in self-criticism on behalf of the Church, remembering all the instances through history in which it offered the world, "instead of the testimony of faith, the spectacle of ways of think-ing and acting which were actual forms of anti-testimony and scandal". According to Wojtyla, the Church "cannot cross the threshold of the new millennium without encouraging its children to purify themselves, through repentance, of any errors, unfaithfulness, inconsistencies, delays ..."; "a painful chapter ... is the acquiescence shown, especially in some cen-turies, to methods of intolerance and even violence in the service of truth ...", whereas "truth can only be imposed by the force of truth itself, which penetrates the mind softly and strongly at the same time ...[8]". John Paul II also suggests that at present we have to complain bitterly about the "lack of discernment, which sometimes has become even acquiescence, of many Christians when faced with the violation of fun-damental human rights by totalitarian regimes ... the co-responsibility of many Christians in serious forms of injustice and social marginaliza-tion ...".

The movement toward self-denunciation of the dark periods in the history of the Church, initiated by John Paul II, seems to be destined to a continuous deepening, balanced only by the accompanying demand

[6] In this connection, see, among other things, John Paul II, "The Role of lay believ-ers", speech to the Bishops of the Nord 1 Region of Brazil on the occasion of their *ad Limina* visit on 30 May 1995.

[7] John Paul II, *Crossing the threshold of hope*, Milan, 1994.

[8] Cited apostolic letter *Tertio Millennio*.

to examine ever more thoroughly the need to take a stance on the principal contemporary international issues.

A final very positive element of Karol Wojtyla's teaching is the compelling and concrete commitment to truly achieving equal rights for women, and to elaborating a program for renewed and universal promotion of the role of women within the life of the peoples and the international community.

4.2. The Holy See and the International Need to Reflect upon Truth

Sure of her competence as the bearer of the Revelation of Jesus Christ, the Church reaffirms, – under the Pontificate of John Paul II –, the need to reflect upon truth.

This is why Wojtyla has decided to address, with the Encyclical Letter *Fides et ratio*(adopted on September 14, 1998*)* on the relationship between faith and religion, bishops (with whom he shares the mission of "proclaiming the truth openly") as also theologians and philosophers ("whose duty it is to explore the different aspects of truth") and "all those who are searching".

His purpose is to offer some reflections on the path "which leads to true wisdom, so that those who love truth may take the sure path leading to it and so find rest from their labours and joy for their spirit".

Wojtyla felt impelled to undertake this task above all because of the Second Vatican Council's insistence that the Bishops are "witnesses of divine and catholic truth".

As the Pope declares: "To bear witness to the truth is therefore a task entrusted to us Bishops; we cannot renounce this task without failing in the ministry which we have received. In reaffirming the truth of faith, we can both restore to our contemporaries a genuine trust in their capacity to know and challenge philosophy to recover and develop its own full dignity".

According to John Paul II, the need for "a foundation for personal and communal life becomes all the more pressing at a time when we are faced with the patent inadequacy of perspectives in which the ephemeral is affirmed as a value and the possibility of discovering the real meaning of life is cast into doubt".

This is why many people "stumble through life to the very edge of the abyss without knowing where they are going. At times, this happens because those whose vocation it is to give cultural expression to their thinking no longer look to truth, preferring quick success to the toil of patient enquiry into what makes life worth living".

With its "enduring appeal to the search for truth, philosophy has the great responsibility of forming thought and culture; and now it must strive resolutely to recover its original vocation". This is why Wojtyla has felt "both the need and the duty to address this theme so that, on the threshold of the third millennium of the Christian era, humanity may come to a clearer sense of the great resources with which it has been endowed and may commit itself with renewed courage to implement the plan of salvation of which its history is part".

4.3. Future Outlook

According to the Pope, the Holy See has a series of priority objectives.

First of all, the advancement – through doctrinal dialogue and ecumenical prayer – of the process leading towards the complete unity of Christians, whose "divisions ... are ... a scandal for the world". The jubilee of 2000 should find the Christians, "if not completely united, at least much closer to overcoming the divisions of the second millennium[9]".

Another main objective is the further promotion of dialogue with the great religions, "giving priority in particular to Jews and Muslims". In this context, joint meetings will take place in the most significant places for the religions of the Book – Bethlehem, Jerusalem, Mount Sinai. John Paul II has declared, however, that he wants to be on the watch for the "risk of syncretism and of an easy and deceptive sort of irenics[10]".

Finally, the commitment to the "confrontation with the century" remains firm, and it will be made easier by a greater communion among Christians themselves and between them and the followers of other religions. This contrast will have to be aimed at further spreading the international social doctrine of the Church, more strongly emphasizing the preferential option for the poor and the outcast, and dealing with the vast issues of the crisis of civilization, especially in the technologically advanced Western world. Moreover, Wojtyla also puts forward the opportunity to think – on the occasion of the jubilee – "of a remarkable

---

[9] Cited apostolic letter *Tertio Millennio.* See also: John Paul II, *Crossing the threshold of hope*, op. cit.
[10] Ibid.

reduction, if not a complete remission, of the international debt that hangs over the destiny of many nations[11]".

The acknowledgment of the renewed vigor of the Holy See leads us to meditate on its implications for a future increase in the interventions of the Church in international politics. It seems inevitable: the bigger the need in today's world for mediation and negotiations – which are the only alternative to war – the more useful a legal entity of a spiritual nature like the Holy See. It must be kept in mind, in fact, that the Holy See is today the only legal entity capable of acting as a bridge between the first, the second, the third, and the fourth worlds, and, therefore, of having – beyond the boundaries of its confessional universality – room for action all over the world.

We think, however, that the critical point is a different one, and it is linked to the ways in which this ever increasing presence is carried out.

In order to "be present in the world of international relations", the Holy See must be careful, in exercising its "political" influence (a word that for the Holy See means "careful attention to the common good"), to always distinguish moral denunciation – which is legitimate and essential – from a superficial moralistic approach to complex international issues[12]. In fact, the social doctrine of the Church teaches that immediate solicitousness can negatively affect the respect for this distinction and harm international peace and justice, with prejudice to the interests of the Church itself in the medium and long run[13]. As it was recently written, when the importance of religion in politics exceeds a certain level, a just war inevitably becomes a holy war[14]. God is recruited, and religion turns into a powerful means of propaganda and mobilization[15]. Just wars become crusades and every value assessment becomes ambiguous[16].

The above-mentioned risk is always latent, but in our opinion it is very effectively controlled by Catholicism itself: in particular, John Paul II fully reconfirmed the validity of the Second Vatican Council doctrine according to which the State and the Church are autonomous

[11] Cited apostolic letter *Tertio Millennio*.

[12] Editorial, "Interesse nazionale e interesse cattolico", in the issue "Le città di Dio. Il mondo secondo il Vaticano", of the journal *Limes,* Rome.

[13] Ibid.

[14] Jean, C."Guerre giuste e guerre ingiuste, ovvero i rischi del moralismo", in the issue "Le città di Dio – Il mondo secondo il Vaticano" of the journal *Limes*, Rome, 1993.

[15] Ibid.

[16] Ibid.

and independent from each other, having in common only that they are both at the service of man. This precludes a priori that an increased involvement by the Pope in international political issues may end up being a totalitarian mixture of ethics and politics – a result which the Pope has repeatedly condemned, in his teaching, as being contrary to the Gospel[17].

---

[17] The Pope has recently said (in "Crossing the threshold of hope", cited) that "in those countries where the fundamentalist groups come to power, human rights and the principle of religious freedom are unfortunately given a very unilateral interpretation: the freedom of faith is understood as the freedom to impose on all citizens the "true religion".

REFERENCES

Sources

1435, Eugene IV, *Dudum Nostras.*
1537, Paul III, *Veritas Ipsa.*
1639, Urban VIII, *Commissum Nobis.*
1791, Pius VI, *Quod Aliquantum.*
1814, Pius VII, *Post Tam Diuturnitas.*
1832, Gregory XVI, *Mirari Vos.*
1849, Pius IX, *Noscitis et Nobiscum.*
1864, Pius IX, *Quanta Cura.*
1865–1908, *Acta Sanctae Sedis* (A.S.S.), *Commentarium Officiale, Romae.*
1870, First Vatican Council: Dogmatic Constitution *Pastor Aeternus.*
1889, Leo XIII, *Libertas.*
1891, Leo XIII, *Rerum Novarum.*
1909 et seq., *Acta Apostolicae Sedis* (A.S.S.), *Commentarium Officiale, Romae.*
1929, Pius XI, *Divini Illius Magistri.*
1931, Pius XI, *Quadragesimo Anno.*
1939, Pius XII, *Summi Pontificatus.*
1941, 1942, 1944, 1945, Pius XII, Christmas radio messages.
1961, John XXIII, *Mater et Magistra.*
1962–1965, Second Vatican Council: dogmatic constitution on the Church, *Lumen Gentium*; pastoral constitution on the Church in the contemporary world, *Gaudium et Spes*; decree on the lay apostolate, *Apostolicam Actuositatem*; declaration on Christian education, *Gravissimum Educationis*; declaration on religious freedom, *Dignitatis Humanae*; decree on the missionary activity of the Church, *Ad Gentes*; decree on ecumenism, *Unitatis Redintegratio.*
1963, John XXIII, *Pacem in Terris.*
1963, Paul VI, *Ecclesiam Suam.*
1967, Paul VI, *Populorum Progressio.*
1969, Paul VI, *Sollicitudo Omnium Ecclesiarum de Muneribus Legatorum Romani Pontificis.*
1975, Commission Pontificale "Iustitia et Pax", "L'Eglise et le droits de l'homme", document de travail N. 1, Cité du Vatican.
1976, Commission Pontificale "Iustitia et Pax", *Le Saint-Siège et le désarmement*, Cité du Vatican.
1977, Commission Pontificale "Iustitia et Pax", "La déstination universelle des biens: A propos de la Conférence du droit de la mer", Instrument de travail N. 2, Cité du Vatican.

1978 Commission Pontificale "Iustitia et Pax", "Self-reliance: compter sur soi. Vers la troisième décennie du devéloppement", Instrument de travail N. 3, Cité du Vatican.

1979, John Paul II, *Redemptor Hominis*.

1980, John Paul II, *Dives in Misericordia*.

1981, John Paul II, *Laborem Exercens*.

1981, Commission Pontificale "Iustitia et Pax", "Aspects généraux de la Catéchèse sociale de Jean-Paul II", Instrument de travail N. 1, Cité du Vatican.

1982, Pontificia Commissione "Iustitia et Pax", *Le vere dimensioni dello sviluppo oggi*, Vatican City.

1984 Pontifical Commission "Iustitia et Pax", "International economics: interdependence and dialogue", Instrument de travail N. 5, Cité du Vatican.

1984, S. Congregazione per la dottrina della Fede, *Istruzione su alcuni aspetti della "Teologia della liberazione"*, Vatican City.

1985, John Paul II, *Slavorum Apostoli*.

1986, John Paul II, *Dominum et Vivificantem*.

1986, Pontificia Commissione "Iustitia et Pax", *Al servizio della comunità umana: un approccio etico del debito internazionale*, Vatican City.

1987, John Paul II, *Redemptoris Mater*.

1987, John Paul II, *Sollicitudo Rei Socialis*.

1987, *Church's Statistical Yearbook*, Vatican City.

1988, Pontificia Commissione "Iustitia et Pax", *La Chiesa di fronte al razzismo: per una società più fraterna*, Vatican City.

1988, Pontifical Council for Justice and Peace, *Human rights and the Church: Historical and theological reflections*, Vatican City.

1990, John Paul II, *Redemptoris Missio*.

1991, John Paul II, *Centesimus Annus*.

1992, Pontifical Council for Justice and Peace, *Social and ethical aspects of economics*, Vatican City.

1992, Pontificio Consiglio Cor Unum, *La fondazione Populorum Progressio: Al servizio del popoli indigeni contadini dell'America Latina*, Vatican City.

1992, Pontificia Commissione "Pro Russia", *Principi e norme pratiche per coordinare l'azione evangelizzatrice e l'impegno ecumenico della Chiesa Cattolica in Russia e negli altri paesi della Comunità degli Stati Indipendenti*, Vatican City.

1992, John Paul II, apostolic constitution *Fidei Depositum*, for the publication of the Catechism of the Catholic Church.

1992, *Catechismo della Chiesa Cattolica*, Vatican City.

1992, Pontificio Consiglio "Cor Unum" and Pontificio Consiglio della Pastorale per i Migranti e gli Itineranti, *I rifugiati - una sfida alla solidarietà*, Vatican City.

1992, Conseil Pontifical "Justice et Paix" and Fédération Internationale des Universités Catholiques, *Les Droits de l'homme dans l'enseignement de l'Eglise: de Jean XXIII à Jean Paul II, recueil systématique des textes du Magistère conciliaire et pontifical (1961–1991)*, Vatican City.

1993 *Annuario Pontificio*, Vatican City.

1993, John Paul II, *Veritatis Splendor*.

1993, Secrétariat de la Conférence des Evèques de France, *Où en est l'endettement international? Nouvelles approches éthiques*, Bulletin N. 10, Paris.

1994 Pontificio Consiglio della Giustizia e della Pace, *Il commercio internazionale delle armi: Una riflessione etica*, Vatican City.

1994 Conseil Pontifical "Justice et Paix", *Le développement moderne des activités financières au regard des exigences éthiques du Christianisme*, Vatican City.

1994, Pontifical Council for Justice and Peace, *World development and economic institutions*, Vatican City.

1994, John Paul II, motu proprio *Vitae Mysterium*.

1994, John Paul II, apostolic letter *Tertio Millennio Adveniente*.

1994, John Paul II, *Varcare la soglia della speranza*, Milan.

1995, John Paul II, *Evangelium Vitae*.

1995, John Paul II, apostolic letter *Orientale Lumen*.

1995, John Paul II, *Ut Unum Sint*.

1995, post-synod apostolic exhortation *Ecclesia in Africa*.

1995, Message for the 50th anniversary of the end of World War II in Europe.

1998, John Paul II, *Fides et ratio*

Literature

1970, L. Capovilla, *Giovanni XXIII: Quindici letture*, Rome.

1974, Card. A. Casaroli, "La Santa Sede e le Organizzazioni internazionali", conference at the SIOI, Rome.

1979, Piero Monni, *ONU quale libertà? Trent'anni di dibattito sulla libertà religiosa*, Rome.

1979, "I principi ispiratori del nuovo pontificato nell'enciclica 'Redemptor hominis'", editorial in the journal *La Civiltà Cattolica*.

1980, B. Sorge, "Aprire l'uomo a Dio e la giustizia all'amore: Il messaggio dell'enciclica 'Dives in Misericordia'", in *La Civiltà Cattolica*.

1981, "Scoprire i nuovi significati del lavoro umano: L'enciclica sociale di Giovanni Paolo II", editorial in *La Civiltà Cattolica*.

1981, P. Nichols, *Le divisioni del Papa: La Chiesa Cattolica oggi*, Milan.

1982, M. Olivieri, "Natura e funzioni dei legati pontifici nella storia e nel contesto ecclesiologico del Vaticano II".

1984, C. Oderisi, "Il nuovo Concordato tra l'Italia e la Santa Sede", in the journal *Affari Esteri*.

1985, G. W. Maccotta, "La Chiesa di Giovanni Paolo II nel mondo di oggi", in the journal *Rivista Marittima*.

1986, "L'enciclica di Giovanni Paolo II sullo Spirito Santo", editorial in *La Civiltà Cattolica*.

1987, "Maria 'pellegrina nella fede' secondo la nuova enciclica", editorial in *La Civiltà Cattolica*.

1987, A. Fonseca, "Debito internazionale e principi etici: A proposito del documento della Pontificia Commissione 'Iustitia et Pax'", in *La Civiltà Cattolica*.

1988, "La dottrina sociale della Chiesa oggi", editorial in *La Civiltà Cattolica*.

1988, P. Poupard, "Politica e religione", in *Grande Dizionario delle Religioni*, Casale Monferrato.

1988, C. Bressolette, "Libertà religiosa: Dichiarazione Vaticano II", in *Grande Dizionario delle Religioni*, Casale Monferrato.

1988, "La Chiesa e il problema dello sviluppo: Dalla 'Populorum progressio' alla 'Sollicitudo rei socialis'", editorial in *La Civiltà Cattolica*.

1988, G. Verucci, *La Chiesa nella società contemporanea -Dal primo dopoguerra al Concilio Vaticano II*, Rome-Bari.

1988, J. Delors, "Jacques Delors et le message européen de Jean Paul II", in the newspaper *Le Monde*, 11 October.

1989, J.-B. d'Onorio, ed., *Le Saint-Siège dans les relations internationales*, 1989, Paris.

1990, P. Fantò, *Una diplomazia per la Chiesa nel mondo*, Rome.

1990, M. Martin, *The Keys of This Blood: the Struggle for World Dominion between Pope John Paul II, Mikhail Gorbachev and the Capitalist West*, New York.

1990, E. Cantero Núñez, *La Concepción de los Derechos Humanos en Juan Pablo II*, Madrid.

1990, G. Alberigo and A. Riccardi, eds., *Chiesa e Papato nel Mondo Contemporaneo*, Rome-Bari.

1990, A. C. de Montclos, *Les voyages de Jean-Paul II: Dimensions Sociales et Politiques*, Paris.

1991, L. Di Liegro and F. Pittau, "Dalla Rerum Novarum alla Centesimus Annus", in the journal *Affari Sociali Internazionali*.

1991, J.-P. Willaime, *Strasbourg, Jean Paul II et l'Europe*, Paris.

1991, L. Negri, *L'insegnamento di Giovanni Paolo II*, Milan.

1991, "La 'Centesimus Annus', attualizzazione della 'Rerum Novarum'", editorial in *La Civiltà Cattolica*.

1991, P. Laurent, "Per un'etica dei mercati finanziari", in *La Civiltà Cattolica*.

1991, N. Bobbio, "I diritti dell' uomo oggi", speech to the Accademia Nazionale dei Lincei, June 14th.

1991, O. F. Williams and J. W. Houck, *The Making of an Economic Vision: John Paul II's on Social Concern*, Lanham, Md.

1992, A. Spinosa, *Pio XII: L'ultimo Papa*, Milan.

1992, G. Gutiérrez and A. Grados Bertorini, "De la *Rerum Novarum* a la *Centesimus Annus*: los Cambios en el Perú y el Mundo", proceedings from the 31st meeting of Intercampus, Lima.

1992, R. Sánchez Medal, *La Presencia en México de Juan Pablo II y la Relación Iglesia-Estado*, Mexico City.

1992, J.-B. d'Onorio and Z. Grocholewski, *Jean Paul II et l'éthique politique*, Paris.

1992, R. J. Neuhaus, *Doing Well and Doing Good: the Challenge to the Christian Capitalist*, New York.

1992, G. Weigel, *A Newly Worldly Order: John Paul II and Human Freedom*, Washington D.C.

1992, R. M. Hogan and J. M. LeVoir, *Covenant of love: Pope John Paul II on Sexuality, Marriage and Family in the Modern World*, San Francisco.

1992, J. Wilson, *Pope John Paul II*, New York.

1992, D. Willey, *Il politico di Dio: Giovanni Paolo II e la funzione del Vaticano sulla scena internazionale*, Milan/New York.

1992, W. Kessler, "Les riches deviennent de plus en plus riches...Des rideaux de fer à l'Etat social international ou La recherche d'un ordre économique mondial plus juste", in the journal *Concilium*.

1992, G. Barberini, ed., *La politica internazionale della Santa Sede 1965–1990*, Naples.

1992, E. Dal Covolo and A. M. Triacca, *La Missione del Redentore: studi sull'enciclica missionaria di Giovanni Paolo II*, Turin.

1992, E. Balboni and A. Liserre, "Introduzione alla Centesimus annus: aspetti economici e giuridici", papers from a meeting held at the Facoltà di Economia e Commercio of the Università Cattolica, Milan.

1992, "Dalla parte dei poveri e degli oppressi-La presenza della Chiesa nel mondo di oggi", editorial in *La Civiltà Cattolica*.

1992, "Il mondo dopo il crollo del comunismo e la guerra del Golfo-Verso un nuovo ordine mondiale?", editorial in *La Civiltà Cattolica*.

1992, G. Zizola, "La politica estera di Papa Wojtyla", in the journal *Views*.

1993, G. Zizola, "Sulla morale la Chiesa sfida il mondo: dopo il crollo del comunismo la politica internazionale della Santa Sede è volta a rilanciare i valori umani", in the newspaper *Il Sole-24 Ore*, January 5th.

1993, A. Riccardi, *Il Vaticano e Mosca 1940–1990*, Rome-Bari.

1993, Msgr. G. Marra, "L'esigenza della pace e della legittima difesa nei contenuti del nuovo Catechismo Universale della Chiesa Cattolica", conference organized by the CASD, Rome.

1993, P. Laurent, "A che punto è l'indebitamento internazionale?", in *La Civiltà Cattolica*.

1993, M. Camdessus, "Mercato-Regno la doppia appartenenza", in the journal *Studi Sociali*.

1993, L. Prezzi, "La dottrina sociale nei cinque continenti", in the journal *Il Regno*.

1993, E. Benvenuto, "Dottrina sociale-magistero papale: l'accidentato percorso", in the journal *Il Regno*.

1993, L. Caracciolo, ed., "Le Città di Dio: Il Mondo secondo il Vaticano", in the journal *Limes*.

1993, G. Colzani, "Il catechismo della Chiesa Cattolica", in the journal *Il Mulino*.

1993, E. Fazio, "Economia e Società", speech at the II Conference on "Ethics and Economy": Dottrina economica e dottrina sociale - un confronto, Foligno.

1993, F. Colombo, "Il giovane popolo di Wojtyla", in *La Stampa*, 14 August.

1993, "The Pope in Africa", *America*, vol. 168, no. 8, March 6.

1993, "La publication de l'encyclique 'Veritatis Splendor'", in *Le Monde*, 6 October.

1993, J.-M. Lustiger, "Encyclique morale: Pour défendre l'humanité du désespoir", in *Le Monde*, cit.

1993, V. Possenti, "La verità è uguale per tutti-La Chiesa propone un'alleanza per dare ospitalità a valori che per secoli erano stati utilizzati per combatterla", in *Il Sole-24 Ore*, October 6th.

1993, G. Concetti, *Il diritto di ingerenza umanitario*, Vigodarzere (Padua).

1993, H. Tincq, *L'étoile et la croix: Jean Paul II-Israel, l'explication*, Paris.

1993, K. L. Schmitz, *At the center of the human drama: the philosophical anthropology of Karol Wojtyla/Pope John Paul II*, Washington D.C.

1993, L. J. Donovan and J. P. Langan, "Catholic Universities in Church and Society: a dialogue on *Ex Corde Ecclesiae*", papers from a symposium held at Georgetown University in April.

1994, A. Macchi, "L'Accordo Fondamentale' tra la Santa Sede e lo Stato d'Israele", in *La Civiltà Cattolica*.

1994, G. Brunelli, "Helsinki vista da Sarajevo", in the journal *Il Regno-Attualità*.

1994, R. Wright, "What Would the World be Like Without Him", *Atlantic Monthly*, vol. 274, no. 1, July.

1994, "Pope lands on bestseller list", *Christianity Today*, vol. 38, no. 14, December 12.

1994, Elson, J. and K. Fedarko, "Lives of the pope", *Time*, vol. 144, no. 26, December 26.

1994, C. de Montclos, "Le Saint-Siège et l' ingerence humanitaire", in the journal *Études,* Paris.

1994, J. Joblin, "Rapporti tra governi, istituzioni internazionali e organizzazioni non governative", in *La Civiltà Cattolica*.

1994, M. Walsh, *John Paul II*, London.

1994, J. Pérez Pellón, *Wojtyla, el ultimo cruzado: un papado medieval en el fin del milenio*, Madrid.

1994, A. Vircondelet, *Jean-Paul II: Biographie*, Paris.

1995, P. Hebblethwaite, *The next Pope: a behind-the scenes look at the forces that will choose the successor to John Paul II and decide the future of the Catholic Church*, San Francisco.

1995, P. Hebblethwaite, *Pope John Paul II and the Church*, Kansas City.

1995, J. Saward, *Christ is the answer: the Christ-centered teaching of Pope John Paul II*, New York.

1995, T. Szulc, *Pope John Paul II: the biography*, New York.

1995, W. Houck, *John Paul II and the New Evangelization: How You Can Bring the Good News to Others*, San Francisco.

1995, K. Wildes, "In the Name of the Father", *New Republic*, vol. 211, no. 26, December 26.

1995, "Papal challenge in Asia", *Christian Century*, vol. 112, no. 4, February 1.

1995, L. D. Lefebvre, "John Paul II: the philosopher pope", *Christian Century*, vol. 112, no. 5, February 15.

1995, D. Butler, "Pope condemns 'immoral' embryo research", *Nature*, vol. 374, no. 6522, April 6.

1995, "The pope: A see change", *The Economist*, vol. 335, no. 7912, April 29.

1995, J. Bryan Hehir, "Get a (culture of) life: the pope's moral vision", *Commonweal*, vol. 122, no. 10, May 19.

1995, G. S. Johnston, "Pope culture", *American Spectator*, vol. 28, no. 7, July.

1995, J. Nilson, "John Paul II ecumenist", *Commonweal*, vol. 122, no. 13, July 14.

1995, J. Maxwell, "Pope issues call for Christian unity", *Christianity Today*, vol. 39, no. 8, July 17.

1995, J. Moody, "A true culture of freedom", *Time*, vol. 146, no. 16, October 16.

1995, "The pope at the UN", *Commonweal*, vol. 122, no. 18, October 20.

1995, J. Chelini, *Jean-Paul II au Vatican*, Paris.

1995, W. F. Buckley Jr., "Understanding the Papal Bull", *National Review*, vol. 47, no. 21, November 6.

1995, L. Klenicki and E. J. Fisher, *Spiritual Pilgrimage: texts on Jews and Judaism 1979–1995 /Pope John Paul II*, New York.

1995, M. Allsopp and J. J. O'Keefe, *Veritatis Splendor: American Responses*, Kansas City.

1995, C. Lawliss, *John Paul II: 1920–199?*, New York.

1995, R. M. Hogan and J. M. Le Voir, *Faith for today: Pope John Paul II's catechetical teaching*, Boston.

1996, M. Bellini and G. De Carli, *"Quando la Chiesa é donna"*, Milano.

1996, G. Giansanti, *"Giovanni Paolo II. Ritratto di un pontefice"*, Roma.

1996, T. Buccheri, *"La Chiesa, il papa e le donne"*, Milano.

1996, "Il cristianesimo e le altre religioni. Il dibattito sul dialogo interreligioso", editorial, in *La Civiltà Cattolica*.

1996, G. Arroyo S.J., "Globalizacion del capitalismo actual: nuevos dilemas eticos", in *Mensaye*, n. 447.

1996, "La concezione di Dio nell'induismo", editorial in *La Civiltà Cattolica*.

1996, "Quale posto ha Dio nel buddismo", editorial, in *La Civiltà Cattolica*.

1996, "Dio nel Corano", editorial, in *La Civiltà Cattolica*.

1996, E. Casale, "Banca etica, la finanza alternativa", in *Aggiornamenti Sociali* n.5.

1996, I. Camacho S.J., "Dimension etica de las actividades financieras", in *Fomento Social*, n. 201.

1996, W.C.C. Programme Unit on Justice, "Work in a Sustainable Society", in *The Ecumenical Review*, vol. 48, n.3.

1996, V. Cable, "The New Trade Agenda: Universal Rules amid Cultural Diversity", in *International Affairs*, vol. 72, n.2.

1996, J. Joblin S. J., "Etica, morale e debito internazionale", in *La Civiltà Cattolica*.

1996, L. Bouckaert, "Economics, Politics and Ethics: in Search of a New Balance", in *Ethical Perspectives*, vol. 3, n.3.

1996, A. Caloia, *L'imprenditore sociale*, Casale Monferrato.

1996, Movimento Ecclesiale di Impegno Culturale (MEIC), *"Una buona società in cui vivere"*, Roma.

1996, M. Albert, "Pour la construction d'un ordre financier", in *Communio*, n.4.

1996, A.A.V.V., "Tutta un'altra banca", in *Nigrizia*.

1996, H. Puel, *Les paradoxes de l'économie. L'éthique au défi*, Paris.

1996, Institut International Jacques Maritain, *Poverty and Development. The Call of the Catholic Church in Asia*, Roma.

1996, Institut International Jacques Maritain, *Ethique et dévelopment. L'apport des communautés chrétiennes en Afrique*, Yaoundé/Roma.

1996, C. Bernstein and M. Politi, *Sua Santità Giovanni Paolo II e la storia segreta del nostro tempo*, Milano.

1996, G.P. Salvini S.I., "IX Simposio dei vescovi europei", in *Civiltà Cattolica*.

1996, Kevin P. Doran, *Solidarity: a Synthesis of Personalism and Communalism in the Thought of Karol Wojtyla*, New York

1996, U. Colombo Sacco, *I valori della cultura e dell'arte nel pensiero di Giovanni Paolo II*, in Cahiers d'Art, N.12

1997, J. Mathews, "The Age of Nonstate Actors", in *Foreign Affairs*, vol. 76, n.1.

1997, G. Zizola, *La chiesa nei media*, Torino.

1997, Z. Karabell, "Fundamental Misconceptions: Islamic Foreign Policy", in *Foreign Policy*, n.105.

1997, J. Moody, *Pope John Paul II: Biography*, New York.

1997, R. Buttiglione, *Karol Wojtyla: the Thought of the Man who became Pope John Paul II*, Grand Rapids.

1997, J. Kwitny, *Man of the Century: the Life and Times of Pope John Paul II*, New York.

1997, U. Colombo Sacco, *Giovanni Paolo II e la nuova proiezione internazionale della Santa Sede: 1978-1996*, Milano.

1997, H. Tincq, *Defis au Pape du troisieme millenaire: le pontificat de Jean Paul II - les dossiers du succeseur*, Paris.

1997, G. Concetti, *Con Giovanni Paolo II una nuova dimensione internazionale della Santa Sede*, in *L'Osservatore Romano*, July 19th

1997, G. Beigel, *Faith and Social Justice in the Teachings of Pope John Paul II*, New York.

1998, U. Colombo Sacco, Kyo Ko Yohane Paulo Ni-sei to SeKai Seiji, NagasaKi.

APPENDIX

Selection of Holy See Documents
On International Issues *
1978-1998

*

For better introcing the reader to the Holy See's increasing involvement in international politics, the author has hereby selected some of the principal documents (in full or privileging some passages of particular interest) published during the pontificate of John Paul II. Specific emphasis has been put on geographical areas out of Europe.

<u>The Author warns the reader that</u> whenever the Appendix present some passages isolated from the doctrinal content of a single text that is due to the necessity to keep a small size for this introductory book. For this very same reason the foot notes of the documents have been suppressed. Off course, a correct understanding and application of the teaching embodied in such texts, as a guide to Christian behaviour, can only be achieved through the <u>integral</u> reading of the original versions.

ENCYCLICAL LETTER
CENTESIMUS ANNUS
ADDRESSED BY
THE SUPREME PONTIFF
JOHN PAUL II
TO HIS VENERABLE BROTHERS
IN THE EPISCOPATE
THE PRIESTS AND DEACONS
FAMILIES OF MEN AND WOMEN RELIGIOUS
ALL THE CHRISTIAN FAITHFUL
AND TO ALL MEN AND WOMEN
OF GOOD WILL
ON THE HUNDREDTH ANNIVERSARY OF
*RERUM NOVARUM**

*copyright: Vatican Information Service

. . . .
. . . .
. . . .
. . . .

II. TOWARDS THE "NEW THINGS" OF TODAY

12. The commemoration of *Rerum novarum* would be incomplete unless reference were also made to the situation of the world today. The document lends itself to such a reference, because the historical picture and the prognosis which it suggests have proved to be surprisingly accurate in the light of what has happened since then.

This is especially confirmed by the events which took place near the end of 1989 and at the beginning of 1990. These events, and the radical transformations which followed, can only be explained by the preceding situations which, to a certain extent, crystallized or institutionalized Leo XIII's predictions and the increasingly disturbing signs noted by his Successors. Pope Leo foresaw the negative consequences – political, social and economic – of the social order proposed by "socialism", which at that time was still only a social philosophy and not yet a fully structured movement. It may seem surprising that "socialism" appeared at the beginning of the Pope's critique of solutions to the "question of the working class" at a time when "socialism" was not yet in the form of a strong and powerful State, with all the resources which that implies, as was later to happen. However, he correctly judged the danger posed to the masses by the attractive presentation of this simple and radical solution to the "question of the working class" of the time – all the more so when one considers the terrible situation of injustice in which the working classes of the recently industrialized nations found themselves.

Two things must be emphasized here: first, the great clarity in perceiving, in all its harshness, the actual condition of the working class – men, women and children; secondly, equal clarity in recognizing the evil of a solution which, by appearing to reverse the positions of the poor and the rich, was in reality detrimental to the very people whom it was meant to help. The remedy would prove worse than the sickness. By defining the nature of the socialism of his day as the suppression of private property, Leo XIII arrived at the crux of the problem. His words deserve to be re-read attentively: "To remedy these wrongs (the unjust distribution of wealth and the poverty of the workers), the Socialists encourage the poor man's envy of the rich and strive to do away with private property, contending that individual possessions should become the common property of all...; but their contentions are so clearly powerless to end the controversy that, were they carried into effect, the working man himself would be among the first to suffer. They are moreover emphatically unjust, for they would rob the lawful possessor, distort the functions of the State, and create utter confusion in the community".39 The evils caused by the setting up of this type of socialism as a State system – what would later be called "Real Socialism" – could not be better expressed.

13. Continuing our reflections, and referring also to what has been said in the Encyclicals *Laborem exercens* and *Sollicitudo rei socialis,* we have to add that the fundamental error of socialism is anthropological in nature. Socialism considers the individual person simply as an element, a molecule within the social organism, so that the good of the individual is completely subordinated to the functioning of the socio-economic mechanism. Socialism likewise maintains that the good of the individual can be realized without reference to his free choice, to the unique and exclusive responsibility which he exercises in the face of good or evil. Man is thus reduced to a series of social relationships, and the concept of the person as the autonomous subject of moral decision disappears, the very subject whose decisions build the social order. From this mistaken conception of the person there arise both a distortion of law, which defines the sphere of the exercise of freedom, and an opposition to private property. A person who is deprived of something he can call "his own", and of the possibility of earning a living through his own initiative, comes to depend on the social machine and on those who control it. This makes it much more difficult for him to recognize his dignity as a person, and hinders progress towards the building up of an authentic human community.

In contrast, from the Christian vision of the human person there necessarily follows a correct picture of society. According to *Rerum novarum* and the whole

social doctrine of the Church, the social nature of man is not completely fulfilled in the State, but is realized in various intermediary groups, beginning
with the family and including economic, social, political and cultural groups
which stem from human nature itself and have their own autonomy, always
with a view to the common good. This is what I have called the "subjectivity"
of society which, together with the subjectivity of the individual, was cancelled
out by "Real Socialism".40

If we then inquire as to the source of this mistaken concept of the nature of the
person and the "subjectivity" of society, we must reply that its first cause is
atheism. It is by responding to the call of God contained in the being of things
that man becomes aware of his transcendent dignity. Every individual must give
this response, which constitutes the apex of his humanity, and no social mechanism or collective subject can substitute for it. The denial of God deprives the
person of his foundation, and consequently leads to a reorganization of the
social order without reference to the person's dignity and responsibility.

The atheism of which we are speaking is also closely connected with the rationalism
of the Enlightenment, which views human and social reality in a mechanistic
way. Thus there is a denial of the supreme insight concerning man's true greatness,
his transcendence in respect to earthly realities, the contradiction in his heart
between the desire for the fullness of what is good and his own inability to
attain it and, above all, the need for salvation which results from this situation.

14. From the same atheistic source, socialism also derives its choice of the
means of action condemned in *Rerum novarum,* namely, class struggle. The
Pope does not, of course, intend to condemn every possible form of social
conflict. The Church is well aware that in the course of history conflicts of
interest between different social groups inevitably arise, and that in the face of
such conflicts Christians must often take a position, honestly and decisively.
The Encyclical *Laborem exercens* moreover clearly recognized the positive role of
conflict when it takes the form of a "struggle for social justice";41 *Quadragesimo anno* had already stated that "if the class struggle abstains from enmities
and mutual hatred, it gradually changes into an honest discussion of differences
founded on a desire for justice".42

However, what is condemned in class struggle is the idea that conflict is
not restrained by ethical or juridical considerations, or by respect for the
dignity of others (and consequently of oneself); a reasonable compromise is
thus excluded, and what is pursued is not the general good of society, but a
partisan interest which replaces the common good and sets out to destroy
whatever stands in its way. In a word, it is a question of transferring to the
sphere of internal conflict between social groups the doctrine of "total war",
which the militarism and imperialism of that time brought to bear on international relations. As a result of this doctrine, the search for a proper balance
between the interests of the various nations was replaced by attempts to impose

the absolute domination of one's own side through the destruction of the other side's capacity to resist, using every possible means, not excluding the use of lies, terror tactics against citizens, and weapons of utter destruction (which precisely in those years were beginning to be designed). Therefore class struggle in the Marxist sense and militarism have the same root, namely, atheism and contempt for the human person, which place the principle of force above that of reason and law.

15. *Rerum novarum* is opposed to State control of the means of production, which would reduce every citizen to being a "cog" in the State machine. It is no less forceful in criticizing a concept of the State which completely excludes the economic sector from the State's range of interest and action. There is certainly a legitimate sphere of autonomy in economic life which the State should not enter. The State, however, has the task of determining the juridical framework within which economic affairs are to be conducted, and thus of safeguarding the prerequisites of a free economy, which presumes a certain equality between the parties, such that one party would not be so powerful as practically to reduce the other to subservience.43

In this regard, *Rerum novarum* points the way to just reforms which can restore dignity to work as the free activity of man. These reforms imply that society and the State will both assume responsibility, especially for protecting the worker from the nightmare of unemployment. Historically, this has happened in two converging ways: either through economic policies aimed at ensuring balanced growth and full employment, or through unemployment insurance and retraining programmes capable of ensuring a smooth transfer of workers from crisis sectors to those in expansion.

Furthermore, society and the State must ensure wage levels adequate for the maintenance of the worker and his family, including a certain amount for savings. This requires a continuous effort to improve workers' training and capability so that their work will be more skilled and productive, as well as careful controls and adequate legislative measures to block shameful forms of exploitation, especially to the disadvantage of the most vulnerable workers, of immigrants and of those on the margins of society. The role of trade unions in negotiating minimum salaries and working conditions is decisive in this area. Finally, "humane" working hours and adequate free-time need to be guaranteed, as well as the right to express one's own personality at the work-place without suffering any affront to one's conscience or personal dignity. This is the place to mention once more the role of trade unions, not only in negotiating contracts, but also as "places" where workers can express themselves. They serve the development of an authentic culture of work and help workers to share in a fully human way in the life of their place of employment.44

The State must contribute to the achievement of these goals both directly and indirectly. Indirectly and according to the *principle of subsidiarity*, by creating

favourable conditions for the free exercise of economic activity, which will lead
to abundant opportunities for employment and sources of wealth. Directly and
according to the *principle of solidarity*, by defending the weakest, by placing certain limits on the autonomy of the parties who determine working conditions,
and by ensuring in every case the necessary minimum support for the unem-
ployed worker.45
The Encyclical and the related social teaching of the Church had far-reaching
influence in the years bridging the nineteenth and twentieth centuries. This
influence is evident in the numerous reforms which were introduced in the
areas of social security, pensions, health insurance and compensation in the case of
accidents, within the framework of greater respect for the rights of workers.46

16. These reforms were carried out in part by States, but in the struggle to
achieve them *the role of the workers' movement* was an important one. This
movement, which began as a response of moral conscience to unjust and harmful situations, conducted a widespread campaign for reform, far removed from
vague ideology and closer to the daily needs of workers. In this context its
efforts were often joined to those of Christians in order to improve workers' living conditions. Later on, this movement was dominated to a certain extent by
the Marxist ideology against which *Rerum novarum* had spoken.
These same reforms were also partly the result of *an open process by which society
organized itself* through the establishment of effective instruments of solidarity,
which were capable of sustaining an economic growth more respectful of the
values of the person. Here we should remember the numerous efforts to which
Christians made a notable contribution in establishing producers', consumers'
and credit cooperatives, in promoting general education and professional training, in experimenting with various forms of participation in the life of the
work-place and in the life of society in general.
Thus, as we look at the past, there is good reason to thank God that the great
Encyclical was not without an echo in human hearts and indeed led to a generous response on the practical level. Still, we must acknowledge that its
prophetic message was not fully accepted by people at the time. Precisely for
this reason there ensued some very serious tragedies.

17. Reading the Encyclical within the context of Pope Leo's whole magisterium,47 we see how it points essentially to the socio-economic consequences
of an error which has even greater implications. As has been mentioned, this
error consists in an understanding of human freedom which detaches it from
obedience to the truth, and consequently from the duty to respect the rights of
others. The essence of freedom then becomes self-love carried to the point of
contempt for God and neighbour, a self-love which leads to an unbridled
affirmation of self-interest and which refuses to be limited by any demand of
justice.48

This very error had extreme consequences in the tragic series of wars which ravaged Europe and the world between 1914 and 1945. Some of these resulted from militarism and exaggerated nationalism, and from related forms of totalitarianism; some derived from the class struggle; still others were civil wars or wars of an ideological nature. Without the terrible burden of hatred and resentment which had built up as a result of so many injustices both on the international level and within individual States, such cruel wars would not have been possible, in which great nations invested their energies and in which there was no hesitation to violate the most sacred human rights, with the extermination of entire peoples and social groups being planned and carried out. Here we recall the Jewish people in particular, whose terrible fate has become a symbol of the aberration of which man is capable when he turns against God.

However, it is only when hatred and injustice are sanctioned and organized by the ideologies based on them, rather than on the truth about man, that they take possession of entire nations and drive them to act.49 *Rerum novarum* opposed ideologies of hatred and showed how violence and resentment could be overcome by justice. May the memory of those terrible events guide the actions of everyone, particularly the leaders of nations in our own time, when other forms of injustice are fuelling new hatreds and when new ideologies which exalt violence are appearing on the horizon.

18. While it is true that since 1945 weapons have been silent on the European continent, it must be remembered that true peace is never simply the result of military victory, but rather implies both the removal of the causes of war and genuine reconciliation between peoples. For many years there has been in Europe and the world a situation of non-war rather than genuine peace. Half of the continent fell under the domination of a Communist dictatorship, while the other half organized itself in defence against this threat. Many peoples lost the ability to control their own destiny and were enclosed within the suffocating boundaries of an empire in which efforts were made to destroy their historical memory and the centuries-old roots of their culture. As a result of this violent division of Europe, enormous masses of people were compelled to leave their homeland or were forcibly deported.

An insane arms race swallowed up the resources needed for the development of national economies and for assistance to the less developed nations. Scientific and technological progress, which should have contributed to man's well-being, was transformed into an instrument of war: science and technology were directed to the production of ever more efficient and destructive weapons. Meanwhile, an ideology, a perversion of authentic philosophy, was called upon to provide doctrinal justification for the new war. And this war was not simply expected and prepared for, but was actually fought with enormous bloodshed in various parts of the world. The logic of power blocs or empires, denounced in various Church documents and recently in the Encyclical *Sollicitudo rei socialis,50* led to a situation in which controversies and disagreements among Third World countries were systematically aggravated and exploited in order to create difficulties for the adversary.

Extremist groups, seeking to resolve such controversies through the use of arms, found ready political and military support and were equipped and trained for war; those who tried to find peaceful and humane solutions, with respect for the legitimate interests of all parties, remained isolated and often fell victim to their opponents. In addition, the precariousness of the peace which followed the Second World War was one of the principal causes of the militarization of many Third World countries and the fratricidal conflicts which afflicted them, as well as of the spread of terrorism and of increasingly barbaric means of political and military conflict. Moreover, the whole world was oppressed by the threat of an atomic war capable of leading to the extinction of humanity. Science used for military purposes had placed this decisive instrument at the disposal of hatred, strengthened by ideology. But if war can end without winners or losers in a suicide of humanity, then we must repudiate the logic which leads to it: the idea that the effort to destroy the enemy, confrontation and war itself are factors of progress and historical advancement.51 When the need for this repudiation is understood, the concepts of "total war" and "class struggle" must necessarily be called into question.

19. At the end of the Second World War, however, such a development was still being formed in people's consciences. What received attention was the spread of Communist totalitarianism over more than half of Europe and over other parts of the world. The war, which should have re-established freedom and restored the right of nations, ended without having attained these goals. Indeed, in a way, for many peoples, especially those which had suffered most during the war, it openly contradicted these goals. It may be said that the situation which arose has evoked different responses.

Following the destruction caused by the war, we see in some countries and under certain aspects a positive effort to rebuild a democratic society inspired by social justice, so as to deprive Communism of the revolutionary potential represented by masses of people subjected to exploitation and oppression. In general, such attempts endeavour to preserve free market mechanisms, ensuring, by means of a stable currency and the harmony of social relations, the conditions for steady and healthy economic growth in which people through their own work can build a better future for themselves and their families. At the same time, these attempts try to avoid making market mechanisms the only point of reference for social life, and they tend to subject them to public control which upholds the principle of the common destination of material goods. In this context, an abundance of work opportunities, a solid system of social security and professional training, the freedom to join trade unions and the effective action of unions, the assistance provided in cases of unemployment, the opportunities for democratic participation in the life of society – all these are meant to deliver work from the mere condition of "a commodity", and to guarantee its dignity.

Then there are the other social forces and ideological movements which oppose Marxism by setting up systems of "national security", aimed at controlling the whole of society in a systematic way, in order to make Marxist infiltration impossible. By emphasizing and increasing the power of the State, they wish to protect their people from Communism, but in doing so they run the grave risk of destroying the freedom and values of the person, the very things for whose sake it is necessary to oppose Communism.

Another kind of response, practical in nature, is represented by the affluent society or the consumer society. It seeks to defeat Marxism on the level of pure materialism by showing how a free-market society can achieve a greater satisfaction of material human needs than Communism, while equally excluding spiritual values. In reality, while on the one hand it is true that this social model shows the failure of Marxism to contribute to a humane and better society, on the other hand, insofar as it denies an autonomous existence and value to morality, law, culture and religion, it agrees with Marxism, in the sense that it totally reduces man to the sphere of economics and the satisfaction of material needs.

20. During the same period a widespread process of "decolonization" occurred, by which many countries gained or regained their independence and the right freely to determine their own destiny. With the formal re-acquisition of State sovereignty, however, these countries often find themselves merely at the beginning of the journey towards the construction of genuine independence. Decisive sectors of the economy still remain *de facto* in the hands of large foreign companies which are unwilling to commit themselves to the long-term development of the host country. Political life itself is controlled by foreign powers, while within the national boundaries there are tribal groups not yet amalgamated into a genuine national community. Also lacking is a class of competent professional people capable of running the State apparatus in an honest and just way, nor are there qualified personnel for managing the economy in an efficient and responsible manner.

Given this situation, many think that Marxism can offer a sort of short-cut for building up the nation and the State; thus many variants of socialism emerge with specific national characteristics. Legitimate demands for national recovery, forms of nationalism and also of militarism, principles drawn from ancient popular traditions (which are sometimes in harmony with Christian social doctrine) and Marxist-Leninist concepts and ideas – all these mingle in the many ideologies which take shape in ways that differ from case to case.

21. Lastly, it should be remembered that after the Second World War, and in reaction to its horrors, there arose a more lively sense of human rights, which

found recognition in a number of *International Documents52* and, one might
say, in the drawing up of a new "right of nations", to which the Holy See has
constantly contributed. The focal point of this evolution has been the United
Nations Organization. Not only has there been a development in awareness of
the rights of individuals, but also in awareness of the rights of nations, as well as
a clearer realization of the need to act in order to remedy the grave imbalances
that exist between the various geographical areas of the world. In a certain
sense, these imbalances have shifted the centre of the social question from the
national to the international level.53
While noting this process with satisfaction, nevertheless one cannot ignore the
fact that the overall balance of the various policies of aid for development has
not always been positive. The United Nations, moreover, has not yet succeeded
in establishing, as alternatives to war, effective means for the resolution of international conflicts. This seems to be the most urgent problem which the international community has yet to resolve.

III. THE YEAR 1989

22. It is on the basis of the world situation just described, and already elaborated in the Encyclical *Sollicitudo rei socialis,* that the unexpected and promising significance of the events of recent years can be understood. Although they
certainly reached their climax in 1989 in the countries of Central and Eastern
Europe, they embrace a longer period of time and a wider geographical area. In
the course of the 80s, certain dictatorial and oppressive regimes fell one by one
in some countries of Latin America and also of Africa and Asia. In other cases
there began a difficult but productive transition towards more participatory
and more just political structures. An important, even decisive, contribution
was made by *the Church's commitment to defend and promote human rights.* In
situations strongly influenced by ideology, in which polarization obscured the
awareness of a human dignity common to all, the Church affirmed clearly and
forcefully that every individual – whatever his or her personal convictions –
bears the image of God and therefore deserves respect. Often, the vast majority
of people identified themselves with this kind of affirmation, and this led to a
search for forms of protest and for political solutions more respectful of the
dignity of the person.
From this historical process new forms of democracy have emerged which offer
a hope for change in fragile political and social structures weighed down by a
painful series of injustices and resentments, as well as by a heavily damaged
economy and serious social conflicts. Together with the whole Church, I thank
God for the often heroic witness borne in such difficult circumstances by many
Pastors, entire Christian communities, individual members of the faithful, and
other people of good will; at the same time I pray that he will sustain the

efforts being made by everyone to build a better future. This is, in fact, a responsibility which falls not only to the citizens of the countries in question, but to all Christians and people of good will. It is a question of showing that the complex problems faced by those peoples can be resolved through dialogue and solidarity, rather than by a struggle to destroy the enemy through war.

23. Among the many factors involved in the fall of oppressive regimes, some deserve special mention. Certainly, the decisive factor which gave rise to the changes was the violation of the rights of workers. It cannot be forgotten that the fundamental crisis of systems claiming to express the rule and indeed the dictatorship of the working class began with the great upheavals which took place in Poland in the name of solidarity. It was the throngs of working people which foreswore the ideology which presumed to speak in their name. On the basis of a hard, lived experience of work and of oppression, it was they who recovered and, in a sense, rediscovered the content and principles of the Church's social doctrine.

Also worthy of emphasis is the fact that the fall of this kind of "bloc" or empire was accomplished almost everywhere by means of peaceful protest, using only the weapons of truth and justice. While Marxism held that only by exacerbating social conflicts was it possible to resolve them through violent confrontation, the protests which led to the collapse of Marxism tenaciously insisted on trying every avenue of negotiation, dialogue, and witness to the truth, appealing to the conscience of the adversary and seeking to reawaken in him a sense of shared human dignity.

It seemed that the European order resulting from the Second World War and sanctioned by the *Yalta Agreements* could only be overturned by another war. Instead, it has been overcome by the non-violent commitment of people who, while always refusing to yield to the force of power, succeeded time after time in finding effective ways of bearing witness to the truth. This disarmed the adversary, since violence always needs to justify itself through deceit, and to appear, however falsely, to be defending a right or responding to a threat posed by others.54 Once again I thank God for having sustained people's hearts amid difficult trials, and I pray that this example will prevail in other places and other circumstances. May people learn to fight for justice without violence, renouncing class struggle in their internal disputes, and war in international ones.

24. The second factor in the crisis was certainly the inefficiency of the economic system, which is not to be considered simply as a technical problem, but rather a consequence of the violation of the human rights to private initiative, to ownership of property and to freedom in the economic sector. To this must be added the cultural and national dimension: it is not possible to understand man on the basis of economics alone, nor to define him simply on the basis of

class membership. Man is understood in a more complete way when he is
situated within the sphere of culture through his language, history, and the
position he takes towards the fundamental events of life, such as birth, love,
work and death. At the heart of every culture lies the attitude man takes to the
greatest mystery: the mystery of God. Different cultures are basically different
ways of facing the question of the meaning of personal existence. When this
question is eliminated, the culture and moral life of nations are corrupted. For
this reason the struggle to defend work was spontaneously linked to the struggle
for culture and for national rights.
But the true cause of the new developments was the spiritual void brought
about by atheism, which deprived the younger generations of a sense of direction
and in many cases led them, in the irrepressible search for personal identity
and for the meaning of life, to rediscover the religious roots of their national
cultures, and to rediscover the person of Christ himself as the existentially
adequate response to the desire in every human heart for goodness, truth and
life. This search was supported by the witness of those who, in difficult circumstances and under persecution, remained faithful to God. Marxism had
promised to uproot the need for God from the human heart, but the results
have shown that it is not possible to succeed in this without throwing the heart
into turmoil.

25. The events of 1989 are an example of the success of willingness to negoti-
ate and of the Gospel spirit in the face of an adversary determined not to be
bound by moral principles. These events are a warning to those who, in the
name of political realism, wish to banish law and morality from the political
arena. Undoubtedly, the struggle which led to the changes of 1989 called for
clarity, moderation, suffering and sacrifice. In a certain sense, it was a struggle
born of prayer, and it would have been unthinkable without immense trust in
God, the Lord of history, who carries the human heart in his hands. It is by
uniting his own sufferings for the sake of truth and freedom to the sufferings
of Christ on the Cross that man is able to accomplish the miracle of peace and
is in a position to discern the often narrow path between the cowardice which
gives in to evil and the violence which, under the illusion of fighting evil, only
makes it worse.
Nevertheless, it cannot be forgotten that the manner in which the individual
exercises his freedom is conditioned in innumerable ways. While these certainly
have an influence on freedom, they do not determine it; they make the exercise
of freedom more difficult or less difficult, but they cannot destroy it. Not only
is it wrong from the ethical point of view to disregard human nature, which is
made for freedom, but in practice it is impossible to do so. Where society is so
organized as to reduce arbitrarily or even suppress the sphere in which freedom
is legitimately exercised, the result is that the life of society becomes progressively disorganized and goes into decline.

Moreover, man, who was created for freedom, bears within himself the wound of original sin, which constantly draws him towards evil and puts him in need of redemption. Not only is *this doctrine an integral part of Christian revelation;* it also has great hermeneutical value insofar as it helps one to understand human reality. Man tends towards good, but he is also capable of evil. He can transcend his immediate interest and still remain bound to it. The social order will be all the more stable, the more it takes this fact into account and does not place in opposition personal interest and the interests of society as a whole, but rather seeks ways to bring them into fruitful harmony. In fact, where self-interest is violently suppressed, it is replaced by a burdensome system of bureaucratic control which dries up the wellsprings of initiative and creativity. When people think they possess the secret of a perfect social organization which makes evil impossible, they also think that they can use any means, including violence and deceit, in order to bring that organization into being. Politics then becomes a "secular religion" which operates under the illusion of creating paradise in this world. But no political society – which possesses its own autonomy and laws55 – can ever be confused with the Kingdom of God. The Gospel parable of the weeds among the wheat (cf. Mt 13:24-30; 36-43) teaches that it is for God alone to separate the subjects of the Kingdom from the subjects of the Evil One, and that this judgment will take place at the end of time. By presuming to anticipate judgment here and now, man puts himself in the place of God and sets himself against the patience of God.

Through Christ's sacrifice on the Cross, the victory of the Kingdom of God has been achieved once and for all. Nevertheless, the Christian life involves a struggle against temptation and the forces of evil. Only at the end of history will the Lord return in glory for the final judgment (cf. Mt 25:31) with the establishment of a new heaven and a new earth (cf. 2 Pt 3:13; Rev 21:1); but as long as time lasts the struggle between good and evil continues even in the human heart itself.

What Sacred Scripture teaches us about the prospects of the Kingdom of God is not without consequences for the life of temporal societies, which, as the adjective indicates, belong to the realm of time, with all that this implies of imperfection and impermanence. The Kingdom of God, being *in* the world without being *of* the world, throws light on the order of human society, while the power of grace penetrates that order and gives it life. In this way the requirements of a society worthy of man are better perceived, deviations are corrected, the courage to work for what is good is reinforced. In union with all people of good will, Christians, especially the laity, are called to this task of imbuing human realities with the Gospel.56

26. The events of 1989 took place principally in the countries of Eastern and Central Europe. However, they have worldwide importance because they have positive and negative consequences which concern the whole human family.

These consequences are not mechanistic or fatalistic in character, but rather are opportunities for human freedom to cooperate with the merciful plan of God who acts within history.

The first consequence was *an encounter* in some countries *between the Church and the workers' movement*, which came about as a result of an ethical and explicitly Christian reaction against a widespread situation of injustice. For about a century the workers' movement had fallen in part under the dominance of Marxism, in the conviction that the working class, in order to struggle effectively against oppression, had to appropriate its economic and materialistic theories.

In the crisis of Marxism, the natural dictates of the consciences of workers have re-emerged in a demand for justice and a recognition of the dignity of work, in conformity with the social doctrine of the Church.57 The worker movement is part of a more general movement among workers and other people of good will for the liberation of the human person and for the affirmation of human rights. It is a movement which today has spread to many countries, and which, far from opposing the Catholic Church, looks to her with interest.

The crisis of Marxism does not rid the world of the situations of injustice and oppression which Marxism itself exploited and on which it fed. To those who are searching today for a new and authentic theory and praxis of liberation, the Church offers not only her social doctrine and, in general, her teaching about the human person redeemed in Christ, but also her concrete commitment and material assistance in the struggle against marginalization and suffering.

In the recent past, the sincere desire to be on the side of the oppressed and not to be cut off from the course of history has led many believers to seek in various ways an impossible compromise between Marxism and Christianity. Moving beyond all that was short-lived in these attempts, present circumstances are leading to a reaffirmation of the positive value of an authentic theology of integral human liberation.58 Considered from this point of view, the events of 1989 are proving to be important also for the countries of the Third World, which are searching for their own path to development, just as they were important for the countries of Central and Eastern Europe.

27. The second consequence concerns the peoples of Europe themselves. Many individual, social, regional and national injustices were committed during and prior to the years in which Communism dominated; much hatred and ill-will have accumulated. There is a real danger that these will re-explode after the collapse of dictatorship, provoking serious conflicts and casualties, should there be a lessening of the moral commitment and conscious striving to bear witness to the truth which were the inspiration for past efforts. It is to be hoped that hatred and violence will not triumph in people's hearts, especially among those who are struggling for justice, and that all people will grow in the spirit of peace and forgiveness.

What is needed are concrete steps to create or consolidate international structures capable of intervening through appropriate arbitration in the conflicts which arise between nations, so that each nation can uphold its own rights and reach a just agreement and peaceful settlement vis-à-vis the rights of others. This is especially needed for the nations of Europe, which are closely united in a bond of common culture and an ageold history. A great effort is needed to rebuild morally and economically the countries which have abandoned Communism. For a long time the most elementary economic relationships were distorted, and basic virtues of economic life, such as truthfulness, trustworthiness and hard work were denigrated. A patient material and moral reconstruction is needed, even as people, exhausted by longstanding privation, are asking their governments for tangible and immediate results in the form of material benefits and an adequate fulfilment of their legitimate aspirations.

The fall of Marxism has naturally had a great impact on the division of the planet into worlds which are closed to one another and in jealous competition. It has further highlighted the reality of interdependence among peoples, as well as the fact that human work, by its nature, is meant to unite peoples, not divide them. Peace and prosperity, in fact, are goods which belong to the whole human race: it is not possible to enjoy them in a proper and lasting way if they are achieved and maintained at the cost of other peoples and nations, by violating their rights or excluding them from the sources of well-being.

28. In a sense, for some countries of Europe the real post-war period is just beginning. The radical reordering of economic systems, hitherto collectivized, entails problems and sacrifices comparable to those which the countries of Western Europe had to face in order to rebuild after the Second World War. It is right that in the present difficulties the formerly Communist countries should be aided by the united effort of other nations. Obviously they themselves must be the primary agents of their own development, but they must also be given a reasonable opportunity to accomplish this goal, something that cannot happen without the help of other countries. Moreover, their present condition, marked by difficulties and shortages, is the result of an historical process in which the formerly Communist countries were often objects and not subjects. Thus they find themselves in the present situation not as a result of free choice or mistakes which were made, but as a consequence of tragic historical events which were violently imposed on them, and which prevented them from following the path of economic and social development.

Assistance from other countries, especially the countries of Europe which were part of that history and which bear responsibility for it, represents a debt in justice. But it also corresponds to the interest and welfare of Europe as a whole, since Europe cannot live in peace if the various conflicts which have arisen as a result of the past are to become more acute because of a situation of economic disorder, spiritual dissatisfaction and desperation.

This need, however, must not lead to a slackening of efforts to sustain and assist the countries of the Third World, which often suffer even more serious conditions of poverty and want.59 What is called for is a special effort to mobilize resources, which are not lacking in the world as a whole, for the purpose of economic growth and common development, redefining the priorities and hierarchies of values on the basis of which economic and political choices are made. Enormous resources can be made available by disarming the huge military machines which were constructed for the conflict between East and West. These resources could become even more abundant if, in place of war, reliable procedures for the resolution of conflicts could be set up, with the resulting spread of the principle of arms control and arms reduction, also in the countries of the Third World, through the adoption of appropriate measures against the arms trade.60 But it will be necessary above all to abandon a mentality in which the poor – as individuals and as peoples – are considered a burden, as irksome intruders trying to consume what others have produced. The poor ask for the right to share in enjoying material goods and to make good use of their capacity for work, thus creating a world that is more just and prosperous for all. The advancement of the poor constitutes a great opportunity for the moral, cultural and even economic growth of all humanity.

29. Finally, development must not be understood solely in economic terms, but in a way that is fully human.61 It is not only a question of raising all peoples to the level currently enjoyed by the richest countries, but rather of building up a more decent life through united labour, of concretely enhancing every individual's dignity and creativity, as well as his capacity to respond to his personal vocation, and thus to God's call. The apex of development is the exercise of the right and duty to seek God, to know him and to live in accordance with that knowledge.62 In the totalitarian and authoritarian regimes, the principle that force predominates over reason was carried to the extreme. Man was compelled to submit to a conception of reality imposed on him by coercion, and not reached by virtue of his own reason and the exercise of his own freedom. This principle must be overturned and total recognition must be given to *the rights of the human conscience,* which is bound only to the truth, both natural and revealed. The recognition of these rights represents the primary foundation of every authentically free political order.63 It is important to reaffirm this latter principle for several reasons:

a) because the old forms of totalitarianism and authoritarianism are not yet completely vanquished; indeed there is a risk that they will regain their strength. This demands renewed efforts of cooperation and solidarity between all countries;

b) because in the developed countries there is sometimes an excessive promotion of purely utilitarian values, with an appeal to the appetites and inclinations towards immediate gratification, making it difficult to recognize and respect the hierarchy of the true values of human existence;

c) because in some countries new forms of religious fundamentalism are emerging which covertly, or even openly, deny to citizens of faiths other than that of the majority the full exercise of their civil and religious rights, preventing them from taking part in the cultural process, and restricting both the Church's right to preach the Gospel and the rights of those who hear this preaching to accept it and to be converted to Christ. No authentic progress is possible without respect for the natural and fundamental right to know the truth and live according to that truth. The exercise and development of this right includes the right to discover and freely to accept Jesus Christ, who is man's true good.64

IV. PRIVATE PROPERTY AND THE UNIVERSAL DESTINATION OF MATERIAL GOODS

30. In *Rerum novarum,* Leo XIII strongly affirmed the natural character of the right to private property, using various arguments against the socialism of his time.65 This right, which is fundamental for the autonomy and development of the person, has always been defended by the Church up to our own day. At the same time, the Church teaches that the possession of material goods is not an absolute right, and that its limits are inscribed in its very nature as a human right.

While the Pope proclaimed the right to private ownership, he affirmed with equal clarity that the "use" of goods, while marked by freedom, is subordinated to their original common destination as created goods, as well as to the will of Jesus Christ as expressed in the Gospel. Pope Leo wrote: "those whom fortune favours are admonished ... that they should tremble at the warnings of Jesus Christ ... and that a most strict account must be given to the Supreme Judge for the use of all they possess"; and quoting Saint Thomas Aquinas, he added: "But if the question be asked, how must one's possessions be used? the Church replies without hesitation that man should not consider his material possessions as his own, but as common to all...", because "above the laws and judgments of men stands the law, the judgment of Christ".66

The Successors of Leo XIII have repeated this twofold affirmation: the necessity and therefore the legitimacy of private ownership, as well as the limits which are imposed on it.67 The Second Vatican Council likewise clearly restated the traditional doctrine in words which bear repeating: "In making use of the exterior things we lawfully possess, we ought to regard them not just as our own but also as common, in the sense that they can profit not only the owners but others too"; and a little later we read: "Private property or some ownership of external goods affords each person the scope needed for personal and family autonomy, and should be regarded as an extension of human freedom ... Of its nature private property also has a social function which is based on the law of the *common purpose of goods*".68 I have returned to this same doctrine, first in my address to the Third Conference of the Latin American Bishops at Puebla, and later in the Encyclicals *Laborem exercens* and *Sollicitudo rei socialis.69*

31. Re-reading this teaching on the right to property and the common destination of material wealth as it applies to the present time, the question can be raised concerning the origin of the material goods which sustain human life, satisfy people's needs and are an object of their rights.
The original source of all that is good is the very act of God, who created both the earth and man, and who gave the earth to man so that he might have dominion over it by his work and enjoy its fruits (Gen 1:28). God gave the earth to the whole human race for the sustenance of all its members, without excluding or favouring anyone. This is *the foundation of the universal destination of the earth's goods.* The earth, by reason of its fruitfulness and its capacity to satisfy human needs, is God's first gift for the sustenance of human life. But the earth does not yield its fruits without a particular human response to God's gift, that is to say, without work. It is through work that man, using his intelligence and exercising his freedom, succeeds in dominating the earth and making it a fitting home. In this way, he makes part of the earth his own, precisely the part which he has acquired through work; this is *the origin of individual property.* Obviously, he also has the responsibility not to hinder others from having their own part of God's gift; indeed, he must cooperate with others so that together all can dominate the earth.
In history, these two factors – *work* and *the land* – are to be found at the beginning of every human society. However, they do not always stand in the same relationship to each other. At one time *the natural fruitfulness of the earth* appeared to be, and was in fact, the primary factor of wealth, while work was, as it were, the help and support for this fruitfulness. In our time, *the role of human work* is becoming increasingly important as the productive factor both of non-material and of material wealth. Moreover, it is becoming clearer how a person's work is naturally interrelated with the work of others. More than ever, work is *work with others* and *work for others:* it is a matter of doing something for someone else. Work becomes ever more fruitful and productive to the extent that people become more knowledgeable of the productive potentialities of the earth and more profoundly cognisant of the needs of those for whom their work is done.

32. In our time, in particular, there exists another form of ownership which is becoming no less important than land: *the possession of know-how, technology and skill.* The wealth of the industrialized nations is based much more on this kind of ownership than on natural resources.
Mention has just been made of the fact that *people work with each other,* sharing in a "community of work" which embraces ever widening circles. A person

who produces something other than for his own use generally does so in order that others may use it after they have paid a just price, mutually agreed upon through free bargaining. It is precisely the ability to foresee both the needs of others and the combinations of productive factors most adapted to satisfying those needs that constitutes another important source of wealth in modern society. Besides, many goods cannot be adequately produced through the work of an isolated individual; they require the cooperation of many people in working towards a common goal. Organizing such a productive effort, planning its duration in time, making sure that it corresponds in a positive way to the demands which it must satisfy, and taking the necessary risks – all this too is a source of wealth in today's society. In this way, the *role* of disciplined and creative *human work* and, as an essential part of that work, *initiative and entrepreneurial ability* becomes increasingly evident and decisive.70

This process, which throws practical light on a truth about the person which Christianity has constantly affirmed, should be viewed carefully and favourably. Indeed, besides the earth, man's principal resource is *man himself*. His intelligence enables him to discover the earth's productive potential and the many different ways in which human needs can be satisfied. It is his disciplined work in close collaboration with others that makes possible the creation of ever more extensive *working communities* which can be relied upon to transform man's natural and human environments. Important virtues are involved in this process, such as diligence, industriousness, prudence in undertaking reasonable risks, reliability and fidelity in interpersonal relationships, as well as courage in carrying out decisions which are difficult and painful but necessary, both for the overall working of a business and in meeting possible set-backs.

The modern *business economy* has positive aspects. Its basis is human freedom exercised in the economic field, just as it is exercised in many other fields. Economic activity is indeed but one sector in a great variety of human activities, and like every other sector, it includes the right to freedom, as well as the duty of making responsible use of freedom. But it is important to note that there are specific differences between the trends of modern society and those of the past, even the recent past. Whereas at one time the decisive factor of production was *the land*, and later capital – understood as a total complex of the instruments of production – today the decisive factor is increasingly *man himself*, that is, his knowledge, especially his scientific knowledge, his capacity for interrelated and compact organization, as well as his ability to perceive the needs of others and to satisfy them.

33. However, the risks and problems connected with this kind of process should be pointed out. The fact is that many people, perhaps the majority today, do not have the means which would enable them to take their place in an effective and humanly dignified way within a productive system in which work is truly central. They have no possibility of acquiring the basic knowledge

which would enable them to express their creativity and develop their potential. They have no way of entering the network of knowledge and intercommunication which would enable them to see their qualities appreciated and utilized. Thus, if not actually exploited, they are to a great extent marginalized; economic development takes place over their heads, so to speak, when it does not actually reduce the already narrow scope of their old subsistence economies. They are unable to compete against the goods which are produced in ways which are new and which properly respond to needs, needs which they had previously been accustomed to meeting through traditional forms of organization. Allured by the dazzle of an opulence which is beyond their reach, and at the same time driven by necessity, these people crowd the cities of the Third World where they are often without cultural roots, and where they are exposed to situations of violent uncertainty, without the possibility of becoming integrated. Their dignity is not acknowledged in any real way, and sometimes there are even attempts to eliminate them from history through coercive forms of demographic control which are contrary to human dignity.

Many other people, while not completely marginalized, live in situations in which the struggle for a bare minimum is uppermost. These are situations in which the rules of the earliest period of capitalism still flourish in conditions of "ruthlessness" in no way inferior to the darkest moments of the first phase of industrialization. In other cases the land is still the central element in the economic process, but those who cultivate it are excluded from ownership and are reduced to a state of quasi-servitude.71 In these cases, it is still possible today, as in the days of *Rerum novarum,* to speak of inhuman exploitation. In spite of the great changes which have taken place in the more advanced societies, the human inadequacies of capitalism and the resulting domination of things over people are far from disappearing. In fact, for the poor, to the lack of material goods has been added a lack of knowledge and training which prevents them from escaping their state of humiliating subjection.

Unfortunately, the great majority of people in the Third World still live in such conditions. It would be a mistake, however, to understand this *"world"* in purely geographic terms. In some regions and in some social sectors of that world, development programmes have been set up which are centered on the use not so much of the material resources available but of the "human resources". Even in recent years it was thought that the poorest countries would develop by isolating themselves from the world market and by depending only on their own resources. Recent experience has shown that countries which did this have suffered stagnation and recession, while the countries which experienced development were those which succeeded in taking part in the general interrelated economic activities at the international level. It seems therefore that the chief problem is that of gaining fair access to the international market, based not on the unilateral principle of the exploitation of the natural resources of these countries but on the proper use of human resources.72

However, aspects typical of the Third World also appear in developed countries, where the constant transformation of the methods of production and
consumption devalues certain acquired skills and professional expertise, and
thus requires a continual effort of re-training and updating. Those who fail to
keep up with the times can easily be marginalized, as can the elderly, the young
people who are incapable of finding their place in the life of society and, in general,
those who are weakest or part of the so-called Fourth World. The situation of
women too is far from easy in these conditions.

34. It would appear that, on the level of individual nations and of international
relations, the *free market* is the most efficient instrument for utilizing resources
and effectively responding to needs. But this is true only for those needs which
are "solvent", insofar as they are endowed with purchasing power, and for those
resources which are "marketable", insofar as they are capable of obtaining a satisfactory price. But there are many human needs which find no place on the
market. It is a strict duty of justice and truth not to allow fundamental human
needs to remain unsatisfied, and not to allow those burdened by such needs to
perish. It is also necessary to help these needy people to acquire expertise, to
enter the circle of exchange, and to develop their skills in order to make the
best use of their capacities and resources. Even prior to the logic of a fair
exchange of goods and the forms of justice appropriate to it, there exists *something which is due to man because he is man,* by reason of his lofty dignity. Inseparable from that required "something" is the possibility to survive and, at the
same time, to make an active contribution to the common good of humanity.
In Third World contexts, certain objectives stated by *Rerum novarum* remain
valid, and, in some cases, still constitute a goal yet to be reached, if man's work
and his very being are not to be reduced to the level of a mere commodity.
These objectives include a sufficient wage for the support of the family, social
insurance for old age and unemployment, and adequate protection for the
conditions of employment.

35. Here we find a wide range of *opportunities for commitment and effort* in the
name of justice on the part of trade unions and other workers' organizations.
These defend workers' rights and protect their interests as persons, while fulfilling a vital cultural role, so as to enable workers to participate more fully and
honourably in the life of their nation and to assist them along the path of
development.
In this sense, it is right to speak of a struggle against an economic system, if the
latter is understood as a method of upholding the absolute predominance of
capital, the possession of the means of production and of the land, in contrast
to the free and personal nature of human work.73 In the struggle against such
a system, what is being proposed as an alternative is not the socialist system,
which in fact turns out to be State capitalism, but rather *a society of free work,*

of enterprise and of participation. Such a society is not directed against the market, but demands that the market be appropriately controlled by the forces of society and by the State, so as to guarantee that the basic needs of the whole of society are satisfied.

The Church acknowledges the legitimate *role of profit* as an indication that a business is functioning well. When a firm makes a profit, this means that productive factors have been properly employed and corresponding human needs have been duly satisfied. But profitability is not the only indicator of a firm's condition. It is possible for the financial accounts to be in order, and yet for the people – who make up the firm's most valuable asset – to be humiliated and their dignity offended. Besides being morally inadmissible, this will eventually have negative repercussions on the firm's economic efficiency. In fact, the purpose of a business firm is not simply to make a profit, but is to be found in its very existence as a *community of persons* who in various ways are endeavouring to satisfy their basic needs, and who form a particular group at the service of the whole of society. Profit is a regulator of the life of a business, but it is not the only one; *other human and moral factors* must also be considered which, in the long term, are at least equally important for the life of a business.

We have seen that it is unacceptable to say that the defeat of so-called "Real Socialism" leaves capitalism as the only model of economic organization. It is necessary to break down the barriers and monopolies which leave so many countries on the margins of development, and to provide all individuals and nations with the basic conditions which will enable them to share in development. This goal calls for programmed and responsible efforts on the part of the entire international community. Stronger nations must offer weaker ones opportunities for taking their place in international life, and the latter must learn how to use these opportunities by making the necessary efforts and sacrifices and by ensuring political and economic stability, the certainty of better prospects for the future, the improvement of workers' skills, and the training of competent business leaders who are conscious of their responsibilities.74

At present, the positive efforts which have been made along these lines are being affected by the still largely unsolved problem of the foreign debt of the poorer countries. The principle that debts must be paid is certainly just. However, it is not right to demand or expect payment when the effect would be the imposition of political choices leading to hunger and despair for entire peoples. It cannot be expected that the debts which have been contracted should be paid at the price of unbearable sacrifices. In such cases it is necessary to find – as in fact is partly happening – ways to lighten, defer or even cancel the debt, compatible with the fundamental right of peoples to subsistence and progress.

36. It would now be helpful to direct our attention to the specific problems and threats emerging within the more advanced economies and which are related to their particular characteristics. In earlier stages of development, man

always lived under the weight of necessity. His needs were few and were deter-mined, to a degree, by the objective structures of his physical make-up. Economic activity was directed towards satisfying these needs. It is clear that today the problem is not only one of supplying people with a sufficient quan-tity of goods, but also of responding to a *demand for quality:* the quality of the goods to be produced and consumed, the quality of the services to be enjoyed, the quality of the environment and of life in general.

To call for an existence which is qualitatively more satisfying is of itself legiti-mate, but one cannot fail to draw attention to the new responsibilities and dan-gers connected with this phase of history. The manner in which new needs arise and are defined is always marked by a more or less appropriate concept of man and of his true good. A given culture reveals its overall understanding of life through the choices it makes in production and consumption. It is here that *the phenomenon of consumerism* arises. In singling out new needs and new means to meet them, one must be guided by a comprehensive picture of man which respects all the dimensions of his being and which subordinates his material and instinctive dimensions to his interior and spiritual ones. If, on the contrary, a direct appeal is made to his instincts – while ignoring in various ways the reality of the person as intelligent and free – then *consumer attitudes* and *life-styles* can be created which are objectively improper and often damag-ing to his physical and spiritual health. Of itself, an economic system does not possess criteria for correctly distinguishing new and higher forms of satisfying human needs from artificial new needs which hinder the formation of a mature personality. *Thus a great deal of educational and cultural work* is urgently needed, including the education of consumers in the responsible use of their power of choice, the formation of a strong sense of responsibility among producers and among people in the mass media in particular, as well as the necessary intervention by public authorities.

A striking example of artificial consumption contrary to the health and dignity of the human person, and certainly not easy to control, is the use of drugs. Widespread drug use is a sign of a serious malfunction in the social system; it also implies a materialistic and, in a certain sense, destructive "reading" of human needs. In this way the innovative capacity of a free economy is brought to a one-sided and inadequate conclusion. Drugs, as well as pornography and other forms of consumerism which exploit the frailty of the weak, tend to fill the resulting spiritual void.

It is not wrong to want to live better; what is wrong is a style of life which is presumed to be better when it is directed towards "having" rather than "being", and which wants to have more, not in order to be more but in order to spend life in enjoyment as an end in itself.75 It is therefore necessary to create life-styles in which the quest for truth, beauty, goodness and communion with others for the sake of common growth are the factors which determine con-sumer choices, savings and investments. In this regard, it is not a matter of the duty of charity alone, that is, the duty to give from one's "abundance", and sometimes even out of one's needs, in order to provide what is essential for the life of a poor person. I am referring to the fact that even the decision to invest in one place rather than another, in one productive sector rather than another, is always *a moral and cultural choice*. Given the utter necessity of certain economic conditions and of political stability, the decision to invest, that is, to offer people an opportunity to make good use of their own labour, is also determined by an attitude of human sympathy and trust in Providence, which reveal the human quality of the person making such decisions.

37. Equally worrying is *the ecological question* which accompanies the problem of consumerism and which is closely connected to it. In his desire to have and to enjoy rather than to be and to grow, man consumes the resources of the earth and his own life in an excessive and disordered way. At the root of the senseless destruction of the natural environment lies an anthropological error, which unfortunately is widespread in our day. Man, who discovers his capacity to transform and in a certain sense create the world through his own work, forgets that this is always based on God's prior and original gift of the things that are. Man thinks that he can make arbitrary use of the earth, subjecting it without restraint to his will, as though it did not have its own requisites and a prior God-given purpose, which man can indeed develop but must not betray. Instead of carrying out his role as a co-operator with God in the work of creation, man sets himself up in place of God and thus ends up provoking a rebellion on the part of nature, which is more tyrannized than governed by him.76
In all this, one notes first the poverty or narrowness of man's outlook, motivated as he is by a desire to possess things rather than to relate them to the truth, and lacking that disinterested, unselfish and aesthetic attitude that is born of wonder in the presence of being and of the beauty which enables one to see in visible things the message of the invisible God who created them. In this regard, humanity today must be conscious of its duties and obligations towards future generations.

38. In addition to the irrational destruction of the natural environment, we must also mention the more serious destruction of the *human environment,* something which is by no means receiving the attention it deserves. Although people are rightly worried – though much less than they should be – about preserving the natural habitats of the various animal species threatened with extinction, because they realize that each of these species makes its particular contribution to the balance of nature in general, too little effort is made to *safeguard the moral conditions for an authentic "human ecology"*. Not only has God given the earth to man, who must use it with respect for the original good purpose for which it was given to him, but man too is God's gift to man. He must

therefore respect the natural and moral structure with which he has been endowed. In this context, mention should be made of the serious problems of modern urbanization, of the need for urban planning which is concerned with how people are to live, and of the attention which should be given to a "social ecology" of work.

Man receives from God his essential dignity and with it the capacity to transcend every social order so as to move towards truth and goodness. But he is also conditioned by the social structure in which he lives, by the education he has received and by his environment. These elements can either help or hinder his living in accordance with the truth. The decisions which create a human environment can give rise to specific structures of sin which impede the full realization of those who are in any way oppressed by them. To destroy such structures and replace them with more authentic forms of living in community is a task which demands courage and patience.77

39. The first and fundamental structure for "human ecology" is the family, in which man receives his first formative ideas about truth and goodness, and learns what it means to love and to be loved, and thus what it actually means to be a person. Here we mean the *family founded on marriage,* in which the mutual gift of self by husband and wife creates an environment in which children can be born and develop their potentialities, become aware of their dignity and prepare to face their unique and individual destiny. But it often happens that people are discouraged from creating the proper conditions for human reproduction and are led to consider themselves and their lives as a series of sensations to be experienced rather than as a work to be accomplished. The result is a lack of freedom, which causes a person to reject a commitment to enter into a stable relationship with another person and to bring children into the world, or which leads people to consider children as one of the many "things" which an individual can have or not have, according to taste, and which compete with other possibilities.

It is necessary to go back to seeing the family as the *sanctuary of life.* The family is indeed sacred: it is the place in which life – the gift of God – can be properly welcomed and protected against the many attacks to which it is exposed, and can develop in accordance with what constitutes authentic human growth. In the face of the so-called culture of death, the family is the heart of the culture of life.

Human ingenuity seems to be directed more towards limiting, suppressing or destroying the sources of life – including recourse to abortion, which unfortunately is so widespread in the world – than towards defending and opening up the possibilities of life. The Encyclical *Sollicitudo rei socialis* denounced systematic anti-childbearing campaigns which, on the basis of a distorted view of the demographic problem and in a climate of "absolute lack of respect for the freedom of choice of the parties involved", often subject them "to intolerable

pressures ... in order to force them to submit to this new form of oppression".78 These policies are extending their field of action by the use of new
techniques, to the point of poisoning the lives of millions of defenceless human
beings, as if in a form of "chemical warfare".

These criticisms are directed not so much against an economic system as
against an ethical and cultural system. The economy in fact is only one aspect
and one dimension of the whole of human activity. If economic life is absolu-
tized, if the production and consumption of goods become the centre of social
life and society's only value, not subject to any other value, the reason is to be
found not so much in the economic system itself as in the fact that the entire
socio-cultural system, by ignoring the ethical and religious dimension, has been
weakened, and ends by limiting itself to the production of goods and services
alone.79

All of this can be summed up by repeating once more that economic freedom
is only one element of human freedom. When it becomes autonomous, when
man is seen more as a producer or consumer of goods than as a subject who
produces and consumes in order to live, then economic freedom loses its necessary relationship to the human person and ends up by alienating and oppressing
him.80

40. It is the task of the State to provide for the defence and preservation of
common goods such as the natural and human environments, which cannot be
safeguarded simply by market forces. Just as in the time of primitive capitalism
the State had the duty of defending the basic rights of workers, so now, with
the new capitalism, the State and all of society have the duty of *defending those
collective goods* which, among others, constitute the essential framework for the
legitimate pursuit of personal goals on the part of each individual.

Here we find a new limit on the market: there are collective and qualitative
needs which cannot be satisfied by market mechanisms. There are important
human needs which escape its logic. There are goods which by their very
nature cannot and must not be bought or sold. Certainly the mechanisms of
the market offer secure advantages: they help to utilize resources better; they
promote the exchange of products; above all they give central place to the
person's desires and preferences, which, in a contract, meet the desires and preferences of another person. Nevertheless, these mechanisms carry the risk of an
"idolatry" of the market, an idolatry which ignores the existence of goods
which by their nature are not and cannot be mere commodities.

41. Marxism criticized capitalist bourgeois societies, blaming them for the
commercialization and alienation of human existence. This rebuke is of course
based on a mistaken and inadequate idea of alienation, derived solely from the
sphere of relationships of production and ownership, that is, giving them a
materialistic foundation and moreover denying the legitimacy and positive

value of market relationships even in their own sphere. Marxism thus ends up by affirming that only in a collective society can alienation be eliminated. However, the historical experience of socialist countries has sadly demonstrated that collectivism does not do away with alienation but rather increases it, adding to it a lack of basic necessities and economic inefficiency.

The historical experience of the West, for its part, shows that even if the Marxist analysis and its foundation of alienation are false, nevertheless alienation – and the loss of the authentic meaning of life – is a reality in Western societies too. This happens in consumerism, when people are ensnared in a web of false and superficial gratifications rather than being helped to experience their person-hood in an authentic and concrete way. Alienation is found also in work, when it is organized so as to ensure maximum returns and profits with no concern whether the worker, through his own labour, grows or diminishes as a person, either through increased sharing in a genuinely supportive community or through increased isolation in a maze of relationships marked by destructive competitiveness and estrangement, in which he is considered only a means and not an end.

The concept of alienation needs to be led back to the Christian vision of reality, by recognizing in alienation a reversal of means and ends. When man does not recognize in himself and in others the value and grandeur of the human person, he effectively deprives himself of the possibility of benefitting from his human-ity and of entering into that relationship of solidarity and communion with others for which God created him. Indeed, it is through the free gift of self that man truly finds himself.81 This gift is made possible by the human person's essential "capacity for transcendence". Man cannot give himself to a purely human plan for reality, to an abstract ideal or to a false utopia. As a person, he can give himself to another person or to other persons, and ultimately to God, who is the author of his being and who alone can fully accept his gift.82 A man is alienated if he refuses to transcend himself and to live the experience of self-giving and of the formation of an authentic human community oriented towards his final destiny, which is God. A society is alienated if its forms of social organization, production and consumption make it more difficult to offer this gift of self and to establish this solidarity between people.

Exploitation, at least in the forms analyzed and described by Karl Marx, has been overcome in Western society. Alienation, however, has not been overcome as it exists in various forms of exploitation, when people use one another, and when they seek an ever more refined satisfaction of their individual and secondary needs, while ignoring the principal and authentic needs which ought to regulate the manner of satisfying the other ones too.83 A person who is con-cerned solely or primarily with possessing and enjoying, who is no longer able to control his instincts and passions, or to subordinate them by obedience to the truth, cannot be free: *obedience to the truth* about God and man is the first condition of freedom, making it possible for a person to order his needs and desires and to choose the means of satisfying them according to a correct scale of values, so that the ownership of things may become an occasion of growth for him. This growth can be hindered as a result of manipulation by the means of mass communication, which impose fashions and trends of opinion through carefully orchestrated repetition, without it being possible to subject to critical scrutiny the premises on which these fashions and trends are based.

42. Returning now to the initial question: can it perhaps be said that, after the failure of Communism, capitalism is the victorious social system, and that capitalism should be the goal of the countries now making efforts to rebuild their economy and society? Is this the model which ought to be proposed to the countries of the Third World which are searching for the path to true economic and civil progress?

The answer is obviously complex. If by "capitalism" is meant an economic system which recognizes the fundamental and positive role of business, the market, private property and the resulting responsibility for the means of production, as well as free human creativity in the economic sector, then the answer is certainly in the affirmative, even though it would perhaps be more appropriate to speak of a "business economy", "market economy" or simply "free economy". But if by "capitalism" is meant a system in which freedom in the economic sector is not circumscribed within a strong juridical framework which places it at the service of human freedom in its totality, and which sees it as a particular aspect of that freedom, the core of which is ethical and religious, then the reply is certainly negative.

The Marxist solution has failed, but the realities of marginalization and exploitation remain in the world, especially the Third World, as does the reality of human alienation, especially in the more advanced countries. Against these phenomena the Church strongly raises her voice. Vast multitudes are still living in conditions of great material and moral poverty. The collapse of the Communist system in so many countries certainly removes an obstacle to facing these problems in an appropriate and realistic way, but it is not enough to bring about their solution. Indeed, there is a risk that a radical capitalistic ideology could spread which refuses even to consider these problems, in the *a priori* belief that any attempt to solve them is doomed to failure, and which blindly entrusts their solution to the free development of market forces.

43. The Church has no models to present; models that are real and truly effective can only arise within the framework of different historical situations, through the efforts of all those who responsibly confront concrete problems in all their social, economic, political and cultural aspects, as these interact with one another.84 For such a task the Church offers her social teaching as an *indispensable and ideal orientation,* a teaching which, as already mentioned,

recognizes the positive value of the market and of enterprise, but which at the same time points out that these need to be oriented towards the common good. This teaching also recognizes the legitimacy of workers' efforts to obtain full respect for their dignity and to gain broader areas of participation in the life of industrial enterprises so that, while cooperating with others and under the direction of others, they can in a certain sense "work for themselves"85 through the exercise of their intelligence and freedom.

The integral development of the human person through work does not impede but rather promotes the greater productivity and efficiency of work itself, even though it may weaken consolidated power structures. A business cannot be considered only as a "society of capital goods"; it is also a "society of persons" in which people participate in different ways and with specific responsibilities, whether they supply the necessary capital for the company's activities or take part in such activities through their labour. To achieve these goals there is still need for a broad associated workers' movement, directed towards the liberation and promotion of the whole person.

In the light of today's "new things", we have re-read *the relationship between individual or private property and the universal destination of material wealth.* Man fulfils himself by using his intelligence and freedom. In so doing he utilizes the things of this world as objects and instruments and makes them his own. The foundation of the right to private initiative and ownership is to be found in this activity. By means of his work man commits himself, not only for his own sake but also *for others* and *with others*. Each person collaborates in the work of others and for their good. Man works in order to provide for the needs of his family, his community, his nation, and ultimately all humanity.86 Moreover, he collaborates in the work of his fellow employees, as well as in the work of suppliers and in the customers' use of goods, in a progressively expanding chain of solidarity. Ownership of the means of production, whether in industry or agriculture, is just and legitimate if it serves useful work. It becomes illegitimate, however, when it is not utilized or when it serves to impede the work of others, in an effort to gain a profit which is not the result of the overall expansion of work and the wealth of society, but rather is the result of curbing them or of illicit exploitation, speculation or the breaking of solidarity among working people.87 Ownership of this kind has no justification, and represents an abuse in the sight of God and man.

The obligation to earn one's bread by the sweat of one's brow also presumes the right to do so. A society in which this right is systematically denied, in which economic policies do not allow workers to reach satisfactory levels of employment, cannot be justified from an ethical point of view, nor can that society attain social peace.88 Just as the person fully realizes himself in the free gift of self, so too ownership morally justifies itself in the creation, at the proper time and in the proper way, of opportunities for work and human growth for all.

V. STATE AND CULTURE

44. Pope Leo XIII was aware of the need for a sound *theory of the State* in order to ensure the normal development of man's spiritual and temporal activities, both of which are indispensable.89 For this reason, in one passage of *Rerum novarum* he presents the organization of society according to the three powers – legislative, executive and judicial –, something which at the time represented a novelty in Church teaching.90 Such an ordering reflects a realistic vision of man's social nature, which calls for legislation capable of protecting the freedom of all. To that end, it is preferable that each power be balanced by other powers and by other spheres of responsibility which keep it within proper bounds. This is the principle of the "rule of law", in which the law is sovereign, and not the arbitrary will of individuals.

In modern times, this concept has been opposed by totalitarianism, which, in its Marxist-Leninist form, maintains that some people, by virtue of a deeper knowledge of the laws of the development of society, or through membership of a particular class or through contact with the deeper sources of the collective consciousness, are exempt from error and can therefore arrogate to themselves the exercise of absolute power. It must be added that totalitarianism arises out of a denial of truth in the objective sense. If there is no transcendent truth, in obedience to which man achieves his full identity, then there is no sure principle for guaranteeing just relations between people. Their self-interest as a class, group or nation would inevitably set them in opposition to one another. If one does not acknowledge transcendent truth, then the force of power takes over, and each person tends to make full use of the means at his disposal in order to impose his own interests or his own opinion, with no regard for the rights of others. People are then respected only to the extent that they can be exploited for selfish ends. Thus, the root of modern totalitarianism is to be found in the denial of the transcendent dignity of the human person who, as the visible image of the invisible God, is therefore by his very nature the subject of rights which no one may violate – no individual, group, class, nation or State. Not even the majority of a social body may violate these rights, by going against the minority, by isolating, oppressing, or exploiting it, or by attempting to annihilate it.91

45. The culture and praxis of totalitarianism also involve a rejection of the Church. The State or the party which claims to be able to lead history towards perfect goodness, and which sets itself above all values, cannot tolerate the affirmation of an *objective criterion of good and evil* beyond the will of those in power, since such a criterion, in given circumstances, could be used to judge their actions. This explains why totalitarianism attempts to destroy the Church, or at least to reduce her to submission, making her an instrument of its own ideological apparatus.92

Furthermore, the totalitarian State tends to absorb within itself the nation, society, the family, religious groups and individuals themselves. In defending her own freedom, the Church is also defending the human person, who must obey God rather than men (cf. Acts 5:29), as well as defending the family, the various social organizations and nations – all of which enjoy their own spheres of autonomy and sovereignty.

46. The Church values the democratic system inasmuch as it ensures the participation of citizens in making political choices, guarantees to the governed the possibility both of electing and holding accountable those who govern them, and of replacing them through peaceful means when appropriate.[93] Thus she cannot encourage the formation of narrow ruling groups which usurp the power of the State for individual interests or for ideological ends.

Authentic democracy is possible only in a State ruled by law, and on the basis of a correct conception of the human person. It requires that the necessary conditions be present for the advancement both of the individual through education and formation in true ideals, and of the "subjectivity" of society through the creation of structures of participation and shared responsibility. Nowadays there is a tendency to claim that agnosticism and sceptical relativism are the philosophy and the basic attitude which correspond to democratic forms of political life. Those who are convinced that they know the truth and firmly adhere to it are considered unreliable from a democratic point of view, since they do not accept that truth is determined by the majority, or that it is subject to variation according to different political trends. It must be observed in this regard that if there is no ultimate truth to guide and direct political activity, then ideas and convictions can easily be manipulated for reasons of power. As history demonstrates, a democracy without values easily turns into open or thinly disguised totalitarianism.

Nor does the Church close her eyes to the danger of fanaticism or fundamentalism among those who, in the name of an ideology which purports to be scientific or religious, claim the right to impose on others their own concept of what is true and good. *Christian truth* is not of this kind. Since it is not an ideology, the Christian faith does not presume to imprison changing socio-political realities in a rigid schema, and it recognizes that human life is realized in history in conditions that are diverse and imperfect. Furthermore, in constantly reaffirming the transcendent dignity of the person, the Church's method is always that of respect for freedom.[94]

But freedom attains its full development only by accepting the truth. In a world without truth, freedom loses its foundation and man is exposed to the violence of passion and to manipulation, both open and hidden. The Christian upholds freedom and serves it, constantly offering to others the truth which he has known (cf. Jn 8:31-32), in accordance with the missionary nature of his vocation. While paying heed to every fragment of truth which he encounters in the life experience and in the culture of individuals and of nations, he will not fail to affirm in dialogue with others all that his faith and the correct use of reason have enabled him to understand.95

47. Following the collapse of Communist totalitarianism and of many other totalitarian and "national security" regimes, today we are witnessing a predominance, not without signs of opposition, of the democratic ideal, together with lively attention to and concern for human rights. But for this very reason it is necessary for peoples in the process of reforming their systems to give democracy an authentic and solid foundation through the explicit recognition of those rights.96 Among the most important of these rights, mention must be made of the right to life, an integral part of which is the right of the child to develop in the mother's womb from the moment of conception; the right to live in a united family and in a moral environment conducive to the growth of the child's personality; the right to develop one's intelligence and freedom in seeking and knowing the truth; the right to share in the work which makes wise use of the earth's material resources, and to derive from that work the means to support oneself and one's dependents; and the right freely to establish a family, to have and to rear children through the responsible exercise of one's sexuality. In a certain sense, the source and synthesis of these rights is religious freedom, understood as the right to live in the truth of one's faith and in conformity with one's transcendent dignity as a person.97
Even in countries with democratic forms of government, these rights are not always fully respected. Here we are referring not only to the scandal of abortion, but also to different aspects of a crisis within democracies themselves, which seem at times to have lost the ability to make decisions aimed at the common good. Certain demands which arise within society are sometimes not examined in accordance with criteria of justice and morality, but rather on the basis of the electoral or financial power of the groups promoting them. With time, such distortions of political conduct create distrust and apathy, with a subsequent decline in the political participation and civic spirit of the general population, which feels abused and disillusioned. As a result, there is a growing inability to situate particular interests within the framework of a coherent vision of the common good. The latter is not simply the sum total of particular interests; rather it involves an assessment and integration of those interests on the basis of a balanced hierarchy of values; ultimately, it demands a correct understanding of the dignity and the rights of the person.98
The Church respects *the legitimate autonomy of the democratic order* and is not entitled to express preferences for this or that institutional or constitutional solution. Her contribution to the political order is precisely her vision of the dignity of the person revealed in all its fulness in the mystery of the Incarnate Word.99

48. These general observations also apply to the *role of the State in the economic sector*. Economic activity, especially the activity of a market economy, cannot be conducted in an institutional, juridical or political vacuum. On the contrary, it presupposes sure guarantees of individual freedom and private property, as well as a stable currency and efficient public services. Hence the principle task of the State is to guarantee this security, so that those who work and produce can enjoy the fruits of their labours and thus feel encouraged to work efficiently and honestly. The absence of stability, together with the corruption of public officials and the spread of improper sources of growing rich and of easy profits deriving from illegal or purely speculative activities, constitutes one of the chief obstacles to development and to the economic order.

Another task of the State is that of overseeing and directing the exercise of human rights in the economic sector. However, primary responsibility in this area belongs not to the State but to individuals and to the various groups and associations which make up society. The State could not directly ensure the right to work for all its citizens unless it controlled every aspect of economic life and restricted the free initiative of individuals. This does not mean, however, that the State has no competence in this domain, as was claimed by those who argued against any rules in the economic sphere. Rather, the State has a duty to sustain business activities by creating conditions which will ensure job opportunities, by stimulating those activities where they are lacking or by supporting them in moments of crisis.

The State has the further right to intervene when particular monopolies create delays or obstacles to development. In addition to the tasks of harmonizing and guiding development, in exceptional circumstances the State can also exercise *a substitute function*, when social sectors or business systems are too weak or are just getting under way, and are not equal to the task at hand. Such supplementary interventions, which are justified by urgent reasons touching the common good, must be as brief as possible, so as to avoid removing permanently from society and business systems the functions which are properly theirs, and so as to avoid enlarging excessively the sphere of State intervention to the detriment of both economic and civil freedom.

In recent years the range of such intervention has vastly expanded, to the point of creating a new type of State, the so-called "Welfare State". This has happened in some countries in order to respond better to many needs and demands, by remedying forms of poverty and deprivation unworthy of the human person. However, excesses and abuses, especially in recent years, have provoked very harsh criticisms of the Welfare State, dubbed the "Social Assistance State". Malfunctions and defects in the Social Assistance State are the result of an inadequate understanding of the tasks proper to the State. Here again *the principle of subsidiarity* must be respected: a community of a higher order should not interfere in the internal life of a community of a lower order, depriving the latter of its functions, but rather should support it in case of need and help to coordinate its activity with the activities of the rest of society, always with a view to the common good.100

By intervening directly and depriving society of its responsibility, the Social Assistance State leads to a loss of human energies and an inordinate increase of public agencies, which are dominated more by bureaucratic ways of thinking than by concern for serving their clients, and which are accompanied by an enormous increase in spending. In fact, it would appear that needs are best understood and satisfied by people who are closest to them and who act as neighbours to those in need. It should be added that certain kinds of demands often call for a response which is not simply material but which is capable of perceiving the deeper human need. One thinks of the condition of refugees, immigrants, the elderly, the sick, and all those in circumstances which call for assistance, such as drug abusers: all these people can be helped effectively only by those who offer them genuine fraternal support, in addition to the necessary care.

49. Faithful to the mission received from Christ her Founder, the Church has always been present and active among the needy, offering them material assistance in ways that neither humiliate nor reduce them to mere objects of assistance, but which help them to escape their precarious situation by promoting their dignity as persons. With heartfelt gratitude to God it must be pointed out that active charity has never ceased to be practised in the Church; indeed, today it is showing a manifold and gratifying increase. In this regard, special mention must be made of *volunteer work,* which the Church favours and promotes by urging everyone to cooperate in supporting and encouraging its undertakings.

In order to overcome today's widespread individualistic mentality, what is required is *a concrete commitment to solidarity and charity,* beginning in the family with the mutual support of husband and wife and the care which the different generations give to one another. In this sense the family too can be called a community of work and solidarity. It can happen, however, that when a family does decide to live up fully to its vocation, it finds itself without the necessary support from the State and without sufficient resources. It is urgent therefore to promote not only family policies, but also those social policies which have the family as their principle object, policies which assist the family by providing adequate resources and efficient means of support, both for bringing up children and for looking after the elderly, so as to avoid distancing the latter from the family unit and in order to strengthen relations between generations.101

Apart from the family, other intermediate communities exercise primary functions and give life to specific networks of solidarity. These develop as real communities of persons and strengthen the social fabric, preventing society from becoming an anonymous and impersonal mass, as unfortunately often happens today.

It is in interrelationships on many levels that a person lives, and that society becomes more "personalized". The individual today is often suffocated between two poles represented by the State and the marketplace. At times it seems as though he exists only as a producer and consumer of goods, or as an object of State administration. People lose sight of the fact that life in society has neither the market nor the State as its final purpose, since life itself has a unique value which the State and the market must serve. Man remains above all a being who seeks the truth and strives to live in that truth, deepening his understanding of it through a dialogue which involves past and future generations.102

50. From this open search for truth, which is renewed in every generation, *the culture of a nation* derives its character. Indeed, the heritage of values which has been received and handed down is always challenged by the young. To challenge does not necessarily mean to destroy or reject *a priori,* but above all to put these values to the test in one's own life, and through this existential verification to make them more real, relevant and personal, distinguishing the valid elements in the tradition from false and erroneous ones, or from obsolete forms which can be usefully replaced by others more suited to the times.
In this context, it is appropriate *to recall that evangelization too plays a role in the culture of the various nations,* sustaining culture in its progress towards the truth, and assisting in the work of its purification and enrichment.103 However, when a culture becomes inward looking, and tries to perpetuate obsolete ways of living by rejecting any exchange or debate with regard to the truth about man, then it becomes sterile and is heading for decadence.

51. All human activity takes place within a culture and interacts with culture. For an adequate formation of a culture, the involvement of the whole man is required, whereby he exercises his creativity, intelligence, and knowledge of the world and of people. Furthermore, he displays his capacity for self-control, personal sacrifice, solidarity and readiness to promote the common good. Thus the first and most important task is accomplished within man's heart. The way in which he is involved in building his own future depends on the understanding he has of himself and of his own destiny. It is on this level that *the Church's specific and decisive contribution to true culture* is to be found. The Church promotes those aspects of human behaviour which favour a true culture of peace, as opposed to models in which the individual is lost in the crowd, in which the role of his initiative and freedom is neglected, and in which his greatness is posited in the arts of conflict and war. The Church renders this service to human society *by preaching the truth about the creation of the world,* which God has placed in human hands so that people may make it fruitful and more perfect through their work; and *by preaching the truth about the Redemption,* whereby the Son of God has saved mankind and at the same time has united all people, making them responsible for one another. Sacred Scripture continually

speaks to us of an active commitment to our neighbour and demands of us a shared responsibility for all of humanity.

This duty is not limited to one's own family, nation or State, but extends progressively to all mankind, since no one can consider himself extraneous or indifferent to the lot of another member of the human family. No one can say that he is not responsible for the well-being of his brother or sister (cf. Gen 4:9; Lk 10:29-37; Mt 25:31-46). Attentive and pressing concern for one's neighbour in a moment of need – made easier today because of the new means of communication which have brought people closer together – is especially important with regard to in the search for ways to resolve international conflicts other than by war. It is not hard to see that the terrifying power of the means of destruction – to which even medium and small-sized countries have access – and the ever closer links between the peoples of the whole world make it very difficult or practically impossible to limit the consequences of a conflict.

52. Pope Benedict XV and his Successors clearly understood this danger.104 I myself, on the occasion of the recent tragic war in the Persian Gulf, repeated the cry: "Never again war!". No, never again war, which destroys the lives of innocent people, teaches how to kill, throws into upheaval even the lives of those who do the killing and leaves behind a trail of resentment and hatred, thus making it all the more difficult to find a just solution of the very problems which provoked the war. Just as the time has finally come when in individual States a system of private vendetta and reprisal has given way to the rule of law, so too a similar step forward is now urgently needed in the international community. Furthermore, it must not be forgotten that at the root of war there are usually real and serious grievances: injustices suffered, legitimate aspirations frustrated, poverty, and the exploitation of multitudes of desperate people who see no real possibility of improving their lot by peaceful means.

For this reason, another name for peace is *development*.105 Just as there is a collective responsibility for avoiding war, so too there is a collective responsibility for promoting development. Just as within individual societies it is possible and right to organize a solid economy which will direct the functioning of the market to the common good, so too there is a similar need for adequate interventions on the international level. For this to happen, *a great effort must be made to enhance mutual understanding and knowledge, and to increase the sensitivity of consciences.* This is the culture which is hoped for, one which fosters trust in the human potential of the poor, and consequently in their ability to improve their condition through work or to make a positive contribution to economic prosperity. But to accomplish this, the poor – be they individuals or nations – need to be provided with realistic opportunities. Creating such conditions calls for a *concerted worldwide effort to promote development,* an effort which also involves sacrificing the positions of income and of power enjoyed by the more developed economies.106

This may mean making important changes in established life-styles, in order to limit the waste of environmental and human resources, thus enabling every individual and all the peoples of the earth to have a sufficient share of those resources. In addition, the new material and spiritual resources must be utilized which are the result of the work and culture of peoples who today are on the margins of the international community, so as to obtain an overall human enrichment of the family of nations.

VI. MAN IS THE WAY OF THE CHURCH

53. Faced with the poverty of the working class, Pope Leo XIII wrote: "We approach this subject with confidence, and in the exercise of the rights which manifestly pertain to us ... By keeping silence we would seem to neglect the duty incumbent on us".107 During the last hundred years the Church has repeatedly expressed her thinking, while closely following the continuing development of the social question. She has certainly not done this in order to recover former privileges or to impose her own vision. Her sole purpose has been *care and responsibility* for man, who has been entrusted to her by Christ himself: for *this man,* whom, as the Second Vatican Council recalls, is the only creature on earth which God willed for its own sake, and for which God has his plan, that is, a share in eternal salvation. We are not dealing here with man in the "abstract", but with the real, "concrete", "historical" man. We are dealing with *each individual,* since each one is included in the mystery of Redemption, and through this mystery Christ has united himself with each one for ever.108 It follows that the Church cannot abandon man, and that *"this man* is the primary route that the Church must travel in fulfilling her mission ... the way traced out by Christ himself, the way that leads invariably through the mystery of the Incarnation and the Redemption".109

This, and this alone, is the principle which inspires the Church's social doctrine. The Church has gradually developed that doctrine in a systematic way, above all in the century that has followed the date we are commemorating, precisely because the horizon of the Church's whole wealth of doctrine is man in his concrete reality as sinful and righteous.

54. Today, the Church's social doctrine focuses especially *on man* as he is involved in a complex network of relationships within modern societies. The human sciences and philosophy are helpful for interpreting *man's central place within society* and for enabling him to understand himself better as a "social being". However, man's true identity is only fully revealed to him through faith, and it is precisely from faith that the Church's social teaching begins. While drawing upon all the contributions made by the sciences and philosophy, her social teaching is aimed at helping man on the path of salvation.

The Encyclical *Rerum novarum* can be read as a valid contribution to socio-economic analysis at the end of the nineteenth century, but its specific value derives from the fact that it is a document of the Magisterium and is fully a part of the Church's evangelizing mission, together with many other documents of this nature. Thus the Church's *social teaching* is itself a valid *instrument of evangelization*. As such, it proclaims God and his mystery of salvation in Christ to every human being, and for that very reason reveals man to himself. In this light, and only in this light, does it concern itself with everything else: the human rights of the individual, and in particular of the "working class", the family and education, the duties of the State, the ordering of national and international society, economic life, culture, war and peace, and respect for life from the moment of conception until death.

55. The Church receives "the meaning of man" from Divine Revelation. "In order to know man, authentic man, man in his fullness, one must know God", said Pope Paul VI, and he went on to quote Saint Catherine of Siena, who, in prayer, expressed the same idea: "In your nature, O eternal Godhead, I shall know my own nature".110
Christian anthropology therefore is really a chapter of theology, and for this reason, the Church's social doctrine, by its concern for man and by its interest in him and in the way he conducts himself in the world, "belongs to the field ... of theology and particularly of moral theology".111 The theological dimension is needed both for interpreting and solving present-day problems in human society. It is worth noting that this is true in contrast both to the "atheistic" solution, which deprives man of one of his basic dimensions, namely the spiritual one, and to permissive and consumerist solutions, which under various pretexts seek to convince man that he is free from every law and from God himself, thus imprisoning him within a selfishness which ultimately harms both him and others.
When the Church proclaims God's salvation *to man,* when she offers and communicates the life of God through the sacraments, when she gives direction to human life through the commandments of love of God and neighbour, she contributes to the enrichment of human dignity. But just as the Church can never abandon her religious and transcendent mission on behalf of man, so too she is aware that today her activity meets with particular difficulties and obstacles. That is why she devotes herself with ever new energies and methods to an evangelization which promotes the whole human being. Even on the eve of the third Millennium she continues to be "a sign and safeguard of the transcendence of the human person",112 as indeed she has always sought to be from the beginning of her existence, walking together with man through history. The Encyclical *Rerum novarum* itself is a significant sign of this.

56. On the hundredth anniversary of that Encyclical I wish to thank all those who have devoted themselves to studying, expounding and making better

known Christian social teaching. To this end, the cooperation of the local Churches is indispensable, and I would hope that the present anniversary will be a source of fresh enthusiasm for studying, spreading and applying that teaching in various contexts.

In particular, I wish this teaching to be made known and applied in the countries which, following the collapse of "Real Socialism", are experiencing a serious lack of direction in the work of rebuilding. The Western countries, in turn, run the risk of seeing this collapse as a one-sided victory of their own economic system, and thereby failing to make necessary corrections in that system. Meanwhile, the countries of the Third World are experiencing more than ever the tragedy of underdevelopment, which is becoming more serious with each passing day.

After formulating principles and guidelines for the solution of the worker question, Pope Leo XIII made this incisive statement: "Everyone should put his hand to the work which falls to his share, and that at once and straightway, lest the evil which is already so great become through delay absolutely beyond remedy", and he added, "in regard to the Church, her cooperation will never be found lacking".113

57. As far as the Church is concerned, the social message of the Gospel must not be considered a theory, but above all else a basis and a motivation for action. Inspired by this message, some of the first Christians distributed their goods to the poor, bearing witness to the fact that, despite different social origins, it was possible for people to live together in peace and harmony. Through the power of the Gospel, down the centuries monks tilled the land, men and women Religious founded hospitals and shelters for the poor, Confraternities as well as individual men and women of all states of life devoted themselves to the needy and to those on the margins of society, convinced as they were that Christ's words "as you did it to one of the least of these my brethren, you did it to me" (Mt 25:40) were not intended to remain a pious wish, but were meant to become a concrete life commitment.

Today more than ever, the Church is aware that her social message will gain credibility more immediately from the *witness of actions* than as a result of its internal logic and consistency. This awareness is also a source of her preferential option for the poor, which is never exclusive or discriminatory towards other groups. This option is not limited to material poverty, since it is well known that there are many other forms of poverty, especially in modern society – not only economic but cultural and spiritual poverty as well. The Church's love for the poor, which is essential for her and a part of her constant tradition, impels her to give attention to a world in which poverty is threatening to assume massive proportions in spite of technological and economic progress. In the countries of the West, different forms of poverty are being experienced by groups which live on the margins of society, by the elderly and the sick, by the victims of consumerism, and even more immediately by so many refugees and migrants. In the developing countries, tragic crises loom on the horizon unless internationally coordinated measures are taken before it is too late.

58. Love for others, and in the first place love for the poor, in whom the Church sees Christ himself, is made concrete in the *promotion of justice.* Justice will never be fully attained unless people see in the poor person, who is asking for help in order to survive, not an annoyance or a burden, but an opportunity for showing kindness and a chance for greater enrichment. Only such an awareness can give the courage needed to face the risk and the change involved in every authentic attempt to come to the aid of another. It is not merely a matter of "giving from one's surplus", but of helping entire peoples which are presently excluded or marginalized to enter into the sphere of economic and human development. For this to happen, it is not enough to draw on the surplus goods which in fact our world abundantly produces; it requires above all a change of life-styles, of models of production and consumption, and of the established structures of power which today govern societies. Nor is it a matter of eliminating instruments of social organization which have proved useful, but rather of orienting them according to an adequate notion of the common good in relation to the whole human family. Today we are facing the so-called "globalization" of the economy, a phenomenon which is not to be dismissed, since it can create unusual opportunities for greater prosperity. There is a growing feeling, however, that this increasing internationalization of the economy ought to be accompanied by effective international agencies which will oversee and direct the economy to the common good, something that an individual State, even if it were the most powerful on earth, would not be in a position to do. In order to achieve this result, it is necessary that there be increased coordination among the more powerful countries, and that in international agencies the interests of the whole human family be equally represented. It is also necessary that in evaluating the consequences of their decisions, these agencies always give sufficient consideration to peoples and countries which have little weight in the international market, but which are burdened by the most acute and desperate needs, and are thus more dependent on support for their development. Much remains to be done in this area.

59. Therefore, in order that the demands of justice may be met, and attempts to achieve this goal may succeed, what is needed is *the gift of grace, a gift* which comes from God. Grace, in cooperation with human freedom, constitutes that mysterious presence of God in history which is Providence.
The newness which is experienced in following Christ demands to be communicated to other people in their concrete difficulties, struggles, problems and challenges, so that these can then be illuminated and made more human in the

light of faith. Faith not only helps people to find solutions; it makes even situations of suffering humanly bearable, so that in these situations people will not become lost or forget their dignity and vocation.

In addition, the Church's social teaching has an important interdisciplinary dimension. In order better to incarnate the one truth about man in different and constantly changing social, economic and political contexts, this teaching enters into dialogue with the various disciplines concerned with man. It assimilates what these disciplines have to contribute, and helps them to open themselves to a broader horizon, aimed at serving the individual person who is acknowledged and loved in the fullness of his or her vocation.

Parallel with the interdisciplinary aspect, mention should also be made of the practical and as it were experiential dimension of this teaching, which is to be found at the crossroads where Christian life and conscience come into contact with the real world. This teaching is seen in the efforts of individuals, families, people involved in cultural and social life, as well as politicians and statesmen to give it a concrete form and application in history.

60. In proclaiming the principles for a solution of the worker question, Pope Leo XIII wrote: "This most serious question demands the attention and the efforts of others". 114 He was convinced that the grave problems caused by industrial society could be solved only by cooperation between all forces. This affirmation has become a permanent element of the Church's social teaching, and also explains why Pope John XXIII addressed his Encyclical on peace to "all people of good will".

Pope Leo, however, acknowledged with sorrow that the ideologies of his time, especially Liberalism and Marxism, rejected such cooperation. Since then, many things have changed, especially in recent years. The world today is ever more aware that solving serious national and international problems is not just a matter of economic production or of juridical or social organization, but also calls for specific ethical and religious values, as well as changes of mentality, behaviour and structures. The Church feels a particular responsibility to offer this contribution and, as I have written in the Encyclical *Sollicitudo rei socialis,* there is a reasonable hope that the many people who profess no religion will also contribute to providing the social question with the necessary ethical foundation.115

In that same Encyclical I also addressed an appeal to the Christian Churches and to all the great world religions, inviting them to offer the unanimous witness of our common convictions regarding the dignity of man, created by God.116 In fact I am convinced that the various religions, now and in the future, will have a preeminent role in preserving peace and in building a society worthy of man.

Indeed, openness to dialogue and to cooperation is required of all people of good will, and in particular of individuals and groups with specific responsibilities in the areas of politics, economics and social life, at both the national and international levels.

61. At the beginning of industrialized society, it was "a yoke little better than that of slavery itself" which led my Predecessor to speak out *in defence of man.* Over the past hundred years the Church has remained faithful to this duty. Indeed, she intervened in the turbulent period of class struggle after the First World War in order to defend man from economic exploitation and from the tyranny of the totalitarian systems. After the Second World War, she put the dignity of the person at the centre of her social messages, insisting that material goods were meant for all, and that the social order ought to be free of oppression and based on a spirit of cooperation and solidarity. The Church has constantly repeated that the person and society need not only material goods but spiritual and religious values as well. Furthermore, as she has become more aware of the fact that too many people live, not in the prosperity of the Western world, but in the poverty of the developing countries amid conditions which are still "a yoke little better than that of slavery itself", she has felt and continues to feel obliged to denounce this fact with absolute clarity and frankness, although she knows that her call will not always win favour with everyone.
One hundred years after the publication of *Rerum novarum,* the Church finds herself still facing "new things" and new challenges. The centenary celebration should therefore confirm the commitment of all people of good will and of believers in particular.

. . . .
. . . .
. . . .

APOSTOLIC LETTER
TERTIO MILLENNIO ADVENIENTE
OF HIS HOLINESS
POPE JOHN PAUL II
TO THE BISHOPS, CLERGY
AND LAY FAITHFUL
ON PREPARATION
FOR THE JUBILEE OF THE YEAR 2000*

. . . .
. . . .
. . . .
. . . .

17. *In the Church's history every jubilee is prepared for by Divine Providence.* This is true also of the Great Jubilee of the Year 2000. With this conviction, we look today with a sense of gratitude and yet with a sense of responsibility at all that has happened in human history since the Birth of Christ, particularly the events which have occurred between the years 1000 and 2000. But in a very particular way, we look with the eyes of faith to our own century, searching out whatever bears witness not only to man's history but also to God's intervention in human affairs.

18. From this point of view we can affirm that *the Second Vatican Council was a providential event, whereby the Church began the more immediate preparation* for the Jubilee of the Second Millennium. It was a Council similar to earlier ones, yet very different; it was a Council *focused on the mystery of Christ and his Church and at the same time open to the world.* This openness was an evangelical response to recent changes in the world, including the profoundly disturbing experiences of the Twentieth Century, a century scarred by the First and Second World Wars, by the experience of concentration camps and by horrendous massacres. All these events demonstrate most vividly that the world needs purification; it needs to be converted.
The Second Vatican Council is often considered as the beginning of a new era in the life of the Church. This is true, but at the same time it is difficult to overlook the fact that *the Council drew much from the experiences and reflections of the immediate past,* especially from the intellectual legacy left by Pius XII. In the history of the Church, the "old" and the "new" are always closely interwoven. The "new" grows out of the "old", and the "old" finds a fuller expression in the "new". Thus it was for the Second Vatican Council and for the activity of the

Popes connected with the Council, starting with John XXIII, continuing with
Paul VI and John Paul I, up to the present Pope.

What these Popes have accomplished during and since the Council, in their
Magisterium no less than in their pastoral activity, has certainly made a significant contribution to the *preparation of that new springtime of Christian life*
which will be revealed by the Great Jubilee, if Christians are docile to the
action of the Holy Spirit.

19. The Council, while not imitating the sternness of John the Baptist who
called for repentance and conversion on the banks of the Jordan (cf. *Lk* 3:1-7),
did show something of the Prophet of old, pointing out with fresh vigour to
the men and women of today that Jesus Christ is the "Lamb of God who takes
away the sin of the world" (*Jn* 1:29), the Redeemer of humanity and the Lord
of history. During the Council, precisely out of a desire to be fully faithful to
her Master, the Church questioned herself about her own identity, and discovered anew the depth of her mystery as the Body and the Bride of Christ.
Humbly heeding the word of God, she reaffirmed the universal call to holiness;
she made provision for the reform of the liturgy, the "origin and summit" of
her life; she gave impetus to the renewal of many aspects of her life at the
universal level and in the local Churches; she strove to promote the various
Christian vocations, from those of the laity to those of Religious, from the
ministry of deacons to that of priests and Bishops; and in a particular way
she rediscovered episcopal collegiality, that privileged expression of the pastoral
service carried out by the Bishops in communion with the Successor of Peter.
On the basis of this profound renewal, the Council opened itself to Christians
of other denominations, to the followers of other religions and to all the people of our time. No Council had ever spoken so clearly about Christian unity,
about dialogue with non-Christian religions, about the specific meaning of the
Old Covenant and of Israel, about the dignity of each person's conscience,
about the principle of religious liberty, about the different cultural traditions
within which the Church carries out her missionary mandate, and about the
means of social communication.

20. The Council's enormously rich body of teaching and *the striking new tone*
in the way it presented this content constitute as it were a proclamation of new
times. The Council Fathers spoke in the language of the Gospel, the language
of the Sermon on the Mount and the Beatitudes. In the Council's message God
is presented *in his absolute lordship over all things,* but also as *the One who
ensures the authentic autonomy of earthly realities.*

The best preparation for the new millennium, therefore, can only be expressed
in a renewed commitment *to apply,* as faithfully as possible, *the teachings of Vatican II to the life of every individual and of the whole Church.* It was with the Second Vatican Council that, in the broadest sense of the term, the immediate

preparations for the Great Jubilee of the Year 2000 were really begun. If we look for an analogy in the liturgy, it could be said that the yearly *Advent liturgy* is the season nearest to the spirit of the Council. For Advent prepares us to meet the One who was, who is and who is to come (cf. *Rev* 4:8).

21. Part of the preparation for the approach of the Year 2000 is the *series of Synods* begun after the Second Vatican Council: general Synods together with continental, regional, national and diocesan Synods. The theme underlying them all is *evangelization,* or rather the new evangelization, the foundations of which were laid down in the Apostolic Exhortation *Evangelii Nuntiandi* of Pope Paul VI, issued in 1975 following the Third General Assembly of the Synod of Bishops. These Synods themselves are part of the new evangelization: they were born of the Second Vatican Council's vision of the Church. They open up broad areas for the participation of the laity, whose specific responsibilities in the Church they define. They are an expression of the strength which Christ has given to the entire People of God, making it a sharer in his own Messianic mission as Prophet, Priest and King. Very eloquent in this regard are the statements of the Dogmatic Constitution *Lumen Gentium. The preparation for the Jubilee Year 2000 is thus taking place throughout the whole Church, on the universal and local levels,* giving her a new awareness of the salvific mission she has received from Christ. This awareness is particularly evident in the Post-Synodal Exhortations devoted to the mission of the laity, the formation of priests, catechesis, the family, the value of penance and reconciliation in the life of the Church and of humanity in general, as well as in the forth coming one to be devoted to the consecrated life.

22. Special tasks and responsibilities with regard to the Great Jubilee of the Year 2000 belong to the *ministry of the Bishop of Rome.* In a certain sense, all the Popes of the past century have prepared for this Jubilee. With his programme to renew all things in Christ, Saint Pius X tried to forestall the tragic developments which arose from the international situation at the beginning of this century. The Church was aware of her duty to act decisively to promote and defend the basic values of peace and justice in the face of contrary tendencies in our time. The Popes of the period before the Council acted with firm commitment, each in his own way: Benedict XV found himself faced with the tragedy of the First World War; Pius XI had to contend with the threats of totalitarian systems or systems which did not respect human freedom in Germany, in Russia, in Italy, in Spain, and even earlier still in Mexico. Pius XII took steps to counter the very grave injustice brought about by a total contempt for human dignity at the time of the Second World War. He also provided enlightened guidelines for the birth of a new world order after the fall of the previous political systems.

Furthermore, in the course of this century the Popes, following in the footsteps of Leo XIII, systematically developed the themes of Catholic social doctrine, expounding the characteristics of a *just system* in the area of relations between labour and capital. We may recall the Encyclical *Quadragesimo Anno* of Pius XI, the numerous interventions of Pius XII, the Encyclicals *Mater et Magistra* and *Pacem in Terris* of John XXIII, the Encyclical *Populorum Progressio* and the Apostolic Letter *Octogesima Adveniens* of Paul VI. I too have frequently dealt with this subject: I specifically devoted the Encyclical *Laborem Exercens* to the importance of human labour, while in *Centesimus Annus* I wished to reaffirm the relevance, one hundred years later, of the doctrine presented in *Rerum Novarum*. In my Encyclical *Sollicitudo Rei Socialis* I had earlier offered a systematic reformulation of the Church's entire social doctrine against the background of the East-West confrontation and the danger of nuclear war. The two elements of the Church's social doctrine – the *safeguarding of human dignity and rights* in the sphere of a just relation between labour and capital and *the promotion of peace* – were closely joined in this text. The Papal Messages of 1 January each year, begun in 1968 in the pontificate of Paul VI, are also meant to serve the cause of peace.

23. Since the publication of the very first document of my Pontificate, *I have spoken explicitly of the Great Jubilee*, suggesting that the time leading up to it be lived as "a new Advent".9 This theme has since reappeared many times, and was dwelt upon at length in the Encyclical *Dominum et Vivificantem*.10 In fact, preparing for the *Year 2000 has become as it were a hermeneutical key of my Pontificate*. It is certainly not a matter of indulging in a new millenarianism, as occurred in some quarters at the end of the first millennium; rather, it is *aimed at an increased sensitivity to all that the Spirit is saying to the Church and to the Churches* (cf. *Rev* 2:7 ff.), as well as to individuals through charisms meant to serve the whole community. The purpose is to emphasize what the Spirit is suggesting to the different communities, from the smallest ones, such as the family, to the largest ones, such as nations and international organizations, taking into account cultures, societies and sound traditions. Despite appearances, humanity continues to await the revelation of the children of God, and lives by this hope, like a mother in labour, to use the image employed so powerfully by Saint Paul in his Letter to the Romans (cf. 8:19-22).

24. *Papal Journeys* have become an important element in the work of implementing the Second Vatican Council. Begun by John XXIII on the eve of the Council with a memorable pilgrimage to Loreto and Assisi (1962), they notably increased under Paul VI who, after first visiting the Holy Land (1964), undertook nine other great apostolic journeys which brought him into direct contact with the peoples of the different continents.

The current Pontificate has widened this programme of travels even further, starting with Mexico, on the occasion of the Third General Conference of the

Latin American Episcopate held in Puebla in 1979. In that same year, there was also the trip to Poland for the Jubilee of the nine hundredth anniversary of the death of Saint Stanislaus, Bishop and Martyr.

The successive stages of these travels are well known. Papal journeys have become a regular occurrence, taking in the particular Churches in every continent and showing concern *for the development of ecumenical relationships* with Christians of various denominations. Particularly important in this regard were the visits to Turkey (1979), Germany (1980), England, Scotland and Wales (1982), Switzerland (1984), the Scandinavian countries (1989), and most recently the Baltic countries (1993).

At present, it is my fervent wish to visit Sarajevo in Bosnia-Hercegovina and the Middle East: Lebanon, Jerusalem and the Holy Land. It would be very significant if in the Year 2000 it were possible to visit the *places on the road taken by the People of God of the Old Covenant,* starting from the places associated with Abraham and Moses, through Egypt and Mount Sinai, as far as Damascus, the city which witnessed the conversion of Saint Paul.

25. In preparing for the Year 2000, *the individual Churches* have their own role to play, as they celebrate with their own Jubilees significant stages in the salvation history of the various peoples. Among these regional or *local Jubilees,* events of great importance have included the millennium of the Baptism of Rus' in 1988 11 as also the five hundredth anniversary of the beginning of evangelization in America (1492). Besides events of such wide-ranging impact, we may recall others which, although not of universal importance, are no less significant: for example, the millennium of the Baptism of Poland in 1966 and of the Baptism of Hungary in 1968, together with the six hundredth anniversary of the Baptism of Lithuania in 1987. There will soon also be celebrated the 1500th anniversary of the Baptism of Clovis (496), king of the Franks, and the 1400th anniversary of the arrival of Saint Augustine in Canterbury (597), marking the beginning of the evangelization of the Anglo-Saxon world.

As far as Asia is concerned, the Jubilee will remind us of the Apostle Thomas, who, according to tradition, brought the proclamation of the Gospel at the very beginning of the Christian era to India, where missionaries from Portugal would not arrive until about the year 1500. The current year also marks the seventh centenary of the evangelization of China (1294), and we are preparing to commemorate the spread of missionary work in the Philippines with the erection of the Metropolitan See of Manila (1595). We likewise look forward to the fourth centenary of the first martyrs in Japan (1597).

In Africa, where the first proclamation of the Gospel also dates back to Apostolic times, together with the 1650th anniversary of the episcopal consecration of the first Bishop of the Ethiopians, Saint Frumentius (c. 340), and the five hundredth anniversary of the beginning of the evangelization of Angola in the ancient Kingdom of the Congo (1491), nations such as Cameroon, Côte d'Ivoire, the Central African Republic, Burundi and Burkina Faso are celebrating the centenaries of the arrival of the first missionaries in their respective territories. Other African nations have recently celebrated such centenaries.

And how can we fail to mention the Eastern Churches, whose ancient Patriarchates are so closely linked to the apostolic heritage and whose venerable theological, liturgical and spiritual traditions constitute a tremendous wealth which is the common patrimony of the whole of Christianity? The many jubilee celebrations in these Churches, and in the Communities which acknowledge them as the origin of their own apostolicity, recall the journey of Christ down the centuries, leading to the Great Jubilee at the end of the second millennium. Seen in this light, the whole of Christian history appears to us as a single river, into which many tributaries pour their waters. The Year 2000 invites us to gather with renewed fidelity and ever deeper communion *along the banks of this great river:* the river of Revelation, of Christianity and of the Church, a river which flows through human history starting from the event which took place at Nazareth and then at Bethlehem two thousand years ago. This is truly the "river" which with its "streams", in the expression of the Psalm, "make glad the city of God" (46:4).

. . . .
. . . .

32. A Jubilee is always an occasion of special grace, "a day blessed by the Lord". As has already been noted, it is thus a time of joy. The Jubilee of the Year 2000 is meant to be a great *prayer of praise and thanksgiving,* especially for the *gift of the Incarnation of the Son of God and of the Redemption* which he accomplished. In the Jubilee Year Christians will stand with the renewed wonder of faith before the love of the Father, who *gave his Son,* "that whoever believes in him should not perish but have eternal life" (*Jn* 3:16). With a profound sense of commitment, they will likewise express their gratitude for the *gift of the Church,* established by Christ as "a kind of sacrament or sign of intimate union with God, and of the unity of all mankind".14 Their thanksgiving will embrace the *fruits of holiness* which have matured in the life of all those many men and women who in every generation and every period of history have fully welcomed the gift of Redemption.

Nevertheless, the joy of every Jubilee is above all a *joy based upon the forgiveness of sins, the joy of conversion.* It therefore seems appropriate to emphasize once more the theme of the *Synod of Bishops in 1984: penance and reconciliation.*15 That Synod was an event of extraordinary significance in the life of the post-conciliar Church. It took up the ever topical question of conversion ("*metanoia*"), which is the pre-condition for reconciliation with God on the part of both individuals and communities.

33. Hence it is appropriate that, as the Second Millennium of Christianity draws to a close, the Church should become more fully conscious of the

sinfulness of her children, recalling all those times in history when they departed from the spirit of Christ and his Gospel and, instead of offering to the world the witness of a life inspired by the values of faith, indulged in ways of thinking and acting which were truly *forms of counter-witness and scandal.*

Although she is holy because of her incorporation into Christ, the Church does not tire of doing penance: before God and man *she always acknowledges as her own her sinful sons and daughters.* As *Lumen Gentium* affirms: "The Church, embracing sinners to her bosom, is at the same time holy and always in need of being purified, and incessantly pursues the path of penance and renewal".16 The Holy Door of the Jubilee of the Year 2000 should be symbolically wider than those of previous Jubilees, because humanity, upon reaching this goal, will leave behind not just a century but a millennium. It is fitting that the Church should make this passage with a clear awareness of what has happened to her during the last ten centuries. She cannot cross the threshold of the new millennium without encouraging her children to purify themselves, through repentance, of past errors and instances of infidelity, inconsistency, and slowness to act. Acknowledging the weaknesses of the past is an act of honesty and courage which helps us to strengthen our faith, which alerts us to face today's temptations and challenges and prepares us to meet them.

34. Among the sins which require a greater commitment to repentance and conversion should certainly be counted those which *have been detrimental to the unity willed by God for his People.* In the course of the thousand years now drawing to a close, even more than in the first millennium, ecclesial communion has been painfully wounded, a fact "for which, at times, men of both sides were to blame".17 Such wounds openly contradict the will of Christ and are a cause of scandal to the world.18 These sins of the past unfortunately still burden us and remain ever present temptations. It is necessary to make amends for them, and earnestly to beseech Christ's forgiveness.

In these last years of the millennium, the Church should invoke the Holy Spirit with ever greater insistence, imploring from him the grace of *Christian unity.* This is a crucial matter for our testimony to the Gospel before the world. Especially since the Second Vatican Council many ecumenical initiatives have been undertaken with generosity and commitment: it can be said that the whole activity of the local Churches and of the Apostolic See has taken on an ecumenical dimension in recent years. The *Pontifical Council for the Promotion of Christian Unity* has become an important catalyst in the movement towards full unity.

We are all however aware that the attainment of this goal cannot be the fruit of human efforts alone, vital though they are. *Unity, after all, is a gift of the Holy Spirit.* We are asked to respond to this gift responsibly, without compromise in our witness to the truth, generously implementing the guidelines laid down by the Council and in subsequent documents of the Holy See, which are also highly regarded by many Christians not in full communion with the Catholic Church.

This then is one of the tasks of Christians as we make our way to the Year 2000. The approaching end of the second millennium demands of everyone an *examination of conscience* and the promotion of fitting ecumenical initiatives, so that we can celebrate the Great Jubilee, if not completely united, *at least much closer to overcoming the divisions of the second millennium.* As everyone recognizes, an enormous effort is needed in this regard. It is essential not only to continue along the path of dialogue on doctrinal matters, but above all to be more committed to *prayer for Christian unity.* Such prayer has become much more intense after the Council, but it must increase still more, involving an ever greater number of Christians, in unison with the great petition of Christ before his Passion: "Father ... that they also may all be one in us" (*Jn* 17:21).

35. Another painful chapter of history to which the sons and daughters of the Church must return with a spirit of repentance is that of the acquiescence given, especially in certain centuries, to *intolerance and even the use of violence* in the service of truth.

It is true that an accurate historical judgment cannot prescind from careful study of the cultural conditioning of the times, as a result of which many people may have held in good faith that an authentic witness to the truth could include suppressing the opinions of others or at least paying no attention to them. Many factors frequently converged to create assumptions which justified intolerance and fostered an emotional climate from which only great spirits, truly free and filled with God, were in some way able to break free. Yet the consideration of mitigating factors does not exonerate the Church from the obligation to express profound regret for the weaknesses of so many of her sons and daughters who sullied her face, preventing her from fully mirroring the image of her crucified Lord, the supreme witness of patient love and of humble meekness. From these painful moments of the past a lesson can be drawn for the future, leading all Christians to adhere fully to the sublime principle stated by the Council: "The truth cannot impose itself except by virtue of its own truth, as it wins over the mind with both gentleness and power".19

36. Many Cardinals and Bishops expressed the desire for a serious examination of conscience above all on the part of *the Church of today.* On the threshold of the new Millennium Christians need to place themselves humbly before the Lord and examine themselves on *the responsibility which they too have for the evils of our day.* The present age in fact, together with much light, also presents not a few shadows.

How can we remain silent, for example, about the *religious indifference* which causes many people today to live as if God did not exist, or to be content with a vague religiosity, incapable of coming to grips with the question of truth and the requirement of consistency? To this must also be added the widespread loss of the transcendent sense of human life, and confusion in the ethical sphere, even about the fundamental values of respect for life and the family. The sons and daughters of the Church too need to examine themselves in this regard. To what extent have they been shaped by the climate of secularism and ethical relativism? And what responsibility do they bear, in view of the increasing lack of religion, for not having shown the true face of God, by having "failed in their religious, moral, or social life"? 20

It cannot be denied that, for many Christians, the spiritual life is passing through *a time of uncertainty* which affects not only their moral life but also their life of prayer and the *theological correctness of their faith*. Faith, already put to the test by the challenges of our times, is sometimes disoriented by erroneous theological views, the spread of which is abetted by the crisis of obedience vis-à-vis the Church's Magisterium.

And with respect to the Church of our time, how can we not lament *the lack of discernment*, which at times became even acquiescence, shown by many Christians concerning the violation of fundamental human rights by totalitarian regimes? And should we not also regret, among the shadows of our own day, the responsibility shared by so many Christians *for grave forms of injustice and exclusion?* It must be asked how many Christians really know and put into practice the principles of the Church's social doctrine.

An examination of conscience must also consider the *reception given to the Council,* this great gift of the Spirit to the Church at the end of the second millennium. To what extent has the word of God become more fully the soul of theology and the inspiration of the whole of Christian living, as *Dei Verbum* sought? Is the liturgy lived as the "origin and summit" of ecclesial life, in accordance with the teaching of *Sacrosanctum Concilium?* In the universal Church and in the particular Churches, is the ecclesiology of communion described in *Lumen Gentium* being strengthened? Does it leave room for charisms, ministries, and different forms of participation by the People of God, without adopting notions borrowed from democracy and sociology which do not reflect the Catholic vision of the Church and the authentic spirit of Vatican II? Another serious question is raised by the nature of relations between the Church and the world. The Council's guidelines – set forth in *Gaudium et Spes* and other documents – of open, respectful and cordial dialogue, yet accompanied by careful discernment and courageous witness to the truth, remain valid and call us to a greater commitment.

37. The Church of the first millennium was born of the blood of the martyrs: *"Sanguis martyrum – semen christianorum".*21 The historical events linked to the figure of Constantine the Great could never have ensured the development of the Church as it occurred during the first millennium if it had not been for the *seeds sown by the martyrs and the heritage of sanctity which marked the first*

Christian generations. At the end of the second millennium, *the Church has once
again become a Church of martyrs.* The persecutions of believers – priests, Religious and laity – has caused a great sowing of martyrdom in different parts of
the world. The witness to Christ borne even to the shedding of blood has
become a common inheritance of Catholics, Orthodox, Anglicans and Protes-
tants, as Pope Paul VI pointed out in his Homily for the Canonization of the
Ugandan Martyrs.22

This witness must not be forgotten. The Church of the first centuries, although
facing considerable organizational difficulties, took care to write down in
special martyrologies the witness of the martyrs. These martyrologies have been
constantly updated through the centuries, and the register of the saints and the
blessed bears the names not only of those who have shed their blood for Christ
but also of teachers of the faith, missionaries, confessors, bishops, priests,
virgins, married couples, widows and children.

In our own century the martyrs have returned, many of them nameless, *"unknown
soldiers"* as it were *of God's great cause.* As far as possible, their witness should
not be lost to the Church. As was recommended in the Consistory, *the local
Churches should do everything possible to ensure that the memory of those who have
suffered martyrdom should be safeguarded, gathering the necessary documentation.*
This gesture cannot fail to have an ecumenical character and expression. Perhaps the most convincing form of ecumenism is *the ecumenism of the saints* and
of the martyrs. The *communio sanctorum* speaks louder than the things which
divide us. The *martyrologium* of the first centuries was the basis of the veneration of the Saints. By proclaiming and venerating the holiness of her sons and
daughters, the Church gave supreme honour to God himself; in the martyrs
she venerated Christ, who was at the origin of their martyrdom and of their
holiness. In later times there developed the practice of canonization, a practice
which still continues in the Catholic Church and in the Orthodox Churches.
In recent years the number of canonizations and beatifications has increased.
These show the *vitality of the local Churches,* which are much more numerous
today than in the first centuries and in the first millennium. The greatest
homage which all the Churches can give to Christ on the threshold of the third
millennium will be to manifest the Redeemer's all-powerful presence through
the fruits of faith, hope and charity present in men and women of many
different tongues and races who have followed Christ in the various forms of
the Christian vocation.

It will be the task of the Apostolic See, in preparation for the Year 2000, *to
update the martyrologies* for the universal Church, paying careful attention to
the holiness of those who *in our own time* lived fully by the truth of Christ. In
particular, there is a need to foster the recognition of the heroic virtues of men
and women who have lived their Christian vocation *in marriage.* Precisely
because we are convinced of the abundant fruits of holiness in the married
state, we need to find the most appropriate means for discerning them and

proposing them to the whole Church as a model and encouragement for other Christian spouses.

38. A further need emphasized by the Cardinals and Bishops is that of *Continental Synods,* following the example of those already held for Europe and Africa. The last General Conference of the Latin American Episcopate accepted, in agreement with the Bishops of North America, the proposal for *a Synod for the Americas* on the problems of the new evangelization in both parts of the same continent, so different in origin and history, and on issues of justice and of international economic relations, in view of the enormous gap between North and South.

Another plan for a continent-wide Synod will concern *Asia,* where the issue of the encounter of Christianity with ancient local cultures and religions is a pressing one. This is a great challenge for evangelization, since religious systems such as Buddhism or Hinduism have a clearly soteriological character. There is also an urgent need for a Synod on the occasion of the Great Jubilee in order to illustrate and explain more fully the truth that Christ is the one Mediator between God and man and the sole Redeemer of the world, to be clearly distinguished from the founders of other great religions. With sincere esteem, the Church regards the elements of truth found in those religions as a reflection of the Truth which enlightens all men and women.23 *"Ecce natus est nobis Salvator mundi"*: in the Year 2000 the proclamation of this truth should resound with renewed power.

Also for *Oceania* a Regional Synod could be useful. In this region there arises the question, among others, of the Aboriginal People, who in a unique way evoke aspects of human prehistory. In this Synod a matter not to be overlooked, together with other problems of the region, would be the encounter of Christianity with the most ancient forms of religion, profoundly marked by a monotheistic orientation.

. . . .
. . . .
. . . .
. . . .

52. Recalling that "Christ ... by the revelation of the mystery of the Father and his love, fully reveals man to man himself and makes his supreme calling clear",34 two commitments should characterize in a special way the third preparatory year: *meeting the challenge of secularism and dialogue with the great religions.*

With regard to the former, it will be fitting to broach the vast subject of the *crisis of civilization,* which has become apparent especially in the West, which is highly developed from the standpoint of technology but is interiorly impoverished by its tendency to forget God or to keep him at a distance. This crisis of civilization must be countered by *the civilization of love,* founded on the universal values of peace, solidarity, justice and liberty, which find their full attainment in Christ.

53. On the other hand, as far as the field of religious awareness is concerned, the eve of the Year 2000 will provide a great opportunity, especially in view of the events of recent decades, for *interreligious dialogue,* in accordance with the specific guidelines set down by the Second Vatican Council in its Declaration *Nostra Aetate* on the relationship of the Church to non-Christian religions.

In this dialogue the Jews and the Muslims ought to have a pre-eminent place. God grant that as a confirmation of these intentions it may also be possible to hold *joint meetings* in places of significance for the great monotheistic religions. In this regard, attention is being given to finding ways of arranging historic meetings in places of exceptional symbolic importance like Bethlehem, Jerusalem and Mount Sinai as a means of furthering dialogue with Jews and the followers of Islam, and to arranging similar meetings elsewhere with the leaders of the great world religions. However, care will always have be taken not to cause harmful misunderstandings, avoiding the risk of syncretism and of a facile and deceptive irenicism.

. . . .
. . . .

57. Therefore, ever since the apostolic age, *the Church's mission* has continued without interruption within the whole human family. The first evangelization took place above all in the region of the Mediterranean. In the course of the first millennium, missions setting out from Rome and Constantinople brought Christianity to *the whole continent of Europe.* At the same time they made their way to the heart of *Asia,* as far as India and China. The end of the fifteenth century marked both the discovery of *America* and the beginning of the evangelization of that great continent, North and South. Simultaneously, while the sub-Saharan coasts of Africa welcomed the light of Christ, Saint Francis Xavier, Patron of the Missions, reached Japan. At the end of the eighteenth century and the beginning of the nineteenth, a layman, Andrew Kim, brought Christianity to Korea. In the same period the proclamation of the Gospel reached Indochina, as well as *Australia and the Islands of the Pacific.*

The nineteenth century witnessed vast missionary activity among the *peoples of Africa.* All these efforts bore fruit which has lasted up to the present day. The Second Vatican Council gives an account of this in the Decree *Ad Gentes* on Missionary Activity. After the Council the question of missionary work was dealt with in the Encyclical *Redemptoris Missio,* in the light of the problems of the missions in these final years of our century. In the future too, the Church must continue to be missionary: indeed missionary outreach is part of her very nature. With the fall of the great anti-Christian systems in Europe, first of Nazism and then of Communism, there is urgent need to bring once more the liberating message of the Gospel to the men and women of Europe.39 Furthermore, as the Encyclical *Redemptoris Missio* affirms, the modern world reflects the situation of the *Areopagus of Athens,* where Saint Paul spoke40. Today there are many "areopagi", and very different ones: these are the vast sectors of contemporary civilization and culture, of politics and economics. *The more the West is becoming estranged from its Christian roots, the more it is becoming missionary territory,* taking the form of many different "areopagi".

. . . .
. . . .

ADDRESS OF HIS HOLINESS POPE JOHN PAUL II TO THE FIFTIETH GENERAL ASSEMBLY OF THE UNITED NATIONS ORGANIZATION*

* Copyright: Vatican Information Service

. . . .
. . . .
. . . .
. . . .

A Common Human Patrimony

2. Ladies and Gentlemen! On the threshold of a new millennium we are witnessing an extraordinary global acceleration of that quest for freedom which is one of the great dynamics of human history. This phenomenon is not limited to any one part of the world; nor is it the expression of any single culture. Men and women throughout the world, even when threatened by violence, have taken the risk of freedom, asking to be given a place in social, political, and economic life which is commensurate with their dignity as free human beings. This universal longing for freedom is truly one of the distinguishing marks of our time.

During my previous Visit to the United Nations on 2 October 1979, I noted that the quest for freedom in our time has its basis in those universal rights which human beings enjoy by the very fact of their humanity. It was precisely outrages against human dignity which led the United Nations Organization to formulate, barely three years after its establishment, that Universal Declaration of Human Rights which remains one of the highest expressions of the human conscience of our time. In Asia and Africa, in the Americas, in Oceania and Europe, men and women of conviction and courage have appealed to this Declaration in support of their claims for a fuller share in the life of society.

3. It is important for us to grasp what might be called the inner structure of this worldwide movement. It is precisely its global character which offers us its first and fundamental "key" and confirms that there are indeed universal human rights, rooted in the nature of the person, rights which reflect the objective and inviolable demands of a universal moral law. These are not abstract points; rather, these rights tell us something important about the actual life of every individual and of every social group. They also remind us that we do not

live in an irrational or meaningless world. On the contrary, there is a moral logic which is built into human life and which makes possible dialogue between individuals and peoples. If we want a century of violent coercion to be succeeded by a century of persuasion, we must find a way to discuss the human future intelligibly. The universal moral law written on the human heart is precisely that kind of "grammar" which is needed if the world is to engage this discussion of its future.

In this sense, it is a matter for serious concern that some people today deny the universality of human rights, just as they deny that there is a human nature shared by everyone. To be sure, there is no single model for organizing the politics and economics of human freedom; different cultures and different historical experiences give rise to different institutional forms of public life in a free and responsible society. But it is one thing to affirm a legitimate pluralism of "forms of freedom", and another to deny any universality or intelligibility to the nature of man or to the human experience. The latter makes the international politics of persuasion extremely difficult, if not impossible.

Taking the Risk of Freedom

4. The moral dynamics of this universal quest for freedom clearly appeared in Central and Eastern Europe during the non-violent revolutions of 1989. Unfolding in specific times and places, those historical events nonetheless taught a lesson which goes far beyond a specific geographical location. For the non-violent revolutions of 1989 demonstrated that the quest for freedom cannot be suppressed. It arises from a recognition of the inestimable dignity and value of the human person, and it cannot fail to be accompanied by a commitment on behalf of the human person. Modern totalitarianism has been, first and foremost, an assault on the dignity of the person, an assault which has gone even to the point of denying the inalienable value of the individual's life. The revolutions of 1989 were made possible by the commitment of brave men and women inspired by a different, and ultimately more profound and powerful, vision: the vision of man as a creature of intelligence and free will, immersed in a mystery which transcends his own being and endowed with the ability to reflect and the ability to choose – and thus capable of wisdom and virtue. A decisive factor in the success of those non-violent revolutions was the experience of social solidarity: in the face of regimes backed by the power of propaganda and terror, that solidarity was the moral core of the "power of the powerless", a beacon of hope and an enduring reminder that it is possible for man's historical journey to follow a path which is true to the finest aspirations of the human spirit.

Viewing those events from this privileged international forum, one cannot fail to grasp the connection between the values which inspired those people's liberation movements and many of the moral commitments inscribed in the United Nations Charter: I am thinking for example of the commitment to "reaffirm faith in fundamental human rights (and) in the dignity and worth of the human person"; and also the commitment "to promote social progress and better standards of life in larger freedom" (Preamble). The fifty-one States which founded this Organization in 1945 truly lit a lamp whose light can scatter the darkness caused by tyranny – a light which can show the way to freedom, peace, and solidarity.

The Rights of Nations

5. The quest for freedom in the second half of the twentieth century has engaged not only individuals but nations as well. Fifty years after the end of the Second World War, it is important to remember that that war was fought because of violations of the rights of nations. Many of those nations suffered grievously for no other reason than that they were deemed "other". Terrible crimes were committed in the name of lethal doctrines which taught the "inferiority" of some nations and cultures. In a certain sense, the United Nations Organization was born from a conviction that such doctrines were antithetical to peace; and the Charter's commitment to "save future generations from the scourge of war" (Preamble) surely implied a moral commitment to defend every nation and culture from unjust and violent aggression.

Unfortunately, even after the end of the Second World War, the rights of nations continued to be violated. To take but one set of examples, the Baltic States and extensive territories in Ukraine and Belarus were absorbed into the Soviet Union, as had already happened to Armenia, Azerbaijan, and Georgia in the Caucasus. At the same time the so-called "People's Democracies" of Central and Eastern Europe effectively lost their sovereignty and were required to submit to the will dominating the entire bloc. The result of this artificial division of Europe was the "cold war", a situation of international tension in which the threat of a nuclear holocaust hung over humanity. It was only when freedom was restored to the nations of Central and Eastern Europe that the promise of the peace which should have come with the end of the war began to be realized for many of the victims of that conflict.

6. The Universal Declaration of Human Rights, adopted in 1948, spoke eloquently of the rights of persons; but no similar international agreement has yet adequately addressed the rights of nations. This situation must be carefully pondered, for it raises urgent questions about justice and freedom in the world today.

In reality the problem of the full recognition of the rights of peoples and nations has presented itself repeatedly to the conscience of humanity, and has also given rise to considerable ethical and juridical reflection. I am reminded of the debate which took place at the Council of Constance in the fifteenth century, when the representatives of the Academy of Krakow, headed by Pawel Wlodkowic, courageously defended the right of certain European peoples to existence and independence. Still better known is the discussion which went on in that same period at the University of Salamanca with regard to the peoples of the New World. And in our own century, how can I fail to mention the prophetic words of my predecessor, Pope Benedict XV, who in the midst of the First World War reminded everyone that "nations do not die", and invited them "to ponder with serene conscience the rights and the just aspirations of peoples" (To the Peoples at War and their Leaders, 28 July 1915)?

7. Today the problem of nationalities forms part of a new world horizon marked by a great "mobility" which has blurred the ethnic and cultural frontiers of the different peoples, as a result of a variety of processes such as migrations, mass-media and the globalization of the economy. And yet, precisely against this horizon of universality we see the powerful re-emergence of a certain ethnic and cultural consciousness, as it were an explosive need for identity and survival, a sort of counterweight to the tendency toward uniformity. This is a phenomenon which must not be underestimated or regarded as a simple left-over of the past. It demands serious interpretation, and a closer examination on the levels of anthropology, ethics and law.

This tension between the particular and the universal can be considered immanent in human beings. By virtue of sharing in the same human nature, people automatically feel that they are members of one great family, as is in fact the case. But as a result of the concrete historical conditioning of this same nature, they are necessarily bound in a more intense way to particular human groups, beginning with the family and going on to the various groups to which they belong and up to the whole of their ethnic and cultural group, which is called, not by accident, a "nation", from the Latin word "nasci": "to be born". This term, enriched with another one, "patria" (fatherland/motherland), evokes the reality of the family. The human condition thus finds itself between these two poles – universality and particularity – with a vital tension between them; an inevitable tension, but singularly fruitful if they are lived in a calm and balanced way.

8. Upon this anthropological foundation there also rest the "rights of nations", which are nothing but "human rights" fostered at the specific level of community life. A study of these rights is certainly not easy, if we consider the difficulty of defining the very concept of "nation", which cannot be identified a priori and necessarily with the State. Such a study must nonetheless be made, if we wish to avoid the errors of the past and ensure a just world order.

A presupposition of a nation's rights is certainly its right to exist: therefore no one – neither a State nor another nation, nor an international organization – is ever justified in asserting that an individual nation is not worthy of existence. This fundamental right to existence does not necessarily call for sovereignty as a state, since various forms of juridical aggregation between different nations are possible, as for example occurs in Federal States, in Confederations or in States characterized by broad regional autonomies. There can be historical circumstances in which aggregations different from single state sovereignty can even prove advisable, but only on condition that this takes place in a climate of true freedom, guaranteed by the exercise of the self-determination of the peoples concerned. Its right to exist naturally implies that every nation also enjoys the right to its own language and culture, through which a people expresses and promotes that which I would call its fundamental spiritual "sovereignty". History shows that in extreme circumstances (such as those which occurred in the land where I was born) it is precisely its culture that enables a nation to survive the loss of political and economic independence. Every nation therefore has also the right to shape its life according to its own traditions, excluding, of course, every abuse of basic human rights and in particular the oppression of minorities. Every nation has the right to build its future by providing an appropriate education for the younger generation.

But while the "rights of the nation" express the vital requirements of "particularity", it is no less important to emphasize the requirements of universality, expressed through a clear awareness of the duties which nations have vis-à-vis other nations and humanity as a whole. Foremost among these duties is certainly that of living in a spirit of peace, respect and solidarity with other nations. Thus the exercise of the rights of nations, balanced by the acknowledgement and the practice of duties, promotes a fruitful "exchange of gifts", which strengthens the unity of all mankind.

Respect for Differences

9. During my pastoral pilgrimages to the communities of the Catholic Church over the past seventeen years, I have been able to enter into dialogue with the rich diversity of nations and cultures in every part of the world. Unhappily, the world has yet to learn how to live with diversity, as recent events in the Balkans and Central Africa have painfully reminded us. The fact of "difference", and the reality of "the other", can sometimes be felt as a burden, or even as a threat. Amplified by historic grievances and exacerbated by the manipulations of the unscrupulous, the fear of "difference" can lead to a denial of the very humanity of "the other": with the result that people fall into a cycle of violence in which no one is spared, not even the children. We are all very familiar today with such situations; at this moment my heart and my prayers turn in a special way to the sufferings of the sorely tried peoples of Bosnia-Hercegovina.

From bitter experience, then, we know that the fear of "difference", especially when it expresses itself in a narrow and exclusive nationalism which denies any rights to "the other", can lead to a true nightmare of violence and terror. And yet if we make the effort to look at matters objectively, we can see that, transcending all the differences which distinguish individuals and peoples, there is a fundamental commonality. For different cultures are but different ways of facing the question of the meaning of personal existence. And it is precisely here that we find one source of the respect which is due to every culture and every nation: every culture is an effort to ponder the mystery of the world and in particular of the human person: it is a way of giving expression to the transcendent dimension of human life. The heart of every culture is its approach to the greatest of all mysteries: the mystery of God.

10. Our respect for the culture of others is therefore rooted in our respect for each community's attempt to answer the question of human life. And here we can see how important it is to safeguard the fundamental right to freedom of religion and freedom of conscience, as the cornerstones of the structure of human rights and the foundation of every truly free society. No one is permitted to suppress those rights by using coercive power to impose an answer to the mystery of man.
To cut oneself off from the reality of difference – or, worse, to attempt to stamp out that difference – is to cut oneself off from the possibility of sounding the depths of the mystery of human life. The truth about man is the unchangeable standard by which all cultures are judged; but every culture has something to teach us about one or other dimension of that complex truth. Thus the "difference" which some find so threatening can, through respectful dialogue, become the source of a deeper understanding of the mystery of human existence.

11. In this context, we need to clarify the essential difference between an unhealthy form of nationalism, which teaches contempt for other nations or cultures, and patriotism, which is a proper love of one's country. True patriotism never seeks to advance the well-being of one's own nation at the expense of others. For in the end this would harm one's own nation as well: doing wrong damages both aggressor and victim. Nationalism, particularly in its most radical forms, is thus the antithesis of true patriotism, and today we must ensure that extreme nationalism does not continue to give rise to new forms of the aberrations of totalitarianism. This is a commitment which also holds true, obviously, in cases where religion itself is made the basis of nationalism, as unfortunately happens in certain manifestations of so-called "fundamentalism".

Freedom and Moral Truth

12. Ladies and Gentlemen! Freedom is the measure of man's dignity and greatness. Living the freedom sought by individuals and peoples is a great challenge

to man's spiritual growth and to the moral vitality of nations. The basic question which we must all face today is the responsible use of freedom, in both its personal and social dimensions. Our reflection must turn then to the question of the moral structure of freedom, which is the inner architecture of the culture of freedom.

Freedom is not simply the absence of tyranny or oppression. Nor is freedom a licence to do whatever we like. Freedom has an inner "logic" which distinguishes it and ennobles it: freedom is ordered to the truth, and is fulfilled in man's quest for truth and in man's living in the truth. Detached from the truth about the human person, freedom deteriorates into license in the lives of individuals, and, in political life, it becomes the caprice of the most powerful and the arrogance of power. Far from being a limitation upon freedom or a threat to it, reference to the truth about the human person – a truth universally knowable through the moral law written on the hearts of all – is, in fact, the guarantor of freedom's future.

13. In the light of what has been said we understand how utilitarianism, the doctrine which defines morality not in terms of what is good but of what is advantageous, threatens the freedom of individuals and nations and obstructs the building of a true culture of freedom. Utilitarianism often has devastating political consequences, because it inspires an aggressive nationalism on the basis of which the subjugation, for example, of a smaller or weaker nation is claimed to be a good thing solely because it corresponds to the national interest. No less grave are the results of economic utilitarianism, which drives more powerful countries to manipulate and exploit weaker ones.

Nationalistic and economic utilitarianism are sometimes combined, a phenomenon which has too often characterized relations between the "North" and the "South". For the emerging countries, the achievement of political independence has too frequently been accompanied by a situation of de facto economic dependence on other countries; indeed, in some cases, the developing world has suffered a regression, such that some countries lack the means of satisfying the essential needs of their people. Such situations offend the conscience of humanity and pose a formidable moral challenge to the human family. Meeting this challenge will obviously require changes in both developing and developed countries. If developing countries are able to offer sure guarantees of the proper management of resources and of assistance received, as well as respect for human rights, by replacing where necessary unjust, corrupt, or authoritarian forms of government with participatory and democratic ones, will they not in this way unleash the best civil and economic energies of their people? And must not the developed countries, for their part, come to renounce strictly utilitarian approaches and develop new approaches inspired by greater justice and solidarity?

Yes, distinguished Ladies and Gentlemen! The international economic scene needs an ethic of solidarity, if participation, economic growth, and a just distribution of goods are to characterize the future of humanity. The international cooperation called for by the Charter of the United Nations for "solving international problems of an economic, social, cultural, or humanitarian character" (art. 1.3) cannot be conceived exclusively in terms of help and assistance, or even by considering the eventual returns on the resources provided. When millions of people are suffering from a poverty which means hunger, malnutrition, sickness, illiteracy, and degradation, we must not only remind ourselves that no one has a right to exploit another for his own advantage, but also and above all we must recommit ourselves to that solidarity which enables others to live out, in the actual circumstances of their economic and political lives, the creativity which is a distinguishing mark of the human person and the true source of the wealth of nations in today's world.

The United Nations and the Future of Freedom

14. As we face these enormous challenges, how can we fail to acknowledge the role of the United Nations Organization? Fifty years after its founding, the need for such an Organization is even more obvious, but we also have a better understanding, on the basis of experience, that the effectiveness of this great instrument for harmonizing and coordinating international life depends on the international culture and ethic which it supports and expresses. The United Nations Organization needs to rise more and more above the cold status of an administrative institution and to become a moral centre where all the nations of the world feel at home and develop a shared awareness of being, as it were, a "family of nations". The idea of "family" immediately evokes something more than simple functional relations or a mere convergence of interests. The family is by nature a community based on mutual trust, mutual support and sincere respect. In an authentic family the strong do not dominate; instead, the weaker members, because of their very weakness, are all the more welcomed and served. Raised to the level of the "family of nations", these sentiments ought to be, even before law itself, the very fabric of relations between peoples. The United Nations has the historic, even momentous, task of promoting this qualitative leap in international life, not only by serving as a centre of effective mediation for the resolution of conflicts but also by fostering values, attitudes and concrete initiatives of solidarity which prove capable of raising the level of relations between nations from the "organizational" to a more "organic" level, from simple "existence with" others to "existence for" others, in a fruitful exchange of gifts, primarily for the good of the weaker nations but even so, a clear harbinger of greater good for everyone.

15. Only on this condition shall we attain an end not only to "wars of combat" but also to "cold wars". It will ensure not only the legal equality of all peoples

but also their active participation in the building of a better future, and not only respect for individual cultural identities, but full esteem for them as a common treasure belonging to the cultural patrimony of mankind. Is this not the ideal held up by the Charter of the United Nations when it sets as the basis of the Organization "the principle of the sovereign equality of all its Members" (art. 2.1), or when it commits it to "develop friendly relations between nations based on respect for the principle of equal rights and of self-determination" (art. 1.2)? This is the high road which must be followed to the end, even if this involves, when necessary, appropriate modifications in the operating model of the United Nations, so as to take into account everything that has happened in this half century, with so many new peoples experiencing freedom and legitimately aspiring to "be" and to "count for" more.

None of this should appear an unattainable utopia. Now is the time for new hope, which calls us to expel the paralyzing burden of cynicism from the future of politics and of human life. The anniversary which we are celebrating invites us to do this by reminding us of the idea of "united nations", an idea which bespeaks mutual trust, security and solidarity. Inspired by the example of all those who have taken the risk of freedom, can we not recommit ourselves also to taking the risk of solidarity – and thus the risk of peace?

Beyond Fear: the Civilization of Love

16. It is one of the great paradoxes of our time that man, who began the period we call "modernity" with a self-confident assertion of his "coming of age" and "autonomy", approaches the end of the twentieth century fearful of himself, fearful of what he might be capable of, fearful for the future. Indeed, the second half of the twentieth century has seen the unprecedented phenomenon of a humanity uncertain about the very likelihood of a future, given the threat of nuclear war. That danger, mercifully, appears to have receded – and everything that might make it return needs to be rejected firmly and universally; all the same, fear for the future and of the future remains.

In order to ensure that the new millennium now approaching will witness a new flourishing of the human spirit, mediated through an authentic culture of freedom, men and women must learn to conquer fear. We must learn not to be afraid, we must rediscover a spirit of hope and a spirit of trust. Hope is not empty optimism springing from a naive confidence that the future will necessarily be better than the past. Hope and trust are the premise of responsible activity and are nurtured in that inner sanctuary of conscience where "man is alone with God" (Gaudium et Spes, 16) and he thus perceives that he is not alone amid the enigmas of existence, for he is surrounded by the love of the Creator!

Hope and trust: these may seem matters beyond the purview of the United Nations. But they are not. The politics of nations, with which your Organization is principally concerned, can never ignore the transcendent, spiritual dimension of the human experience, and could never ignore it without harming the cause of man and the cause of human freedom. Whatever diminishes man – whatever shortens the horizon of man's aspiration to goodness – harms the cause of freedom. In order to recover our hope and our trust at the end of this century of sorrows, we must regain sight of that transcendent horizon of possibility to which the soul of man aspires.

17. As a Christian, my hope and trust are centered on Jesus Christ, the two thousandth anniversary of whose birth will be celebrated at the coming of the new millennium. We Christians believe that in his Death and Resurrection were fully revealed God's love and his care for all creation. Jesus Christ is for us God made man, and made a part of the history of humanity. Precisely for this reason, Christian hope for the world and its future extends to every human person. Because of the radiant humanity of Christ, nothing genuinely human fails to touch the hearts of Christians. Faith in Christ does not impel us to intolerance. On the contrary, it obliges us to engage others in a respectful dialogue. Love of Christ does not distract us from interest in others, but rather invites us to responsibility for them, to the exclusion of no one and indeed, if anything, with a special concern for the weakest and the suffering. Thus, as we approach the two thousandth anniversary of the birth of Christ, the Church asks only to be able to propose respectfully this message of salvation, and to be able to promote, in charity and service, the solidarity of the entire human family. Ladies and Gentlemen! I come before you, as did my predecessor Pope Paul VI exactly thirty years ago, not as one who exercises temporal power – these are his words – nor as a religious leader seeking special privileges for his community. I come before you as a witness: a witness to human dignity, a witness to hope, a witness to the conviction that the destiny of all nations lies in the hands of a merciful Providence.

18. We must overcome our fear of the future. But we will not be able to overcome it completely unless we do so together. The "answer" to that fear is neither coercion nor repression, nor the imposition of one social "model" on the entire world. The answer to the fear which darkens human existence at the end of the twentieth century is the common effort to build the civilization of love, founded on the universal values of peace, solidarity, justice, and liberty. And the "soul" of the civilization of love is the culture of freedom: the freedom of individuals and the freedom of nations, lived in self-giving solidarity and responsibility.

We must not be afraid of the future. We must not be afraid of man. It is no accident that we are here. Each and every human person has been created in the "image and likeness" of the One who is the origin of all that is. We have within us the capacities for wisdom and virtue. With these gifts, and with the help of God's grace, we can build in the next century and the next millennium a civilization worthy of the human person, a true culture of freedom. We can and must do so! And in doing so, we shall see that the tears of this century have prepared the ground for a new springtime of the human spirit.

. . . .
. . . .

POST-SYNODAL
APOSTOLIC EXHORTATION
ECCLESIA IN AFRICA
OF THE HOLY FATHER
JOHN PAUL II
TO THE BISHOPS
PRIESTS AND DEACONS
MEN AND WOMEN RELIGIOUS
AND ALL THE LAY FAITHFUL
ON THE CHURCH IN AFRICA
AND ITS EVANGELIZING MISSION
TOWARDS THE YEAR 2000 *

A relevant and credible message

21. According to the Synod Fathers, the main question facing the Church in Africa consists in delineating as clearly as possible what it is and what it must fully carry out, in order that its message may be relevant and credible.24 All the discussions at the Assembly referred to this truly essential and fundamental need, which is *a real challenge for the Church in Africa.*
It is of course true "that the Holy Spirit is the principal agent of evangelization: it is he who impels each individual to proclaim the Gospel, and it is he who in the depths of consciences causes the word of salvation to be accepted and understood".25 After reaffirming this truth, the Special Assembly rightly went on to add that evangelization is also a mission which the Lord Jesus entrusted to his Church under the guidance and in the power of the Holy Spirit. Our cooperation is necessary through fervent prayer, serious reflection, suitable planning and the mobilization of resources.26
The Synod's debate on the *relevance* and *credibility* of the Church's message in Africa inescapably entailed consideration of the *very credibility of the proclaimers of this message.* The Synod Fathers faced the question directly, with genuine frankness and devoid of any complacency. Pope Paul VI had already addressed this question in memorable words when he stated: "It is often said nowadays that the present century thirsts for authen- ticity. Especially in regard to young

people, it is said that they have a horror of the artificial or false and that they are searching above all for truth and honesty. These *signs of the times* should find us vigilant. Either tacitly or aloud – but always forcefully – we are being asked: Do you really believe what you are proclaiming? Do you live what you believe? Do you really preach what you live? The witness of life has become more than ever an essential condition for real effectiveness in preaching. Precisely because of this we are, to a certain extent, responsible for the progress of the Gospel that we proclaim".27

That is why, with reference to the Church's evangelizing mission in the field of justice and peace, I have said: "Today more than ever, the Church is aware that her social doctrine will gain credibility more immediately from *witness of action* than as a result of its internal logic and consistency".28

. . . .
. . . .

I. BRIEF HISTORY OF THE CONTINENT'S EVANGELIZATION

30. On the opening day of the Special Assembly for Africa of the Synod of Bishops, the first meeting of this kind in history, the Synod Fathers recalled some of the marvels wrought by God in the course of Africa's evangelization. It is a history which goes back to the period of the Church's very birth. The spread of the Gospel has taken place in different phases. The first centuries of Christianity saw the evangelization of Egypt and North Africa. A second phase, involving the parts of the Continent south of the Sahara, took place in the fifteenth and sixteenth centuries. A third phase, marked by an extraordinary missionary effort, began in the nineteenth century.

First phase

31. In a message to the Bishops and to all the peoples of Africa concerning the promotion of the religious, civil and social well-being of the Continent, my venerable Predecessor Paul VI recalled in memorable words the glorious splendour of Africa's Christian past: "We think of the Christian Churches of Africa whose origins go back to the times of the Apostles and are traditionally associated with the name and teaching of Mark the Evangelist. We think of their countless Saints, Martyrs, Confessors, and Virgins, and recall the fact that from the second to the fourth centuries Christian life in the North of Africa was most vigorous and had a leading place in theological study and literary production. The names of the great doctors and writers come to mind, men like Origen, Saint Athanasius, and Saint Cyril, leaders of the Alexandrian school, and at the other end of the North African coastline, Tertullian, Saint Cyprian

and above all Saint Augustine, one of the most brilliant lights of the Christian world. We shall mention the great Saints of the desert, Paul, Anthony, and Pachomius, the first founders of the monastic life, which later spread through their example in both the East and the West. And among many others we want also to mention Saint Frumentius, known by the name of Abba Salama, who was consecrated Bishop by Saint Athanasius and became the first Apostle of Ethiopia".37 During these first centuries of the Church in Africa, certain women also bore their own witness to Christ. Among them Saints Perpetua and Felicitas, Saint Monica and Saint Thecla are particularly deserving of mention. "These noble examples, as also the saintly African Popes, Victor I, Melchiades and Gelasius I, belong to the common heritage of the Church, and the Christian writers of Africa remain today a basic source for deepening our knowledge of the history of salvation in the light of the Word of God. In recalling the ancient glories of Christian Africa, we wish to express our profound respect for the Churches with which we are not in full communion: the Greek Church of the Patriarchate of Alexandria, the Coptic Church of Egypt and the Church of Ethiopia, which share with the Catholic Church a common origin and the doctrinal and spiritual heritage of the great Fathers and Saints, not only of their own land, but of all the early Church. They have laboured much and suffered much to keep the Christian name alive in Africa through all the vicissitudes of history".38 These Churches continue to give evidence down to our own times of the Christian vitality which flows from their Apostolic origins. This is especially true in Egypt, in Ethiopia and, until the seventeenth century, in Nubia. At that time a new phase of evangelization was beginning on the rest of the Continent.

Second phase

32. In the fifteenth and sixteenth centuries, the exploration of the African coast by the Portuguese was soon accompanied by the evangelization of the regions of Sub-Saharan Africa. That endeavour included the regions of present-day Benin, São Tomé, Angola, Mozambique and Madagascar.
On Pentecost Sunday, 7 June 1992, for the commemoration of the five hundred years of the evangelization of Angola, I said in Luanda: "The Acts of the Apostles indicate by name the inhabitants of the places who participated directly in the birth of the Church and the work of the breath of the Holy Spirit. They all said: ?We hear them telling in our own tongues the mighty works of God' (*Acts* 2:11). Five hundred years ago the people of Angola were added to this chorus of languages. In that moment, in your African homeland the Pentecost of Jerusalem was renewed. Your ancestors heard the message of the Good News which is the language of the Spirit. Their hearts accepted this message for the first time, and they bowed their heads to the waters of the

baptismal font in which, by the power of the Holy Spirit, a person dies with Christ and is born again to new life in his Resurrection ... It was certainly the same Spirit who moved those men of faith, the first missionaries, who in 1491 sailed into the mouth of the Zaire River, at Pinda, beginning a genuine missionary saga. It was the Holy Spirit, who works as he wills in people's hearts, who moved the great King of the Congo, Nzinga-a-Nkuwu, to ask for missionaries to proclaim the Gospel. It was the Holy Spirit who sustained the life of those four first Angolan Christians who, returning from Europe, testified to the Christian faith. After the first missionaries, many others came from Portugal and other European countries to continue, expand and strengthen the work that had been begun".39

A certain number of Episcopal Sees were erected during this period, and one of the first fruits of that missionary endeavour was the consecration in Rome, by Pope Leo X in 1518, of Don Henrique, the son of Don Alfonso I, King of the Congo, as Titular Bishop of Utica. Don Henrique thus became the first native Bishop of Black Africa.

It was during this period, in 1622, that my Predecessor Pope Gregory XV permanently erected the Congregation *de Propaganda Fide* for the purpose of better organizing and expanding the missions.

Because of various difficulties, the second phase of the evangelization of Africa came to an end in the eighteenth century, with the disappearance of practically all the missions south of the Sahara.

Third phase

33. The third phase of Africa's systematic evangelization began in the nineteenth century, a period marked by an extraordinary effort organized by the great apostles and promoters of the African mission. It was a period of rapid growth, as the statistics presented to the Synodal Assembly by the Congregation for the Evangelization of Peoples clearly demonstrate.40 Africa has responded with great generosity to Christ's call. In recent decades many African countries have celebrated the first centenary of the beginning of their evangelization. Indeed, the growth of the Church in Africa over the last hundred years is a marvellous work of divine grace.

The glory and splendour of the present period of Africa's evangelization are illustrated in a truly admirable way by the Saints whom modern Africa has given to the Church. Pope Paul VI eloquently expressed this when he canonized the Ugandan Martyrs in Saint Peter's Basilica on World Mission Day, 1964: "These African Martyrs add a new page to that list of victorious men and women that we call the martyrology, in which we find the most magnificent as well as the most tragic stories. The page that they add is worthy to take its place alongside those wonderful stories of ancient Africa ... For from the

Africa that was sprinkled with the blood of these Martyrs, the first of this new age (and, God willing, the last, so sublime, so precious was their sacrifice), there is emerging a free and redeemed Africa".41

34. The list of Saints that Africa gives to the Church, the list that is its greatest title of honour, continues to grow. How could we fail to mention, among the most recent, Blessed Clementine Anwarite, Virgin and Martyr of Zaire, whom I beatified on African soil in 1985, Blessed Victoria Rasoamanarivo of Madagascar, and Blessed Josephine Bakhita of the Sudan, also beatified during my Pontificate? And how can we not recall Blessed Isidore Bakanja, Martyr of Zaire, whom I had the privilege of raising to the honours of the altar in the course of the Special Assembly for Africa? "Other causes are reaching their final stages. *The Church in Africa must furnish and write her own Martyrology,* adding to the outstanding figures of the first centuries ... the Martyrs and Saints of our own day".42

Faced with the tremendous growth of the Church in Africa over the last hundred years and the fruits of holiness that it has borne, there is only one possible explanation: all this is a gift of God, for no human effort alone could have performed this work in the course of such a relatively short period of time. There is however no reason for worldly triumphalism. In recalling the glorious splendour of the Church in Africa, the Synod Fathers only wished to celebrate God's marvellous deeds for Africa's liberation and salvation.

> "This is the Lord's doing;
> it is marvellous in our eyes" (*Ps* 118:23).
> "He who is mighty has done great things for
> me, and holy is his name" (*Lk* 1:49).

. . . .
. . . .

Deeper roots and growth of the Church

38. The fact that in the course of almost two centuries the number of African Catholics has grown quickly is an outstanding achievement by any standard. In particular, the building up of the Church on the Continent is confirmed by facts such as the noteworthy and rapid increase in the number of ecclesiastical circumscriptions, the growth of a native clergy, of seminarians and candidates for Institutes of Consecrated Life, and the steady increase in the network of catechists, whose contribution to the spread of the Gospel among the African peoples is well known. Finally, of fundamental importance is the high percentage of indigenous Bishops who now make up the Hierarchy on the Continent. The Synod Fathers identified many very significant accomplishments of the

Church in Africa in the areas of inculturation and ecumenical dialogue.46 The outstanding and meritorious achievements in the field of education are universally acknowledged.

Although Catholics constitute only fourteen per cent of the population of Africa, Catholic health facilities make up seventeen per cent of the health-care institutions of the entire Continent.

The initiatives boldly undertaken by the young Churches of Africa in order to bring the Gospel "to the ends of the earth" (*Acts* 1:8) are certainly worthy of note. The missionary Institutes founded in Africa have grown in number, and have begun to supply missionaries not only for the countries of the Continent but also for other areas of the world. A slowly increasing number of African diocesan priests are beginning to make themselves available, for limited periods, as *fidei donum* priests in other needy Dioceses – in their own countries or abroad. The African provinces of Religious Institutes of pontifical right, both of men and of women, have also recorded a growth in membership. In this way the Church offers her ministry to the peoples of Africa; but she also accepts involvement in the "exchange of gifts" with other particular Churches which make up the People of God. All this manifests, in a tangible way, the maturity which the Church in Africa has attained: this is what made possible the celebration of the Special Assembly of the Synod of Bishops.

What has become of Africa?

39. A little less than thirty years ago many African countries gained their independence from the colonial powers. This gave rise to great hopes with regard to the political, economic, social and cultural development of the African peoples. However, "in some countries the internal situation has unfortunately not yet been consolidated, and violence has had, or in some cases still has, the upper hand. But this does not justify a general condemnation involving a whole people or a whole nation or, even worse, a whole continent".47

40. But what is the true overall situation of the African Continent today, especially from the point of view of the Church's evangelizing mission? In this regard the Synod Fathers first of all asked: "In a Continent full of bad news, how is the Christian message 'Good News' for our people? In the midst of an all-pervading despair, where lie the hope and optimism which the Gospel brings? Evangelization stands for many of those essential values which our Continent very much lacks: hope, peace, joy, harmony, love and unity".48

After correctly noting that Africa is a huge Continent where very diverse situations are found, and that it is necessary to avoid generalizations both in evaluating problems and suggesting solutions, the Synodal Assembly sadly had to say: "One common situation, without any doubt, is that Africa is full of problems.

In almost all our nations, there is abject poverty, tragic mismanagement of available scarce resources, political instability and social disorientation. The results stare us in the face: misery, wars, despair. In a world controlled by rich and powerful nations, Africa has practically become an irrelevant appendix, often forgotten and neglected".49

41. For many Synod Fathers contemporary Africa can be compared to the man who went down from Jerusalem to Jericho; he fell among robbers who stripped him, beat him and departed, leaving him half dead (cf. *Lk* 10:30-37). Africa is a Continent where countless human beings – men and women, children and young people – are lying, as it were, on the edge of the road, sick, injured, disabled, marginalized and abandoned. They are in dire need of Good Samaritans who will come to their aid.

For my part, I express the hope that the Church will continue patiently and tirelessly its work as a Good Samaritan. Indeed, for a long period certain regimes, which have now come to an end, were a great trial for Africans and weakened their ability to respond to situations: an injured person has to rediscover all the resources of his own humanity. The sons and daughters of Africa need an understanding presence and pastoral concern. They need to be helped to recoup their energies so as to put them at the service of the common good.

Positive values of African culture

42. Although Africa is very rich in natural resources, it remains economically poor. At the same time, it is endowed with a wealth of cultural values and priceless human qualities which it can offer to the Churches and to humanity as a whole. The Synod Fathers highlighted some of these cultural values, which are truly a providential preparation for the transmission of the Gospel. They are values which can contribute to an effective reversal of the Continent's dramatic situation and facilitate that worldwide revival on which the desired development of individual nations depends.

Africans have a profound religious sense, a sense of the sacred, of the existence of God the Creator and of a spiritual world. The reality of sin in its individual and social forms is very much present in the consciousness of these peoples, as is also the need for rites of purification and expiation.

43. In African culture and tradition the role of the family is everywhere held to be fundamental. Open to this sense of the family, of love and respect for life, the African loves children, who are joyfully welcomed as gifts of God. *"The sons and daughters of Africa love life.* It is precisely this love for life that leads them to give such great importance to the veneration of their ancestors. They believe intuitively that the dead continue to live and remain in communion with them.

Is this not in some way *a preparation for belief in the Communion of the Saints?*
The peoples of Africa respect the life which is conceived and born. They rejoice in
this life. They reject the idea that it can be destroyed, even when the so-called
'progressive civilizations' would like to lead them in this direction. And practices hostile to life are imposed on them by means of economic systems which
serve the selfishness of the rich".50 Africans show their respect for human life
until its natural end, and keep elderly parents and relatives within the family.
African cultures have an acute sense of solidarity and community life. In Africa
it is unthinkable to celebrate a feast without the participation of the whole village. Indeed, community life in African societies expresses the extended family.
It is my ardent hope and prayer that Africa will always preserve this priceless
cultural heritage and never succumb to the temptation to individualism, which
is so alien to its best traditions.

Some choices of the African peoples

44. While the shadows and the dark side of the African situation described
above can in no way be minimized, it is worth recalling here a number of positive achievements of the peoples of the Continent which deserve to be praised
and encouraged. For example, the Synod Fathers in their *Message* to the People
of God were pleased to mention the beginning of the democratic process in
many African countries, expressing the hope that this process would be consolidated, and that all obstacles and resistance to the establishment of the rule of
law would be promptly removed through the concerted action of all those
involved and through their sense of the common good.51
The "winds of change" are blowing strongly in many parts of Africa, and people
are demanding ever more insistently the recognition and promotion of human
rights and freedoms. In this regard I note with satisfaction that the Church in
Africa, faithful to its vocation, stands resolutely on the side of the oppressed
and of voiceless and marginalized peoples. I strongly encourage it to continue
to bear this witness. *The preferential option for the poor* is "a special form of primacy in the exercise of Christian charity, to which the whole Tradition of the
Church bears witness ... The motivating concern for the poor – who are in the
very meaning of the term 'the Lord's poor' – must be translated at all levels into
concrete actions, until it decisively attains a series of necessary reforms".52

45. In spite of its poverty and the meagre means at its disposal, the Church in
Africa plays a leading role in what touches upon integral human development.
Its remarkable achievements in this regard are often recognized by governments
and international experts.
The Special Assembly for Africa expressed deep gratitude "to all Christians and
to all men and women of good will who are working in the fields of assistance

and health-care with *Caritas* and other development organizations".53 The assistance which they, as Good Samaritans, give to the African victims of wars and disasters, to refugees and displaced persons, deserves the admiration, gratitude and support of all.

I feel it my duty to express heartfelt thanks to the Church in Africa for the role which it has played over the years as a promoter of peace and reconciliation in many situations of conflict, political turmoil and civil war.

II. PRESENT-DAY PROBLEMS OF THE CHURCH IN AFRICA

46. The Bishops of Africa are faced with two fundamental questions. How must the Church carry out her evangelizing mission as the Year 2000 approaches? How can African Christians become ever more faithful witnesses to the Lord Jesus? In order to provide adequate responses to these questions the Bishops, both before and during the Special Assembly, examined the major challenges that the Ecclesial Community in Africa must face today.

More profound evangelization

47. The primary and most fundamental fact noted by the Synod Fathers is the thirst for God felt by the peoples of Africa. In order not to disappoint this expectation, the members of the Church must first of all deepen their faith.54 Indeed, precisely because she evangelizes, the Church must "begin by being evangelized herself".55 She needs to meet the challenge raised by "this theme of the Church which is evangelized by constant conversion and renewal, in order to evangelize the world with credibility".56

The Synod recognized the urgency of proclaiming the Good News to the millions of people in Africa who are not yet evangelized. The Church certainly respects and esteems the non-Christian religions professed by very many Africans, for these religions are the living expression of the soul of vast groups of people. However, "neither respect and esteem for these religions nor the complexity of the questions raised is an invitation to the Church to withhold from these non-Christians the proclamation of Jesus Christ. On the contrary the Church holds that these multitudes have the right to know the riches of the mystery of Christ (cf. *Eph* 3:8) – riches in which we believe that the whole of humanity can find, in unsuspected fullness, everything that it is gropingly searching for concerning God, man and his destiny, life and death, and truth".57

48. The Synod Fathers rightly affirmed that "a serious concern for a true and balanced inculturation is necessary in order to avoid cultural confusion and

alienation in our fast evolving society".58 During my visit to Malawi I made the same point: "*I put before you today a challenge* – a challenge to reject a way of living which does not correspond to the best of your traditions, and your Christian faith. Many people in Africa look beyond Africa for the so-called 'freedom of the modern way of life'. Today I urge you *to look inside yourselves. Look to the riches of your own traditions, look to the faith* which we are celebrating in this assembly. Here you will find genuine freedom – here you will find Christ who will lead you to the truth".59

Overcoming divisions

49. Another challenge identified by the Synod Fathers concerns the various forms of division which need to be healed through honest dialogue.60 It has been rightly noted that, within the borders left behind by the colonial powers, the co-existence of ethnic groups with different traditions, languages, and even religions often meets obstacles arising from serious mutual hostility. "*Tribal oppositions* at times endanger if not peace, at least the pursuit of the common good of the society. They also create difficulties for the life of the Churches and the acceptance of Pastors from other ethnic groups".61 This is why the Church in Africa feels challenged by the specific responsibility of healing these divisions. For the same reason the Special Assembly emphasized the importance of ecumenical dialogue with other Churches and Ecclesial Communities, and of dialogue with African traditional religion and Islam. The Fathers also considered the means to be used to achieve this goal.

Marriage and vocations

50. A major challenge emphasized almost unanimously by the Episcopal Conferences of Africa in their replies to the *Lineamenta* concerned Christian marriage and family life.62 What is at stake is extremely serious: truly "the future of the world and of the Church passes through the family".63
Another fundamental responsibility which the Special Assembly highlighted is concern for vocations to the priesthood and consecrated life. It is necessary to discern them wisely, to provide competent directors and to oversee the quality of the formation offered. The fulfilment of the hope for a flowering of African missionary vocations depends on the attention given to the solution of this problem, a flowering that is required if the Gospel is to be proclaimed in every part of the Continent and beyond.

Social and political difficulties

51. "In Africa, the need to apply the Gospel to concrete life is felt strongly. How could one proclaim Christ on that immense Continent while forgetting

that it is one of the world's poorest regions? How could one fail to take into account the anguished history of a land where many nations are still in the grip of famine, war, racial and tribal tensions, political instability and the violation of human rights? This is all a challenge to evangelization".64

All the preparatory documents of the Synod, as well as the discussions in the Assembly, clearly showed that issues in Africa such as increasing poverty, urbanization, the international debt, the arms trade, the problem of refugees and displaced persons, demographic concerns and threats to the family, the liberation of women, the spread of AIDS, the survival of the practice of slavery in some places, ethnocentricity and tribal opposition figure among the fundamental challenges addressed by the Synod.

Intrusiveness of the mass media

52. Finally, the Special Assembly addressed the means of social communication, an issue which is of the greatest importance because it concerns both the instruments of evangelization and the means of spreading a new culture which needs to be evangelized.65 The Synod Fathers were thus faced with the sad fact that "the developing nations, instead of becoming *autonomous nations* concerned with their own progress towards a just sharing in the goods and services meant for all, become parts of a machine, cogs on a gigantic wheel. This is often true also in the field of social communications which, being run by centres mostly in the northern hemisphere, do not always give due consideration to the priorities and problems of such countries or respect their cultural make-up. They frequently impose a distorted vision of life and of man, and thus fail to respond to the demands of true development".66

III. FORMATION OF THE AGENTS OF EVANGELIZATION

53. With what resources will the Church in Africa succeed in meeting the challenges just mentioned? "The most important [resource], after the grace of Christ, is the people. The whole People of God in the theological understanding of *Lumen Gentium* – this People, which comprises the members of the Body of Christ in its entirety – has received the mandate, which is both an honour and a duty, to proclaim the Gospel ... The whole community needs to be trained, motivated and empowered for evangelization, each according to his or her specific role within the Church".67 For this reason the Synod strongly emphasized the training of the agents of evangelization in Africa. I have already referred to the necessity of formation for candidates to the priesthood and those called to the consecrated life. The Assembly also paid due attention to the formation of the lay faithful, appropriately recognizing their indispensable role in the evangelization of Africa. In particular, the training of lay catechists received the emphasis which it rightly deserves.

54. A last question must be asked: Has the Church in Africa sufficiently formed the lay faithful, enabling them to assume competently their civic responsibilities and to consider socio-political problems in the light of the Gospel and of faith in God? This is certainly a task belonging to Christians: to bring to bear upon the social fabric an influence aimed at changing not only ways of thinking but also the very structures of society, so that they will better reflect God's plan for the human family. Consequently I have called for the thorough formation of the lay faithful, a formation which will help them to lead a fully integrated life. Faith, hope and charity must influence the actions of the true follower of Christ in every activity, situation and responsibility. Since "evangelizing means bringing the Good News into all the strata of humanity, and through its influence transforming humanity from within and making it new",68 Christians must be formed to live the social implications of the Gospel in such a way that their witness will become a prophetic challenge to whatever hinders the true good of the men and women of Africa and of every other continent.

. . . .
. . . .
. . . .
. . . .

Urgent need for inculturation

59. On several occasions the Synod Fathers stressed the particular importance for evangelization of inculturation, the process by which "catechesis '*takes flesh*' in the various cultures".86 Inculturation includes two dimensions: on the one hand, "the intimate transformation of authentic cultural values through their integration in Christianity" and, on the other, "the insertion of Christianity in the various human cultures".87 The Synod considers inculturation an urgent priority in the life of the particular Churches, for a firm rooting of the Gospel in Africa.88 It is "a requirement for evangelization",89 "a path towards full evangelization",90 and one of the greatest challenges for the Church on the Continent on the eve of the Third Millennium.91

Theological foundations

60. "But when the time had fully come" (Gal 4:4), the Word, the Second Person of the Blessed Trinity, the Only Son of God, "by the power of the Holy Spirit he became incarnate from the Virgin Mary, and was made man".92 This is the sublime mystery of the Incarnation of the Word, a mystery which took place *in history:* in clearly defined circumstances of time and space, amidst a

people with its own culture, a people that God had chosen and accompanied throughout the entire history of salvation, in order to show through what he did for them what he intended to do for the whole human race.

Jesus Christ is the unmistakable proof of God's love for humanity (cf. *Rom* 5:8). By his life, his preaching of the Good News to the poor, his Passion, Death and glorious Resurrection, he brought about the remission of our sins and our reconciliation with God, his Father and, thanks to him, our Father too. The Word that the Church proclaims is precisely the Word of God made man, who is himself the subject and object of this Word. *The Good News is Jesus Christ.*

Just as "the Word became flesh and dwelt among us" (*Jn* 1:14), so too the Good News, the Word of Jesus Christ proclaimed to the nations, *must take root* in the life-situation of the hearers of the Word. Inculturation is precisely this insertion of the Gospel message into cultures.93 For the Incarnation of the Son of God, precisely because it was complete and concrete,94 was also an incarnation in a particular culture.

61. Given the close and organic relationship that exists between Jesus Christ and the Word that the Church proclaims, the inculturation of the revealed message cannot but follow the "logic" proper to the *Mystery of the Redemption.* Indeed, the Incarnation of the Word is not an isolated moment but tends towards Jesus' "Hour" and the Paschal Mystery: "Unless a grain of wheat falls into the earth and dies, it remains alone; but if it dies, it bears much fruit" (*Jn* 12:24). Jesus says: "And I, when I am lifted up from the earth, will draw all men to myself" (*Jn* 12:32). This emptying of self, this *kenosis* necessary for exaltation, which is the way of Christ and of each of his disciples (cf. *Phil* 2:6-9), sheds light on the encounter of cultures with Christ and his *Gospel.* "Every culture needs to be transformed by Gospel values in the light of the Paschal Mystery".95

It is by looking at the Mystery of the Incarnation and of the Redemption that the values and counter-values of cultures are to be discerned. Just as the Word of God became like us in everything but sin, so too the inculturation of the Good News takes on all authentic human values, purifying them from sin and restoring to them their full meaning.

Inculturation also has profound links with the *Mystery of Pentecost.* Thanks to the outpouring and action of the Spirit, who draws gifts and talents into unity, all the peoples of the earth when they enter the Church live a new Pentecost, profess in their own tongue the one faith in Jesus, and proclaim the marvels that the Lord has done for them. The Spirit, who on the natural level is the true source of the wisdom of peoples, leads the Church with a supernatural light into knowl- edge of the whole truth. In her turn the Church takes on the values of different cultures, becoming the "*sponsa ornata monilibus suis*", "the bride who adorns herself with her jewels" (cf. *Is* 61:10).

Criteria and areas of inculturation

62. Inculturation is a difficult and delicate task, since it raises the question of the Church's fidelity to the Gospel and the Apostolic Tradition amidst the constant evolution of cultures. Rightly therefore the Synod Fathers observed: "Considering the rapid changes in the cultural, social, economic and political domains, our local Churches must be involved in the process of inculturation in an ongoing manner, respecting the two following criteria: compatibility with the Christian message and communion with the universal Church … In all cases, care must be taken to avoid syncretism".96

"Inculturation is a movement towards full evangelization. It seeks to dispose people to receive Jesus Christ in an integral manner. It touches them on the personal, cultural, economic and political levels so that they can live a holy life in total union with God the Father, through the action of the Holy Spirit".97 Thanking God for the fruits which the efforts at inculturation have already brought forth in the life of the Churches of the Continent, notably in the ancient Eastern Churches of Africa, the Synod recommended "to the Bishops and to the Episcopal Conferences to take note that inculturation includes the whole life of the Church and the whole process of evangelization. It includes theology, liturgy, the Church's life and structures. All this underlines the need for research in the field of African cultures in all their complexity". Precisely for this reason the Synod invited Pastors "to exploit to the maximum the numerous possibilities which the Church's present discipline provides in this matter".98

. . . .

. . . .

Dialogue

65. "Openness to dialogue is the Christian's attitude inside the community as well as with other believers and with men and women of good will".107 *Dialogue is to be practised first of all within the family of the Church* at all levels: between Bishops, Episcopal Conferences or Hierarchical Assemblies and the Apostolic See, between Conferences or Episcopal Assemblies of the different nations of the same continent and those of other continents, and within each particular Church between the Bishop, the presbyterate, consecrated persons, pastoral workers and the lay faithful; and also between different rites within the same Church. SECAM is to establish "structures and means which will ensure the exercise of this dialogue",108 especially in order to foster an organic pastoral solidarity.

"United to Jesus Christ by their witness in Africa, Catholics are invited to develop an *ecumenical dialogue* with all their baptized brothers and sisters of other Christian denominations, in order that the unity for which Christ prayed may be achieved, and in order that their service to the peoples of the Continent may make the Gospel more credible in the eyes of those who are searching for God".109 Such dialogue can be conducted through initiatives such as ecumenical translations of the Bible, theological study of various dimensions of the Christian faith or by bearing common evangelical witness to justice, peace and respect for human dignity. For this purpose care will be taken to set up national and diocesan commissions for ecumenism.110 Together Christians are responsible for the witness to be borne to the Gospel on the Continent. Advances in ecumenism are also aimed at making this witness more effective.

66. "Commitment to dialogue must also embrace all Muslims of good will. Christians cannot forget that many Muslims try to imitate the faith of Abraham and to live the demands of the Decalogue".111 In this regard the *Message of the Synod* emphasizes that the Living God, Creator of heaven and earth and the Lord of history, is the Father of the one great human family to which we all belong. As such, he wants us to bear witness to him through our respect for the values and religious traditions of each person, working together for human progress and development at all levels. Far from wishing to be the one in whose name a person would kill other people, he requires believers to join together in the service of life in justice and peace.112 Particular care will therefore be taken so that Islamic-Christian dialogue respects on both sides the principle of religious freedom with all that this involves, also including external and public manifestations of faith.113 Christians and Muslims are called to commit themselves to promoting a dialogue free from the risks of false irenicism or militant fundamentalism, and to raising their voices against unfair policies and practices, as well as against the lack of reciprocity in matters of religious freedom.114

67. With regard to African traditional religion, a serene and prudent dialogue will be able, on the one hand, to protect Catholics from negative influences which condition the way of life of many of them and, on the other hand, to foster the assimilation of positive values such as belief in a Supreme Being who is Eternal, Creator, Provident and Just Judge, values which are readily harmonized with the content of the faith. They can even be seen as a *preparation for the Gospel*, because they contain precious *semina Verbi* which can lead, as already happened in the past, a great number of people "to be open to the fullness of Revelation in Jesus Christ through the proclamation of the Gospel".115 The adherents of African traditional religion should therefore be treated with great respect and esteem, and all inaccurate and disrespectful language should be avoided. For this purpose, suitable courses in African traditional religion should be given in houses of formation for priests and religious.116

. . . .
. . . .

Becoming the voice of the voiceless

70. Strengthened by faith and hope in the saving power of Jesus, the Synod Fathers concluded their work by renewing their commitment to accept the challenge of being instruments of salvation in every area of the life of the peoples of Africa. "The Church", they declared, "must continue to exercise her prophetic role and be the voice of the voiceless",130 so that everywhere the human dignity of every individual will be acknowledged, and that people will always be at the centre of all government programmes. The Synod "challenges the consciences of Heads of State and those responsible for the public domain to guarantee ever more the liberation and development of their peoples".131 Only at this price is peace established between nations.

Evangelization must promote initiatives which contribute to the development and *ennoblement* of individuals in their spiritual and material existence. This involves the development of every person and of the whole person, considered not only individually but also and especially in the context of the common and harmonious development of all the members of a nation and of all the peoples of the world.132

Finally, evangelization must denounce and combat all that degrades and destroys the person. "The condemnation of evils and injustices is also part of that *ministry of evangelization* in the social field which is an aspect of the Church's *prophetic role.* But it should be made clear that proclamation is always more important than condemnation, and the latter cannot ignore the former, which gives it true solidity and the force of higher motivation".133

Means of social communication

71. "From the beginning it has been a characteristic of God to want to communicate. This he does by various means. He has bestowed being upon every created thing, animate or inanimate. He enters into relationships with human beings in a very special way. "In many and various ways God spoke of old to our fathers by the prophets; but in these last days he as spoken to us by a Son" (*Heb* 1:1-2)".134 The Word of God is by nature word, dialogue and communication. He came to restore on the one hand communication and relations between God and humanity, and on the other hand those of people with one another.

The Synod paid great attention to the mass media under two important and complementary aspects: as a new and emerging cultural world and as a series of means serving communication. First of all, they constitute a new culture that has its own language and above all its own specific values and counter-values. For this reason, like any culture, the mass media need to be evangelized.135 Today in fact the mass media constitute not only a world but also a culture and civilization. And it is also to this world that the Church is sent to bring the Good News of salvation. The heralds of the Gospel must therefore *enter this world* in order to *allow themselves to be permeated* by this new civilization and culture for the purpose of learning how to make good *use* of them. "The first Areopagus of the modern age is the world of communications, which is unifying humanity and turning it into what is known as a 'global village'. The means of social communication have become so important as to be for many the chief means of information and education, of guidance and inspiration in their behaviour as individuals, families and within society at large".136

Training in the use of the mass media is therefore a necessity not only *for the preacher* of the Gospel, who must master, among other things, the media *style* of communication but also for the *reader,* the *listener* and the *viewer.* Trained to understand this kind of communication, they must be able to make use of its contributions with discernment and a critical mind.

In Africa, where *oral transmission* is one of the characteristics of culture, such training is of capital importance. This same kind of communication must remind pastors, especially Bishops and priests, that the Church is sent to *speak,* to preach the Gospel in words and deeds. Thus she *cannot remain silent,* at the risk of failing in her mission, except in cases where silence itself would be a way of speaking and bearing witness. We must therefore always preach in season and out of season (cf. *2 Tim* 4:2), in order to build up, in charity and truth.

. . . .
. . . .

Saving the African family

84. Many interventions in the Synod Hall highlighted present-day threats to the African family. The concerns of the Synod Fathers were all the more justified in that the preparatory document of a United Nations Conference held in September 1994 in Cairo – on African soil – clearly seemed to wish to adopt resolutions contradicting many values of the African family. The Synod Fathers, accepting my concerns previously expressed to the Conference and to all the world's Heads of State,164 launched an urgent appeal to safeguard the family. They pleaded: "Do not allow the African family to be ridiculed on its own soil! Do not allow the International Year of the Family to become the year of the destruction of the family!"165

The family as open to society

85. By its nature marriage, which has the special mission of perpetuating humanity, transcends the couple. In the same way, by its nature, the family

extends beyond the individual household: it is oriented towards society. "The family has vital and organic links with society, since it is its foundation and nourishes it continually through its role of service to life: it is from the family that citizens come to birth and it is within the family that they find the first school of the social virtues that are the animating principle of the existence and development of society itself. Thus, far from being closed in on itself, the family is by nature and vocation open to other families and to society, and undertakes its social role".166

Along these lines, the Special Assembly for Africa affirmed that the goal of evangelization is to build up the Church as the Family of God, an anticipation on earth, though imperfect, of the Kingdom. The Christian families of Africa will thus become true "domestic churches", contribut- ing to society's progress towards a more fraternal life. This is how African societies will be transformed through the Gospel!

. . . .
. . . .

Cooperation with other believers

109. The obligation to commit oneself to the development of peoples is not just an *individual* duty, and still less an *individualistic* one, as if it were possible to achieve this development through the isolated efforts of each person. It is a responsibility which obliges *each and every man and woman*, as well as *societies and nations*. In particular, it obliges the Catholic Church and the other Churches and Ecclesial Communities, with which Catholics are willing to cooperate in this field.213 In this sense, just as Catholics invite their Christian brothers and sisters to share in their initiatives, so, when they accept invitations offered to them, Catholics show that they are ready to cooperate in projects undertaken by other Christians. In the promotion of integral human development Catholics can also cooperate with the believers of other religions, as in fact they are already doing in various places.214

Good administration of public affairs

110. The Synod Fathers were unanimous in acknowledging that the greatest challenge for bringing about justice and peace in Africa consists in a good administration of public affairs in the two interrelated areas of politics and the economy. Certain problems have their roots outside the Continent and therefore are not entirely under the control of those in power or of national leaders. But the Synodal Assembly acknowledged that many of the Continent's problems are the result of a manner of governing often stained by corruption.

A serious reawakening of conscience linked to a firm determination of will is necessary, in order to put into effect solutions which can no longer be put off.

Building the nation

111. On the political front, the arduous process of building national unity encounters particular problems in the Continent where most of the States are relatively young political entities. To reconcile profound differences, overcome long- standing ethnic animosities and become integrated into international life demands a high degree of competence in the art of governing. That is why the Synod prayed fervently to the Lord that there would arise in Africa *holy politicians* – both men and women – and that there would be saintly Heads of State, who profoundly love their own people and wish to serve rather than be served.215

The rule of law

112. The foundation of good government must be established on the sound basis of laws which protect the rights and define the obligations of the citizens.216 I must note with great sadness that many African nations still labour under authoritarian and oppressive regimes which deny their subjects personal freedom and fundamental human rights, especially the freedom of association and of political expression, as well as the right to choose their governments by free and honest elections. Such political injustices provoke tensions which often degenerate into armed conflicts and internal wars, bringing with them serious consequences such as famine, epidemics and destruction, not to mention massacres and the scandal and tragedy of refugees. That is why the Synod rightly considered that an authentic democracy, which respects pluralism, "is one of the principal routes along which the Church travels together with the people ... The lay Christian, engaged in the democratic struggle according to the spirit of the Gospel, is the sign of a Church which participates in the promotion of the rule of law everywhere in Africa".217

Administering the common patrimony

113. The Synod also called on African governments to establish the appropriate policies needed to increase economic growth and investment in order to create new jobs.218 This involves the commitment to pursue sound economic policies, adopting the right priorities for the exploitation and distribution of often scarce national resources in such a way as to provide for people's basic

needs, and to ensure an honest and equitable sharing of benefits and burdens. In particular, governments have the binding duty to protect the *common patrimony* against all forms of waste and embezzlement by citizens lacking public spirit or by unscrupulous foreigners. It is also the duty of governments to undertake suitable initiatives to improve the conditions of international commerce.

Africa's economic problems are compounded by the dishonesty of corrupt government leaders who, in connivance with domestic or foreign private interests, divert national resources for their own profit and transfer public funds to private accounts in foreign banks. This is plain theft, whatever the legal camouflage may be. I earnestly hope that international bodies and people of integrity in Africa and elsewhere will be able to investigate suitable legal ways of having these embezzled funds returned. In the granting of loans, it is important to make sure of the responsibility and forthrightness of the beneficiaries.219

The international dimension

114. As an Assembly of Bishops of the universal Church presided over by the Successor of Peter, the Synod furnished a providential occasion to evaluate positively the place and role of Africa in the universal Church and the world community. Since we live in a world that is increasingly interdependent, the destinies and problems of the different regions are linked together. As God's Family on earth, the Church should be the living sign and efficacious instrument of universal solidarity for building a world-wide community of justice and peace. A better world will come about only if it is built on the solid foundation of sound ethical and spiritual principles.

In the present world order, the African nations are among the most disadvantaged. Rich countries must become clearly aware of their duty to support the efforts of the countries struggling to rise from their poverty and misery. In fact, it is in the interest of the rich countries to choose the path of solidarity, for only in this way can lasting peace and harmony for humanity be ensured. Moreover, the Church in the developed countries cannot ignore the added responsibility arising from the Christian commitment to justice and charity. Because all men and women bear God's image and are called to belong to the same family redeemed by Christ's Blood, each individual should be guaranteed just access to the world's resources which God has put at the everyone's disposal.220

It is not hard to see the many practical implications of this. In the first place it involves working for improved socio-political relations among nations, ensuring greater justice and dignity for those countries which, after gaining independence, have been members of the international community for less time. A compassionate ear must also be lent to the anguished cries of the poor nations asking for help in areas of particular importance: malnutrition, the widespread deterioration in the standard of living, the insufficiency of means for educating the young, the lack of elementary health and social services with the resulting persistence of endemic diseases, the spread of the terrible scourge of AIDS, the heavy and often unbearable burden of international debt, the horror of fratricidal wars fomented by unscrupulous arms trafficking, the shameful and pitiable spectacle of refugees and displaced persons. These are some of the areas where prompt interventions are necessary and expedient, even if in the overall situation they seem to be inadequate.

I. SOME WORRISOME PROBLEMS

Restoring hope to youth

115. The economic situation of poverty has a particularly negative impact on the young. They embark on adult life with very little enthusiasm for a present riddled with frustrations and they look with still less hope to a future which to them seems sad and sombre. That is why they tend to flee the neglected rural areas and gather in cities which in fact do not have much more to offer them. Many of them go to foreign countries where, as if in exile, they live a precarious existence as economic refugees. With the Synod Fathers I feel the duty to plead their cause: it is urgently necessary to find a solution for their impatience to take part in the life of the nation and of the Church.221
But at the same time I also wish to appeal to the youth: Dear young people, the Synod asks you to take in hand the development of your countries, to love the culture of your people, and to work for its renewal with fidelity to your cultural heritage, through a sharpening of your scientific and technical expertise, and above all through the witness of your Christian faith.222

The scourge of AIDS

116. Against the background of widespread poverty and inadequate medical services the Synod considered the tragic scourge of AIDS which is sowing suffering and death in many parts of Africa. It noted the role played in the spread of this disease by irresponsible sexual behaviour and drafted this strong recommendation: "The companionship, joy, happiness and peace which Christian marriage and fidelity provide, and the safeguard which chastity gives, must be continuously presented to the faithful, particularly the young".223
The battle against AIDS ought to be everyone's battle. Echoing the voice of the Synod Fathers, I too ask pastoral workers to bring to their brothers and sisters affected by AIDS all possible material, moral and spiritual comfort. I urgently ask the world's scientists and political leaders, moved by the love and respect due to every human person, to use every means available in order to put an end to this scourge.

"Beat your swords into ploughshares" (Is 2:4): no more wars!

117. The Synod incisively described the tragedy of wars which are tearing Africa apart: "For some decades now Africa has been the theatre of fratricidal wars which are decimating peoples and destroying their natural and cultural resources".224 This very sad situation, in addition to causes external to Africa, also has internal causes such as "tribalism, nepotism, racism, religious intolerance and the thirst for power taken to the extreme by totalitarian regimes which trample with impunity the rights and dignity of the person. Peoples crushed and reduced to silence suffer as innocent and resigned victims all these situations of injustice".225
I cannot fail to join my voice to that of the members of the Synodal Assembly in order to deplore the situations of unspeakable suffering caused by so many conflicts now taking place or about to break out, and to ask all those who can do so to make every effort to put an end to such tragedies.
Together with the Synod Fathers, I likewise urge a serious commitment to foster on the Continent conditions of greater social justice and good government, in order thereby to prepare the ground for peace. "If you want peace, work for justice".226 It is much better – and also easier – to prevent wars than to try to stop them after they have broken out. It is time that peoples beat their swords into ploughshares, and their spears into pruning hooks (cf. *Is* 2:4).

118. The Church in Africa – especially through some of its leaders – has been in the front line of the search for negotiated solutions to the armed conflicts in many parts of the Continent. This mission of pacification must continue, encouraged by the Lord's promise in the Beatitudes: "Blessed are the peacemakers, they shall be called sons of God" (*Mt* 5:9).
Those who foment wars in Africa by the arms trade are accomplices in abominable crimes against humanity. I make my own the Synod's recommendations on this subject. Having said that "the sale of arms is a scandal since it sows the seed of death", the Synod appealed to all countries that sell arms to Africa to stop doing so, and it asked African governments "to move away from huge military expenditures and put the emphasis on the education, health and well-being of their people".227
Africa must continue to seek peaceful and effective means so that military regimes will transfer authority to civilians. But it is also true that the military are called to play a distinctive role in the nation. Thus, while the Synod praised the "brothers in the military for the service that they assume in the name of our countries",228 it immediately warned them forcefully that "they will have to answer before God for every act of violence against the lives of innocent people".229

Refugees and displaced persons

119. One of the most bitter fruits of wars and economic hardships is the sad phenomenon of refugees and displaced persons, a phenomenon which, as the Synod mentioned, has reached tragic dimensions. The ideal solution is the re-establishment of a just peace, reconciliation and economic development. It is therefore urgent that national, regional and international organizations should find equitable and long-lasting solutions to the problems of refugees and displaced persons.230 In the meantime, since the Continent continues to suffer from the massive displacement of refugees, I make a pressing appeal that these people be given material help and offered pastoral support wherever they may be, whether in Africa or on other Continents.

The burden of the international debt

120. The question of the indebtedness of poor nations towards rich ones is a matter of great concern for the Church, as expressed in many official documents and interventions of the Holy See.231
Taking up the words of the Synod Fathers, I particularly feel it is my duty to urge "the Heads of State and their governments in Africa not to crush their peoples with internal and external debts".232 I also make a pressing appeal to "the International Monetary Fund and the World Bank and all foreign creditors to alleviate the crushing debts of the African nations".233 Finally, I earnestly ask "the Episcopal Conferences of the industrialized countries to present this issue consistently to their governments and to the organizations concerned".234 The situation of many African countries is so serious as to leave no room for attitudes of indifference and complacency.

Dignity of the African woman

121. One of the characteristic signs of our times is the growing awareness of women's dignity and of their specific role in the Church and in society at large. "So God created man in his own image, in the image of God he created him; male and female he created them" (*Gen* 1:27).
I have repeatedly affirmed the fundamental equality and enriching complementarity that exist between man and woman.235 The Synod applied these principles to the condition of women in Africa. Their rights and duties in building up the family and in taking full part in the development of the Church and society were strongly affirmed. With specific regard to the Church, women should be properly trained so that they can participate at appropriate levels in her apostolic activity.

The Church deplores and condemns, to the extent that they are still found in some African societies, all "the customs and practices which deprive women of their rights and the respect due to them".236 It is recommended that Episcopal Conferences establish special commissions to study further women's problems in cooperation with interested government agencies, wherever this is possible.237

II. COMMUNICATING THE GOOD NEWS

Following Christ, the Communicator "par excellence"

122. The Synod had much to say about social communications in the context of the evangelization of Africa, carefully taking into account present circumstances. The theological point of departure is Christ, the Communicator *par excellence* who shares with those who believe in him the truth, the life and the love which he shares with his Heavenly Father and the Holy Spirit. That is why "the Church is aware of her duty of fostering social communications *ad intra* and *ad extra*. The Church should promote communication from within through a better diffusion of information among her members".238 This will put her in a more advantageous position to communicate to the world the Good News of the love of God revealed in Jesus Christ.

Traditional forms of communication

123. The traditional forms of social communication must never be underestimated. In many places in Africa they are still very useful and effective. Moreover, they are "less costly and more accessible".239 These forms include songs and music, mimes and the theatre, proverbs and fables. As vehicles of the wisdom and soul of the people, they are a precious source of material and of inspiration for the modern media.

Evangelization of the world of the media

124. The modern mass media are not only instruments of communication, but also a world to be evangelized. In terms of the message they transmit, it is necessary to ensure that they propagate the good, the true and the beautiful. Echoing the preoccupation of the Synod Fathers I express my deep concern about the moral content of very many programmes with which the media flood the African Continent. In particular I warn against the pornography and violence which are inundating poor countries. In addition, the Synod rightly deplored "the very negative portrayal of the African in the media and called for its immediate cessation".240

Every Christian should be concerned that the communications media are a vehicle of evangelization. But Christians who are professionals in this sector have a special part to play. It is their duty to ensure that Christian principles influence the practice of the profession, including the technical and administrative sector. To enable them to exercise this role properly, they need to be provided with a wholesome human, religious and spiritual training.

Using the means of social communication

125. Today the Church has at her disposal a variety of means of social communication, traditional as well as modern. It is her duty to make the best possible use of them in order to spread the message of salvation. In the Church in Africa many obstacles impede easy access to these means, not the least of which is their high cost. Moreover, in many places government regulations impose undue control on them. Every possible effort should be made to remove these obstacles. The media, whether private or public, should serve all people without exception. Therefore I invite the particular Churches of Africa to do everything in their power to meet this objective.241

Cooperation and coordination in the mass media

126. The media, especially in their most modern forms, have a wide-ranging impact. Consequently, closer cooperation is needed in this area, in order to ensure more effective coordination at all levels: diocesan, national, continental and worldwide. In Africa, the Church has a great need for solidarity with sister Churches in the richer and technologically more advanced countries. Programmes of continental cooperation which already exist in Africa, such as the Pan African Episcopal Committee for Social Communications, should be encouraged and revitalized. As the Synod suggested, it is necessary to establish closer cooperation in other areas, such as professional training, structures of radio and television production, and stations that transmit to the whole Continent.242

. . . .
. . . .

Putting solidarity into practice

138. In bearing witness to Christ "to the ends of the earth", the Church in Africa will no doubt be assisted by the conviction of the "*positive* and *moral value* of the growing awareness of *interdependence* among individuals and

nations. The fact that men and women in various parts of the world feel personally affected by the injustices and violations of human rights committed in distant countries, countries which perhaps they will never visit, is a further sign of a reality transformed into *awareness*, thus acquiring a *moral* connotation".265 It is my desire that Christians in Africa will become ever more aware of this interdependence among individuals and nations, and will be ready to respond to it by practising the virtue of *solidarity*. The fruit of solidarity is peace, an inestimable good for peoples and nations in every part of the world. For it is precisely by means of fostering and strengthening solidarity that the Church can make a specific and decisive contribution to a true culture of peace.

139. By entering into contact with all the peoples of the world through her dialogue with the various cultures, the Church brings them closer to one another, enabling each people to assume, in faith, the authentic values of others. Ready to cooperate with all people of good will and with the international community, the Church in Africa does not seek advantages for itself. The solidarity which it expresses "seeks to go beyond itself, to take on the *specifically Christian* dimensions of total gratuity, forgiveness and reconciliation".266 The Church seeks to contribute to humanity's conversion, leading it to acceptance of God's salvific plan through her witness to the Gospel, accompanied by charitable work on behalf of the poor and the neediest. In so doing she never loses sight of the primacy of the transcendent and of those spiritual realities which are the first fruits of man's eternal salvation.

In their discussion on the Church's solidarity with peoples and nations, the Synod Fathers were at all times fully aware that "earthly progress must be carefully distinguished from the growth of Christ's Kingdom. Nevertheless, to the extent that the former can contribute to the better ordering of human society, it is of vital concern to the Kingdom of God".267 Precisely for this reason the Church in Africa is convinced – as the work of the Special Assembly clearly demonstrated – that waiting for Christ's final return "can never be an excuse for lack of concern for people in their concrete personal situations and in their social, national and international life",268 since these earthly conditions have a bearing upon humanity's pilgrimage towards eternity.

. . . .
. . . .

SYNOD OF BISHOPS
SPECIAL ASSEMBLY FOR AMERICA
ENCOUNTER WITH THE LIVING JESUS CHRIST:
THE WAY TO
CONVERSION, COMMUNION AND SOLIDARITY
IN AMERICA
INSTRUMENTUM LABORIS *

The Topic of the Special Assembly

1. While all the People of God prepare to celebrate with joy the beginning of the Third Millennium marking 2000 years since the Birth of the Lord Jesus Christ, the Pastors of the Church in the American hemisphere, responding to the call of the Holy Father, are to gather for the first time in the Special Assembly of the Synod of Bishops for America to treat the topic: **Encounter with the Living Jesus Christ: the Way to Conversion, Communion and Solidarity in America.**(1) This topic provides the framework for coming to a knowledge of the present state of the Church in all America and how the Church can prepare herself better to face the new challenges of evangelization in the future, while bearing in mind the aims proposed by the Supreme Pontiff for this synodal assembly.(2)

– to foster a **new evangelization on the whole continent as an expression of episcopal** communion;
– **to increase** solidarity among the various particular Churches in different fields of **pastoral activity**; and
– to shed light on the problems of **justice and international economic relations** among the nations of America, considering the enormous imbalances between the North, Central and South of the American continent.

2. The structural parts of the topic for the Special Assembly are inter- related. The three elements – conversion, communion and solidarity – are directed to, and intrinsically connected with, the main topic of the encounter with Jesus

Christ from which they flow and on which they are based. As the Word of God clearly demonstrates, these three basic concepts result from the personal encounter with the Son of God made man. This Jesus invites all men and women of all time to a change of life (*metanoia* – cf. *Mk* 1:15), which is the first step for entering into communion (*koinonia*) with the Lord himself and his disciples (cf. *Acts* 2:42). The communion of those who believe in Christ is directed, following in the footsteps of the Servant of God, towards living with all in a spirit of solidarity and service (*diaconia*), above all with the least of humankind (cf. *Mt* 25:40).

Since the encounter with Jesus Christ is the origin of conversion, communion and solidarity, each one of the three respective parts of the present text will place particular emphasis on the encounter with Jesus and the effect of this encounter on the life of individuals and the community of believers. Further-more, the three sections of this document are also inter- related:

• only through conversion to the Gospel of Jesus Christ is there a possibility for true communion and genuine solidarity;
• communion with Christ and his Church is at the same time the basis for an ongoing personal conversion and the foundation for achieving solidarity;
• solidarity, insofar as it is an expression of the essential values of the Kingdom of God, manifests the goal and point of convergence to which both conver-sion and communion are directed.

. . . .
. . . .

The Religious Identity of America

3. At first glance, it might seem artificial to use the simple term "America" to designate the extensive territories of the hemisphere (North, Central and South America and the Caribbean) as a single geographic entity, without at the same time acknowledging the great variety of historical, ethnic, cultural and economic differences which characterize the various nations making up that immense land mass. However, from a religious point of view, it may be said that the American hemisphere has a common **Christian identity**, based on the procla-mation of the Gospel in the New World after the discovery of the continent more than 500 years ago. At that time, the planting of a cross in American soil by Christopher Columbus upon his landing on the Island of El Salvador,(3) was a prophetic sign foreshadowing how subsequent centuries, with their accomplishments and failings, would be intrinsically united to the mystery of redemption in the Lord Jesus Christ.(4)

From the time of that discovery, this new land witnessed the arrival of colonists and immigrants coming from various European nations and a considerable number of Africans who were victims of the slave trade. This influx was common historical fact for all parts of the continent, even though different characteristics accompanied this series of events in each region. This movement of people, coming in contact with indigenous American peoples, produced in many cases new cultural expressions, often reflecting the characteristic marks of each civilization. In the last century, waves of immigrants came from Europe, and in more recent times from Asia and Oceania, moved by the ideal and hope of a better life. In many areas of the continent the greater part of the immigrants were Catholic, whereas in other areas Catholics were in the minority, with the majority consisting of members of other Christian confessions coming from the Protestant reform of the 16th Century.

4. As a result of these factors, the various nations of America today are a rich multi-ethnic and multi-cultural family, in which the following fundamental elements – among others – may be distinguished:

- **common Christian roots**, with which the majority of people with their various traditions and cultural expressions can identify despite human and temporal diversity. This common heritage is understood with different shades of meaning. In Latin America, the common Christian root, in addition to being Christian, is Catholic, while the rest of the continent is united in a predominantly Christian identity, without excluding, in minor proportions, the feature of Catholicism;
- a history rich in ancient civilizations, yet marked by the proclamation of the Gospel for only 500 years, so that, from this point of view, it may be said that the common Christian roots have a relatively young history. Consequently, the Church in this hemisphere is a **young Church**, marked by a great vitality and a force of renewal, which is a source of hope and joy;
- these common Christian roots are incarnated in a **plurality of cultural expressions** which include a wide range of realities, those having social, political and economic aspects as well as highly ethnic ones. This heterogeneity is a richness providing a fertile field for undertaking the work of communion and solidarity, a work which can profit from the Church's new evangelization.

Moreover, these aspects of the American identity imply a great responsibility for the Church, calling on her to be the light of the world and the salt of the earth (cf. *Matt* 5:14) as she brings her message and witness to the work of building a more just society, thus preparing for the coming of the Kingdom of Heaven.

5. The *Instrumentum laboris*, in summarizing the responses to the questions proposed in the *Lineamenta*, presents the first-fruits of the process of preparation and in this way serves as the basis for synodal discussion in the Special Assembly of the Synod of Bishops for America. Therefore, the present document presents for consideration and reflection the principal common points

and contrasting elements in the responses, the aspects which need to be examined further and the observations related to the synodal topic, in view of the dialogue to be undertaken by the Synod Fathers, called together by the Holy Father.

. . . .
. . . .

CHAPTER II: THE ANNOUNCEMENT OF JESUS CHRIST IN THE CULTURAL CONTEXT OF AMERICA

The Gospel and Culture

12. In summarizing responses related to the evangelization of culture, certain general tendencies stand out in the present-day societies of the American hemisphere. These same tendencies can also be detected in cultural trends at the international level. Among them are:

- a **pluralism** presenting itself in all America under many forms: an affirmation of identity based on various ethnic, linguistic and national groups; a diversity of mentalities as a manifestation of freedom of expression; the co-existence in the same area of many different cultural and religious traditions; an openness through the world of communications to a wealth of information for enlarging the horizons of human knowledge, etc.;
- a **secularism** proposing a vision of life which lacks transcendent values, while at the same time indirectly stimulating the person of today to search for the ultimate purpose of life;
- a **subjectivism and moral relativism**, producing in the person of today a great crisis and confusion of conscience, which consequently leads to a devaluation of the objective moral order and an over- emphasis on personal subjectivity. These characteristics lead to the loss of a sense of sin;
- a **globalization** of culture having positive aspects which offer the possibility of enrichment through inter-communication, while at the same time leading cultures towards an homogenization of contents and values, with the consequent loss of individual identity. This effect may be especially worrying when the Christian, and particularly Catholic, profile of local cultures is at stake;
- an awareness of the importance of certain **values**, some of which are connected with the dignity of the human person, such as freedom, life and justice; others relate to the innate desire of each human being towards spiritual and transcendent realities; and
- an **urbanization** raising new challenges for evangelization, not only because it creates new problems coming from urban culture (poverty and indigence of marginalized groups, uprooting, anonymity, loneliness, immorality and violence, etc.) but also because the present urban structure requires new pastoral methods, including the use of modern means and techniques of communication.

It could be said that the above characteristics are common to the whole continent, even if they are present in various ways in different regional and local settings. For example, the phenomenon of urbanization raises the problem of social marginalization, both in the poor sectors of the "favelas" in Latin America as well as the disadvantaged areas of the big cities of North America. Similarly, the awareness of certain values – such as justice, freedom and life – is manifested in various cultural expressions according to the degree of economic development and the political situation in the respective society, though in fact the basic ideals are the same.

The Gospel and Indigenous and Afro-American Cultures

13. In the responses to the *Lineamenta* on the subject of evangelization, the interest in the relationship between the Gospel and culture is extended to include indigenous and Afro-American cultures, which, to varying degrees, are a part of all the countries in the American hemisphere. These cultures are a legacy of the civilizations which existed on the continent before the arrival of the first evangelizers, or are the fruit of an immigration immediately following their arrival. In either case, it could be said that, from the outset, both these cultures welcomed the message of the Good News with a simplicity of heart. Nevertheless, the task of evangelization of these cultures was not completed with the first announcement of the *kerygma*. Today still, as clearly seen from the replies to the questions of the preparatory document for the synodal assembly, a greater presence of the Church is required in the cultures of these peoples so as to transform inwardly their authentic cultural values, through integrating the various cultures into Christianity and enlightening them by the faith.

14. Among the indigenous and Afro-American groups, there is a growing awareness of the right to conserve one's cultural identity. The Church in all America, in communion with the Magisterium of the Holy Father, is conscious of the importance of such rights and makes every effort to bring to these people the Gospel message, while at the same time concerning herself with promoting their legitimate claims.(25) According to the answers to the *Lineamenta* questions, among the values of these cultures compatible with the Christian faith are the following: a great love for one's own land, a respect for ancestors and community traditions, the religious sense of life and death as expressed in ritual celebrations enlivened with dancing, music and singing as well as the belief in a life beyond this one. At the same time, these answers underscore aspects which need to be purified, since all cultures are a product of mankind and thus marked by sin. Some of the habits and attitudes needing purification are the following: a high rate of alcoholism (frequently connected with the holding of festivities), fetishism, superstition, casting of spells, religious syncretism, fatalism,

black magic, witch doctoring and other mythical ideas which take the form of practices incompatible with the Christian faith.

The Gospel and the Cultures of Immigrant Peoples

15. No less important than the evangelization of indigenous and Afro- American cultures is the evangelization of the cultures of immigrants, which constitutes a reality in almost all societies in the American hemisphere since the end of the last century. The answers to the *Lineamenta* indicate the presence of two main immigration currents: one coming basically from Europe and to a lesser extent from Asia; and the other, a movement within the American hemisphere itself. The first immigrant movement occurred with greater intensity in some countries more than others, but generally speaking it may be said that the immigrants brought with them authentic human values, such as: the sense of family and work, a love of their country of origin, a solidarity with those poorer than themselves, the value of a promise given, the sense of justice, and also certain religious values, whether Catholic (mainly from the Latin Church, though also from Oriental Churches) or from other Christian religions (various Protestant communities and also Orthodox Churches) and including non-Christian religions (Judaism and to a lesser extent Islam). While in certain countries like Canada and above all the United States the immigration flow consisted of many currents mainly coming from various European and to a lesser extent Asian countries and cultures, in the rest of the continent this same phenomenon reflects the presence of predominantly Spanish and Italian immigrants.

16. The second current includes massive immigration from the South, Central and Caribbean parts of the continent to the North. Many answers to the *Lineamenta* agree that more collaboration is needed between the *a quo* and *ad quem* Churches in order to provide adequate pastoral care of immigrants in which, for example, immigrant persons might receive assistance from priests coming from their own region. In the same way, suggestions are made to promote the forms of popular piety which the immigrants bring with them, such as: family festivities, religious holidays and patron saints' days, traditional celebrations associated with Christmas and Holy Week, as well as processions and devotions associated with special titles for Christ, the Blessed Virgin and the saints. In the United States of America the significantly increasing presence of Latin American immigrants represents in many instances an enriching element for this country's culture. Many immigrants, the majority of which were Catholic, brought with them authentic values: the sense of family, popular piety, folklore and local traditions. The bishops of this country recognize the value of this style of life and the customs which manifest the Catholic faith, while at the same time point out the need continually to evangelize these

popular expressions of Latin American piety to purify them and integrate them appropriately in accomplishing a major enrichment of the local Christian culture.

The Gospel and Popular Piety

17. Another aspect emerging from the answers to the *Lineamenta* on the subject of the evangelization of culture is popular piety. In the people of Latin America and Latin American groups living in North America, this expression of culture is basically the expression of the Catholic faith, while in the rest of the continent it can be said that such religious sentiment is generally Christian. In any case, it is noted that recently the simple, but no less profound, religious character of these people has received special attention in the pastoral initiatives of local Churches throughout all America.

Some signs which indicate the importance of popular religious culture are: the increasing participation of people in pilgrimages to shrines (especially Marian shrines), the tradition in families of baptizing children, the giving of alms for the souls in Purgatory and celebrating Masses for the deceased, patronal feasts with their characteristic processions and the celebration of Holy Mass (generally attended by large numbers of people), devotion to the saints, not only those of the universal Church but also those of the American continent, etc..(26) These and many other expressions of popular piety offer excellent opportunities for the faithful to encounter the living Jesus Christ. In fact, the ecclesial community, in coming together for the celebration of the Word and Sacrament in memory of the saints, remembers in a particular way those who faithfully imitated in their lives the Savior of the world, and that same community enters into communion with those who are part of the heavenly Church. It is for this reason that popular piety – purified and duly catechized – may come to be a decisive element in the new evangelization. This is a point on which most of the answers to the *Lineamenta* agree.

. . . .
. . . .

Positive Aspects of Contemporary Society and the Gospel

27. Responding to the invitation of the Second Vatican Council to know and understand the world with its hopes and aspirations,(44) the questions of the *Lineamenta* propose looking at temporal realities so as to discover in them some positive signs predisposing the person of today to encounter Jesus Christ. The answers contain the following elements:

- a growing awareness of the **dignity of the human person** and his**inalienable rights** as well as a **sense of justice**, finding expression, among others, in the refusal of all social discrimination as a consequence of respect for the person and in a search for an ever greater forthrightness in the administration of justice;
- a **respect for nature** expressed in an attentive consideration of**ecological problems**. This is a positive aspect in that it properly predisposes persons to become aware of their being part of creation, thus eliciting a respect for the Creator's work;
- a pronounced interest in **spiritual values** and a concern for**transcendent realities**. While, at times, this interest takes the form of syncretic and pseudo-religious practices, it continues to serve as the basis for the Church's dialogue with people today, who are thirsting for the Word of Life; and
- a strong **feeling of solidarity and generosity**, expressed in a growing sensitivity to the needs of others. This positive sign, reflected in many humanitarian organizations, characterizes not only various national situations but also international relations.

Aspects of Today's Society Requiring Conversion

28. Certain aspects also exist in the societies of the American continent requiring conversion and a change in attitudes. The Church in all America attentive to the social situation has expressed in numerous documents of the Pastors her continuing desire to offer enlightenment to temporal matters through the teachings of the Gospel. From the answers to the *Lineamenta* the following points emerge as social aspects necessitating conversion:

- in the **family context**, both a concept of freedom and an ideal of human love without obligations are often detected. Separation and divorce have become more and more frequent with the consequent break-up of families. Contraceptive practice and abortion are leading to the loss of a sense of the value of life and to the spread of a "culture of death." Family violence is very real and on the increase. A feminine and masculine identity is being lost, and, at the same time, an inadequate formation in sexuality is being indiscriminately promoted in the field of education. Childhood, women, youth and the elderly are areas requiring greater attention;
- in the **economic sphere**, many societies in the American hemisphere are marked by the lack of a greater distributive justice. Unemployment is on the rise, wages are low, and the distance between rich and poor continues to grow. In the entire American continent, there are indications of the difference mentioned by Pope John Paul II in his Encyclical Letter *Redemptoris missio*: "the North has constructed (a development model) which is now spreading to the South, where a sense of religion as well as human values are in danger of being overwhelmed by a wave of consumerism."(45) Various

answers point to the urgent need to find a solution to the problem of the foreign debt in the context of the celebration of the Great Jubilee of the Year 2000, as proposed by the Holy Father in his Apostolic Letter *Tertio millenio adveniente*.(46)

- on the **social level**, the process of urbanization continues to accelerate in connection with the appearance of an industrial society and demographic growth. The development of big cities, often uncontrolled and lacking order, brings with it serious social problems such as poverty, uprooting of persons and whole families, drug trafficking and addiction, child and youth prostitution, alcoholism, de- personalization, etc.
- on the **political level**, a concept of politics is becoming prominent which does not take into account the common good. It is not unusual for upper class people to live in remote contact with the needs of other people and to be guided by partisan interests. Frequently, a spirit of **demagogy** is seen with the increased **corruption** of the structures of power. This situation leads to a lack of confidence regarding political institutions, above all affecting the administration of justice, which is not always forthright, equal and effective.
- on the **cultural level**, an atheistic lay culture is sometimes manifested in scholarly and cultural circles by the presence of only a few committed Christian lay men and women in universities and among intellectuals, professionals and artists. There is a need for a greater presence of the Christian laity in the means of social communication. In some cases, a scarce application of ethical principles leads certain agents of social communications to lack objectivity in presenting the truth. Shortcomings in the educational field are evidenced, above all in illiteracy and in the reduction of education to mere instruction, where there is little space for transcendent values.

. . . .
. . . .

The Social Doctrine of the Church

57. The Christian reality is complex because the ethic of justice and the requirement of fraternal solidarity must both be met. The Christian faith calls for a Christian social ethic which the Church's social doctrine proposes in a systematic way as directives for Christ's disciples in their personal, family, cultural and social life. The responses to the questions in the *Lineamenta* speak of a general conviction on the part of bishops in the particular Churches in all America that the social doctrine of the Church is a useful and necessary instrument to carry forward a pastoral program of Christian solidarity. The social doctrine formulates the basic principles for viewing real situations and the criteria of moral judgement for evaluating the social conflict between the human reality and the Christian ideal as well as the rules capable of guiding the concrete

actions of individuals and communities for the promotion of the common good and the overcoming of moral disorder and social injustice.(77) Moreover, the fundamental principles of the Church's social doctrine, founded on the dignity of the person, are the principles of solidarity and subsidiarity. According to the first principle, each individual is called upon to contribute to the common good of society; according to the second, the State cannot substitute for the free initiatives and responsibility either of individuals or intermediary social groups on the level where each is able to act.(78)

58. With regard to the diffusion of the Church's social doctrine, many answers to the *Lineamenta* report various initiatives being undertaken by local Churches and episcopal conferences, such as: the organization of courses, workshops, conferences and study weeks; articles and essays in local newspapers, magazines and Church publications; courses in seminaries, universities and Catholic schools; etc.. Furthermore, numerous ecclesial institutions are turning towards the Church's social doctrine though study for a fuller understanding and in applying its principles. Many episcopal conferences have commissions designated to promote socio-pastoral activity. Their involvement in the social problems of their given country is usually very positive, since it contributes to bringing the principles of the Church's social doctrine into the dialogue between trade unions and business men as well as government and workers. The mediation task of the Church in these cases is generally well accepted by both parties.
Nevertheless, in addition to the extensive work being done in this area, the responses acknowledge that much still needs to be done in the Church in the American hemisphere to foster knowledge and application of the Church's social doctrine. The answers to the *Lineamenta* indicate that this situation results from the little account given in some cases to the social implications of the faith, which, in turn, is reflected in an incomplete formation in both laity and clergy. The subject of the essential unity between the faith and works (cf. *James* 2:14), between worship and Christian living (cf. *Mt* 5:23-24), between the spiritual life and putting into practice the Gospel principle of love of neighbor still needs to be more deeply rooted in the consciences of many members of the People of God.

. . . .
. . . .

CHAPTER III: AREAS OF SOLIDARITY IN ALL AMERICA

The Challenge of the Gospel

59. The intended receiver of the plan of communion and salvation in Christ is the person, "the primary and fundamental way for the Church, the way traced out by Christ himself, the way that leads invariably through the mystery of the incarnation and redemption."(79) The Gospel cannot be proclaimed as if it

were separated from the problems of the human condition, both in its spiritual and temporal aspects.(80) The community of Jesus' disciples continues to be the Church of the Good Samaritan, who seeks to do whatever is necessary for the afflicted (cf. *Lk* 10:25-37). Human promotion is intimately united to evangelization, since the person to whom the Gospel is addressed is not an abstract concept but a subject affected by concrete social and economic problems.(81)

60. Answers coming from the Latin American countries point to various distressing situations which afflict many peoples in this geographic and cultural region, such as: the ever widening gap between the rich and the poor; the complex situation created by the international debt,(82) the absence of employment and an insufficient salary, a situation unable to be overcome except through a rousing of conscience which gives rise to a general movement of solidarity;(83) economic recession and inflation; financial speculation and draining of capital; sale of arms and tensions coming from war; the problem of drug trafficking; corruption of public administration and a disinterest in the common good,(84) conditions of poverty in which many families live (hunger, sickness and a lack of social aid and health assistance, a want of a decent home and education). All this is seen not only as a serious ethical disorder which cries out for a change in mentality, but also an invitation to the whole Church to have as her goal in her evangelizing mission the human person in this concrete, integral reality.

61. In other countries in the American hemisphere, principally in Canada and the United States of America, social situations exist which are in a certain way similar to those previously described. These are also a source of concern for the Church, principally in two cultural areas: immigrants and those living in isolated areas of big cities where complex social problems exist, such as: unemployment, impoverished conditions of life (hunger, lack of decent living conditions and hygiene), drug addiction and violence, the inadequacy of many immigrants to insert themselves in society, juvenile delinquency, etc.. In these cases, Christian communities live these problems in response to the Gospel's duty of service to one's neighbor and attempt to give an appropriate response in view of material assistance, which is, at one and the same time, the message of charity and the Gospel's witness of charity. In these social activities, there is evidence of a good spirit of collaboration between the Catholic Church and other Christian confessions as well as with other religions. The same cannot be said of the sects and similar religious movements.

Solidarity and Love for the Poor

62. The words of Pope John XXIII have a perennial force, especially in the American hemisphere, in his declaring that the Church, embracing everyone, wishes above all to be the Church of the poor.(85) The discussion on the

Church and the poor during the Second Vatican Council was particularly poignant. The Church sees in the poor – as if in a moral mirror – the image of her divine Founder, poor and humble, and she seeks to alleviate the poor's suffering as a service to Christ.(86) The call to action in response to poverty continues with insistence. Paul VI, speaking to the farmers in Colombia, spoke of the poor as a "sacrament of Christ;"(87) and in the Apostolic Exhortation *Evangelii nuntiandi* confirmed the link between the Gospel of Christ and the question of the liberation from misery as a demand of justice and Christian charity.(88)

63. The Pastors of the particular Churches in all America, supported by the Holy Father's Magisterium, encourage all members of the Church to fulfill better their Christian duties in order to overcome the distressing situation of misery resulting from sinful structures, which lead to the rich becoming richer and the poor becoming poorer. John Paul II, while in apostolic visitation to the American hemisphere, recommended a social commitment to justice and called for a just distribution of goods.(89) The particular Churches in all America, following the invitation of the Successor of Peter, developed intensive pastoral activity on Christian solidarity towards infants and women, farmers and workers, the sick and imprisoned, emigrants and immigrants, the poor and the abandoned. On several occasions, the bishops in Latin America have invited the whole People of God to occupy themselves in a particular way with the problem of poverty. They proclaimed that authentic evangelization is manifested in a love for the needy, which calls for a commitment of service to people who are suffering, and a taking on of a clear preferential option and solidarity towards the poor.(90)

Ecclesial Communities and Solidarity

64. The II General Conference of the Latin American Bishops, in Medellin, defined basic Church communities (*comunidad ecclesial de base*) as the primary cells in the Church structure, which, on their proper level, are responsible for the richness of the faith and its expansion as well as for the promotion of the person and development.(91) The concept of basic Church communities returned as a point of discussion at the III General Conference of the Latin American Bishops, which noted three distinctive characteristics: the communal dimension through which members enter into an intimate inter-personal relationship of faith; the ecclesial dimension of the community, according to which the community, while celebrating the sacraments, seeks to live the implications of the new commandment in fraternal solidarity and commitment of life; the structural dimension through which the community formed by a few members in a permanent way of living is understood to be the vibrant and fundamental

cell of a larger community.(92) To these fundamental elements, Pope Paul VI, explaining the ecclesial dimension implicit in these communities, added two essential characteristics: communion with the Church (local and universal) and communion with the Pastors and the Magisterium of the Church.(93)

In many Churches in Latin America, these small Christian communities have been considered a decisive pastoral option for the renewal of Church life, given the enormous dimensions and demands of the diocesan and parochial structure. Nevertheless, the same magisterial documents of the Latin American bishops recognize that in some places these basic communities have been manipulated by political interests and isolated from communion with the bishops, losing in this way the ecclesial dimension.(94) However, the responses to the *Lineamenta* praise basic Church communities as groups where many Christians can experience ecclesial communion and fraternal solidarity.

The Foreign Debt and Balance in the Global Economy

65. The Church in all America seeks in announcing the Gospel to provide guidance to the men and women of the continent in their work of constructing fraternal solidarity, where justice and peace are the determining principles. The bonds of solidarity acquire particular importance in reference to the relation between the North and South, above all concerning the question of the foreign debt. The responses to the *Lineamenta* suggest that the way to address this complex problem in the context of the globalization of the international economy can only be found in fundamental ethical principles with which each party assumes in solidarity their responsibilities in the construction of the future.(95)

Even though the international debt is not the sole cause of poverty in many developing countries, it cannot be denied that it has contributed to creating conditions of extreme privation which constitute today an urgent challenge appealing to the conscience of the People of God. Many characteristics are listed in the responses to the preparatory document: famine and misery; lack of the basic necessities for living, health and nourishment; unemployment; absence of proper housing and education, etc.. This situation of suffering for so many poor families in all America is witnessed among farming populations and workers in cities, among Afro- Americans and American Indians. A Christianity committed to justice stands before a wide field of action. Many of the answers to the *Lineamenta* re- affirm the call of Pope John Paul II to find a solution to the problem of the international debt "proposing the Jubilee as an appropriate time to give thought, among other things, to reducing substantially, if not cancelling outright the international debt."(96)' Moreover, the suggestion is made to discuss the subject in the wider context of the globalization of the international economy in the prospects of a proper re-establishment of the order of social justice.

Solidarity and the Promotion of the Culture of Life

66. The human person called to the fullness of life consisting in the participation of divine life is the one to whom the Church announces the salvation accomplished in Christ through his Pascal Mystery. In recent times, the pontifical Magisterium has shown its special concern for the family and the protection of human life in all its stages.(97) The Church in the American hemisphere has also manifested through her many pastoral initiatives her adhesion to the concern of the Holy Father concerning the promotion of human life. In his Encyclical Letter *Evangelium Vitae*, Pope John Paul II recalled the responsibility which every human being has before God for one's life and the life of one's neighbor.(98) Among the principle concerns indicated in the *Lineamenta* for promoting human life are the following:

- The **family** as the privileged place where life is born and the person develops.(99) In this area there exists, at the diocesan and national level, different Church institutions and organizations which promote in families the meaning of conjugal fidelity, responsible parenthood, the Christian education of children, solidarity with other families and, in general, the development of the nuclear family as a "domestic Church" after the example of the Holy Family at Nazareth. In this regard, special attention needs to be given to: the diffusion of information on the natural means of family planning and the care of unmarried mothers and the elderly without the joy of a family.

- **Health assistance** directed to all stages of human life. In this area, the Church carries out work not only in offering spiritual care to the sick but also, in some cases, healthcare services in collaboration with the civil initiatives in hospitals and healthcare centers. Among other areas of action, the following can be mentioned: the cases of serious illnesses such as cancer and AIDS, drug addiction, alcoholism; those persons who are physically and mentally handicapped; etc.

- **Christian bio-ethics** as the set of ethical principles related to human life. In this field, it is a question of bringing the Gospel to bear on new problems which science is posing because of its new discoveries. In this regard, initiatives are indicated such as: the creation of centers on bioethics, the preparation of specialized pastoral personnel, inclusion of this subject matter in the programs of Catholic seminaries and universities, etc.. The answers show that there is still much to be done to address this great challenge of our time.

- The promotion of the **culture of life** in response to "a culture which denies solidarity and in many cases takes the form of a veritable culture of death."(100) Many negative signs are manifesting themselves in a denial of life in the societies of all America, for example: the violation of human rights, the legalization of abortion, the acceptance of euthanasia, sterilization programs, etc. On many occasions, the bishops have spoken out individually and collegially through their own preaching and through documents from the episcopal conferences, directing their words as Pastors to the People of God and to all people of good will, so as to make them aware of the individual and social responsibility associated with the divine gift of life.

. . . .
. . . .
. . . .

SYNOD OF BISHOPS
SPECIAL ASSEMBLY FOR OCEANIA
JESUS CHRIST
AND
THE PEOPLES OF OCEANIA:
WALKING HIS WAY,
TELLING HIS TRUTH,
LIVING HIS LIFE
LINEAMENTA
VATICAN CITY
1997 *

. . . .
. . . .
. . . .
. . . .

Oceania and its peoples

1. On the world-map Oceania ranks as the fifth great division of the globe. Because so distant from other countries, it was the last area discovered by European navigators on their voyages of exploration. But the last discovered are now the newest arrivals in whom the Church rejoices. Oceania has been a challenge to explorers and missionaries and to its own people because of its immense size. It covers millions of square kilometers of the greatest ocean on earth as well as the continental landmass of Australia. Its name, of course, is taken from the ocean that connects the islands and landmasses together into one geographical zone. The early navigators found that after a treacherous storm they could be becalmed because of its "peaceful character" which left them motionless on the water, without wind to fill their sails. And so this great ocean became the Pacific Ocean.
The word "pacific", however, indicates more than a name; the term can also be said to characterise the manner of life of the peoples of the region. The *Pacific*

Way suggests the typical manner in which the area's peoples deal with their problems. But much more than this, it indicates how deeply the people treasure peace and desire it. Peace resulting from dialogue and consensus is generally preferred to imposing violent solutions. Though this sense of peace was violated many times in history and in the subsequent struggle for self-sufficiency, it still endures as the traditional ideal and rule for most peoples in the area. Since the end of the Second World War, great political, economic and social changes have swept through the region. In some cases, these changes in Oceania are taking place in a relatively peaceful way. In others, the tendency to use force and violence is on the increase, as painfully witnessed in Papua New Guinea.(1)

Oceania is home to a rich variety of peoples. For the sake of this synodal assembly, the term "Oceania" refers to all the peoples living in the geographical area of Australia, New Zealand, and the Pacific Islands grouped together as Melanesia, Polynesia and Micronesia.(2) Some Asian ethnic groups, like Indians, Chinese, Vietnamese, Koreans, Filipinos and Javanese, coming originally as an imported or indentured immigrant labour force, are now inhabitants of Oceania. Even after many years of residency – sometimes for more than a century – these groups still retain their original and characteristic identity.

Many Island people have moved to Australia or New Zealand and have formed a cultural group of their own. The original people of Australia, the Aborigines, and of New Zealand, the Maoris (who call their country *Aotearoa*), now find themselves minorities in their own countries, a situation which resulted from colonisation in these two countries by European settlers, mainly from England, Ireland and Scotland. Many Europeans have also settled on various islands in the Pacific. In the last 50 years, other ethnic groups from Europe and Asia have also migrated to Oceania.

From the point of view of historical discovery, Oceania – apart from the Marianas, colonised and Christianised in the 16th century – was the geographical area last touched by European colonisation and Christian missionary activity. The colonial powers were aware that the discovery of a continent under the Southern Cross would complete their world map. They named it "the Southern Land (*Terra Australis*) of the Holy Spirit", referring to the One who completes the communion of the Trinity. The generous service of so many missionaries moved by the Holy Spirit contributed to bringing the Gospel of Christ to the region, thus making the Spirit's presence felt in Oceania and manifesting His many fruits among its peoples.

Today, the peoples of Oceania are facing significant changes which have begun since the Second World War when the Pacific became a battleground and a militarily strategic part of the world. Until that time, the peoples of the region had lived, for the most part, in a relatively routine manner with little outside attention. In the aftermath of this Great War, however, the situation began to change: the idea of democracy was introduced; many small island countries became politicarhy independent; the Cold War ended and the Pacific Rim grew in economic importance. In many cases, Oceania is presently attempting to find its own identity in relation to Europe, America and Asia. After many years of dependence on colonial powers, the region is looking at ways to achieve a greater self-sufficiency through unity in diversity, cooperation amidst friendly competition, and interdependence with autonomy. Realistically speaking, however, most realise that true political and economic self-sufficiency as well as a proper cultural identity must take into account the other parts of the globe and their peoples

. . . .
. . . .

Initiatives of The Holy See

6. A full scale missionary outreach of the Catholic Church to Oceania was organised at the end of the 18th Century, but was not begun until the early 19th Century. The Roman Pontiffs and the Congregation for the Propagation of the Faith (now: Congregation for the Evangelisation of Peoples) took the initiative and made courageous plans to send missionaries to Oceania.
A first attempt was made in 1827, when Pope Leo XII asked the Society of the Sacred Hearts of Jesus and Mary (SS.C.C.) to establish missions in Hawaii. Though the first priests who arrived in 1831 were soon deported because of Protestant opposition, they returned to stay in 1833. Missionaries gradually went to the other islands and New Zealand, first from Hawaii and Tahiti, and then directly from Europe. A great expansion of mission stations was the result. In this context, only a few pioneering events can be mentioned. In 1837, Bishop Pompallier and the first French Marists reached Wallis and Futuna. Some months later, they landed in New Zealand. An effort to establish a mission in New Britain was made in 1881. A year later, the Missionaries of the Sacred Heart, under Father Navarre, made a second attempt, laying the foundation for a successful mission on the islands of New Guinea. In 1882, their confrere, Father Verjus, and his fellow missionaries landed on Yule Island from where they began preaching the faith on the Papuan coast. In 1896, Father Limbrock led a group of missionaries of the Society of the Divine Word to found a lasting mission on the coast of New Guinea.
The first hierarchy in Oceania was established in Australia in 1842. The apostolic vicariate of New Holland had already been created in 1834 and entrusted to the English Benedictines. They were to serve the religious needs of the convicts and the colonists, many of whom were Irish and Catholic. The "Men of '37" were a group of Irish clergy who arrived in Australia in that year to establish the skeleton of what became the parish system in the country. The spiritual needs of Christians of other denominations were already being

attended by clergy sent from Great Britain. The Catholic missionaries were not always welcome in Australia. In the early days, the colonial authorities often persecuted them or hindered their efforts to serve the Catholic people.

After the successful missionary efforts of European and American Protestant Communities in the Pacific Islands, Catholic missionaries arrived. These missionaries, oftentimes enduring great difficulties, succeeded in contacting the indigenous people and making converts. They saw the importance not only to convert the peoples of Oceania from a belief in their gods and spirits to faith in Jesus Christ, but to teach them Catholic doctrine and to receive them into the communion of the Catholic Church with Her sacraments, liturgy and devotions. Where at the beginning there were difficulties in the relations between Christian leaders in these missionary attempts, there is presently a greater ecumenical spirit of cooperation and movement towards communion in accordance with Jesus' prayer and desire.

Work of Missionary Congregations and Institutes

7. The great workers in the missions of Oceania were largely members of religious orders and congregations. The first were the Spanish Franciscans and the Jesuits in the 17th century. In the 19th century, the English Benedictines went to Australia. As the century passed, the recently founded apostolic congregations, especially those from France, began sending their missionaries, priests, sisters and brothers to Oceania. The pioneering efforts of the Franciscans, the Jesuits, the Society of Mary (Marists), the Pontifical Institute for Foreign Mission of Milan (PIME), and the Missionaries of the Sacred Heart and the Society of the Divine Word, were assisted by the missionary work of many other congregations of priests, brothers and sisters related to these initial groups, and by the arrival of similar self-sacrificing persons from still other religious orders and congregations.

In 1672, after four years of missionary work on the shores of Guam, Blessed Diego Luis de San Vitores, a Spanish Jesuit priest was killed for baptising the dying daughter of a local chief. He is considered the *protomartyr* of the Marianas. A French Marist priest, St. Peter Chanel, was martyred in 1841 on Futuna, after a brief apostolate on the island. He is regarded as the first saint and patron of Oceania. Another missionary and martyr of Oceania is Blessed Giovanni Mazzucconi of the Pontifical Institute for Foreign Missions of Milan (PIME), who was martyred in 1855 on Woodlark Island in Papua New Guinea. Bishop Jean-Baptiste Epalle, a Marist and first Vicar Apostolic of Melanesia, was the first bishop to be the victim of violence. After being attacked by indigenous tribesmen on the island, he died in 1844 on the ship which brought him to San Isabel in the Solomon Islands.

The martyrdom of these missionaries points to the many sacrifices which men and women endured for the sake of spreading God's Kingdom, e.g., long and difficult sea voyages, separation from distant homelands, isolation and loneliness, the tropical climate with its devastating sicknesses, thick forests and mountainous terrain, unfamiliar food and poor housing, and often violence from the indigenous tribes, all of which sometimes led to an untimely death. Some missionaries drowned while attempting to cross rivers and seas to bring the sacraments or medical help to those in need.

At present, international orders and congregations, oftentimes having indigenous members, continue to work side by side with indigenous congregations in various parts of Oceania, so as to contribute to the growth and the vitality of the Church and Her mission to human society. An outstanding example of apostolic activity and religious life was given by Mother Mary McKillop (1842-1909), an Australian, beatified in 1995. Foundress of the Sisters of St. Joseph of the Sacred Heart, she and her sisters, along with many other men and women religious, particularly from Ireland, England and France, responded generously to the great need for Catholic education in Australia and the colonies of the region. Until well after the Second World War, the Catholic school system in Oceania was almost entirely staffed by religious men and women.

So many others – known and unknown – illustrate through their life and work the heroism of the missionaries in founding and serving Catholic Communities in Oceania. Many died or suffered greatly in the service of evangelisation as they endured times of hardship, the most recent being the Second World War. Their lives of sacrifice and generosity will always be recalled by Christians of any age as a lasting, encouraging example to live the faith, and their prayerful intercession will be a sustaining force in the preparation and celebration of this Special Assembly of the Synod of Bishops for Oceania.

Oceanians as Missionaries

8. Since the beginning of the Church's missionary efforts in the region, foreign missionaries needed and solicited the help of local men and women. They trained catechists to work with them, to translate their sermons and instructions, to prepare the people for the sacraments, to teach them to pray and to serve the local Christian communities through their spiritual leadership. Often these local men and their families accompanied the missionaries as they established new missions in other parts of Oceania. Like the missionaries from Europe who followed the missionary example of Jesus Christ, they left home and family to live among foreign peoples and cultures.

A great example of these devoted catechists is Peter To Rot of New Britain (Papua New Guinea), beatified in 1995. During the Second World War, many missionaries were imprisoned by the Japanese occupying forces. Many of them were killed or died from wounds or tropical diseases. At the time, catechists were forbidden to do their work among the local people. Peter To Rot lost his life by refusing to cease teaching and offering religious support to converts.

Shortly after 1840, early attempts to train local clergy on the islands were made by Bishop Pierre Bataillon, Vicar Apostolic of Central Oceania. Though the European model of formation often proved too difficult for seminarians, resulting in some initial failures, more and more local candidates – diocesan and religious – were trained and ordained to the priesthood. Encouraged by the example of some outstanding indigenous priests and bishops, they joined their missionary brothers from overseas. For several years now, numerous local priests and religious, brothers and sisters throughout Oceania are serving their own people.

By following the Gospel more and more and fervently receiving the sacraments, people become more aware of the missionary call which is addressed to the whole Church. In this regard, much depends on Christian families. Christian parents have an important role in offering encouragement to their sons and daughters and in supporting them in their desire to become missionaries, not only in the local Church but in other parts of the world. Many men and women born in Oceania have joined the missionary ranks of local or international congregations, working in other parts of Oceania and in other countries across the world. In this way, the local Churches of Oceania manifest the continual challenge to act in solidarity with the worldwide Catholic Church, to bring the Good News to other nations and thus to walk the way of Jesus, their Master and Model.

What Paul VI said to Catholics in Australia, referring them to Oceania as their wider mission field, can be repeated to all Catholics in Oceania: "Lift up your eyes and look at this vast harvest waiting for its reapers to gather it in (cf. *Jn* 4:35). Is it possible that your community which has had the great fortune of receiving the grace of the Gospel, which has responded with fervour to the teaching of your priests and which offers the world a noteworthy testimony of faith, fidelity to doctrine, and generosity towards the upkeep of works of the apostolate – is it possible for it not to be at the same time a land of missionaries?"(5)

. . . .
. . . .

THE WAY TO MANY CULTURES

Introduction

9. Whenever people's lives are touched by the Gospel and the grace of Jesus Christ, they are transformed. This effect is not limited only to persons. The more people accept Christianity and live it in their lives, the more society and culture are transformed. By nature and necessity, a person is a member of a

human society. The values held by the members of that society, the customs which they follow, the beliefs they have, the language they speak, the stories they tell, the way they organise their work, their time, and above all, the way they express their ideological and religious convictions, all comprise their way of life, their **culture**. The Church has a deep respect for every culture. At the same time, the Gospel She preaches makes unique challenges on culture in an attempt to elevate, enrich and purify it. By being received into a particular culture, the Gospel is expressed and lived in a certain manner, which itself becomes a means of proclaiming the Gospel to others.

Cultural Variety

10. Oceania is characterised by a **variety of cultures**. People of various cultures live together in the same territory, often dwelling very close to one another. These cultures are not only the indigenous cultures of the Pacific Islands, New Zealand and Australia, but also the cultures brought from Europe and those developed during the years of colonisation, migration, and the struggle for autonomy. This cultural variety can be illustrated particularly through language. In addition to the hundreds of indigenous languages, some languages have developed and been accepted as communal languages. English and French, though inherited from Western Europe, are for the most part accepted as the official languages in Oceania, each being appropriated in its own way. In Melanesia the pidgin languages, with their own flavour and richness of expression, have developed to bridge the European and the local languages.

This same variety of cultures can also be seen in the Church. The missionaries brought a Catholic faith which was linked to various nations and cultures, primarily European. By necessity, they taught the faith through these cultural models and trained their converts to express the faith in the same manner. In a positive ecumenical climate, the various religious cultures of other denominations have had an impact on the Catholic communities living close to them. These many cultures influence Church life, not only in the words, rites and songs of the liturgy and in prayers and devotional practices, but also in preaching, in expressing theological concepts and in the organisation and leadership of communities.

The Catholic Church seeks to respect the variety of cultures. In the words of Paul VI: "Far from smothering what is good and original in every culture, in every form of human culture She accepts, respects and puts to use the genius of each people, endowing with variety and beauty the one seamless garment of the Church of Christ."(6) It is a great challenge for the Church to welcome and incorporate this cultural variety into Herself and to bring it to unity and harmony through the mystery of communion. Where cultures are respected, contact with each other can be profitable. One culture can learn from another; it can oftentimes be enriched and even made better.

Inculturation

11. Jesus' message and the Gospel as originally preached by the apostles had many features of the Jewish culture of the day. At the same time, their teaching was different from that culture because, with its new values and priorities, it challenged customary practices and beliefs. Wherever the Word of God is preached and welcomed, this dual dynamic is at work. The existing culture with its positive aspects, its "seeds of the Word",(7) its germs of truth and justice, is fostered, becoming, as it were, a new language into which God's Word is translated. At the same time, the existing culture is challenged by the Gospel and is gradually converted. The positive elements of that culture then provide assistance in further preaching God's message to the people of that same culture. This process of **inculturation** is part of the Church's work of evangelisation in all the cultures of Oceania. Pope John Paul II, in his "Allocution to the Aboriginal people of Australia" said: "The Gospel of Our Lord Jesus Christ speaks all languages. It esteems and embraces all cultures. It supports them in everything human and, when necessary, it purifies them. Always and everywhere the Gospel uplifts and enriches cultures with the revealed message of a loving and merciful God."(8)

The Gospel was proclaimed in Oceania by means of European cultural expressions which were foreign to indigenous people. Some forms and elements of this inculturated Gospel have disappeared and have been replaced by indigenous forms and elements. Today, the tendency is to look at these cultural forms and elements to see if they cannot be creatively translated and transformed so as to provide an opportunity for renewal in the local Church. When it was originally preached in Oceania, the Gospel challenged the imperfect or negative elements of the local culture. It required, and still requires, great wisdom to discern the positive and the negative elements in the process of inculturation. According to Pope John Paul II, the two criteria to be followed in sound inculturation are: 1) compatibility with the basic elements of the Gospel, and 2) promotion of communion with the universal Church.(9)

Many positive traditional values are present in Oceania and influence the life of the Church. At the same time, some modern developments are threatening these traditional values. Other developments, if critically appraised and treated, have the potential of breathing new life into them. All such positive values have the potential to enrich and enhance human life and culture in Oceania.

The Church's expression of Her life of faith in symbols and rites is linked to the culture of the person who receives the Gospel of Jesus Christ. Traditional stories and symbols, music and dance, rites and celebrations, all of which are expressions of human memory and imagination, are deeply part of the cultures of Oceania. Through a proper application of inculturation, the Church seeks to incorporate elements of a particular culture into Her liturgy, devotional practices, catechesis and sacred art. In this way, She expresses faith in God and communion among the faithful. While local cultural traditions can be enhanced by their being elevated by the Church, through the dual dynamic of inculturation, they can also be purified of negative elements in the process.

A particular challenge for the Church in Melanesia is the phenomenon of "cargo cult". Economic development and social and political changes in recent times have brought advancement to the indigenous people, but also cultural difficulties. Traditional stories of prosperity, lost or forfeited, are connected with biblical promises of a new world of justice and wealth. "Cargo cult"-thinking expresses itself, at times, in dangerous social, political and religious movements. This phenomenon is a particular challenge for the Church in Oceania in its catechesis and pastoral care of indigenous people.

In theological reflection, a mentality conditioned by a certain culture is a real challenge for the Church. When faithful to the truth as revealed in Jesus Christ and taught by the Church, such an experience can bring positive results, thus enriching the living Catholic theological tradition and allowing the Truth to be expressed in a new, local way.

Theological thinking in Oceania takes into consideration not only the traditional cultures, but also modern developments like industrialisation, secularisation, ecumenical dialogue and the enriching contact with other religions and philosophies. Oceania has a good number of theologians and spiritual writers whose work is recognised internationally. Their contributions to theological research and spiritual reflection are important for the growth of the Church in the area.

Part of the task of evangelisation in Oceania requires committed Christians to go beyond their own culture and encounter various other cultures in the region. In sharing the saving power of God's truth, grace and love with these cultures, they grow in their appreciation and understanding of these same gifts, and thus continue to walk faithfully the way of Jesus Christ.

Ethnic Minorities and Indigenous Peoples

12. Among the various cultural groups of Oceania, some ethnic communities are in the **minority**. Some of these originally made up whole populations, but have become a minority through successive waves of immigration, e.g., the Aborigines in Australia and the Maoris in New Zealand. Others are not strictly a minority, but feel unjustly treated, e.g., the Kanak people in New Caledonia. In some cases, two groups of people, forming almost equal parts of a particular population, feel threatened by each other, e.g., the indigenous Fijians and the Fiji-Indians in Fiji. Other minority groups are clusters of recent immigrants or refugees.

The Church recognizes Her responsibility in this area and is engaged in protecting those who suffer social injustice. Special care for threatened minority groups is a consequence of the *preferential love for the poor* in the Gospel of Jesus Christ. Though the Church is not a political entity, She has a role to play in forming Her faithful in Her social doctrine. She teaches and encourages not only Her members but all civil authorities to be aware of their responsibility to address social injustice against ethnic minorities.(10)

Some ethnic minority groups are painfully struggling to preserve or revive their culture. Pope John Paul II has encouraging words for these groups. Though they were originally addressed to the Aboriginal people and use traditional imagery, they can be applied to others as well: "If you are closely united you are like a tree standing in the middle of a bush fire sweeping through the timber. The leaves are scorched and the tough bark is scarred and burned: but inside the tree, the sap is still flowing and under the ground the roots are still strong. Like that tree you have endured the flames and you still have the power to be reborn. The time of this rebirth is now."(11) Bringing the Gospel to bear on these social and cultural problems is a practical and realistic consequence of walking the way of Jesus Christ.

Migration and Tourism

13. In past centuries, the island people of Oceania were already known for their **migratory movements**. Sometimes, persons moved about on their own accord for reasons of conquest, to prevent over-population or to escape violence. At other times, they were forced to leave their home islands so as to work on plantations or in mining ventures on other islands. In later years, such labourers were recruited from other colonial territories, mainly from Asia. The traditional tendency of the Polynesian people to move from island to island was certainly helpful when missionaries sought local assistants to establish new missions in other parts of Oceania.

Today, there is a great migration of people not simply within the region, but coming from the outside as well. Many Pacific Islanders move to Australia or New Zealand for economic or social reasons. Others are motivated by the prospect of better opportunities in education and work, greater access to modern commodities or more individual freedom and human rights. New Zealand and Australia have traditionally attracted immigrants from Europe, particularly since the end of World War II. At present, more Asians are coming to both countries, thereby contributing to an increasing cultural variety. Among these immigrants are political or economic refugees searching for freedom, justice and prosperity. Many of them find that the Church and Her structures provide a warm environment and a source of security and identity.

In some places, the increasing number of migrants from different cultures is calling for the Church's attention. In the past, the Church has always attempted to provide for the pastoral care of migrants. Consideration needs to be given as to whether these migrants can be said to be a properly constitutive part of the local community in a multi-cultural Church and society. Any pastoral plan would have to determine whether these migrants are on the periphery awaiting assimilation into the predominant culture or whether these migrants are a more permanent part of the culture, requiring their own ministries, e.g., national parishes, or designated parishes which offer as part of their ministry, an apostolate to ethnic groups. As a result of migration, Eastern Catholic Churches, with their own dioceses, parishes and traditions, exist in some parts of Oceania, enriching the Church's witness and presence in society in the area of culture. In Oceania, another increasingly significant social phenomenon related to the movement of peoples is **tourism**. Modern tourism is no longer just an activity for the few, but an industry in which thousands of people participate. For the tourists themselves, this industry provides a service; for the many employees, work and an income. Many places in Australia and New Zealand, not to mention the many Pacific Islands with their splendid features of nature and the traditional culture of hospitality, have become attractive tourist resorts. While the influence of this industry on the local economy has advantages, it is not always beneficial to the environment, the culture, or the moral and spiritual values of the inhabitants.

The Church in Oceania, proclaiming a Gospel of hope and joy, seeks to address these modern realities of migration and tourism. When left outside the traditional pastoral system of parishes and chaplaincies, these movements of people can easily create social areas where the Gospel has little access.

Urbanisation and Industrialisation

14. Relatively speaking, Australia is one of the more **urbanised** countries of the world. New Zealand also has great urban areas, and numerous Pacific Island nations are developing their capital cities. These urban areas are attracting massive numbers of people who believe living in big cities promises ultimate freedom, boundless variety and great prosperity. However, when such people do not succeed in their dream, these same cities suffer not only from a rapid growth in population but also from an increasing percentage of jobless and poor people. Situations created by unemployment, poverty, individualism, tough competition and sometimes inadequate education to attain their goals, are for some people too much to endure. Some young people, coming from rural villages, find in these urban areas an apparent easy solution to their problems by joining criminal gangs or in practicing immoral professions, like prostitution.

After moving to the city, some people fall away from the Church because they perceive the Church as a community for the higher ranks of society. In their present situation, they see themselves as not belonging to any class. Going out

in the footsteps of Jesus, Who Himself became poor, to meet the urban poor is
the concern of every Church member. Where offering material assistance to the
poor is one of the traditional tasks of the Christian community, the Church
also speaks out on the injustice of certain socio-economic developments.
Catholic citizens and politicians are called upon to put the Church's social doctrine into action by devising ways to address socio-economic problems. In this
manner, individual Christians and whole Christian communities can walk the
way of Jesus Christ and meet the needs of the poor.

Today in Oceania, urbanisation goes hand in hand with **secularisation**. In Australia and New Zealand, with a basically Western culture, and in many Pacific
Island nations, there seems to be a tendency among the people to adopt a way
of life in which religion is marginal. A great difference is seen between the sec-
ularised way of life in the big cities and the traditional village or rural life-style.
This trend to secularisation increasingly inclines people towards subjectivism
and freedom from religious authority in many areas of culture, e.g., marriage
and family, morality, education, politics, economy, social communications and
artistic expression. For many people, this movement from village to city leads
to a loss of traditional religious faith and practice. In reference to secularisation,
Pope John Paul II said to the New Zealand bishops: "*The sense of God and of
his loving Providence has diminished* for many individuals and even for whole
sectors of society."(12)

While secularisation creates problems for Christian faith and practice, it also
provides new challenges. The increase in personal and social freedom is an invitation to a greater sense of responsibility and mature decision-making. This situation requires creative theological approaches, meaningful worship and rituals,
a balanced practice of spirituality and devotion, personal rectitude, application
of the Church's social teaching, responsible religious organisation, appropriate
charitable activity and a deeper look at more contemporary forms of ministry.
To face adequately this new cultural reality, the Church has to walk the way of
Jesus Christ with courage, patience and wisdom.

. . . .
. . . .

Today's Challenges

17. In some places in Oceania today, **missionary activity** is in decline and
sometimes put in question. Such a state of affairs was addressed by Pope John
Paul II in his Encyclical Letter *Redemptoris missio*. "For in the Church's history,"
he writes, "missionary drive has always been a sign of vitality, just as its lessening is a sign of a crisis of faith."(18) St. Paul underlines the necessity of telling
the truth of Jesus Christ so that all the peoples of the world, of whatever culture – traditional or secular – may come to the faith and witness to it in their

lives. "But how are men to call upon him in whom they have not believed? And how are they to believe in him of whom they have never heard? And how are they to hear without a preacher?" (*Rom* 10:14). If the Gospel is to grow in the cultures of Oceania, all in the Church need to become more aware of the missionary nature of the Church and find ways to share in the Church's mission. For some generous men and women, this will mean responding to God's call to the vocation to be a missionary who goes forth to tell the truth of Jesus Christ for all to hear.

In a practical way, missionaries are still needed in many places to help the younger Churches achieve more autonomy in terms of local personnel and leadership, and of infra-structure and finance. The developed countries also need evangelisers with a missionary spirit to tell the truth of Jesus Christ, so that their secular cultures may hear His voice – as if for the first time – with joy, welcoming it in the words of the psalm, "O sing to the Lord a new song; sing to the Lord, all the earth" (*Ps* 96:1)!

The problems of evangelisation experienced in developing and developed countries in Oceania are not very different. The secularisation affecting the developed countries is also influencing island and indigenous communities. While most of them still maintain their local cultural identity, which evangelisation must take into account, they too are undergoing modern, secularising trends. Both types of society need missionaries who are able to address each distinct situation. The difficulties facing evangelisation come not only from challenges to the faith but from the crisis in culture as well. When social institutions in a culture experience change, the Church is challenged as well. This is an inevitable consequence of the Church's living in a particular cultural environment Some of the major changes in society, posing real challenges for evangelisation, are the following: the increased impact of government and the economy on life; the over-emphasis on democracy and personal choice; the abuses of a market economy; liberal or individualistic types of philosophy; the strains placed on the institution of marriage and family life; lack of a sense of the spiritual; the negative influence of the mass media on individual and social behaviour, etc..

To deal with these challenges from society, the Church has the truth of the Gospel and Christ's mandate to preach the Gospel to every creature. Her history embraces generations of bishops, clergy, religious and laity dedicated to telling the Good News. She has established innumerable institutions, particularly the Catholic school system, to hand on the faith. Her hospitals and health care programmes are one example of how the Gospel of charity is lived in ways which meet human need, suffering and death. There is "a cloud of witnesses"(*Heb* 12:1) to Gospel values in the home, in the workplace, in the various professions and in civil life. Nevertheless, in many ways the Church is feeling the strain of transmitting the Gospel to this evolving new world.

. . . .
. . . .

Interreligious Dialogue

2. Relationships with **non-Christian religions** is a pressing issue in some areas. For example, leaders from both the Christian and Jewish communities often meet for fruitful discussions. Such theological dialogue has lead to a better insight into Jewish tradition and practice. At the same time, large groups of **Muslims or Hindus**, living in neighbourhoods, cities or countries, are sometimes misunderstood by the wider community as well as by Christians. Dialogue would be a helpful way to break down barriers of mistrust. The **traditional religions** of the peoples of Oceania are not only a cause of interest but a source of inspiration as well. However, they can sometimes become a force rivaling Christianity in a given area. In some cases, a **danger of syncretism** exists in the blending of traditional religion with Christianity. At the same time, studying the religious values of these peoples has led many Christians to a better appreciation of these cultures. For example, the Australian aborigines have a form of religion which is probably the oldest known to humanity. It has monotheistic features which render it of great importance to the Church in Her understanding of indigenous cultures and in Her evangelising mission.(25)

. . . .

. . . .

SECTS

Overview

23. Sects and new religious movements are a common feature in today's world. The Pontifical Council for Inter-religious Dialogue in collaboration with other Offices of the Roman Curia, has included them in its wide field of interests.(26) In Oceania, this phenomenon is an area of concern for the Church because their false doctrines attract many unsuspecting and impressionable persons both in the Church and society, thereby subjecting many families, and sometimes whole communities, to division and difficulties.

Recently, it seems this phenomenon has reached new proportions, particularly as it relates to the Church. In various parts of Oceania, the close-knit groups of the sects seem to offer a warm, emotional experience to some Catholics who have never been able to attain a similar experience at the Church's liturgical services. Music, song, dance, private revelations, visions and speaking in tongues play an important part in attracting persons, particularly youth, to these sects. To persons in search of stability in a rapidly changing world, they teach fundamentalist doctrines which often provide a false security in rigidly unbending moral codes of conduct. Some sects deliberately and aggressively target the Catholic Church and prey on Her weaker members who, for example, can feel "lost" in larger Church congregations where size sometimes limits personal contact. Once assimilated into a sect, persons will try to bring family and friends with them, usually leading to a very deep split in a family and community.

Given the situation, the challenge facing the Church in Oceania is to seek ways to counteract the effect of these sects and new religious movements, some of which might be: through fostering greater fellowship in Church communities; through providing healing ministries which allow the hurt, the alienated and the emotionally injured to re-integrate their lives through conversion experiences within the Catholic community; through better catechesis in the faith, offering persons not only a greater knowledge of the faith, but also explain the errors in the doctrines of the sects and new religious movements.

Many sects use apocalyptic imagery and messages. Dreams and aspirations are connected with biblical messages completely outside their original context. A biblical fundamentalism distorts a meaningful and authentic understanding of the truth of Jesus Christ. Through their use of Christian symbols and expressions, these sects distort people's desire and need for salvation. The existence of such sects shows how much effort should go into proclaiming the truth of Jesus Christ in a sound and liberating way, in accordance with the Church's tradition.

Particular Points

24. Not all the sects and new religious movements in Oceania have Christian roots. Among the more popular are forms of self-improvement that go back to **Eastern traditions**, such as yoga or Buddhist meditation. Ashrams and centres of Zen or Buddhist meditation can be found as welcomed refuges from the frenetic rush of life in the big city. In their acceptable forms, these often offer help to people in need. However, they may also be the cause of Catholics moving away from their faith for various reasons.

A widely diffused form of contemporary spirituality is **New Age**. Linked to the process of secularisation, this movement draws elements from the Jewish and Christian traditions as well as from Gnosticism and Oriental religions. Its followers believe that a new consciousness has dawned on the planet which will make all religion and philosophy out-dated. This would seem to be a radical reaction to the lack of values which has come to characterise an industrialised, technological culture of mass consumption and mass communication.

Some sects and new religious movements use aggressive tactics in proselytizing new adherents among the baptised, thereby often doing injustice to persons. Some leave their followers with serious psychological problems. Oftentimes, when persons are successful in leaving a sect or new religious movement, they have an extremely difficult time making a re-entry into society. Since these groups play on the fear which persons have of a world in which they find it difficult to cope, they are basically turned in upon themselves. On the contrary, the Church, whose Lord promises salvation to each person, "Be of good cheer, I have overcome the world" (*Jn* 16:33), offers Her members Christian optimism in facing life in the world.

In many ways, the sects and the new religious movements with their growing influence are a challenge to the Church. An adequate response to this challenge needs to include an initial proclamation of the Gospel to individuals as well as a catechesis of the Church's members, both of which relate to local experiences and desires, and concentrate on fundamental truths rather than secondary theories. In the planning and celebration of Her liturgies and devotional practices, elements deserving of consideration are the following: the emotional needs of participants, inculturated forms, popular devotions, etc..

. . . .
. . . .

JUSTICE AND PEACE

Working Towards Establishing the Kingdom of God

25. By walking the Way which is Christ, by telling His Truth and Living His Life, the Church contributes to the building of "a civilisation of love", where justice and peace reign. While giving Herself wholeheartedly to this task in the present world, the Church awaits with joyful hope the coming of the final Kingdom when every injustice will be wiped away and all misery will disappear from creation so "that God may be everything to every one" (*1 Cor* 15:28). The Second Vatican Council states, "Christ did not bequeath to the Church a mission in the political, economic, or social order: the purpose He assigned to it was a religious one."(27) Through the Church's preaching the Light of the Gospel shines on people, so that in their becoming believers in Christ, the Saving Light can penetrate and illuminate secular realities through them.

The mission of the Church in the world is summed up in the following statement: "In pursuing Her own salvific purpose not only does the Church communicate divine life to men but in a certain sense She casts the reflected light of that divine life over all the earth, notably in the way She heals and elevates the dignity of the human person, in the way She consolidates society, and empowers the daily activity of men with deeper sense and meaning."(28) The Church's members are to be the leaven in the world so as to renew and transform every worthy part of society according to the will of Christ. "This religious mission can be the source of commitment, direction and vigour to establish and consolidate the community of men according to the law of God."(29)

There are many indications that the Church in Oceania has taken to heart Her mission to transform society and its social structures with the power of the

Gospel. The establishment of many Justice and Peace commissions at local and national levels has lead to programmes which explain and propagate the Church's social teaching. At the practical level, these commissions have defended the human dignity of the person, condemned racial discrimination and fostered human development programmes. Furthermore, they have made submissions to governments, particularly in favour of the poor and disadvantaged, and pointed out the political, social and economic causes of injustice. At the same time, they have confronted some timely subjects in Oceania, e.g., international agreements which leave smaller or weaker nations at an economic and political disadvantage, economic discrimination, a situation where one nation or section of society benefits at the expense of others, the problem in the developed countries of an ever-widening gap between the rich and poor, the need for an ethic of responsibility and social justice in industry, commerce and banking, particularly concerning the wages of workers in relation to world markets, and the attitudes and practices of more developed countries towards lesser developed ones in relation to global economies. In a concrete manner, the Church's social aid agencies in the area have given monetary and material assistance to many groups, families and individuals, especially after natural disasters. Where the phenomenon of a global economy is bringing social and cultural benefits to many parts of Oceania, it is also causing people to make major adjustments in their lives, some of which are difficult to face. For example, unemployment and lack of opportunity for work is on the rise in many areas of Oceania, causing hardship to persons, families and whole communities. Particularly affected in this regard are the young who can easily grow discouraged and disillusioned, and thus turn to unethical forms of behaviour or even to taking their own lives, a trend which is on the rise in some parts of Oceania. The social doctrine of the Church has much to offer governments and companies in their working with others to formulate sound policies and educational programmes in relation to employment practices which can benefit not only the person, but society.

The most significant event in the recent history of Oceania was the Second World War, which caused many changes in the region. As a result, parts of Oceania, because of their geographic position, still maintain political, economic and strategic links with the U.S.A., Japan and South East Asia. At the same time, the countries of the region are increasingly cooperating among themselves and with others in plans for development. In such plans towards development, the Church, according to words of Pope John Paul II,(30) adds to the factor of the economy, those of human values and integral human development, that is, consideration of the spiritual, religious, social, educational, cultural as well as material well-being of the person and whole populations.

In some places in Oceania, the Church has a special and indeed privileged role as peacemaker. Her mediation is being called upon in disputes between tribal or racial groups, sometimes between central governments and separatist movements, sometimes in strike situations and employment disputes. Where possible, in the name of the Gospel, the Church offers Her good services to bring peace to communities through Christ's message of reconciliation and forgiveness. Christ, "Our Peace" (*Eph* 2:14) is the one who can "create in Himself...one body..." (*Eph* 2:15) through the power of His Cross by breaking down the walls of division among peoples.

Responsibility for Creation

26. Persons and groups of persons are not the only concern of Justice and Peace initiatives. Creation, i.e., all life on the planet and the material conditions which sustain it, is also affected by human behaviour, in particular economic activities, e.g., industrialisation, mining, exploration for oil, logging, farming. etc.. Sometimes, if left unchecked, these activities can harm, if not destroy, whole parts of the environment. In Oceania, many animal and plant species have already been destroyed, and others are endangered. In Her teaching on the universal destination of goods, the Church teaches respect and responsibility in the use of creation.

Besides environmental concerns, governments and companies need to take into consideration in their economic policy and practices the culture and customs of the variety of peoples in the Pacific, e.g., cattle grazers, sheep raisers, grain growers, loggers, fishermen, etc.. In her pastoral programmes, the Church also wishes to be sensitive to their unique needs resulting from circumstances related to their work, e.g., feelings of isolation and loneliness, great distances separating them from others, threatened way of life, economic pressure, etc. Pollution of the environment as a side-effect of an industrial society is also a concern, especially since certain parts of Oceania are still in their natural state. At present, with the development of industry, contamination of streams, land and sea is on the increase. Major cities face the ill effects of vehicle emissions on the health of the population. Scientists have raised the critical issue of the depletion of the ozone layer over Antarctica and the Southern Oceans, a concern not only to the people of Oceania but to the entire world population. Still to be evaluated are the long-term effects of nuclear testing in the area.

. . . .
. . . .

Cultural Attitudes Towards Life

32. In Oceania, people who have maintained their **indigenous culture** value human life, not just as an individual or present physical reality, but as a dynamic fullness offered in the ancestral community. They easily conceive of

God as life in its fullness, shared with them through the ancestors in the community. To live in community is to share life. According to this viewpoint, morality is seen as satisfying the desire to bring life to its fullness. The moral life is a person's movement towards fulfillment in God. For these people, morality is lived in community, and individual responsibility is assumed in view of community life and values. Freedom is understood in relation to the community, to its flourishing or diminishment. There can be such a strong sense of community between the people and God that God may be conceived as owning the life they receive and share from Him.

The understanding of human life in a **technological society** is vastly different. In this setting, people also rejoice in life, in beauty, in sport, in good health which is sometimes prised even above intellectual and spiritual talents. In a consumer society, however, human life can easily be reduced to a purely biological reality, living matter which can be manipulated in the laboratory or the operating theatre. With this attitude, what is technologically possible oftentimes is considered premissible without any reference to the wondrous mystery of human life meant to blossom in eternity and to the moral imperatives laid down by God. The "technological imperative" means what can be done, should be done! Some scientists have claimed that no moral limits should be put on research and experimentation because that would harm the progress of science, and thus, of society. This is a claim to absolute freedom for science, superior to every other freedom in society. Any implied moral claim in these matters is usually based on utilitarianism: a calculation of the greatest good for the greatest number. Some mistakenly see this as the fulfillment of the Christian commandment of love. Such a claim, however, puts all accepted moral conceptions into doubt when they cannot successfully pass the utilitarian test. In this mentality, birth and death lose their mystery. They no longer manifest the presence of God as the Lord of creation, personally present to every human person. The human person becomes another material entity to be manipulated at will for material ends.

Moral Issues

33. Modern society in its **social planning and legislative programmes** is increasingly determined to apply technology and the findings of science to as many of its activities as possible. The Church is challenged to find effective ways of making Her moral message heard and applied by governments, scientists and people-at-large.

The Church's concern extends to life in all its stages, aspects and care, from conception to natural death. Bishops' Conferences and individual bishops have spoken on life-issues; they have made submissions to governments and have striven to propagate the Church's teaching in the media. They proclaim the

dignity of the human person and the eternal destiny of each person. They have defended the sacredness of human life and the right to life from the first moment of conception. All types of procured abortion have been condemned as a truly horrendous crime afflicting society. Contraception, because it distorts the personal meaning of human sexuality by dividing the act of love from its fecundity, does not fulfill the criteria of responsible parenthood. The bishops have objected to the wilful manipulation of the embryo and its destruction. They have made known the Church's refusal to accept extra-bodily conception in the form of *in vitro fertilisation* (IVF) as a morally legitimate means of treating infertility.

Euthanasia is the latest issue to surface for public discussion. What is in question is not the legitimate withdrawal of medical treatment of no further benefit to a patient, who is then allowed to die with dignity and in peace. "Euthanasia, in the strict sense, is understood to be an action or omission which, of itself and by intention, causes death, with the purpose of eliminating all suffering."(33) It usually means that another person, usually a doctor, directly and deliberately intervenes to bring about the patient's death. According to God's law, such an action can only be considered either murder or assisted suicide.

The Church's Witness to Life

34. The problems raised by the practice of medicine in hospitals today have lead to the establishment of ethics committees as well as bio-ethics and counseling centres. The **Catholic hospital system** has contributed much to working towards a solution of the health care problems in communities. The pastoral care of those who are ill has received great inspiration from the teachings and implementation of the rite for the sacrament of the anointing of the sick. In various ways, the Church has shown understanding and compassion in Her apostolates directed towards healing the physical and spiritual wounds of a broken humanity. The distribution of health care funds and resources in communities are a burning social justice question. The Church does not want to see the poor, the weak or the elderly disadvantaged in the competition for scarce health care services and facilities. The fact that hospitals are often managed as a business enterprise makes one fear for the fate of those who cannot afford the services they provide.

The Church has encouraged doctors, nurses and everyone of good will to organise in defence of the right of life.(34) They are to use non-violent methods, for "when, in accordance with their principles, such movements act resolutely, but without resorting to violence, they promote a wider and more profound consciousness of the value of life."(35) Nevertheless, certain legislators and persons in the judiciary, regrettably even some Catholics, give in to the pressures of society in seeking legal respectability for actions which are morally indefensible.

There is truth in the principle that violence breeds violence. With the increased killing of the unborn or the terminally ill, there seems to be a proportionate increase in suicides, crimes of assault, domestic violence, sexual exploitation of children and other types of violent acts.

Pope John Paul II in his Encyclical Letter **Evangelium vitae** has treated all the above topics within the framework of Scripture and the tradition of the Church's moral teaching. He says, "One of the specific characteristics of present-day attacks on human life – as has already been said several times – consists in the trend to demand a legal justification for them, as if they were rights which the state, at least under certain conditions, must acknowledge as belonging to citizens."(36) By pointing out the necessary conformity of civil with moral law, the Pope shows that laws which legitimate abortion or euthanasia are unjust and cease to be law because they violate the inviolable and inalienable right of every human being to life. This right has been obscured by moral relativism, which denies any such universal binding force to moral concepts. But "it is easy to see that without an objective moral grounding, not even democracy is capable of ensuing a stable peace."(37)

The practical problem arises when dedicated **Catholic politicians** are faced with voting for or against a bill which would limit the effects of, e.g., an abortion bill already passed. In a pluralistic society, the distinction between **licit and illicit cooperation**(38) with unjust laws can be expected to be a very actual issue for the Church in the future. Catholic politicians are at the forefront to ensure that Christian values will be, and remain, reflected in legislation. Their efforts deserve encouragement and support.

. . . .
. . . .

SYNOD OF BISHOPS
SPECIAL ASSEMBLY FOR ASIA
JESUS CHRIST THE SAVIOUR AND
HIS MISSION OF
LOVE AND SERVICE IN ASIA:
"...THAT THEY MAY HAVE LIFE,
AND HAVE IT ABUNDANTLY" (JN 10:10).
INSTRUMENTUM LABORIS
VATICAN CITY
1998

. . . .
. . . .
. . . .

A Moment of Grace for Asia

2. The Special Assembly for Asia is also an important moment for the people of Asia. During the last fifty years many countries in Asia have gained their independence. A modern and more self-confident Asia is emerging with its ancient cultures, philosophies and religious traditions. The twenty-first century and the Third Millennium will offer new challenges and opportunities to Asian peoples in shaping their own destiny and taking their places on the world scene. The Special Assembly for Asia, therefore, comes at a crucial moment in the history of the Asian continent, coming about in accord with the intention of Pope John Paul II as expressed in his Apostolic Letter *Tertio millennio adveniente(1)* and in his extensive treatment of the subject at the Plenary Assembly of the F.A.B.C. at Manila in January, 1995, in conjunction with his Apostolic Visitation to Asia for World Youth Day.(2)

The Topic of the Synod

3. The topic chosen by the Holy Father for the synod, namely, *Jesus Christ the Saviour and His Mission of Love and Service in Asia: "...that they may have life*

and have it abundantly" (*Jn* 10:10), is most appropriate for Asia, especially in the context of its plurality of religions and cultures, as well as the variety of socio-economic and political situations. This plurality and variety provides fertile ground for the saving message of Jesus Christ the Saviour and opportunity for Church initiatives to demonstrate the Lord's love for Asia's peoples through various acts of loving service aimed at putting into action the Lord's gospel of life. The Church came into being as a result of the salvific act of Jesus Christ in the mystery of his passion, death and resurrection. Her faith in Jesus Christ as the Saviour of the world is the centre of her faith, determining her mission of bringing the gift of eternal life to all. In Christ – the Church believes – all peoples, including those of Asia, can live as brothers and sisters in one large family of God in authentic freedom and newness of life. "For God so loved the world that he gave his only son, so that everyone who believes in him may not perish but may have eternal life" (*Jn* 3:16).

The mission of Jesus is to give fullness of life to all, especially to those in circumstances where life is threatened by sin, evil, selfishness, injustice and exploitation. In every human instance, Jesus wants to bring his life to bear. His mission concerns the life of the Spirit, the gift of eternal life: "Indeed, just as the Father raises the dead and gives life, so also the Son gives life to whomever he wishes...Very truly, I tell you, the hour is coming, and is now here, when the dead will hear the voice of the son of God, and those who hear will live" (*Jn* 5:21, 25).

A Mission of Love and Service to Life in Asia

4. The Gospels attest that Jesus offered life through deeds of love and service on behalf of all. Love and service take specific forms in Asia. They mean having a genuine regard for all Asia's peoples, appreciating their deep religious nature as well as their many cultures. This love is translated into action through various forms of service to the many peoples of Asia, especially the poor and those in need, so that all might share in the fullness of life which Jesus came to offer. Jesus' mission is that of bringing to all those in any form of captivity the glorious freedom of the children of God.

Such is also the mission of the Church as she seeks to renew herself through the celebration of the Jubilee of Redemption in Jesus Christ and as she prepares to enter the Third Millennium. Her mission today in Asia is to be at the service of life, particularly as lived by those suffering from the effects of sin and injustice.

The Synodal Pilgrimage

5. The Church in Asia is presently involved in a synodal journey, a journey which, it is hoped, will lead to internal renewal and a revitalization of the

commitment to proclaim the saving message of Jesus Christ through a new evangelization. In keeping with the etymological meaning of the word, *syn-odos*, "a walking together", this synodal journey is done in the company of Jesus Christ, in communion with all the particular Churches of Asia and with the worldwide Church, and in a spirit of unity not only with the Christian Churches and communities in Asia but also with the followers of the Great Religions and religious traditions in Asia.

Along the way, the Church wants to recognise the presence of the Spirit who reveals Jesus Christ in Asian realities. She wants to recognise the presence of Jesus Christ through humbly sharing in the life-experiences of the Asian peoples and through service to all. The Church in Asia seeks to do this, not as a stranger in a foreign cultural, organisational and liturgical garb but through means of Asian cultures, making her own "the joys and hopes, the griefs and anxieties of the people(3) of Asia.

CHAPTER I
ASIAN REALITIES
Asia in General

Geographic Area and Population

6. The vast continent of Asia extends from West Asia and the Gulf countries to the East Asian countries. The southern portion includes South Asia, Southeast Asia and East Asia. In the north, there are the Central Asian Republics and in the north east, Siberia and Mongolia. In this large land mass, the great distances are gapped by a multiplicity of races, religions and cultures.

The responses to the *Lineamenta* confirmed that Asia is a continent with numerous populations. Three-fourths of the world's population is in Asia, a significant number of which is youth. In this way, Asia is rich in human life and human potential.

Contrasts within Asia are equally striking at the level of social organisation, political life and patterns of economy and standards of life, both within the countries of Asia and between the countries themselves. Various responses point to the fact that where there is human life, the Church is present in varying ways and seeking to increase that presence in response to her mission of spreading the Gospel of Life.

Religions, Cultures and Ancient Civilisations

7. Asia is home to the great religions of the world such as Hinduism, Buddhism, Judaism, Christianity and Islam. It is also the birthplace of other religious

traditions such as Taoism, Confucianism, Zoroastrianism, Jainism, Sikhism, Shintoism, etc. Most are soteriological in character(4) and offer interpretations of the Absolute, the universe, the human person and his existential situation as well as evil and the means of liberation. It is in this religious context that the Church in Asia lives and bears witness to Jesus Christ.

Analysis of Asian realities would be incomplete without reference to what is today called Primal Religion or Traditional Religion. Across Asia there are millions of people who belong to Traditional Religion and other Primal Religions. Some of them have accepted the Christian faith. Many responses point to this fact and mention that the Church needs to enter into dialogue with the followers of Traditional Religion and seek to apply to the cultures which have developed in association with these religions the principles of inculturation in areas of theology, liturgy and spirituality, as a tool in announcing and living the message of life in Jesus Christ.

The religions of Asia have moulded the lives and cultures of Asian people for several millennia and continue to give meaning and direction for their lives even today.(5) In this sense, many responses indicate that the religions of Asia are indeed living religions, permeating every aspect of the life of the individual, family and society. A deep religious nature is one of the main characteristics of the Asian people, expressed in various ways in the family and social life at critical moments through rites of passage such as birth, marriage and death. Such moments are accompanied by prayer, rituals, sacrifices, reading of the Scriptures, fasting, pilgrimages and almsgiving. According to various responses, these positive elements of religion in Asia readily dispose the people to the saving message of Jesus Christ.

Asia is also the cradle of many ancient civilisations. They have had a significant influence not only on Asian cultures, but also on many cultures outside of Asia. Furthermore, some of them still show an extraordinary vitality today. These also require attention in the Church's mission on the continent.

Distinctive Characteristics and Situations Socio-economic

8. As expected, the responses to the *Lineamenta* portray a continent with many unique characteristics and a vast variety of situations.(6) From country to country, and even within countries themselves, many contrasting differences exist among peoples, cultures, and the circumstances and details of life.

Though a few countries of Asia have made considerable economic progress, a degrading and inhuman poverty, along with its consequent inequalities in many parts of Asia, is perhaps one of the most glaring and saddening phenomena of the continent. Though today's poverty can sometimes be traced back centuries, even millennia, certain injustices and other circumstances seem to be perpetuating this state of affairs. Certain responses have suggested the following: an unjust distribution of resources, unequal opportunities, unwillingness to carry out land reform, poor literacy campaigns, concentration of wealth in the hands of a few, state socialism which inevitably leads to corruption, economic waste and poor governance.

In some areas of Asia, despite rapid economic growth and development, poverty still remains the fate of whole sections of the population. In an ironic twist, in some countries of Asia where the living standard is increasing, cultural values are gradually being eroded, leading to egoism and the breakdown of family and social relationships. In such circumstances, many insist that the Church, besides providing a voice for the poor and oppressed, needs to provide pastoral services which will assist people, not only materially but spiritually in their course of development.

Industrialisation and urbanisation also figure into this situation. Rapid industrialisation, absence of land reform, diminishing prospects for livelihood in rural areas, the attraction of great cities and other such causes are changing the economic and demographic landscape of many Asian cities. Forced eviction of rural people to make room for mega industries and projects, financial and economic policies that favour the urban elite ignore the rights of the poor. Unplanned urbanisation is turning some cities of Asia into large slums where human dignity is oftentimes being lost.

Introduced into the economic situation is the question of bonded labour and child labour. All across Asia there are instances of several million bonded labourers, that is, workers under bond to work even for a lifetime for debts incurred in the past. Bonded labour is prevalent mostly in the brick- making industry, in stone quarries, the tobacco-cigarette industry, the carpet industry, etc. Despite national and international legislation, and commercial and political pressure, the problems related to the socio-economic situation in many countries of Asia remain unchanged, and in some cases, are even worsening. In her mission of love and service of life, the Church's message of the inviolable dignity of each human person and works commensurate with this teaching can serve the cause which can help improve such situations and lead to a process of development which respects human life.

Culture

9. Some responses indicate that the economic state of affairs is having collateral effects. New forms of culture are resulting from an over exposure to the mass media, books, magazines, music, films and other forms of entertainment. Although the media has the potential of being a great force for good, many responses mention that what seems to be reaching the Asian market is having an opposite effect. Its images of violence, hedonism, unbridled individualism and materialism is striking at the heart of Asian cultures, at the religious character

of the people, families and whole societies. Many responses lament the fact that the sacredness of marriage, the stability of family, and other traditional values are being threatened by the media and entertainment industries on the Asian continent. Such a situation is posing a serious challenges to the Church's message.

Influences from outside Asia are resulting from the movement of peoples for various reasons. Tourism, for example, is a legitimate industry and has its own cultural and educational values. However, in some countries the situation is described where it is having a devastating influence upon the moral and physical landscape of many Asian countries, manifested in prostitution and the degradation of young women, child abuse and prostitution.

In a similar way, responses indicate that migration within Asian countries, between the countries of Asia and from Asian countries to other continents, is posing increasing human and pastoral problems. Poverty, civil war, ethnic conflicts and economic factors are some of the causes of migration. Migrants, refugees and asylum seekers are often exposed to harsh treatment as well as economic and moral exploitation. Migrant foreign workers are often paid unjust wages and are sometimes required to work in inhuman conditions. They are also exposed to many health hazards and often left without the protection of law. Many call upon the Church in Asia to be sensitive to the pain and human drama caused by migration in and from Asia.

In many parts of Asia, persons belonging to ethnic groups such as tribals, indigenous peoples and minorities based on race, religion, culture, etc., are victims of the injustice of discrimination. In some countries, caste practices have isolated for centuries whole sections of populations, leaving a consequent psychological, cultural and economic trauma on the social conscience. Certain responses give attention to the particular problem created by discrimination against women and girl children. Despite recent efforts from many quarters to lessen this problem, such attitudes still prevail, affecting educational opportunities, work and wages for women. In such situations, the Church, as small as it might be in a given area, is seen as an instrument—through word and deed – of the saving message of Christ which can lead people to a greater awareness of the dignity of each human person and thus to a greater justice and harmony between people.

A number of responses to the *Lineamenta* touch on several other life- threatening and destructive tendencies in Asia. There is a growing lack of respect for human rights and human life itself, abortion, drug trafficking, addiction to various kinds of drugs, spread of AIDS, criminalisation of politics, use of violence to settle disputes, depletion of natural resources, disregard for ecological balance, absence of basic health services, fundamentalism in various forms, etc. These are all new areas in which the Church in Asia has an opportunity to carry out her mission of service of life.

Signs of Hope in Asia

10. Everywhere in Asia there is visible a new awareness carrying the Asian people to liberate themselves from the legacy of negative traditions, social evils and situations associated with the past. The ancient cultures and religions and their collective wisdom form the solid foundation on which to build the Asia of the future. Levels of literacy, education, research and technology are rising daily. Skilled workers, specialists in various sciences, technicians, researchers, inventors are on the increase. Democratic institutions are taking firm root in many countries. Many Asian countries are regaining a sense of self-confidence. There is a growing awareness of human dignity, despite failures in some areas. People are growing in their respect for human rights and they want to demand their rights from governments and institutions of power whether national or international. Regional co-operation is on the increase, especially with continental bodies such as the Association of South East Asian Nations (ASEAN) and the South Asia Association of Regional Cooperation (SAARC). Disputes between countries are more and more frequently settled through negotiations rather than armed conflicts. Mutual cooperation and trans-national investments within Asian countries is growing. These and similar factors provide much hope for the Asia of the future, and consequently, for the Church as well.

CHAPTER II
ECCLESIAL REALITIES OF ASIA
Many Churches

11. The ecclesial situation of Asia is as diverse and distinctive as its secular realities, as seen in the rich variety of Churches. Among the Churches of West Asia special mention must be made of the Churches of Antioch of the Syrians, Antioch of the Greek Melkites and Antioch of the Maronites as well as the Latin Church of Jerusalem. There are also the Chaldean Church of Babylonia and the Armenian Church. Today, most of these Churches live among predominantly Jewish or Islamic populations and cultures, serving their faithful who continue the Christian presence in these countries since the first centuries, and are witnesses to Jesus Christ among other religions.

Many responses mention that their work of evangelization is devoted mostly to works of charity and Christian witness through schools, hospitals and other apostolic works. They seek to project the image of a servant Church. While these Churches are inculturated in Islamic cultures and in the Arabic language, and hence well placed for dialogue with Islam, they are also in a region of conflicts and are threatened by religious fundamentalism.

Apostolic Churches, coming from the Syrian tradition, exist also in India, i.e., the Syro-Malabar Church and the Syro-Malankara Church. Responses indicate

that these Churches are well rooted in the Indian soil and are generally flourishing with a large number of vocations to the priesthood and the religious life.
They have a significant presence in the field of education, social and health services and mass media. Large numbers of faithful from these Churches have
migrated to many parts of India, the Gulf countries, Europe, Canada and the
United States. According to some responses to the *Lineamenta*, however, certain
situations related to liturgical tradition, rites, and synodal forms of Church
organization and administration are still posing difficulties for these Churches.
The Latin Church extends throughout the continent in varying stages of
development. For the most part, her presence has depended on the Church's
missionary efforts which have taken place in the last 500 years. The work of
missionaries has seen varied success in the course of the centuries. Recently, the
Holy Father has established three missions *sui iuris* in the Central Asian
Republics: Tadjikistan, Turkmenistan and Uzbekistan. In Siberia the Church is
happily discovering communities which have kept the faith alive despite the
adverse circumstances created by the past communist regime.

A Variety of Living Situations

12. In addition to the great number of Oriental Churches in Asia, there is a
great variety of situations in which these Churches are required to live.
In some parts of Asia, the Church lives in a predominantly Hindu milieu, posing great philosophical, theological and methodological challenges to the
Church's mission in Asia. At the same time, modern Hindu reformers are great
admirers of the person of Jesus Christ. In some cases, theologians in India have
been attempting to interpret Jesus Christ in terms of the dominant India
philosophy. Some responses mention that, in this and similar situations, the
Church needs to engage in a healthful dialogue and to seek to apply the
principles of inculturation in her attempts at evangelization.
With the exception of Indonesia, the presence of the Church in Muslim countries is small; in some cases communities have to deal with discrimination and
prejudice. Responses mention that certain communities have often to live in
difficult situations where the only type of evangelization which can be done is
daily witnessing to the faith and charitable works. In some countries, the
Church's members are being put to a real test.
In predominantly Buddhist, Confucian and Taoist countries, the Church is for
the most part in the minority. Some responses mention that for the past few
decades communities have been living under many restrictions to freedom of
worship, missionary work, and movement, and even persecutions. Despite
these obvious difficulties, responses mention that in some of these countries
there are signs of growth in the work of evangelization and human development.
In many cases, the championing of the cause of workers and the marginalised

classes as well as the example of the laity in the everyday life of the Church have contributed to a good image of the Church within society.

The Church in the Philippines, the only predominantly Catholic country in Asia, has a unique history of evangelization and growth through different periods of its five hundred year-old history; this has taken place with varying cultural influences. Certain responses mention that various events within the decade have served to assist the Church in a great movement towards renewal. As a result, the Church has a better understanding of evangelisation *ad intra* and *ad extra*, with all its social and spiritual dimensions. The Catholic character of the Philippines is an important factor in the Church's work of evangelisation on the Asian continent.

It is only recently that Central Asian Republics, Siberia and Mongolia began to receive attention at the international level, especially after the disintegration of the Soviet Union. This is true also of the Church. Missionary work has started in these countries. Some responses mention that the occasion of the Special Assembly for Asia is an opportunity to give greater attention to this region and to the work for the evangelization in these countries where there is a very limited Christian presence.

In some countries the Church lives amidst civil wars, caused by ethnic, communal or ideologically inspired conflicts. The Church as a community of communion, harmony and reconciliation has a mission to people in conflict situations, providing a special opportunity for her to preach in action her message in service to life.

A special situation is created for the Church as a result of sects and other religious movements which are becoming increasingly present and active in Asia. As in other parts of the world, certain social patterns and changes are causing people, especially young people, to embark on a search for meaning in their lives, oftentimes looking to the sects and religious movements because they give an immediate sense of well-being, community feeling, and fellowship. Many responses see the great need of the Church to respond this situation, especially in revitalising her pastoral commitment to the spiritual needs of people, strengthen Christian fellowship and education to prayer and use of the Scriptures.

The Image of the Church in Asia

13. Many responses relate that, in the work of evangelisation, the Church in Asia needs to be aware of the image she has among believers of other faiths and non-believers. While the Church is admired for her organisational, administrative, educational, health services, and developmental works, these people often do not see the Church as totally Asian, not simply because much financial support comes from western countries, but also because of her western character in theology, architecture, art, etc. and her association with the past history in

some sections of Asia. Therefore, some people are reluctant to accept Christianity fearing a loss of national identity and culture.

Aware of this fact, the bishops in Asia are attempting to address the matter.

With few exceptions, the Church in Asia is seen as a clerical institution, e.g., in administration, liturgy, formation, etc. Many responses mention that the laity, especially women and young people, are eager to become more actively involved in various levels of the local Churches. They also wish to take part in programs of catechesis and ongoing formation so as to fulfill their role in the mission of the Church in Asia. In some cases, the responses sought a greater cooperation among the various states in the Church so that the evangelising mission of the Church might be more effective.

Christian Mission and Asian Religions

14. The Western Christian missionary approach to other Asian religions, popular devotions and spirituality, with the notable exception of people like Ricci and Valignano in China and Japan, and De Nobili and Beschi in India, oftentimes lacked a full appreciation of these elements. At times, there was also an inadequate regard for Asian cultures. Even though the missionaries efforts met with many successes, it is felt that a proper understanding of these elements in the work of evangelisation would have led to a greater acceptance of the faith by the people of Asia. Therefore, some responses mention that the Church's rediscovered appreciation of other religions and cultures should find greater expression in her missionary approach.

Positive Elements and Signs of Hope
Lay Witness

15. The responses to the *Lineamenta* indicate many positive elements in the particular Churches in Asia. Most of the Church faithful can be termed "practising Catholics," who for the most part give priority to a sacramental and devotional life. The fact that Asians are religious by nature seems to be of assistance in this regard. In many parts of Asia, family prayer, reading of the Scriptures and family devotions nourish the religious life of the faithful. In a particular way, Catholics put their faith in action in moments of natural calamities and communal strife.

The emergence and growth of Basic Christian Communities, charismatic movements and Basic Human Communities are also very positive elements in a number of particular Churches. Some events sponsored by charismatic movements, such as days of spiritual retreat, prayer meetings and gatherings of spiritual renewal, have attracted national interest in which several thousands of the followers of other religions have participated. Ecclesial movements also offer an opportunity to many to enter into dialogue with the followers of other religions.

Certain responses refer to the migration of Christians in and outside Asia whose regular religious practice assists in spreading the faith. In this regard, missionary sisters, brothers and priests from Asia are sent to serve these people and the local Churches in several parts of the world, such as Africa, Latin America, Oceania, etc. This is a most welcome missionary phenomenon in Asia. It is estimated that several thousand priests, religious sisters and brothers, and lay persons are working as missionaries in countries other than their own in Asia and elsewhere.

In a number of particular Churches in Asia, the laity increasingly exercise their role in the life and mission of the Church, as exemplified by lay institutes in Japan and the Philippines. In some countries, the laity play an important role at the national level in politics, education, healthcare, etc. There are permanent structures in many countries of Asia for the formation of the laity in theology, spirituality, and other related subjects. There are also centres where the laity, the clergy and bishops come together for pastoral planning and work. These are very promising initiatives for the future of the Church in Asia.

Consecrated Witness

16. Certain parts of the Church in Asia have shown a steady increase in the number of vocations during the past decades. While many vocations go to traditional religious congregations and institutes which are western in origin, in recent years a number of new local religious congregations have sprung up in Asia. In general, the percentage of vocations to the priesthood, the religious life other forms of consecrated life and missionary institutes is higher than in most other parts of the universal Church.

The Christian witness of love and service to the poor shown by Mother Theresa and her Missionaries of Charity as well as by many other religious women and men have contributed greatly to reveal to the peoples of Asia the authentic countenance of Jesus Christ and the true nature of the Church. Many responses mention how greatly welcomed and appreciated is the Church's presence in homes for the handicapped, orphanages, leprosaria, rural dispensaries and in movements which seek to meet the needs of the marginalised.

In many cases, this service provided by missionaries has led to martyrdom. Their testimony in the history of evangelization has enriched the life of the Church in China, Japan, Korea, Vietnam and many other countries of Asia. The witness of the martyrs of the past and the present is a great means of evangelisation. Therefore, certain responses voice a hope and desire that the Church will consider more Asian martyrs in the canonical process leading to sainthood.

Witness in Asia has also come from a great many of the Church's religious orders and congregations who have made a major contribution to the growth of the local Churches in Asia during the last five hundred years of evangelization. Tens of thousands of religious sisters and brothers, by their love and unselfish service to those who suffer from poverty in its many forms, have contributed to nourishing the faith of many in the Church in Asia. Some of these have given an invaluable service to local Churches by establishing houses of formation, especially seminaries. They have been able to reveal the compassionate, loving and caring face of Jesus to the peoples of Asia. Religious brothers have given an outstanding service to the cause of general education, vocational training, technical education and developmental works Contemplative religious have also made a unique contribution to the Christian mission in Asia by their prayers and their witness of complete dedication to a life of union with God. Some responses refer to missionary institutes of diocesan clergy which have had a great share in the work of evangelization in Asia. Some of them have sent thousands of missionaries to Asia during the last four hundred years. Today, they are followed by several Asian-born missionary institutes. A good number of diocesan priests is volunteering for missionary work in other countries. Some of the earliest seminaries for local clergy in Asia were established by them.

Ecclesial Institutions

17. The Church in Asia has a large network of various kinds of institutions, despite the fact that in some places Christians form a tiny minority of the population. In some countries, where the Christian population is as low as 2%, the percentage of Church related institutions is as high as 30% of non-governmental organisations and voluntary organisations operating in the field of social services. The Church has a formidable instrument in its hands to bear witness to Christ's compassion, love and concern for the poor of Asia. Perhaps the greatest among these are her educational institutions, i.e., primary schools, high schools, colleges and universities. The Church also has healthcare institutions, such as hospitals, medical colleges, dispensaries and other health centres. There are homes for the elderly, the handicapped, the blind and those with speech and hearing disabilities. Moreover, the Church has a good number of publishing centres for books, reviews, news papers, weeklies, popular magazines.

In recent years a number of renewal centres, ashrams, spirituality centres, audio-visual centres and broadcasting stations have also been started by Christians in Asia. Nearly every country in Asia has now pastoral and catechetical centres. Furthermore, the Church has established institutions for human promotion, human rights, inculturation, etc.

The Church in Asia has not only institutions, but a relatively large number of very qualified, dedicated and efficient personnel to run all its institutions.

However, certain responses pose the question: "Are all Church institutions also centres of Christian values and witness in a largely non- Christian environment?" and "How can these institutions serve as a tool of Christian witness and service to life in Asia?"

Conclusion

18. The Asian continent is characterised by a diversity of religions, cultures and peoples as well as of ecclesial realities. Their coming together in Synod is itself a grace and an example for the peoples of Asia which can work for the welfare and progress of the continent and all its peoples. It is in this continent that God has called together Christians in Jesus Christ through the Holy Spirit. It is in the context of the socio-economic realities, its political history and present situation, and in the context of its multi-religious traditions that the little flock of Jesus Christ must live and carry out its saving mission.

CHAPTER III
A BRIEF EVALUATION OF CATHOLIC MISSION HISTORY IN ASIA
The Faith and Its Impact

The Gift of Faith

19. From Apostolic times to the present faith in Jesus Christ is the gift brought by the missionaries and offered to all in Asia. The term 'missionary' includes not simply missionaries from outside Asia, but all native missionaries, clerical and lay, diocesan clergy and those in consecrated life, and Christian communities which witness to Jesus Christ and carry the Good News to their neighbours within the Asian continent or to far off lands. Their example of Christian charity, spirit of dedication, service and sacrifice plants the seeds of faith in the hearts of countless Asians. The fact that tens of thousands of Christians gave their lives in times of persecutions in many Asian countries, especially in Vietnam, Japan, China and Korea, is proof that the faith has taken deep root in the hearts of the Asian people. For this, the Church in Asia rejoices and expresses her gratitude to missionaries who are bringing the faith to various parts of Asia. She also rejoices in the great number of Asian missionaries at work outside their own areas and countries.

Today, in almost every Asian country a Christian presence exists; in some it is a significant number of people, in others, a small minority. By and large, the particular Churches of Asia are well established and have their local clergy and religious to carry out their pastoral and missionary duties. Thanks to missionaries, local communities were established; they were nurtured with continuing catechesis and developed ecclesial structures, a sacramental life and devotions to support their Christian life. At present, these communities have become self-supporting Churches in many ways, though not fully.

Leaven in Society

20. Because of the presence of the local Church in a given country, the Gospel is being announced, becoming a leaven in Asian society, even if not always acknowledged as such. The Gospel has the power to transform Asian societies. It has challenged many social systems and evils in Asian society and acted as an agent of critical judgment. As a result, a number of reform movements within several Asian countries have come about.

Though the Church was not fully involved in independence movements, indirectly she has inspired such movements. In many cases, independence movements were initiated by persons educated in Christian institutions in Asia and abroad. Several outstanding personalities at the highest levels of national life, past and present, were taught in missionary institutions.

Christian mission in general has been an agent of the advancement of culture. In fact, many missionaries were men and women outstanding as linguists, scholars, historians poets and scientists. Many Asian languages were put into writing and foundational books, such a grammars, dictionaries, etc., were done by missionaries. Besides making significant contributions to existing Asian languages, both classical and modern, missionaries also translated many Christian classics into several Asian languages, thus enriching many languages. In this way, they also gained the respect and gratitude many non-Christians. They also became engaged in the publication of popular magazines, scientific reviews, weeklies, daily newspapers, and scholarly books. In some cases, missionaries were also the instruments and channels of introducing modern science into several countries in Asia. Some distinguished themselves as anthropologists, sociologists, and historians of tribal peoples, indigenous peoples, minorities, and marginalised sections of society. In several parts of Asia, missionaries are responsible for the establishment of libraries at the popular and scholarly levels. In a related manner, higher rates of literacy and education have also accompanied the spread of the Gospel, particularly in Asia where in many areas education was limited to the higher classes of society. The Church has undertaken programs to help eliminate illiteracy in Asia and increase the level of education of its people, providing educational opportunities at the elementary level as well as at higher levels of learning. In many places in Asia, girls and women, who were formally excluded from this field, are now receiving an education. Along the same lines, the Church has been instrumental in introducing and encouraging technical, professional, vocational and industrial education in several cases. It has also brought new attitudes and values to manual work and its inherent human dignity.

Human Services

21. Wherever the Church's mission has gone, the care of human life and service to life have followed. Missionaries, particularly religious sisters and Christian

nurses, have distinguished themselves in their evangelical witness to the healing ministry of Jesus. As a result, the Asian continent can boast of hundreds of hospitals and thousands of dispensaries run by the Church, primarily in the midst of the poorer classes. Such action has led to alleviating malnutrition, the curing of various illnesses and the providing of better child care, preventive medicine, diagnostic services, etc.

Missionaries and Christians in general have been present in rescue operations and resettlement works in times of natural calamities like earth quakes, floods and drought. In times of famine they have been very generous with personnel and means. In a number of cases, Christian missionaries have been, and still are, in the forefront for the development of small scale cottage industries, employment schemes, co-operatives, rural banks, etc. By establishing co-operative and rural banks they offer assistance to persons in personal economic matters, with many families benefiting from such self-help projects.

Social Reform

22. The Gospel contains the seeds of human dignity, freedom and human rights. Thus, the Church has been able to show herself on the Asian continent to be a defender of human dignity and rights. In this way, the presence of Christian mission has led to reforms in several areas social life. In a number of cases, the missionaries and their Christian followers have provided the impulse towards the formulation and application of legislation relating to prison reform, total hours of work, the health and safety of workers in mines and health-hazard industries, protection of women and children in certain industries, etc. The support given to marginalised peoples, tribals, fisherfolk, refugees and the working classes is generally acknowledged throughout the Asian continent.

Through introducing the education of girls, the Church in Asia has given a great impetus towards the emancipation of women in general and in many specific areas. It is mainly education that enables women to have an equal status in society. With the entry of religious sisters into the Asian missionary scene, the process of social emancipation of women gained a fresh momentum. In challenging a number of religious and social customs, the announcement of the Christian Gospel has led to legislation against caste practices, permitting temple entry to the so-called untouchables (*Harijans*), and discouraging the practice of self-immolation by widows (*satti*).

Christian mission in Asia has also brought about an increase in vocations among women. They in turn have been instruments of social change through their work as teachers and other educational works, health services as teachers, nurses, dedicated to the service of the poor, the sick and the handicapped.

Critical Aspects

23. Where several Churches in Asia can trace their roots to Apostolic times, the spread of the Gospel in Asia has met with difficulty. The missionary efforts of the early Church towards Central Asia and China made by the Syrian Church did meet with some success. In fact, in the first eight centuries of the Church, the Gospel had reached the farthest ends of Asia, to China as far as Beijing. The western missionary efforts of the Franciscans in the XIII century led by Giovanni da Montecorvino in China also had some limited success. Nevertheless, most of the particular Churches founded as a result of the Syrian missionary efforts and by the Franciscans were practically destroyed because of various causes, such as the Islamic invasions, difficulties in encountering ancient religious traditions, an inadequate appreciation of Asian philosophic, religious and cultural systems, etc.

Most of the present day particular Churches in Asia are the fruit of modern missionary efforts originating in the West from the 16th century. Taking advantage of the European colonial movement, the Church sent missionaries to spread the message of the Gospel. In the course of their work, these missionaries encountered ancient and highly developed philosophical systems, social organisations and religions traditions, such as Hinduism, Buddhism, Confucianism and Taoism, which over the centuries have developed profound religious and philosophical explanations concerning the absolute, the universe and the person, seeking to illuminate humanity's present condition, its final destiny and the ways to reach that destiny. These teachings were supported by deeply moving scriptures, liturgical rites, prayers, methods of contemplation, the practice of virtues for every stage of humanity's pilgrimage to salvation and self-realisation. Sacred art, architecture, and worship also belonged to a highly developed system. The lives of the Asian people of today, at the individual, family and social levels, are deeply permeated by religious sentiments and practices. Popular religious practices, places of pilgrimage, centres of prayer and dialogue, myths and stories bring the philosophical religion to the level of the masses. Thus every aspect of social life is imprinted with a deep sense of religion. On the other hand, there is no compelling hierarchical structures to determine and guide religious beliefs. A wide spectrum of faith and morals is permissible. Religious authority is based not on official position, but on the religious leaders' experience of God and his ability to communicate it to others.

Asian religions propose to give an answer to man's search for the meaning of life, values, and an explanation and interpretation of the universe, his actual state of religious and moral ambivalence, his situation of brokenness, self-alienation, and evil. They also offer concrete means of liberation from the present existential predicament of evil, suffering, death, and provide spiritualities for self-realisation. Moreover, they hold to the nobility of their religious traditions, interpretations and means of liberation- salvation.

This is the context in which the present Christian mission is to take place. Therefore, the new evangelisation is called upon to consider not simply the content of the Gospel message, but those to whom it is directed. This was the conviction of great missionaries like Francis Xavier and Valignano in Japan, Ricci in China, De Nobili and Beschi in India. Among the causes in the past why the efforts of the Church's missionaries in Asia met with limited success, might there be a lack of proper understanding of Asian religions, their inherent values and strengths, their centuries-old teachings, their inner power of self-renewal as well as a reluctance to adopt methods which were suited to the Asian mentality?

In evaluating the Church's program of a new evangelisation in Asia, the question of properly understanding an Asian mentality might also be raised in conjunction with past historical experiences which colour the present situation. Among these are such historically sensitive issues as colonialism, the *padroado*, inculturation of the Gospel, reaction to a perceived Westernisation, etc.

. . . .
. . . .
. . . .
. . . .

Some Perceptions of Christ in Asia

30. As for the image of Christ among other Asians, many responses point out that by natural disposition most Asians have a positive outlook towards Christ, seeing him as a deeply spiritual, compassionate and loving person. Some consider Him a great Teacher. A particularly favourite image for Christ among Buddhists is that of the Sacred Heart.

If some Christians have difficulty in properly understanding the human nature of Christ, most Asians would view him exclusively from this perspective. To respond sufficiently to this fact, the Church needs to place greater emphasis on presenting Christ in the wider context of salvation history and the master plan of God the Creator for the universe, a plan, fulfilled in the Incarnation and Redemption of Christ, and still being worked out in Christ, through His Church, in the present moment in time. To achieve this, some insist that a greater attention should be given to presenting Christ "in Asian garb", that is, using the support of various philosophical and cultural concepts. Such an approach seems all the more important in the context of the Church's dialogue with other religions, especially Hinduism and Buddhism. The question then is: "How can the Church in Asia explain that Christ is the one and only Saviour and unique mediator of salvation distinct from the founders of Asia's other great religions?(9)

In some cases, followers of various Asian religions are increasingly prepared to accept Jesus Christ even as God. However, this does not seem to be a reason for them to accept him as the only Saviour. The trend among the followers of these religions, especially the Hindus, is to consider all religions as equally good. For them, the Hindu gods and Christ are only the different manifestations of the same God. Even those who believe in Christ as God do not see the necessity to embrace the Christian religion, much less the Church, despite the fact that the Church and her institutions do much for society in general.

Asian people, both of the classic religions and traditional and cosmic religions seek to live in harmony between heaven and earth, between the realm of the divine and the human, between the transcendent and the immanent. These apparently contrasting and contradictory realities paradoxically merge into one in many Asian religions. The distance between them is overcome philosophically and liturgically. Christian liturgy expresses it wonderfully when it says: "Would that you rend the heaven and come down" (*Is* 63:19). Such an encounter between the divine and the human, the absolute transcendent and the finite has definitively taken place in Jesus Christ.

Based on the above situation, many responses state that there is a need to present Jesus in the context of this search by Asian religions and cultures for harmony between apparent paradoxes which confront human existence: between transcendence and immanence, emptiness and fullness, death and life, suffering and joy, the finite and the infinite, poverty and riches, weakness and power, the temporal and the eternal, the historical and the cosmic. In Jesus Christ, the incarnate Word of God, crucified and risen, the above paradoxes find a point of convergence. Some responses to the *Lineamenta* speak of a need for developing a Christology of *kenosis*, namely, a Christology based on the self-emptying of Christ in the mystery of the Incarnation and his glorification in the Paschal Mystery.

However, many responses mention that beyond intellectual arguments, true witness to Christ among the Asian people will result when the gap between religion and service is surmounted, in other words, when believers truly become the *living signs of the Lord Jesus Christ* through the exercise of the spiritual and corporal works of mercy. In this way, for the Asian, who sets high priorities on such concepts as community, harmony, peace and deliverance from evil, the faithful's living of the Christian faith will be a compelling form of witness to Christ. At the same time, the rites of the sacraments, devotions, prayers, etc. also reveal, in their own way, the person of Christ, making his saving message known and providing a powerful invitation to the unbeliever towards participation. In this regard, certain responses suggest that greater attention be given to the inculturation of the faith, so as to search for ways among Asian mentalities and cultures – while remaining faithful to the essential content of the faith–to express more clearly and effectively what it means to live in Christ.

. . . .
. . . .
. . . .

The Service of Dialogue

49. The mission of the Church takes place in interaction with others of which dialogue is an important aspect. Dialogue is a means of mutual knowledge, enrichment and communication of the saving message and life of Jesus Christ. True dialogue involves both giving and receiving, speaking and listening. Many responses to the *Lineamenta* have urged that attention be given, in the Church's mission of love and service in Asia, to the service created by dialogue, both with religions and cultures. These responses centre upon the need for dialogue in the present context of Asian societies and the need for a grassroots approach to dialogue, in other words, a dialogue of life.

Modern Asian societies are multi-cultural societies, composed of many different religious, ethnic, and linguistic groups living together. This is true today more than at any time in the past. Increased mobility has resulted in regions where formerly people of only one ethnic or religious group had lived, now manifest plurality in social life. Most urban neighbourhoods and rural villages today are made up of people of various religions and social backgrounds. This has led to a situation in which ethnic, linguistic, and religious groups find themselves trying to maintain and promote their identity, at times creating a danger that national societies become fragmented.

Though various difficulties need to be overcome in the area of dialogue, the Church, committed to being a sign and sacrament of unity among all peoples, pursues the path of dialogue, particularly inter-religious dialogue, on many levels so as to bring good to the many groups which suffer from injustice, discrimination or marginalisation and, at the same time, to contribute through the application of her social doctrine to build societies based on principles of justice, peace and harmony.

In seeking to apply the teachings of the Second Vatican Council and subsequent Magisterium on dialogue in the situations of the local Churches in Asia, some bishops in Asia have placed an emphasis on what they term a "dialogue of life and heart.(43) This type of dialogue refers to Christians and followers of other religions living the highest ideals of their respective faiths in the midst of others. Their lives become the dialogue in which each offers and each receives from the other and in which all are enriched. In the dialogue of life, each strives to express the values derived from their faith, while at the same time remaining open to listening and learning from their neighbours.

The concept of dialogue of life was endorsed by Pope John Paul II in his 1990 encyclical letter *Redemptoris missio*. There he described the dialogue of life as one in which "believers of various religions bear witness to one another in daily life concerning human and spiritual values and help one another to live them in order to build a more just and fraternal society....all the faithful and every Christian community is called to practice dialogue, although not in the same way nor to the same degree."(44)

Several responses to the *Lineamenta* noted that although the term is new, the reality of the dialogue of life has been practised by people of various faiths at the grassroots for centuries in Asia. Other responses noted that the dialogue of life has many applications in Asia. Christian schools can become "laboratories" for students and teachers to learn the dialogue of life. Christian hospitals and other healthcare projects can be places where people of all faiths seek to comfort one another and offer hope from the richness of their respective faiths. Cloistered sisters, who lead lives of prayer and love, in open friendship with their neighbours of other faiths, have shown themselves to be among the most effective practitioners of the dialogue of life.

Dialogue at the grassroots level points up another need for the Church in Asia to come to a greater awareness and appreciation of the religious character of the Asian people. Responses to the Lineamenta insist that there are important spiritual values preserved in popular religiosity which deserve respect and offer values sometimes neglected in the lives of modern Asians, e.g., reverence for nature, the divine presence on earth and the value of familial and communitarian solidarity. A major task of the Church in Asia is to promote respect for cultures and beliefs of Asia's indigenous peoples and demonstrate a greater solidarity towards them through actions of love and service.

The Mission of Bringing the Faith to Culture

50. Inculturation results from the interaction which takes place between faith and culture. In such an interaction, the faith takes visible form and becomes intelligible to believers and others, while positive cultural values are purified and assimilated into the faith. Many responses mention that the new evangelisation in Asia urgently needs to consider the process of inculturation so that the Gospel might take on a real Asian character. True inculturation means "the intimate transformation of authentic cultural values through their integration in Christianity in the various human cultures"(45)

Many responses to the *Lineamenta* deal with the question of inculturation of the Christian faith in the cultures of Asia. The responses from West Asia indicated that inculturation is not so much a problem to be faced today as the natural process by which the Churches in the region developed since the time of the Apostles. There is a centuries-long history of inculturation in language, art, architecture, liturgy, and social organization. Inculturation is expressed today in the continued study by seminarians, clergy, and laity of the Syrian and Arabic traditions of theology, philosophy, spirituality, and liturgy. Inculturation has also meant that Arab culture has been profoundly influenced, over the centuries, by local Christians.

The Eastern Churches in India are engaged in trying to preserve their indigenous traditions and are seeking to assimilate Western artistic and liturgical traditions.

It is felt that inculturation in theology, liturgy, spirituality, art, etc., will emerge only when Christians as a community live the life-style of the masses, understand their ways of thinking and speak their language.

Elsewhere in Asia, inculturation is seen as major challenge for the Church. The approach to inculturation is complicated by the fact that in modern Asia no "pure culture" exists. Asian cultures are continually evolving and incorporating elements from elsewhere. There is an emerging "culture of the city" that often bears little relation to life in the provinces. Some responses are concerned that the power of the Western media and advertising industry are producing a universal "mono-culture" which threatens to drive traditional Asian cultures to extinction. Various experiments in inculturation are producing mixed reactions and effects in the particular Churches. Despite some reservations, the majority of responses regard inculturation as "a major missionary challenge" for the Church.

In its encounter with Asian cultures, dialogue is a two-way process. Religious traditions and symbolic systems of Asian religions can enrich the faith of Christians, but cultural elements cannot be adopted uncritically. Some customs and symbolism will be found to be incompatible with the message that Jesus came to teach and embody. Christians in Asia, as elsewhere in the world, have a duty throughout the world to challenge their cultures and seek to purify them.

The need for inculturation in the field of theology and theological research is often mentioned in the responses. Many maintain that theological expression should draw from the field of culture. A proper application of the process of inculturation would see theological training in seminaries and the work of theological faculties using elements from various Asian philosophical systems, in addition to those already taught in the West, to make more intelligible for the Asian mind the rich theological content of the message of salvation in Jesus Christ. In this way Asian theologians can take more seriously the cultural context, thought patterns, and world views of their regions. This process of inculturation is also important in the area of Christian spirituality through exploring how the richness of Asian spiritual traditions can be lived and transformed through contact with Christ's Paschal mystery.

The efforts in inculturation throughout Asia to move towards giving the Church a truly Asian character offer a sense of richness to the universal Church. Inculturation brings about unity in diversity, in which all local Churches enrich one another by their various attempts to delve deeply to the heart of the Christian mystery and to express that faith in culturally understandable ways.

The Service of Human Promotion

51. The Church, following the example of the Master, is committed to human dignity and promotion in all her evangelizing activities. This ought to be so in

a very special manner in Asia where hundreds of millions of people still live in inhuman poverty. Massive poverty is one of those Asian realities that should help all to widen the concept and scope of evangelization in Asia. The Church in Asia can come to the aid of the poor in various ways. One way is to bring attention to the burden of foreign debts accumulated by some countries of Asia, because of past and present injustices.

The Church's evangelizing mission in Asia is carried out in the context of the triple dialogue with the poor, with people of other religions, and with Asian cultures. As disciples of Jesus, the members of the Church in Asia must turn their attention to all that threatens, weakens, diminishes, and destroys the life of individuals, groups, or peoples. Just as Jesus Christ confronted the forces of sin and enslavement in his day, so today the task of the Church is to struggle constantly against all that enslaves people.

The responses of the Church on human promotion vary according to the concrete situation, the needs and problems of each region and the structures existing in a given society. The Church's contribution to human promotion includes vocally denouncing injustices, supporting victims in their just causes, caring for the marginalised and suffering, joining together with all persons of good will who seek to build a more just and humane society, engaging in the analysis of the given situation in order to arrive at the root causes of poverty and injustice, and faith reflection on pastoral action.

The Church's traditional social works of caring for those in need are expanded today to include new groups of suffering people. Throughout Asia, in addition to orphanages, homes for the elderly, schools, hospitals, and clinics for the destitute, centres for the handicapped and leprosaria, the Church today conducts, for example, drug treatment programs, rehabilitation centres for prostitutes, hospitality centres for seafarers, centres and residences for HIV/AIDS patients, and an apostolate to an increasing number of prisoners who are undocumented workers. While the Church in Asia strives to oppose forces which threaten the dignity and well-being of the individual, she also works to encourage people to form a better society. In Asian countries, the Church has been active in pro-democracy movements aimed at establishing participatory democracies and humane government, in monitoring elections, in working for legislation against graft and corruption, in efforts at reconciliation after communal clashes, and in establishing peace in regions torn by civil war.

In many countries in Asia, the Church has sponsored workshops and training programs aimed at teaching social analysis to get at the root causes of injustice and poverty. In studies on arms proliferation and trade, in communal and interreligious conflicts, in development projects for tourism, logging, mining, and damming, social analysis is used to raise consciousness regarding who is benefiting and who is suffering from such projects. In many instances, Christian activists have discovered that it is primarily local politicians and foreign multinationals who profit, while the local poor are displaced.

The responses to the *Lineamenta* emphasize that in all these expressions of a preferential love for the poor, which are seen as integral aspects of the Church's evangelizing mission, Christians do not act alone. Many of their most devoted and self-sacrificing partners in striving to oppose abuses and build better societies are Muslims, Buddhists, Hindus, followers of Traditional Religions, as well as secular non-religious individuals. Some of the most fruitful forms of dialogue of action are those in which Christians and other believers join hands to address the problems of society and serve the poor in loving cooperation.

The Service to Creation

52. Ecological concerns are gaining in popularity throughout the world. In this area, the Church's teaching on the stewardship of creation, i.e., the responsible use, care and protection of the world created by God has much to offer in both discussion and practise. In Asia there are particular concerns in this area, requiring the pastoral attention of the Church. Consumerism and greed strikes at the root of the sources of life, namely, the seas, rivers, forests, plant and animal life. Unabated technological research and experiments can unsettle eco-systems and balances and endanger future generations and their life on earth. People of today have the responsibility to pass intact to future generations the resources of earth, sea and sky, since they form one support system for life given by the creator God and Sustainer of all things.

Many responses mention that the Church, though a minority, needs to make the faithful aware of the ecological problems facing humanity and find ways to bring these matters to the attention of policy makers of the Asian countries and world organizations. By means of catechesis, pastoral guidance and prophetic declarations the Church can give a very timely service to decision makers in politics, industry, economics, trade and other such areas.

The Means of Social Communication

53. The Church today seeks to preach the perennial saving message of Jesus Christ, crucified and risen, so that the riches of his life might always be communicated to those who will open their hearts in conversion to the promptings of the Spirit.

The responses to the *Lineamenta* note that, since the mass media have a growing influence even in remote areas of the Asian continent, the proclamation of the Gospel message can greatly benefit by better employing this modern technology. Some ask for a more inclusive view of the term "means of social communication", going beyond the customary idea of the technical structures and processes of communication in human society. In speaking of the means of evangelisation, Pope Paul VI listed along with the mass media: witness of life, preaching, personal contact, and popular piety. In the Asian context, all the traditional forms of human communication from Asian cultures can be added, such as dance, theatre, drama, speech, shadow plays etc.. In this way, a particularly rich communication spectrum provides possibilities in the work of evangelisation, far beyond what is possible solely through the restrictive term "mass media".

Responses further maintain that the communications explosion in Asia through satellites, internet, video-conferencing, etc., raise a new challenge for evangelisation. Pope John Paul II states in the encyclical letter *Redemptoris missio*, the means of social communication "have become so important as to be for many the chief means of information and education, of guidance and inspiration in their behaviour as individuals, families and within society at large. In particular the younger generation is growing up in a world conditioned by the mass media."(46) The Holy Father then asks, "Since the very evangelization of modern culture depends to a great extent on the influence of the media, it is not enough to use the media simply to spread the Christian message and the Church's authentic teaching. It is also necessary to integrate that message into the new culture created by modern communication...The new culture originates not just from whatever content is eventually expressed, but from the very fact that there exist new ways of communicating with a new language, new techniques and new psychology."(47) How far is the Church in Asia responding to these "new ways"?

Modern means of social communication challenges the Church in Asia towards three concrete areas of action: 1) the Church in Asia needs to increase her presence in the world of the mass media in order to communicate the Gospel message as well as the social and moral teachings of the Magisterium; 2) the Church needs to enter into the "modern areopagus" through the means of social communications in order to evangelize society and transform, through the values of the Gospel, the new culture being shaped by the means of social communication; and 3) all Church personnel, both clerical and lay, need to receive adequate exposure and training in the use of the mass media and means of social communications. At the same time, the Gospel must be brought into the lives of those who control and those who are engaged in the mass media in different ways.

. . . .
. . . .
. . . .

ENCYCLICAL LETTER
FIDES ET RATIO
OF THE SUPREME PONTIFF
JOHN PAUL II
TO THE BISHOPS
OF THE CATHOLIC CHURCH
ON THE RELATIONSHIP
BETWEEN FAITH AND REASON*

. . . .
. . . .

Faith and reason are like two wings on which the human spirit rises to the contemplation of truth; and God has placed in the human heart a desire to know the truth – in a word, to know himself – so that, by knowing and loving God, men and women may also come to the fullness of truth about themselves (cf. *Ex* 33:18; *Ps* 27:8-9; 63:2-3; *Jn* 14:8; *1 Jn* 3:2).

INTRODUCTION
"KNOW YOURSELF"

1. In both East and West, we may trace a journey which has led humanity down the centuries to meet and engage truth more and more deeply. It is a journey which has unfolded – as it must – within the horizon of personal self-consciousness: the more human beings know reality and the world, the more they know themselves in their uniqueness, with the question of the meaning of things and of their very existence becoming ever more pressing. This is why all that is the object of our knowledge becomes a part of our life. The admonition *Know yourself* was carved on the temple portal at Delphi, as testimony to a basic truth to be adopted as a minimal norm by those who seek to set themselves apart from the rest of creation as "human beings", that is as those who "know themselves".

Moreover, a cursory glance at ancient history shows clearly how in different parts of the world, with their different cultures, there arise at the same time the fundamental questions which pervade human life: *Who am I? Where have I come from and where am I going? Why is there evil? What is there after this life?* These are the questions which we find in the sacred writings of Israel, as also in the Veda and the Avesta; we find them in the writings of Confucius and Lao-Tze, and in the preaching of Tirthankara and Buddha; they appear in the poetry of Homer and in the tragedies of Euripides and Sophocles, as they do in the philosophical writings of Plato and Aristotle. They are questions which have their common source in the quest for meaning which has always compelled the human heart. In fact, the answer given to these questions decides the direction which people seek to give to their lives.

2. The Church is no stranger to this journey of discovery, nor could she ever be. From the moment when, through the Paschal Mystery, she received the gift of the ultimate truth about human life, the Church has made her pilgrim way along the paths of the world to proclaim that Jesus Christ is "the way, and the truth, and the life" (*Jn* 14:6). It is her duty to serve humanity in different ways, but one way in particular imposes a responsibility of a quite special kind: the *diakonia of the truth*.(1) This mission on the one hand makes the believing community a partner in humanity's shared struggle to arrive at truth; (2) and on the other hand it obliges the believing community to proclaim the certitudes arrived at, albeit with a sense that every truth attained is but a step towards that fullness of truth which will appear with the final Revelation of God: "For now we see in a mirror dimly, but then face to face. Now I know in part; then I shall understand fully" (*1 Cor* 13:12).

3. Men and women have at their disposal an array of resources for generating greater knowledge of truth so that their lives may be ever more human. Among these is *philosophy*, which is directly concerned with asking the question of life's meaning and sketching an answer to it. Philosophy emerges, then, as one of noblest of human tasks. According to its Greek etymology, the term philosophy means "love of wisdom". Born and nurtured when the human being first asked questions about the reason for things and their purpose, philosophy shows in different modes and forms that the desire for truth is part of human nature itself. It is an innate property of human reason to ask why things are as they are, even though the answers which gradually emerge are set within a horizon which reveals how the different human cultures are complementary.
Philosophy's powerful influence on the formation and development of the cultures of the West should not obscure the influence it has also had upon the ways of understanding existence found in the East. Every people has its own native and seminal wisdom which, as a true cultural treasure, tends to find voice and develop in forms which are genuinely philosophical. One example of this is the basic form of philosophical knowledge which is evident to this day in the postulates which inspire national and international legal systems in regulating the life of society.

4. Nonetheless, it is true that a single term conceals a variety of meanings. Hence the need for a preliminary clarification. Driven by the desire to discover the ultimate truth of existence, human beings seek to acquire those universal elements of knowledge which enable them to understand themselves better and

to advance in their own self-realization. These fundamental elements of knowledge spring from the *wonder* awakened in them by the contemplation of creation: human beings are astonished to discover themselves as part of the world,
in a relationship with others like them, all sharing a common destiny. Here
begins, then, the journey which will lead them to discover ever new frontiers of
knowledge. Without wonder, men and women would lapse into deadening
routine and little by little would become incapable of a life which is genuinely
personal.

Through philosophy's work, the ability to speculate which is proper to the
human intellect produces a rigorous mode of thought; and then in turn,
through the logical coherence of the affirmations made and the organic unity
of their content, it produces a systematic body of knowledge. In different cultural contexts and at different times, this process has yielded results which have
produced genuine systems of thought. Yet often enough in history this has
brought with it the temptation to identify one single stream with the whole of
philosophy. In such cases, we are clearly dealing with a "philosophical pride"
which seeks to present its own partial and imperfect view as the complete reading of all reality. In effect, every philosophical *system*, while it should always be
respected in its wholeness, without any instrumentalization, must still recognize the primacy of philosophical *enquiry*, from which it stems and which it
ought loyally to serve.

Although times change and knowledge increases, it is possible to discern a core
of philosophical insight within the history of thought as a whole. Consider, for
example, the principles of non-contradiction, finality and causality, as well as
the concept of the person as a free and intelligent subject, with the capacity to
know God, truth and goodness. Consider as well certain fundamental moral
norms which are shared by all. These are among the indications that, beyond
different schools of thought, there exists a body of knowledge which may be
judged a kind of spiritual heritage of humanity. It is as if we had come upon an
implicit philosophy, as a result of which all feel that they possess these principles,
albeit in a general and unreflective way. Precisely because it is shared in some
measure by all, this knowledge should serve as a kind of reference-point for the
different philosophical schools. Once reason successfully intuits and formulates
the first universal principles of being and correctly draws from them conclusions which are coherent both logically and ethically, then it may be called right
reason or, as the ancients called it, *orthós logos, recta ratio*.

5. On her part, the Church cannot but set great value upon reason's drive to
attain goals which render people's lives ever more worthy. She sees in philosophy the way to come to know fundamental truths about human life. At the
same time, the Church considers philosophy an indispensable help for a deeper
understanding of faith and for communicating the truth of the Gospel to those
who do not yet know it.

Therefore, following upon similar initiatives by my Predecessors, I wish to reflect upon this special activity of human reason. I judge it necessary to do so because, at the present time in particular, the search for ultimate truth seems often to be neglected. Modern philosophy clearly has the great merit of focusing attention upon man. From this starting-point, human reason with its many questions has developed further its yearning to know more and to know it ever more deeply. Complex systems of thought have thus been built, yielding results in the different fields of knowledge and fostering the development of culture and history. Anthropology, logic, the natural sciences, history, linguistics and so forth – the whole universe of knowledge has been involved in one way or another. Yet the positive results achieved must not obscure the fact that reason, in its one-sided concern to investigate human subjectivity, seems to have forgotten that men and women are always called to direct their steps towards a truth which transcends them. Sundered from that truth, individuals are at the mercy of caprice, and their state as person ends up being judged by pragmatic criteria based essentially upon experimental data, in the mistaken belief that technology must dominate all. It has happened therefore that reason, rather than voicing the human orientation towards truth, has wilted under the weight of so much knowledge and little by little has lost the capacity to lift its gaze to the heights, not daring to rise to the truth of being. Abandoning the investigation of being, modern philosophical research has concentrated instead upon human knowing. Rather than make use of the human capacity to know the truth, modern philosophy has preferred to accentuate the ways in which this capacity is limited and conditioned.

This has given rise to different forms of agnosticism and relativism which have led philosophical research to lose its way in the shifting sands of widespread scepticism. Recent times have seen the rise to prominence of various doctrines which tend to devalue even the truths which had been judged certain. A legitimate plurality of positions has yielded to an undifferentiated pluralism, based upon the assumption that all positions are equally valid, which is one of today's most widespread symptoms of the lack of confidence in truth. Even certain conceptions of life coming from the East betray this lack of confidence, denying truth its exclusive character and assuming that truth reveals itself equally in different doctrines, even if they contradict one another. On this understanding, everything is reduced to opinion; and there is a sense of being adrift. While, on the one hand, philosophical thinking has succeeded in coming closer to the reality of human life and its forms of expression, it has also tended to pursue issues – existential, hermeneutical or linguistic – which ignore the radical question of the truth about personal existence, about being and about God. Hence we see among the men and women of our time, and not just in some philosophers, attitudes of widespread distrust of the human being's great capacity for knowledge. With a false modesty, people rest content with partial and provisional truths, no longer seeking to ask radical questions about the meaning and ultimate foundation of human, personal and social existence. In short, the hope that philosophy might be able to provide definitive answers to these questions has dwindled.

6. Sure of her competence as the bearer of the Revelation of Jesus Christ, the Church reaffirms the need to reflect upon truth. This is why I have decided to address you, my venerable Brother Bishops, with whom I share the mission of "proclaiming the truth openly" (2 Cor 4:2), as also theologians and philosophers whose duty it is to explore the different aspects of truth, and all those who are searching; and I do so in order to offer some reflections on the path which leads to true wisdom, so that those who love truth may take the sure path leading to it and so find rest from their labours and joy for their spirit. I feel impelled to undertake this task above all because of the Second Vatican Council's insistence that the Bishops are "witnesses of divine and catholic truth".(3) To bear witness to the truth is therefore a task entrusted to us Bishops; we cannot renounce this task without failing in the ministry which we have received. In reaffirming the truth of faith, we can both restore to our contemporaries a genuine trust in their capacity to know and challenge philosophy to recover and develop its own full dignity.

There is a further reason why I write these reflections. In my Encyclical Letter *Veritatis Splendor*, I drew attention to "certain fundamental truths of Catholic doctrine which, in the present circumstances, risk being distorted or denied".(4) In the present Letter, I wish to pursue that reflection by concentrating on the theme of *truth* itself and on its *foundation* in relation to *faith*. For it is undeniable that this time of rapid and complex change can leave especially the younger generation, to whom the future belongs and on whom it depends, with a sense that they have no valid points of reference. The need for a foundation for personal and communal life becomes all the more pressing at a time when we are faced with the patent inadequacy of perspectives in which the ephemeral is affirmed as a value and the possibility of discovering the real meaning of life is cast into doubt. This is why many people stumble through life to the very edge of the abyss without knowing where they are going. At times, this happens because those whose vocation it is to give cultural expression to their thinking no longer look to truth, preferring quick success to the toil of patient enquiry into what makes life worth living. With its enduring appeal to the search for truth, philosophy has the great responsibility of forming thought and culture; and now it must strive resolutely to recover its original vocation. This is why I have felt both the need and the duty to address this theme so that, on the threshold of the third millennium of the Christian era, humanity may come to a clearer sense of the great resources with which it has been endowed and may commit itself with renewed courage to implement the plan of salvation of which its history is part.

. . . .
. . . .

The Magisterium's discernment as diakonia of the truth

49. The Church has no philosophy of her own nor does she canonize any one particular philosophy in preference to others.(54) The underlying reason for this reluctance is that, even when it engages theology, philosophy must remain faithful to its own principles and methods. Otherwise there would be no guarantee that it would remain oriented to truth and that it was moving towards truth by way of a process governed by reason. A philosophy which did not proceed in the light of reason according to its own principles and methods would serve little purpose. At the deepest level, the autonomy which philosophy enjoys is rooted in the fact that reason is by its nature oriented to truth and is equipped moreover with the means necessary to arrive at truth. A philosophy conscious of this as its "constitutive status" cannot but respect the demands and the data of revealed truth.
Yet history shows that philosophy – especially modern philosophy – has taken wrong turns and fallen into error. It is neither the task nor the competence of the Magisterium to intervene in order to make good the lacunas of deficient philosophical discourse. Rather, it is the Magisterium's duty to respond clearly and strongly when controversial philosophical opinions threaten right understanding of what has been revealed, and when false and partial theories which sow the seed of serious error, confusing the pure and simple faith of the People of God, begin to spread more widely.

50. In the light of faith, therefore, the Church's Magisterium can and must authoritatively exercise a critical discernment of opinions and philosophies which contradict Christian doctrine.(55) It is the task of the Magisterium in the first place to indicate which philosophical presuppositions and conclusions are incompatible with revealed truth, thus articulating the demands which faith's point of view makes of philosophy. Moreover, as philosophical learning has developed, different schools of thought have emerged. This pluralism also imposes upon the Magisterium the responsibility of expressing a judgement as to whether or not the basic tenets of these different schools are compatible with the demands of the word of God and theological enquiry.
It is the Church's duty to indicate the elements in a philosophical system which are incompatible with her own faith. In fact, many philosophical opinions – concerning God, the human being, human freedom and ethical behaviour – engage the Church directly, because they touch on the revealed truth of which she is the guardian. In making this discernment, we Bishops have the duty to be "witnesses to the truth", fulfilling a humble but tenacious ministry of service which every philosopher should appreciate, a service in favour of *recta ratio*, or of reason reflecting rightly upon what is true.

51. This discernment, however, should not be seen as primarily negative, as if the Magisterium intended to abolish or limit any possible mediation. On the

contrary, the Magisterium's interventions are intended above all to prompt, promote and encourage philosophical enquiry. Besides, philosophers are the first to understand the need for self-criticism, the correction of errors and the extension of the too restricted terms in which their thinking has been framed. In particular, it is necessary to keep in mind the unity of truth, even if its formulations are shaped by history and produced by human reason wounded and weakened by sin. This is why no historical form of philosophy can legitimately claim to embrace the totality of truth, nor to be the complete explanation of the human being, of the world and of the human being's relationship with God. Today, then, with the proliferation of systems, methods, concepts and philosophical theses which are often extremely complex, the need for a critical discernment in the light of faith becomes more urgent, even if it remains a daunting task. Given all of reason's inherent and historical limitations, it is difficult enough to recognize the inalienable powers proper to it; but it is still more difficult at times to discern in specific philosophical claims what is valid and fruitful from faith's point of view and what is mistaken or dangerous. Yet the Church knows that "the treasures of wisdom and knowledge" are hidden in Christ (*Col* 2:3) and therefore intervenes in order to stimulate philosophical enquiry, lest it stray from the path which leads to recognition of the mystery.

52. It is not only in recent times that the Magisterium of the Church has intervened to make its mind known with regard to particular philosophical teachings. It is enough to recall, by way of example, the pronouncements made through the centuries concerning theories which argued in favour of the pre-existence of the soul,(56) or concerning the different forms of idolatry and esoteric superstition found in astrological speculations,(57) without forgetting the more systematic pronouncements against certain claims of Latin Averroism which were incompatible with the Christian faith.(58)

If the Magisterium has spoken out more frequently since the middle of the last century, it is because in that period not a few Catholics felt it their duty to counter various streams of modern thought with a philosophy of their own. At this point, the Magisterium of the Church was obliged to be vigilant lest these philosophies developed in ways which were themselves erroneous and negative. The censures were delivered even-handedly: on the one hand, *fideism* (59) and *radical traditionalism,*(60) for their distrust of reason's natural capacities, and, on the other, *rationalism* (61) and *ontologism* (62) because they attributed to natural reason a knowledge which only the light of faith could confer. The positive elements of this debate were assembled in the Dogmatic Constitution *Dei Filius*, in which for the first time an Ecumenical Council – in this case, the First Vatican Council – pronounced solemnly on the relationship between reason and faith. The teaching contained in this document strongly and positively marked the philosophical research of many believers and remains today a standard reference-point for correct and coherent Christian thinking in this regard.

53. The Magisterium's pronouncements have been concerned less with individual philosophical theses than with the need for rational and hence ultimately
philosophical knowledge for the understanding of faith. In synthesizing and
solemnly reaffirming the teachings constantly proposed to the faithful by the
ordinary Papal Magisterium, the First Vatican Council showed how inseparable
and at the same time how distinct were faith and reason, Revelation and natural knowledge of God. The Council began with the basic criterion, presup-
posed by Revelation itself, of the natural knowability of the existence of God,
the beginning and end of all things,(63) and concluded with the solemn assertion quoted earlier: "There are two orders of knowledge, distinct not only in
their point of departure, but also in their object".(64) Against all forms of
rationalism, then, there was a need to affirm the distinction between the
mysteries of faith and the findings of philosophy, and the transcendence and
precedence of the mysteries of faith over the findings of philosophy. Against the
temptations of fideism, however, it was necessary to stress the unity of truth
and thus the positive contribution which rational knowledge can and must
make to faith's knowledge: "Even if faith is superior to reason there can never
be a true divergence between faith and reason, since the same God who reveals
the mysteries and bestows the gift of faith has also placed in the human spirit
the light of reason. This God could not deny himself, nor could the truth ever
contradict the truth".(65)

54. In our own century too the Magisterium has revisited the theme on a
number of occasions, warning against the lure of rationalism. Here the pronouncements of Pope Saint Pius X are pertinent, stressing as they did that at
the basis of Modernism were philosophical claims which were phenomenist,
agnostic and immanentist.(66) Nor can the importance of the Catholic rejection
of Marxist philosophy and atheistic Communism be forgotten.(67)
Later, in his Encyclical Letter *Humani Generis*, Pope Pius XII warned against
mistaken interpretations linked to evolutionism, existentialism and historicism.
He made it clear that these theories had not been proposed and developed
by theologians, but had their origins "outside the sheepfold of Christ".(68)
He added, however, that errors of this kind should not simply be rejected but
should be examined critically: "Catholic theologians and philosophers, whose
grave duty it is to defend natural and supernatural truth and instill it in human
hearts, cannot afford to ignore these more or less erroneous opinions. Rather
they must come to understand these theories well, not only because diseases are
properly treated only if rightly diagnosed and because even in these false theories some truth is found at times, but because in the end these theories provoke
a more discriminating discussion and evaluation of philosophical and theological truths".(69)
In accomplishing its specific task in service of the Roman Pontiff's universal
Magisterium,(70) the Congregation for the Doctrine of Faith has more recently

had to intervene to re-emphasize the danger of an uncritical adoption by some liberation theologians of opinions and methods drawn from Marxism.(71)

In the past, then, the Magisterium has on different occasions and in different ways offered its discernment in philosophical matters. My revered Predecessors have thus made an invaluable contribution which must not be forgotten.

55. Surveying the situation today, we see that the problems of other times have returned, but in a new key. It is no longer a matter of questions of interest only to certain individuals and groups, but convictions so widespread that they have become to some extent the common mind. An example of this is the deep-seated distrust of reason which has surfaced in the most recent developments of much of philosophical research, to the point where there is talk at times of "the end of metaphysics". Philosophy is expected to rest content with more modest tasks such as the simple interpretation of facts or an enquiry into restricted fields of human knowing or its structures.

In theology too the temptations of other times have reappeared. In some con-temporary theologies, for instance, a certain *rationalism* is gaining ground, especially when opinions thought to be philosophically well founded are taken as normative for theological research. This happens particularly when theolo-gians, through lack of philosophical competence, allow themselves to be swayed uncritically by assertions which have become part of current parlance and cul-ture but which are poorly grounded in reason.(72)

There are also signs of a resurgence of *fideism*, which fails to recognize the importance of rational knowledge and philosophical discourse for the under-standing of faith, indeed for the very possibility of belief in God. One currently widespread symptom of this fideistic tendency is a "biblicism" which tends to make the reading and exegesis of Sacred Scripture the sole criterion of truth. In consequence, the word of God is identified with Sacred Scripture alone, thus eliminating the doctrine of the Church which the Second Vatican Council stressed quite specifically. Having recalled that the word of God is present in both Scripture and Tradition,(73) the Constitution *Dei Verbum* continues emphatically: "Sacred Tradition and Sacred Scripture comprise a single sacred deposit of the word of God entrusted to the Church. Embracing this deposit and united with their pastors, the People of God remain always faithful to the teaching of the Apostles".(74) Scripture, therefore, is not the Church's sole point of reference. The "supreme rule of her faith" (75) derives from the unity which the Spirit has created between Sacred Tradition, Sacred Scripture and the Magisterium of the Church in a reciprocity which means that none of the three can survive without the others.(76)

Moreover, one should not underestimate the danger inherent in seeking to derive the truth of Sacred Scripture from the use of one method alone, ignoring the need for a more comprehensive exegesis which enables the exegete, together with the whole Church, to arrive at the full sense of the texts. Those who devote themselves to the study of Sacred Scripture should always remember that the various hermeneutical approaches have their own philosophical underpinnings, which need to be carefully evaluated before they are applied to the sacred texts. Other modes of latent fideism appear in the scant consideration accorded to speculative theology, and in disdain for the classical philosophy from which the terms of both the understanding of faith and the actual formulation of dogma have been drawn. My revered Predecessor Pope Pius XII warned against such neglect of the philosophical tradition and against abandonment of the traditional terminology.(77)

56. In brief, there are signs of a widespread distrust of universal and absolute statements, especially among those who think that truth is born of consensus and not of a consonance between intellect and objective reality. In a world subdivided into so many specialized fields, it is not hard to see how difficult it can be to acknowledge the full and ultimate meaning of life which has traditionally been the goal of philosophy. Nonetheless, in the light of faith which finds in Jesus Christ this ultimate meaning, I cannot but encourage philosophers – be they Christian or not – to trust in the power of human reason and not to set themselves goals that are too modest in their philosophizing. The lesson of history in this millennium now drawing to a close shows that this is the path to follow: it is necessary not to abandon the passion for ultimate truth, the eagerness to search for it or the audacity to forge new paths in the search. It is faith which stirs reason to move beyond all isolation and willingly to run risks so that it may attain whatever is beautiful, good and true. Faith thus becomes the convinced and convincing advocate of reason.

. . . .
. . . .

72. In preaching the Gospel, Christianity first encountered Greek philosophy; but this does not mean at all that other approaches are precluded. Today, as the Gospel gradually comes into contact with cultural worlds which once lay beyond Christian influence, there are new tasks of inculturation, which mean that our generation faces problems not unlike those faced by the Church in the first centuries. My thoughts turn immediately to the lands of the East, so rich in religious and philosophical traditions of great antiquity. Among these lands, India has a special place. A great spiritual impulse leads Indian thought to seek an experience which would liberate the spirit from the shackles of time and space and would therefore acquire absolute value. The dynamic of this quest for liberation provides the context for great metaphysical systems.

In India particularly, it is the duty of Christians now to draw from this rich heritage the elements compatible with their faith, in order to enrich Christian thought. In this work of discernment, which finds its inspiration in the Council's Declaration *Nostra Aetate*, certain criteria will have to be kept in mind. The first of these is the universality of the human spirit, whose basic needs are the same in the most disparate cultures. The second, which derives from the first, is this: in engaging great cultures for the first time, the Church cannot abandon what she has gained from her inculturation in the world of Greco-Latin thought. To reject this heritage would be to deny the providential plan of God who guides his Church down the paths of time and history. This criterion is valid for the Church in every age, even for the Church of the future, who will judge herself enriched by all that comes from today's engagement with Eastern cultures and will find in this inheritance fresh cues for fruitful dialogue with the cultures which will emerge as humanity moves into the future. Thirdly, care will need to be taken lest, contrary to the very nature of the human spirit, the legitimate defense of the uniqueness and originality of Indian thought be confused with the idea that a particular cultural tradition should remain closed in its difference and affirm itself by opposing other traditions.

What has been said here of India is no less true for the heritage of the great cultures of China, Japan and the other countries of Asia, as also for the riches of the traditional cultures of Africa, which are for the most part orally transmitted.

. . . .

86. This insistence on the need for a close relationship of continuity between contemporary philosophy and the philosophy developed in the Christian tradition is intended to avert the danger which lies hidden in some currents of thought which are especially prevalent today. It is appropriate, I think, to review them, however briefly, in order to point out their errors and the consequent risks for philosophical work.

The first goes by the name of *eclecticism*, by which is meant the approach of those who, in research, teaching and argumentation, even in theology, tend to use individual ideas drawn from different philosophies, without concern for their internal coherence, their place within a system or their historical context. They therefore run the risk of being unable to distinguish the part of truth of a given doctrine from elements of it which may be erroneous or ill-suited to the task at hand. An extreme form of eclecticism appears also in the rhetorical misuse of philosophical terms to which some theologians are given at times. Such manipulation does not help the search for truth and does not train reason – whether theological or philosophical – to formulate arguments seriously and scientifically. The rigorous and far-reaching study of philosophical doctrines, their particular terminology and the context in which they arose, helps to overcome the danger of eclecticism and makes it possible to integrate them into theological discourse in a way appropriate to the task.

87. Eclecticism is an error of method, but lying hidden within it can also be the claims of *historicism*. To understand a doctrine from the past correctly, it is

necessary to set it within its proper historical and cultural context. The fundamental claim of historicism, however, is that the truth of a philosophy is determined on the basis of its appropriateness to a certain period and a certain historical purpose. At least implicitly, therefore, the enduring validity of truth is denied. What was true in one period, historicists claim, may not be true in another. Thus for them the history of thought becomes little more than an archeological resource useful for illustrating positions once held, but for the most part outmoded and meaningless now. On the contrary, it should not be forgotten that, even if a formulation is bound in some way by time and culture, the truth or the error which it expresses can invariably be identified and evaluated as such despite the distance of space and time.

In theological enquiry, historicism tends to appear for the most part under the guise of "modernism". Rightly concerned to make theological discourse relevant and understandable to our time, some theologians use only the most recent opinions and philosophical language, ignoring the critical evaluation which ought to be made of them in the light of the tradition. By exchanging relevance for truth, this form of modernism shows itself incapable of satisfying the demands of truth to which theology is called to respond.

88. Another threat to be reckoned with is *scientism*. This is the philosophical notion which refuses to admit the validity of forms of knowledge other than those of the positive sciences; and it relegates religious, theological, ethical and aesthetic knowledge to the realm of mere fantasy. In the past, the same idea emerged in positivism and neo-positivism, which considered metaphysical statements to be meaningless. Critical epistemology has discredited such a claim, but now we see it revived in the new guise of scientism, which dismisses values as mere products of the emotions and rejects the notion of being in order to clear the way for pure and simple facticity. Science would thus be poised to dominate all aspects of human life through technological progress. The undeniable triumphs of scientific research and contemporary technology have helped to propagate a scientistic outlook, which now seems boundless, given its inroads into different cultures and the radical changes it has brought.

Regrettably, it must be noted, scientism consigns all that has to do with the question of the meaning of life to the realm of the irrational or imaginary. No less disappointing is the way in which it approaches the other great problems of philosophy which, if they are not ignored, are subjected to analyses based on superficial analogies, lacking all rational foundation. This leads to the impoverishment of human thought, which no longer addresses the ultimate problems which the human being, as the *animal rationale*, has pondered constantly from the beginning of time. And since it leaves no space for the critique offered by ethical judgement, the scientistic mentality has succeeded in leading many to think that if something is technically possible it is therefore morally admissible.

89. No less dangerous is *pragmatism*, an attitude of mind which, in making its choices, precludes theoretical considerations or judgements based on ethical principles. The practical consequences of this mode of thinking are significant. In particular there is growing support for a concept of democracy which is not grounded upon any reference to unchanging values: whether or not a line of action is admissible is decided by the vote of a parliamentary majority. (105) The consequences of this are clear: in practice, the great moral decisions of humanity are subordinated to decisions taken one after another by institutional agencies. Moreover, anthropology itself is severely compromised by a one-dimensional vision of the human being, a vision which excludes the great ethical dilemmas and the existential analyses of the meaning of suffering and sacrifice, of life and death.

90. The positions we have examined lead in turn to a more general conception which appears today as the common framework of many philosophies which have rejected the meaningfulness of being. I am referring to the nihilist inter-pretation, which is at once the denial of all foundations and the negation of all objective truth. Quite apart from the fact that it conflicts with the demands and the content of the word of God, *nihilism* is a denial of the humanity and of the very identity of the human being. It should never be forgotten that the neglect of being inevitably leads to losing touch with objective truth and there-fore with the very ground of human dignity. This in turn makes it possible to erase from the countenance of man and woman the marks of their likeness to God, and thus to lead them little by little either to a destructive will to power or to a solitude without hope. Once the truth is denied to human beings, it is pure illusion to try to set them free. Truth and freedom either go together hand in hand or together they perish in misery. (106)

91. In discussing these currents of thought, it has not been my intention to present a complete picture of the present state of philosophy, which would, in any case, be difficult to reduce to a unified vision. And I certainly wish to stress that our heritage of knowledge and wisdom has indeed been enriched in dif-ferent fields. We need only cite logic, the philosophy of language, epistemology, the philosophy of nature, anthropology, the more penetrating analysis of the affective dimensions of knowledge and the existential approach to the analysis of freedom. Since the last century, however, the affirmation of the principle of immanence, central to the rationalist argument, has provoked a radical reques-tioning of claims once thought indisputable. In response, currents of irrational-ism arose, even as the baselessness of the demand that reason be absolutely self-grounded was being critically demonstrated.
Our age has been termed by some thinkers the age of "postmodernity". Often used in very different contexts, the term designates the emergence of a complex of new factors which, widespread and powerful as they are, have shown them-

selves able to produce important and lasting changes. The term was first used with reference to aesthetic, social and technological phenomena. It was then transposed into the philosophical field, but has remained somewhat ambiguous, both because judgement on what is called "postmodern" is sometimes positive and sometimes negative, and because there is as yet no consensus on the delicate question of the demarcation of the different historical periods. One thing however is certain: the currents of thought which claim to be postmodern merit appropriate attention. According to some of them, the time of certainties is irrevocably past, and the human being must now learn to live in a horizon of total absence of meaning, where everything is provisional and ephemeral. In their destructive critique of every certitude, several authors have failed to make crucial distinctions and have called into question the certitudes of faith.

This nihilism has been justified in a sense by the terrible experience of evil which has marked our age. Such a dramatic experience has ensured the collapse of rationalist optimism, which viewed history as the triumphant progress of reason, the source of all happiness and freedom; and now, at the end of this century, one of our greatest threats is the temptation to despair.

Even so, it remains true that a certain positivist cast of mind continues to nurture the illusion that, thanks to scientific and technical progress, man and woman may live as a demiurge, single-handedly and completely taking charge of their destiny.

. . . .
. . . .

Current tasks for theology

92. As an understanding of Revelation, theology has always had to respond in different historical moments to the demands of different cultures, in order then to mediate the content of faith to those cultures in a coherent and conceptually clear way. Today, too, theology faces a dual task. On the one hand, it must be increasingly committed to the task entrusted to it by the Second Vatican Council, the task of renewing its specific methods in order to serve evangelization more effectively. How can we fail to recall in this regard the words of Pope John XXIII at the opening of the Council? He said then: "In line with the keen expectation of those who sincerely love the Christian, Catholic and apostolic religion, this doctrine must be known more widely and deeply, and souls must be instructed and formed in it more completely; and this certain and unchangeable doctrine, always to be faithfully respected, must be understood more profoundly and presented in a way which meets the needs of our time". (107)

On the other hand, theology must look to the ultimate truth which Revelation entrusts to it, never content to stop short of that goal. Theologians should remember that their work corresponds "to a dynamism found in the faith itself" and that the proper object of their enquiry is "the Truth which is the living God and his plan for salvation revealed in Jesus Christ". (108) This task, which is theology's prime concern, challenges philosophy as well. The array of problems which today need to be tackled demands a joint effort – approached, it is true, with different methods – so that the truth may once again be known and expressed. The Truth, which is Christ, imposes itself as an all-embracing authority which holds out to theology and philosophy alike the prospect of support, stimulation and increase (cf. *Eph* 4:15).

To believe it possible to know a universally valid truth is in no way to encourage intolerance; on the contrary, it is the essential condition for sincere and authentic dialogue between persons. On this basis alone is it possible to overcome divisions and to journey together towards full truth, walking those paths known only to the Spirit of the Risen Lord. (109) I wish at this point to indicate the specific form which the call to unity now takes, given the current tasks of theology.

93. The chief purpose of theology is to *provide an understanding of Revelation and the content of faith*. The very heart of theological enquiry will thus be the contemplation of the mystery of the Triune God. The approach to this mystery begins with reflection upon the mystery of the Incarnation of the Son of God: his coming as man, his going to his Passion and Death, a mystery issuing into his glorious Resurrection and Ascension to the right hand of the Father, whence he would send the Spirit of truth to bring his Church to birth and give her growth. From this vantage-point, the prime commitment of theology is seen to be the understanding of God's *kenosis*, a grand and mysterious truth for the human mind, which finds it inconceivable that suffering and death can express a love which gives itself and seeks nothing in return. In this light, a careful analysis of texts emerges as a basic and urgent need: first the texts of Scripture, and then those which express the Church's living Tradition. On this score, some problems have emerged in recent times, problems which are only partially new; and a coherent solution to them will not be found without philosophy's contribution.

94. An initial problem is that of the relationship between meaning and truth. Like every other text, the sources which the theologian interprets primarily transmit a meaning which needs to be grasped and explained. This meaning presents itself as the truth about God which God himself communicates through the sacred text. Human language thus embodies the language of God, who communicates his own truth with that wonderful "condescension" which mirrors the logic of the Incarnation. (110) In interpreting the sources of Revelation, then, the theologian needs to ask what is the deep and authentic truth which the texts wish to communicate, even within the limits of language.

The truth of the biblical texts, and of the Gospels in particular, is certainly not restricted to the narration of simple historical events or the statement of neutral facts, as historicist positivism would claim. (111) Beyond simple historical occurrence, the truth of the events which these texts relate lies rather in the meaning they have *in* and *for* the history of salvation. This truth is elaborated fully in the Church's constant reading of these texts over the centuries, a reading which preserves intact their original meaning. There is a pressing need, therefore, that the relationship between fact and meaning, a relationship which constitutes the specific sense of history, be examined also from the philosophical point of view.

95. The word of God is not addressed to any one people or to any one period of history. Similarly, dogmatic statements, while reflecting at times the culture of the period in which they were defined, formulate an unchanging and ultimate truth. This prompts the question of how one can reconcile the absoluteness and the universality of truth with the unavoidable historical and cultural conditioning of the formulas which express that truth. The claims of historicism, I noted earlier, are untenable; but the use of a hermeneutic open to the appeal of metaphysics can show how it is possible to move from the historical and contingent circumstances in which the texts developed to the truth which they express, a truth transcending those circumstances.
Human language may be conditioned by history and constricted in other ways, but the human being can still express truths which surpass the phenomenon of language. Truth can never be confined to time and culture; in history it is known, but it also reaches beyond history.

96. To see this is to glimpse the solution of another problem: the problem of the enduring validity of the conceptual language used in Conciliar definitions. This is a question which my revered predecessor Pius XII addressed in his Encyclical Letter *Humani Generis*. (112)
This is a complex theme to ponder, since one must reckon seriously with the meaning which words assume in different times and cultures. Nonetheless, the history of thought shows that across the range of cultures and their development certain basic concepts retain their universal epistemological value and thus retain the truth of the propositions in which they are expressed. (113) Were this not the case, philosophy and the sciences could not communicate with each other, nor could they find a place in cultures different from those in which they were conceived and developed. The hermeneutical problem exists, to be sure; but it is not insoluble. Moreover, the objective value of many concepts does not exclude that their meaning is often imperfect. This is where philosophical speculation can be very helpful. We may hope, then, that philosophy will be especially concerned to deepen the understanding of the relationship between conceptual language and truth, and to propose ways which will lead to a right understanding of that relationship.

97. The interpretation of sources is a vital task for theology; but another still more delicate and demanding task is the *understanding of revealed truth*, or the articulation of the *intellectus fidei*. The *intellectus fidei*, as I have noted, demands the contribution of a philosophy of being which first of all would enable *dogmatic theology* to perform its functions appropriately. The dogmatic pragmatism of the early years of this century, which viewed the truths of faith as nothing more than rules of conduct, has already been refuted and rejected; (114) but the temptation always remains of understanding these truths in purely functional terms. This leads only to an approach which is inadequate, reductive and superficial at the level of speculation. A Christology, for example, which proceeded solely "from below", as is said nowadays, or an ecclesiology developed solely on the model of civil society, would be hard pressed to avoid the danger of such reductionism.

If the *intellectus fidei* wishes to integrate all the wealth of the theological tradition, it must turn to the philosophy of being, which should be able to propose anew the problem of being – and this in harmony with the demands and insights of the entire philosophical tradition, including philosophy of more recent times, without lapsing into sterile repetition of antiquated formulas. Set within the Christian metaphysical tradition, the philosophy of being is a dynamic philosophy which views reality in its ontological, causal and communicative structures. It is strong and enduring because it is based upon the very act of being itself, which allows a full and comprehensive openness to reality as a whole, surpassing every limit in order to reach the One who brings all things to fulfilment. (115) In theology, which draws its principles from Revelation as a new source of knowledge, this perspective is confirmed by the intimate relationship which exists between faith and metaphysical reasoning.

98. These considerations apply equally to *moral theology*. It is no less urgent that philosophy be recovered at the point where the understanding of faith is linked to the moral life of believers. Faced with contemporary challenges in the social, economic, political and scientific fields, the ethical conscience of people is disoriented. In the Encyclical Letter *Veritatis Splendor*, I wrote that many of the problems of the contemporary world stem from a crisis of truth. I noted that "once the idea of a universal truth about the good, knowable by human reason, is lost, inevitably the notion of conscience also changes. Conscience is no longer considered in its prime reality as an act of a person's intelligence, the function of which is to apply the universal knowledge of the good in a specific situation and thus to express a judgment about the right conduct to be chosen here and now. Instead, there is a tendency to grant to the individual conscience the prerogative of independently determining the criteria of good and evil and then acting accordingly. Such an outlook is quite congenial to an individualist ethic, wherein each individual is faced with his own truth different from the truth of others". (116)

Throughout the Encyclical I underscored clearly the fundamental role of truth in the moral field. In the case of the more pressing ethical problems, this truth demands of moral theology a careful enquiry rooted unambiguously in the word of God. In order to fulfil its mission, moral theology must turn to a philosophical ethics which looks to the truth of the good, to an ethics which is neither subjectivist nor utilitarian. Such an ethics implies and presupposes a philosophical anthropology and a metaphysics of the good. Drawing on this organic vision, linked necessarily to Christian holiness and to the practice of the human and supernatural virtues, moral theology will be able to tackle the various problems in its competence, such as peace, social justice, the family, the defence of life and the natural environment, in a more appropriate and effective way.

99. Theological work in the Church is first of all at the service of the proclamation of the faith and of catechesis. (117) Proclamation or kerygma is a call to conversion, announcing the truth of Christ, which reaches its summit in his Paschal Mystery: for only in Christ is it possible to know the fullness of the truth which saves (cf. *Acts* 4:12; 1 *Tm* 2:4-6).

In this respect, it is easy to see why, in addition to theology, reference to *catechesis* is also important, since catechesis has philosophical implications which must be explored more deeply in the light of faith. The teaching imparted in catechesis helps to form the person. As a mode of linguistic communication, catechesis must present the Church's doctrine in its integrity, (118) demonstrating its link with the life of the faithful. (119) The result is a unique bond between teaching and living which is otherwise unattainable, since what is communicated in catechesis is not a body of conceptual truths, but the mystery of the living God. (120)

Philosophical enquiry can help greatly to clarify the relationship between truth and life, between event and doctrinal truth, and above all between transcendent truth and humanly comprehensible language. (121) This involves a reciprocity between the theological disciplines and the insights drawn from the various strands of philosophy; and such a reciprocity can prove genuinely fruitful for the communication and deeper understanding of the faith.

CONCLUSION

100. More than a hundred years after the appearance of Pope Leo XIII's Encyclical *Æterni Patris*, to which I have often referred in these pages, I have sensed the need to revisit in a more systematic way the issue of the relationship between faith and philosophy. The importance of philosophical thought in the development of culture and its influence on patterns of personal and social behaviour is there for all to see. In addition, philosophy exercises a powerful,

though not always obvious, influence on theology and its disciplines. For these reasons, I have judged it appropriate and necessary to emphasize the value of philosophy for the understanding of the faith, as well as the limits which philosophy faces when it neglects or rejects the truths of Revelation. The Church remains profoundly convinced that faith and reason "mutually support each other"; (122) each influences the other, as they offer to each other a purifying critique and a stimulus to pursue the search for deeper understanding.

101. A survey of the history of thought, especially in the West, shows clearly that the encounter between philosophy and theology and the exchange of their respective insights have contributed richly to the progress of humanity. Endowed as it is with an openness and originality which allow it to stand as the science of faith, theology has certainly challenged reason to remain open to the radical newness found in God's Revelation; and this has been an undoubted boon for philosophy which has thus glimpsed new vistas of further meanings which reason is summoned to penetrate.

Precisely in the light of this consideration, and just as I have reaffirmed theology's duty to recover its true relationship with philosophy, I feel equally bound to stress how right it is that, for the benefit and development of human thought, philosophy too should recover its relationship with theology. In theology, philosophy will find not the thinking of a single person which, however rich and profound, still entails the limited perspective of an individual, but the wealth of a communal reflection. For by its very nature, theology is sustained in the search for truth by its *ecclesial context* (123) and by the tradition of the People of God, with its harmony of many different fields of learning and culture within the unity of faith.

102. Insisting on the importance and true range of philosophical thought, the Church promotes both the defence of human dignity and the proclamation of the Gospel message. There is today no more urgent preparation for the performance of these tasks than this: to lead people to discover both their capacity to know the truth (124) and their yearning for the ultimate and definitive meaning of life. In the light of these profound needs, inscribed by God in human nature, the human and humanizing meaning of God's word also emerges more clearly. Through the mediation of a philosophy which is also true wisdom, people today will come to realize that their humanity is all the more affirmed the more they entrust themselves to the Gospel and open themselves to Christ.

103. Philosophy moreover is the mirror which reflects the culture of a people. A philosophy which responds to the challenge of theology's demands and evolves in harmony with faith is part of that "evangelization of culture" which Paul VI proposed as one of the fundamental goals of evangelization. (125) I have unstintingly recalled the pressing need for a *new evangelization*; and I appeal

now to philosophers to explore more comprehensively the dimensions of the true, the good and the beautiful to which the word of God gives access. This task becomes all the more urgent if we consider the challenges which the new millennium seems to entail, and which affect in a particular way regions and cultures which have a long-standing Christian tradition. This attention to philosophy too should be seen as a fundamental and original contribution in service of the new evangelization.

104. Philosophical thought is often the only ground for understanding and dialogue with those who do not share our faith. The current ferment in philosophy demands of believing philosophers an attentive and competent commitment, able to discern the expectations, the points of openness and the key issues of this historical moment. Reflecting in the light of reason and in keeping with its rules, and guided always by the deeper understanding given them by the word of God, Christian philosophers can develop a reflection which will be both comprehensible and appealing to those who do not yet grasp the full truth which divine Revelation declares. Such a ground for understanding and dialogue is all the more vital nowadays, since the most pressing issues facing humanity – ecology, peace and the co-existence of different races and cultures, for instance – may possibly find a solution if there is a clear and honest collaboration between Christians and the followers of other religions and all those who, while not sharing a religious belief, have at heart the renewal of humanity. The Second Vatican Council said as much: "For our part, the desire for such dialogue, undertaken solely out of love for the truth and with all due prudence, excludes no one, neither those who cultivate the values of the human spirit while not yet acknowledging their Source, nor those who are hostile to the Church and persecute her in various ways". (126) A philosophy in which there shines even a glimmer of the truth of Christ, the one definitive answer to humanity's problems, (127) will provide a potent underpinning for the true and planetary ethics which the world now needs.

105. In concluding this Encyclical Letter, my thoughts turn particularly to *theologians*, encouraging them to pay special attention to the philosophical implications of the word of God and to be sure to reflect in their work all the speculative and practical breadth of the science of theology. I wish to thank them for their service to the Church. The intimate bond between theological and philosophical wisdom is one of the Christian tradition's most distinctive treasures in the exploration of revealed truth. This is why I urge them to recover and express to the full the metaphysical dimension of truth in order to enter into a demanding critical dialogue with both contemporary philosophical thought and with the philosophical tradition in all its aspects, whether consonant with the word of God or not. Let theologians always remember the words of that great master of thought and spirituality, Saint Bonaventure, who in

introducing his *Itinerarium Mentis in Deum* invites the reader to recognize the inadequacy of "reading without repentance, knowledge without devotion, research without the impulse of wonder, prudence without the ability to surrender to joy, action divorced from religion, learning sundered from love, intelligence without humility, study unsustained by divine grace, thought without the wisdom inspired by God". (128)

I am thinking too of those *responsible for priestly formation*, whether academic or pastoral. I encourage them to pay special attention to the philosophical preparation of those who will proclaim the Gospel to the men and women of today and, even more, of those who will devote themselves to theological research and teaching. They must make every effort to carry out their work in the light of the directives laid down by the Second Vatican Council (129) and subsequent legislation, which speak clearly of the urgent and binding obligation, incumbent on all, to contribute to a genuine and profound communication of the truths of the faith. The grave responsibility to provide for the appropriate training of those charged with teaching philosophy both in seminaries and ecclesiastical faculties must not be neglected. (130) Teaching in this field necessarily entails a suitable scholarly preparation, a systematic presentation of the great heritage of the Christian tradition and due discernment in the light of the current needs of the Church and the world.

106. I appeal also to *philosophers*, and to all *teachers of philosophy*, asking them to have the courage to recover, in the flow of an enduringly valid philosophical tradition, the range of authentic wisdom and truth – metaphysical truth included – which is proper to philosophical enquiry. They should be open to the impelling questions which arise from the word of God and they should be strong enough to shape their thought and discussion in response to that challenge. Let them always strive for truth, alert to the good which truth contains. Then they will be able to formulate the genuine ethics which humanity needs so urgently at this particular time. The Church follows the work of philosophers with interest and appreciation; and they should rest assured of her respect for the rightful autonomy of their discipline. I would want especially to encourage believers working in the philosophical field to illumine the range of human activity by the exercise of a reason which grows more penetrating and assured because of the support it receives from faith.

Finally, I cannot fail to address a word to *scientists*, whose research offers an ever greater knowledge of the universe as a whole and of the incredibly rich array of its component parts, animate and inanimate, with their complex atomic and molecular structures. So far has science come, especially in this century, that its achievements never cease to amaze us. In expressing my admiration and in offering encouragement to these brave pioneers of scientific research, to whom humanity owes so much of its current development, I would urge them to continue their efforts without ever abandoning the *sapiential* horizon within which scientific and technological achievements are wedded to the philosophical and ethical values which are the distinctive and indelible mark of the human person. Scientists are well aware that "the search for truth, even when it concerns a finite reality of the world or of man, is never-ending, but always points beyond to something higher than the immediate object of study, to the questions which give access to Mystery". (131)

107. I ask *everyone* to look more deeply at man, whom Christ has saved in the mystery of his love, and at the human being's unceasing search for truth and meaning. Different philosophical systems have lured people into believing that they are their own absolute master, able to decide their own destiny and future in complete autonomy, trusting only in themselves and their own powers. But this can never be the grandeur of the human being, who can find fulfilment only in choosing to enter the truth, to make a home under the shade of Wisdom and dwell there. Only within this horizon of truth will people understand their freedom in its fullness and their call to know and love God as the supreme realization of their true self.

108. I turn in the end to the woman whom the prayer of the Church invokes as *Seat of Wisdom,* and whose life itself is a true parable illuminating the reflection contained in these pages. For between the vocation of the Blessed Virgin and the vocation of true philosophy there is a deep harmony. Just as the Virgin was called to offer herself entirely as human being and as woman that God's Word might take flesh and come among us, so too philosophy is called to offer its rational and critical resources that theology, as the understanding of faith, may be fruitful and creative. And just as in giving her assent to Gabriel's word, Mary lost nothing of her true humanity and freedom, so too when philosophy heeds the summons of the Gospel's truth its autonomy is in no way impaired. Indeed, it is then that philosophy sees all its enquiries rise to their highest expression. This was a truth which the holy monks of Christian antiquity understood well when they called Mary "the table at which faith sits in thought". (132) In her they saw a lucid image of true philosophy and they were convinced of the need to *philosophari in Maria.*
May Mary, Seat of Wisdom, be a sure haven for all who devote their lives to the search for wisdom. May their journey into wisdom, sure and final goal of all true knowing, be freed of every hindrance by the intercession of the one who, in giving birth to the Truth and treasuring it in her heart, has shared it forever with all the world.
Given in Rome, at Saint Peter's, on 14 September, the Feast of the Triumph of the Cross, in the year 1998, the twentieth of my Pontificate.

CATECHISM OF THE CATHOLIC CHURCH

. . . .
. . . .

ARTICLE 2 – PARTICIPATION IN SOCIAL LIFE

I. AUTHORITY

1897 "Human society can be neither well-ordered nor prosperous unless it has some people invested with legitimate authority to preserve its institutions and to devote themselves as far as is necessary to work and care for the good of all."[15]

By "authority" one means the quality by virtue of which persons or institutions make laws and give orders to men and expect obedience from them.

1898 Every human community needs an authority to govern it.[16] The foundation of such authority lies in human nature. It is necessary for the unity of the state. Its role is to ensure as far as possible the common good of the society.

1899 The authority required by the moral order derives from God: "Let every person be subject to the governing authorities. For there is no authority except from God, and those that exist have been instituted by God. Therefore he who resists the authorities resists what God has appointed, and those who resist will incur judgment."[17]

1900 The duty of obedience requires all to give due honor to authority and to treat those who are charged to exercise it with respect, and, insofar as it is deserved, with gratitude and good-will.

Pope St. Clement of Rome provides the Church's most ancient prayer for political authorities:[18] "Grant to them, Lord, health, peace, concord, and stability, so that they may exercise without offense the sovereignty that you have given them. Master, heavenly King of the ages, you give glory, honor, and power over the things of earth to the sons of men. Direct, Lord, their counsel, following what is pleasing and acceptable in your sight, so that by exercising with devotion and in peace and gentleness the power that you have given to them, they may find favor with you."[19]

1901 If authority belongs to the order established by God, "the choice of the political regime and the appointment of rulers are left to the free decision of the citizens."[20]

The diversity of political regimes is morally acceptable, provided they serve the legitimate good of the communities that adopt them. Regimes whose nature is contrary to the natural law, to the public order, and to the fundamental rights of persons cannot achieve the common good of the nations on which they have been imposed.

1902 Authority does not derive its moral legitimacy from itself. It must not behave in a despotic manner, but must act for the common good as a "moral force based on freedom and a sense of responsibility":[21]

A human law has the character of law to the extent that it accords with right reason, and thus derives from the eternal law. Insofar as it falls short of right reason it is said to be an unjust law, and thus has not so much the nature of law as of a kind of violence.[22]

1903 Authority is exercised legitimately only when it seeks the common good of the group concerned and if it employs morally licit means to attain it. If rulers were to enact unjust laws or take measures contrary to the moral order, such arrangements would not be binding in conscience. In such a case, "authority breaks down completely and results in shameful abuse."[23]

1904 "It is preferable that each power be balanced by other powers and by other spheres of responsibility which keep it within proper bounds. This is the principle of the 'rule of law,' in which the law is sovereign and not the arbitrary will of men."[24]

II. THE COMMON GOOD

1905 In keeping with the social nature of man, the good of each individual is necessarily related to the common good, which in turn can be defined only in reference to the human person:

Do not live entirely isolated, having retreated into yourselves, as if you were already justified, but gather instead to seek the common good together.[25]

1906 By common good is to be understood "the sum total of social conditions which allow people, either as groups or as individuals, to reach their fulfillment more fully and more easily."[26] The common good concerns the life of all. It calls for prudence from each, and even more from those who exercise the office of authority. It consists of three essential elements:

1907 First, the common good presupposes respect for the person as such. In the name of the common good, public authorities are bound to respect the fundamental and inalienable rights of the human person. Society should permit each of its members to fulfill his vocation. In particular, the common good resides in the conditions for the exercise of the natural freedoms indispensable for the development of the human vocation, such as "the right to act according to a sound norm of conscience and to safeguard ... privacy, and rightful freedom also in matters of religion."[27]

1908 Second, the common good requires the social well-being and development of the group itself. Development is the epitome of all social duties. Certainly, it is the proper function of authority to arbitrate, in the name of the common good, between various particular interests; but it should make accessible to each what is needed to lead a truly human life: food, clothing, health, work, education and culture, suitable information, the right to establish a family, and so on.[28]

1909 Finally, the common good requires peace, that is, the stability and security of a just order. It presupposes that authority should ensure by morally acceptable means the security of society and its members. It is the basis of the right to legitimate personal and collective defence.

1910 Each human community possesses a common good which permits it to be recognized as such; it is in the political community that its most complete realization is found. It is the role of the state to defend and promote the common good of civil society, its citizens, and intermediate bodies.

1911 Human interdependence is increasing and gradually spreading throughout the world. The unity of the human family, embracing people who enjoy equal natural dignity, implies a universal common good. This good calls for an organization of the community of nations able to "provide for the different needs of men; this will involve the sphere of social life to which belong questions of food, hygiene, education, ... and certain situations arising here and there, as for example ... alleviating the miseries of refugees dispersed throughout the world, and assisting migrants and their families."[29]

1912 The common good is always oriented towards the progress of persons: "The order of things must be subordinate to the order of persons, and not the other way around."[30] This order is founded on truth, built up in justice, and animated by love.

III. RESPONSIBILITY AND PARTICIPATION

1913 "Participation" is the voluntary and generous engagement of a person in social interchange. It is necessary that all participate, each according to his position and role, in promoting the common good. This obligation is inherent in the dignity of the human person.

1914 Participation is achieved first of all by taking charge of the areas for which one assumes personal responsibility: by the care taken for the education of his family, by conscientious work, and so forth, man participates in the good of others and of society.[31]

1915 As far as possible citizens should take an active part in public life. The manner of this participation may vary from one country or culture to another. "One must pay tribute to those nations whose systems permit the largest possible number of the citizens to take part in public life in a climate of genuine freedom."[32]

1916 As with any ethical obligation, the participation of all in realizing the common good calls for a continually renewed conversion of the social partners. Fraud and other subterfuges, by which some people evade the constraints of the law and the prescriptions of societal obligation, must be firmly condemned because they are incompatible with the requirements of justice. Much care should be taken to promote institutions that improve the conditions of human life.[33] 1917 It is incumbent on those who exercise authority to strengthen the values that inspire the confidence of the members of the group and encourage them to put themselves at the service of others. Participation begins with education and culture. "One is entitled to think that the future of humanity is in the hands of those who are capable of providing the generations to come with reasons for life and optimism."[34]

IN BRIEF

1918 "There is no authority except from God, and those authorities that exist have been instituted by God" (Rom 13:1).
1919 Every human community needs an authority in order to endure and develop.
1920 "The political community and public authority are based on human nature and therefore ... belong to an order established by God" (GS 74 # 3).
1921 Authority is exercised legitimately if it is committed to the common good of society. To attain this it must employ morally acceptable means.
1922 The diversity of political regimes is legitimate, provided they contribute to the good of the community.
1923 Political authority must be exercised within the limits of the moral order and must guarantee the conditions for the exercise of freedom.
1924 The common good comprises "the sum total of social conditions which allow people, either as groups or as individuals, to reach their fulfillment more fully and more easily" (GS 26 1).
1925 The common good consists of three essential elements: respect for and promotion of the fundamental rights of the person; prosperity, or the development of the spiritual and temporal goods of society; the peace and security of the group and of its members.
1926 The dignity of the human person requires the pursuit of the common good. Everyone should be concerned to create and support institutions that improve the conditions of human life.
1927 It is the role of the state to defend and promote the common good of civil society. The common good of the whole human family calls for an organization of society on the international level.

ARTICLE 3 – SOCIAL JUSTICE

1928 Society ensures social justice when it provides the conditions that allow associations or individuals to obtain what is their due, according to their nature and their vocation. Social justice is linked to the common good and the exercise of authority.

I. RESPECT FOR THE HUMAN PERSON

1929 Social justice can be obtained only in respecting the transcendent dignity of man. The person represents the ultimate end of society, which is ordered to him: What is at stake is the dignity of the human person, whose defense and promotion have been entrusted to us by the Creator, and to whom the men and women at every moment of history are strictly and responsibly in debt.[35]
1930 Respect for the human person entails respect for the rights that flow from his dignity as a creature. These rights are prior to society and must be recognized by it. They are the basis of the moral legitimacy of every authority: by flouting them, or refusing to recognize them in its positive legislation, a society undermines its own moral legitimacy.[36] If it does not respect them, authority can rely only on force or violence to obtain obedience from its subjects. It is the Church's role to remind men of good will of these rights and to distinguish them from unwarranted or false claims.
1931 Respect for the human person proceeds by way of respect for the principle that "everyone should look upon his neighbor (without any exception) as 'another self,' above all bearing in mind his life and the means necessary for living it with dignity."[37] No legislation could by itself do away with the fears, prejudices, and attitudes of pride and selfishness which obstruct the establishment of truly fraternal societies. Such behavior will cease only through the charity that finds in every man a "neighbor," a brother.
1932 The duty of making oneself a neighbor to others and actively serving them becomes even more urgent when it involves the disadvantaged, in whatever area this may be. "As you did it to one of the least of these my brethren, you did it to me."[38]
1933 This same duty extends to those who think or act differently from us. The teaching of Christ goes so far as to require the forgiveness of offenses. He extends the commandment of love, which is that of the New Law, to all enemies.[39] Liberation in the spirit of the Gospel is incompatible with hatred of one's enemy as a person, but not with hatred of the evil that he does as an enemy.

II. EQUALITY AND DIFFERENCES AMONG MEN

1934 Created in the image of the one God and equally endowed with rational souls, all men have the same nature and the same origin. Redeemed by the sacrifice of Christ, all are called to participate in the same divine beatitude: all therefore enjoy an equal dignity.

1935 The equality of men rests essentially on their dignity as persons and the rights that flow from it:

Every form of social or cultural discrimination in fundamental personal rights on the grounds of sex, race, color, social conditions, language, or religion must be curbed and eradicated as incompatible with God's design.[40]

1936 On coming into the world, man is not equipped with everything he needs for developing his bodily and spiritual life. He needs others. Differences appear tied to age, physical abilities, intellectual or moral aptitudes, the benefits derived from social commerce, and the distribution of wealth.[41] The "talents" are not distributed equally.[42]

1937 These differences belong to God's plan, who wills that each receive what he needs from others, and that those endowed with particular "talents" share the benefits with those who need them. These differences encourage and often oblige persons to practice generosity, kindness, and sharing of goods; they foster the mutual enrichment of cultures:

I distribute the virtues quite diversely; I do not give all of them to each person, but some to one, some to others... I shall give principally charity to one; justice to another; humility to this one, a living faith to that one... And so I have given many gifts and graces, both spiritual and temporal, with such diversity that I have not given everything to one single person, so that you may be constrained to practice charity towards one another... I have willed that one should need another and that all should be my ministers in distributing the graces and gifts they have received from me.[43]

1938 There exist also sinful inequalities that affect millions of men and women. These are in open contradiction of the Gospel:

Their equal dignity as persons demands that we strive for fairer and more humane conditions. Excessive economic and social disparity between individuals and peoples of the one human race is a source of scandal and militates against social justice, equity, human dignity, as well as social and international peace.[44]

III. HUMAN SOLIDARITY

1939 The principle of solidarity, also articulated in terms of "friendship" or "social charity," is a direct demand of human and Christian brotherhood.[45] An error, "today abundantly widespread, is disregard for the law of human solidarity and charity, dictated and imposed both by our common origin and by the equality in rational nature of all men, whatever nation they belong to. This law is sealed by the sacrifice of redemption offered by Jesus Christ on the altar of the Cross to his heavenly Father, on behalf of sinful humanity."[46]

1940 Solidarity is manifested in the first place by the distribution of goods and remuneration for work. It also presupposes the effort for a more just social order where tensions are better able to be reduced and conflicts more readily settled by negotiation.

1941 Socio-economic problems can be resolved only with the help of all the forms of solidarity: solidarity of the poor among themselves, between rich and poor, of workers among themselves, between employers and employees in a business, solidarity among nations and peoples. International solidarity is a requirement of the moral order; world peace depends in part upon this.

1942 The virtue of solidarity goes beyond material goods. In spreading the spiritual goods of the faith, the Church has promoted, and often opened new paths for, the development of temporal goods as well. And so throughout the centuries has the Lord's saying been verified: "Seek first his kingdom and his righteousness, and all these things shall be yours as well":[47]

For two thousand years this sentiment has lived and endured in the soul of the Church, impelling souls then and now to the heroic charity of monastic farmers, liberators of slaves, healers of the sick, and messengers of faith, civilization, and science to all generations and all peoples for the sake of creating the social conditions capable of offering to everyone possible a life worthy of man and of a Christian.[48]

IN BRIEF

1943 Society ensures social justice by providing the conditions that allow associations and individuals to obtain their due.

1944 Respect for the human person considers the other "another self." It presupposes respect for the fundamental rights that flow from the dignity intrinsic of the person.

1945 The equality of men concerns their dignity as persons and the rights that flow from it.

1946 The differences among persons belong to God's plan, who wills that we should need one another. These differences should encourage charity.

1947 The equal dignity of human persons requires the effort to reduce excessive social and economic inequalities. It gives urgency to the elimination of sinful inequalities.

1948 Solidarity is an eminently Christian virtue. It practices the sharing of spiritual goods even more than material ones.

. . . .
. . . .

The social duty of religion and the right to religious freedom

2104 "All men are bound to seek the truth, especially in what concerns God and his Church, and to embrace it and hold on to it as they come to know it."[26]

This duty derives from "the very dignity of the human person."[27] It does not contradict a "sincere respect" for different religions which frequently "reflect a ray of that truth which enlightens all men,"[28] nor the requirement of charity, which urges Christians "to treat with love, prudence and patience those who are in error or ignorance with regard to the faith."[29]

2105 The duty of offering God genuine worship concerns man both individually and socially. This is "the traditional Catholic teaching on the moral duty of individuals and societies toward the true religion and the one Church of Christ."[30] By constantly evangelizing men, the Church works toward enabling them "to infuse the Christian spirit into the mentality and mores, laws and structures of the communities in which [they] live."[31] The social duty of Christians is to respect and awaken in each man the love of the true and the good. It requires them to make known the worship of the one true religion which subsists in the Catholic and apostolic Church.[32] Christians are called to be the light of the world. Thus, the Church shows forth the kingship of Christ over all creation and in particular over human societies.[33]

2106 "Nobody may be forced to act against his convictions, nor is anyone to be restrained from acting in accordance with his conscience in religious matters in private or in public, alone or in association with others, within due limits."[34] This right is based on the very nature of the human person, whose dignity enables him freely to assent to the divine truth which transcends the temporal order. For this reason it "continues to exist even in those who do not live up to their obligation of seeking the truth and adhering to it."[35]

2107 "If because of the circumstances of a particular people special civil recognition is given to one religious community in the constitutional organization of a state, the right of all citizens and religious communities to religious freedom must be recognized and respected as well."[36]

2108 The right to religious liberty is neither a moral license to adhere to error, nor a supposed right to error,[37] but rather a natural right of the human person to civil liberty, i.e., immunity, within just limits, from external constraint in religious matters by political authorities. This natural right ought to be acknowledged in the juridical order of society in such a way that it constitutes a civil right.[38]

2109 The right to religious liberty can of itself be neither unlimited nor limited only by a "public order" conceived in a positivist or naturalist manner.[39] The "due limits" which are inherent in it must be determined for each social situation by political prudence, according to the requirements of the common good, and ratified by the civil authority in accordance with "legal principles which are in conformity with the objective moral order."[40]

. . . .
. . . .

V. THE AUTHORITIES IN CIVIL SOCIETY

2234 God's fourth commandment also enjoins us to honor all who for our good have received authority in society from God. It clarifies the duties of those who exercise authority as well as those who benefit from it.

Duties of civil authorities

2235 Those who exercise authority should do so as a service. "Whoever would be great among you must be your servant."[41] The exercise of authority is measured morally in terms of its divine origin, its reasonable nature and its specific object. No one can command or establish what is contrary to the dignity of persons and the natural law.

2236 The exercise of authority is meant to give outward expression to a just hierarchy of values in order to facilitate the exercise of freedom and responsibility by all. Those in authority should practice distributive justice wisely, taking account of the needs and contribution of each, with a view to harmony and peace. They should take care that the regulations and measures they adopt are not a source of temptation by setting personal interest against that of the community.[42]

2237 Political authorities are obliged to respect the fundamental rights of the human person. They will dispense justice humanely by respecting the rights of everyone, especially of families and the disadvantaged.

The political rights attached to citizenship can and should be granted according to the requirements of the common good. They cannot be suspended by public authorities without legitimate and proportionate reasons. Political rights are meant to be exercised for the common good of the nation and the human community.

The duties of citizens

2238 Those subject to authority should regard those in authority as representatives of God, who has made them stewards of his gifts:[43] "Be subject for the Lord's sake to every human institution... Live as free men, yet without using your freedom as a pretext for evil; but live as servants of God."[44] Their loyal collaboration includes the right, and at times the duty, to voice their just criticisms of that which seems harmful to the dignity of persons and to the good of the community.

2239 It is the duty of citizens to contribute along with the civil authorities to the good of society in a spirit of truth, justice, solidarity, and freedom. The love and service of one's country follow from the duty of gratitude and belong to the order of charity. Submission to legitimate authorities and service of the common good require citizens to fulfill their roles in the life of the political community.

2240 Submission to authority and co-responsibility for the common good make it morally obligatory to pay taxes, to exercise the right to vote, and to defend one's country:

Pay to all of them their dues, taxes to whom taxes are due, revenue to whom revenue is due, respect to whom respect is due, honor to whom honor is due.[45]

[Christians] reside in their own nations, but as resident aliens. They participate in all things as citizens and endure all things as foreigners... They obey the established laws and their way of life surpasses the laws... So noble is the position to which God has assigned them that they are not allowed to desert it.[46] The Apostle exhorts us to offer prayers and thanksgiving for kings and all who exercise authority, "that we may lead a quiet and peaceable life, godly and respectful in every way."[47]

2241 The more prosperous nations are obliged, to the extent they are able, to welcome the foreigner in search of the security and the means of livelihood which he cannot find in his country of origin. Public authorities should see to it that the natural right is respected that places a guest under the protection of those who receive him.

Political authorities, for the sake of the common good for which they are responsible, may make the exercise of the right to immigrate subject to various juridical conditions, especially with regard to the immigrants' duties toward their country of adoption. Immigrants are obliged to respect with gratitude the material and spiritual heritage of the country that receives them, to obey its laws and to assist in carrying civic burdens.

2242 The citizen is obliged in conscience not to follow the directives of civil authorities when they are contrary to the demands of the moral order, to the fundamental rights of persons or the teachings of the Gospel. Refusing obedience to civil authorities, when their demands are contrary to those of an upright conscience, finds its justification in the distinction between serving God and serving the political community. "Render therefore to Caesar the things that are Caesar's, and to God the things that are God's."[48] "We must obey God rather than men":[49]

When citizens are under the oppression of a public authority which oversteps its competence, they should still not refuse to give or to do what is objectively demanded of them by the common good; but it is legitimate for them to defend their own rights and those of their fellow citizens against the abuse of this authority within the limits of the natural law and the Law of the Gospel.[50]

2243 Armed resistance to oppression by political authority is not legitimate, unless all the following conditions are met: 1) there is certain, grave, and prolonged violation of fundamental rights; 2) all other means of redress have been exhausted; 3) such resistance will not provoke worse disorders; 4) there is well-founded hope of success; and 5) it is impossible reasonably to foresee any better solution.

The political community and the Church

2244 Every institution is inspired, at least implicitly, by a vision of man and his destiny, from which it derives the point of reference for its judgment, its hierarchy of values, its line of conduct. Most societies have formed their institutions in the recognition of a certain preeminence of man over things. Only the divinely revealed religion has clearly recognized man's origin and destiny in God, the Creator and Redeemer. The Church invites political authorities to measure their judgments and decisions against this inspired truth about God and man:

Societies not recognizing this vision or rejecting it in the name of their independence from God are brought to seek their criteria and goal in themselves or to borrow them from some ideology. Since they do not admit that one can defend an objective criterion of good and evil, they arrogate to themselves an explicit or implicit totalitarian power over man and his destiny, as history shows.[51]

2245 The Church, because of her commission and competence, is not to be confused in any way with the political community. She is both the sign and the safeguard of the transcendent character of the human person. "The Church respects and encourages the political freedom and responsibility of the citizen."[52]

2246 It is a part of the Church's mission "to pass moral judgments even in matters related to politics, whenever the fundamental rights of man or the salvation of souls requires it. The means, the only means, she may use are those which are in accord with the Gospel and the welfare of all men according to the diversity of times and circumstances."[53]

IN BRIEF

. . . .
. . . .

2254 Public authority is obliged to respect the fundamental rights of the human person and the conditions for the exercise of his freedom.

2255 It is the duty of citizens to work with civil authority for building up society in a spirit of truth, justice, solidarity, and freedom.

2256 Citizens are obliged in conscience not to follow the directives of civil authorities when they are contrary to the demands of the moral order. "We must obey God rather than men" (Acts 5:29).

2257 Every society's judgments and conduct reflect a vision of man and his destiny. Without the light the Gospel sheds on God and man, societies easily become totalitarian.

. . . .
. . . .

III. SAFEGUARDING PEACE

Peace

. . . .
. . . .

2304 Respect for and development of human life require peace. Peace is not
merely the absence of war, and it is not limited to maintaining a balance of
powers between adversaries. Peace cannot be attained on earth without safeguarding the goods of persons, free communication among men, respect for the
dignity of persons and peoples, and the assiduous practice of fraternity. Peace is
"the tranquillity of order."[97] Peace is the work of justice and the effect of
charity.[98]
2305 Earthly peace is the image and fruit of the peace of Christ, the messianic
"Prince of Peace."[99] By the blood of his Cross, "in his own person he killed
the hostility,"[100] he reconciled men with God and made his Church the
sacrament of the unity of the human race and of its union with God. "He is
our peace."[101] He has declared: "Blessed are the peacemakers."[102]
2306 Those who renounce violence and bloodshed and, in order to safeguard
human rights, make use of those means of defense available to the weakest,
bear witness to evangelical charity, provided they do so without harming the
rights and obligations of other men and societies. They bear legitimate witness
to the gravity of the physical and moral risks of recourse to violence, with all its
destruction and death.[103]

Avoiding war

2307 The fifth commandment forbids the intentional destruction of human
life. Because of the evils and injustices that accompany all war, the Church
insistently urges everyone to prayer and to action so that the divine Goodness
may free us from the ancient bondage of war.[104]
2308 All citizens and all governments are obliged to work for the avoidance of
war.
However, "as long as the danger of war persists and there is no international
authority with the necessary competence and power, governments cannot be
denied the right of lawful self-defense, once all peace efforts have failed."[105]
2309 The strict conditions for legitimate defense by military force require rigorous consideration. The gravity of such a decision makes it subject to rigorous
conditions of moral legitimacy. At one and the same time:
– the damage inflicted by the aggressor on the nation or community of nations
  must be lasting, grave, and certain;

- all other means of putting an end to it must have been shown to be impractical or ineffective;
- there must be serious prospects of success;
- the use of arms must not produce evils and disorders graver than the evil to be eliminated. The power of modern means of destruction weighs very heavily in evaluating this condition.

These are the traditional elements enumerated in what is called the "just war" doctrine.

The evaluation of these conditions for moral legitimacy belongs to the prudential judgment of those who have responsibility for the common good.

2310 Public authorities, in this case, have the right and duty to impose on citizens the obligations necessary for national defense.

Those who are sworn to serve their country in the armed forces are servants of the security and freedom of nations. If they carry out their duty honorably, they truly contribute to the common good of the nation and the maintenance of peace.[106]

2311 Public authorities should make equitable provision for those who for reasons of conscience refuse to bear arms; these are nonetheless obliged to serve the human community in some other way.[107]

2312 The Church and human reason both assert the permanent validity of the moral law during armed conflict. "The mere fact that war has regrettably broken out does not mean that everything becomes licit between the warring parties."[108]

2313 Non-combatants, wounded soldiers, and prisoners must be respected and treated humanely.

Actions deliberately contrary to the law of nations and to its universal principles are crimes, as are the orders that command such actions. Blind obedience does not suffice to excuse those who carry them out. Thus the extermination of a people, nation, or ethnic minority must be condemned as a mortal sin. One is morally bound to resist orders that command genocide.

2314 "Every act of war directed to the indiscriminate destruction of whole cities or vast areas with their inhabitants is a crime against God and man, which merits firm and unequivocal condemnation."[109] A danger of modern warfare is that it provides the opportunity to those who possess modern scientific weapons especially atomic, biological, or chemical weapons – to commit such crimes.

2315 The accumulation of arms strikes many as a paradoxically suitable way of deterring potential adversaries from war. They see it as the most effective means of ensuring peace among nations. This method of deterrence gives rise to strong moral reservations. The arms race does not ensure peace. Far from eliminating the causes of war, it risks aggravating them. Spending enormous sums to produce ever new types of weapons impedes efforts to aid needy populations;[110] it thwarts the development of peoples. Over-armament multiplies reasons for conflict and increases the danger of escalation.

2316 The production and the sale of arms affect the common good of nations and of the international community. Hence public authorities have the right and duty to regulate them. The short-term pursuit of private or collective interests cannot legitimate undertakings that promote violence and conflict among nations and compromise the international juridical order.

2317 Injustice, excessive economic or social inequalities, envy, distrust, and pride raging among men and nations constantly threaten peace and cause wars. Everything done to overcome these disorders contributes to building up peace and avoiding war:

Insofar as men are sinners, the threat of war hangs over them and will so continue until Christ comes again; but insofar as they can vanquish sin by coming together in charity, violence itself will be vanquished and these words will be fulfilled: "they shall beat their swords into plowshares, and their spears into pruning hooks; nation shall not lift up sword against nation, neither shall they learn war any more."[111]

IN BRIEF

2318 "In [God's] hand is the life of every living thing and the breath of all mankind" (Job 12:10).

2319 Every human life, from the moment of conception until death, is sacred because the human person has been willed for its own sake in the image and likeness of the living and holy God.

2320 The murder of a human being is gravely contrary to the dignity of the person and the holiness of the Creator.

2321 The prohibition of murder does not abrogate the right to render an unjust aggressor unable to inflict harm. Legitimate defense is a grave duty for whoever is responsible for the lives of others or the common good.

2322 From its conception, the child has the right to life. Direct abortion, that is, abortion willed as an end or as a means, is a "criminal" practice (GS 27 # 3), gravely contrary to the moral law. The Church imposes the canonical penalty of excommunication for this crime against human life.

2323 Because it should be treated as a person from conception, the embryo must be defended in its integrity, cared for, and healed like every other human being.

2324 Intentional euthanasia, whatever its forms or motives, is murder. It is gravely contrary to the dignity of the human person and to the respect due to the living God, his Creator.

2325 Suicide is seriously contrary to justice, hope, and charity. It is forbidden by the fifth commandment.

2326 Scandal is a grave offense when by deed or omission it deliberately leads others to sin.

2327 Because of the evils and injustices that all war brings with it, we must do everything reasonably possible to avoid it. The Church prays: "From famine, pestilence, and war, O Lord, deliver us."

2328 The Church and human reason assert the permanent validity of the moral law during armed conflicts. Practices deliberately contrary to the law of nations and to its universal principles are crimes.

2329 "The arms race is one of the greatest curses on the human race and the harm it inflicts on the poor is more than can be endured" (GS 81 # 3).

2330 "Blessed are the peacemakers, for they shall be called sons of God" (Mt 5:9).

. . . .
. . . .

Respect for the integrity of creation

2415 The seventh commandment enjoins respect for the integrity of creation. Animals, like plants and inanimate beings, are by nature destined for the common good of past, present, and future humanity.[194] Use of the mineral, vegetable, and animal resources of the universe cannot be divorced from respect for moral imperatives. Man's dominion over inanimate and other living beings granted by the Creator is not absolute; it is limited by concern for the quality of life of his neighbor, including generations to come; it requires a religious respect for the integrity of creation.[195]

. . . .
. . . .

III. THE SOCIAL DOCTRINE OF THE CHURCH

2419 "Christian revelation … promotes deeper understanding of the laws of social living."[198] The Church receives from the Gospel the full revelation of the truth about man. When she fulfills her mission of proclaiming the Gospel, she bears witness to man, in the name of Christ, to his dignity and his vocation to the communion of persons. She teaches him the demands of justice and peace in conformity with divine wisdom.

2420 The Church makes a moral judgment about economic and social matters, "when the fundamental rights of the person or the salvation of souls requires it."[199] In the moral order she bears a mission distinct from that of political authorities: the Church is concerned with the temporal aspects of the common good because they are ordered to the sovereign Good, our ultimate end. She strives to inspire right attitudes with respect to earthly goods and in socio-economic relationships.

2421 The social doctrine of the Church developed in the nineteenth century when the Gospel encountered modern industrial society with its new structures for the production of consumer goods, its new concept of society, the state and authority, and its new forms of labor and ownership. The development of the doctrine of the Church on economic and social matters attests the permanent value of the Church's teaching at the same time as it attests the true meaning of her Tradition, always living and active.[200]

2422 The Church's social teaching comprises a body of doctrine, which is articulated as the Church interprets events in the course of history, with the assistance of the Holy Spirit, in the light of the whole of what has been revealed by Jesus Christ.[201] This teaching can be more easily accepted by men of good will, the more the faithful let themselves be guided by it.

2423 The Church's social teaching proposes principles for reflection; it provides criteria for judgment; it gives guidelines for action:

Any system in which social relationships are determined entirely by economic factors is contrary to the nature of the human person and his acts.[202]

2424 A theory that makes profit the exclusive norm and ultimate end of economic activity is morally unacceptable. The disordered desire for money cannot but produce perverse effects. It is one of the causes of the many conflicts which disturb the social order.[203]

A system that "subordinates the basic rights of individuals and of groups to the collective organization of production" is contrary to human dignity.[204] Every practice that reduces persons to nothing more than a means of profit enslaves man, leads to idolizing money, and contributes to the spread of atheism. "You cannot serve God and mammon."[205]

2425 The Church has rejected the totalitarian and atheistic ideologies associated in modem times with "communism" or "socialism." She has likewise refused to accept, in the practice of "capitalism," individualism and the absolute primacy of the law of the marketplace over human labor.[206] Regulating the economy solely by centralized planning perverts the basis of social bonds; regulating it solely by the law of the marketplace fails social justice, for "there are many human needs which cannot be satisfied by the market."[207] Reasonable regulation of the marketplace and economic initiatives, in keeping with a just hierarchy of values and a view to the common good, is to be commended.

IV. ECONOMIC ACTIVITY AND SOCIAL JUSTICE

2426 The development of economic activity and growth in production are meant to provide for the needs of human beings. Economic life is not meant solely to multiply goods produced and increase profit or power; it is ordered first of all to the service of persons, of the whole man, and of the entire human community. Economic activity, conducted according to its own proper methods, is to be exercised within the limits of the moral order, in keeping with social justice so as to correspond to God's plan for man.[208]

2427 Human work proceeds directly from persons created in the image of God and called to prolong the work of creation by subduing the earth, both with and for one another.[209] Hence work is a duty: "If any one will not work, let him not eat."[210] Work honors the Creator's gifts and the talents received from him. It can also be redemptive. By enduring the hardship of work[211] in union with Jesus, the carpenter of Nazareth and the one crucified on Calvary, man collaborates in a certain fashion with the Son of God in his redemptive work. He shows himself to be a disciple of Christ by carrying the cross, daily, in the work he is called to accomplish.[212] Work can be a means of sanctification and a way of animating earthly realities with the Spirit of Christ.

2428 In work, the person exercises and fulfills in part the potential inscribed in his nature. The primordial value of labor stems from man himself, its author and its beneficiary. Work is for man, not man for work.[213]

Everyone should be able to draw from work the means of providing for his life and that of his family, and of serving the human community.

2429 Everyone has the right of economic initiative; everyone should make legitimate use of his talents to contribute to the abundance that will benefit all and to harvest the just fruits of his labor. He should seek to observe regulations issued by legitimate authority for the sake of the common good.[214]

2430 Economic life brings into play different interests, often opposed to one another. This explains why the conflicts that characterize it arise.[215] Efforts should be made to reduce these conflicts by negotiation that respects the rights and duties of each social partner: those responsible for business enterprises, representatives of wage- earners (for example, trade unions), and public authorities when appropriate.

2431 The responsibility of the state. "Economic activity, especially the activity of a market economy, cannot be conducted in an institutional, juridical, or political vacuum. On the contrary, it presupposes sure guarantees of individual freedom and private property, as well as a stable currency and efficient public services. Hence the principal task of the state is to guarantee this security, so that those who work and produce can enjoy the fruits of their labors and thus feel encouraged to work efficiently and honestly... Another task of the state is that of overseeing and directing the exercise of human rights in the economic sector. However, primary responsibility in this area belongs not to the state but to individuals and to the various groups and associations which make up society."[216]

2432 Those responsible for business enterprises are responsible to society for the economic and ecological effects of their operations.[217] They have an obligation to consider the good of persons and not only the increase of profits. Profits are necessary, however. They make possible the investments that ensure the future of a business and they guarantee employment.

2433 Access to employment and to professions must be open to all without unjust discrimination: men and women, healthy and disabled, natives and immigrants.[218] For its part society should, according to circumstances, help citizens find work and employment.[219]

2434 A just wage is the legitimate fruit of work. To refuse or withhold it can be a grave injustice.[220] In determining fair pay both the needs and the contributions of each person must be taken into account. "Remuneration for work should guarantee man the opportunity to provide a dignified livelihood for himself and his family on the material, social, cultural and spiritual level, taking into account the role and the productivity of each, the state of the business, and the common good."[221] Agreement between the parties is not sufficient to justify morally the amount to be received in wages.

2435 Recourse to a strike is morally legitimate when it cannot be avoided, or at least when it is necessary to obtain a proportionate benefit. It becomes morally unacceptable when accompanied by violence, or when objectives are included that are not directly linked to working conditions or are contrary to the common good.

. . . .
. . . .

V. JUSTICE AND SOLIDARITY AMONG NATIONS

2437 On the international level, inequality of resources and economic capability is such that it creates a real "gap" between nations.[223] On the one side there are those nations possessing and developing the means of growth and, on the other, those accumulating debts.

2438 Various causes of a religious, political, economic, and financial nature today give "the social question a worldwide dimension."[224] There must be solidarity among nations which are already politically interdependent. It is even more essential when it is a question of dismantling the "perverse mechanisms" that impede the development of the less advanced countries.[225] In place of abusive if not usurious financial systems, iniquitous commercial relations among nations, and the arms race, there must be substituted a common effort to mobilize resources toward objectives of moral, cultural, and economic development, "redefining the priorities and hierarchies of values."[226]

2439 Rich nations have a grave moral responsibility toward those which are unable to ensure the means of their development by themselves or have been prevented from doing so by tragic historical events. It is a duty in solidarity and charity; it is also an obligation in justice if the prosperity of the rich nations has come from resources that have not been paid for fairly.

2440 Direct aid is an appropriate response to immediate, extraordinary needs caused by natural catastrophes, epidemics, and the like. But it does not suffice to repair the grave damage resulting from destitution or to provide a lasting solution to a country's needs. It is also necessary to reform international economic and financial institutions so that they will better promote equitable relationships with less advanced countries.[227] The efforts of poor countries working for growth and liberation must be supported.[228] This doctrine must be applied especially in the area of agricultural labor. Peasants, especially in the Third World, form the overwhelming majority of the poor.

2441 An increased sense of God and increased self-awareness are fundamental to any full development of human society. This development multiplies material goods and puts them at the service of the person and his freedom. It reduces dire poverty and economic exploitation. It makes for growth in respect for cultural identities and openness to the transcendent.[229]

2442 It is not the role of the Pastors of the Church to intervene directly in the political structuring and organization of social life. This task is part of the vocation of the lay faithful, acting on their own initiative with their fellow citizens. Social action can assume various concrete forms. It should always have the common good in view and be in conformity with the message of the Gospel and the teaching of the Church. It is the role of the laity "to animate temporal realities with Christian commitment, by which they show that they are witnesses and agents of peace and justice."[230]

. . . .
. . . .

V. THE USE OF THE SOCIAL COMMUNICATIONS MEDIA

2493 Within modern society the communications media play a major role in information, cultural promotion, and formation. This role is increasing, as a result of technological progress, the extent and diversity of the news transmitted, and the influence exercised on public opinion.

2494 The information provided by the media is at the service of the common good.[284] Society has a right to information based on truth, freedom, justice, and solidarity:

The proper exercise of this right demands that the content of the communication be true and – within the limits set by justice and charity – complete. Further, it should be communicated honestly and properly. This means that in the gathering and in the publication of news, the moral law and the legitimate rights and dignity of man should be upheld.[285]

2495 "It is necessary that all members of society meet the demands of justice and charity in this domain. They should help, through the means of social communication, in the formation and diffusion of sound public opinion."[286] Solidarity is a consequence of genuine and right communication and the free circulation of ideas that further knowledge and respect for others.

2496 The means of social communication (especially the mass media) can give rise to a certain passivity among users, making them less than vigilant consumers of what is said or shown. Users should practice moderation and discipline in their approach to the mass media. They will want to form enlightened and correct consciences the more easily to resist unwholesome influences.

2497 By the very nature of their profession, journalists have an obligation to serve the truth and not offend against charity in disseminating information. They should strive to respect, with equal care, the nature of the facts and the limits of critical judgment concerning individuals. They should not stoop to defamation.

2498 "Civil authorities have particular responsibilities in this field because of the common good... It is for the civil authority ... to defend and safeguard a true and just freedom of information."[287] By promulgating laws and overseeing their application, public authorities should ensure that "public morality and social progress are not gravely endangered" through misuse of the media.[288] Civil authorities should punish any violation of the rights of individuals to their reputation and privacy. They should give timely and reliable reports concerning the general good or respond to the well-founded concerns of the people. Nothing can justify recourse to disinformation for manipulating public opinion through the media. Interventions by public authority should avoid injuring the freedom of individuals or groups.

2499 Moral judgment must condemn the plague of totalitarian states which systematically falsify the truth, exercise political control of opinion through the media, manipulate defendants and witnesses at public trials, and imagine that they secure their tyranny by strangling and repressing everything they consider "thought crimes."

· ·
· ·

EVENTS IN THE PONTIFICATE OF HIS HOLINESS POPE JOHN PAUL II *

* Copyright: Vatican Information Service

1978

Cardinal Karol Wojtyla is elected successor to Pope John Paul I, the 264th Pope of the Catholic Church and takes the name John Paul II. *(Oct. 16)*
First "Urbi et Orbi" radio message of John Paul II.*(Oct. 17)*
Solemn inauguration of his ministry as universal Pastor of the Church.*(Oct. 22)*
John Paul II's historic embrace of Card. Wyszynski. *(Oct. 23)*
First visit of the new Pontiff to Castelgandolfo: visit to the parish church and papal villa. *(Oct. 25)*
First pilgrimage outside Rome to the Shrine of the Blessed Virgin Mary at Mentorella. *(Oct. 29)*
Visit of John Paul II to Assisi to venerate the tomb of St. Francis, patron of Italy, and to the basilica of Santa Maria sopra Minerva to venerate the tomb of St. Catherine, patroness of Italy. *(Nov. 5)*
As Bishop of Rome, John Paul II takes possession of St. John Lateran Basilica. *(Nov. 12)*
John Paul II begins his pastoral visits to the parishes in the diocese of Rome: S. Francesco Saverio at Garbatella. *(Dec. 5)*

1979

John Paul II accepts the request for mediation in the border conflict between Argentina and Chile. *(Jan. 24)*
Audience granted to the Soviet Foreign Minister, Andrei Gromyko.*(Jan. 24)*
First pastoral visit of John Paul II outside Italy: to Santo Domingo, Mexico (for the Third General Conference of the Latin American Bishops, Puebla), and the Bahamas. *(Jan. 25- Feb.)*
First papal encyclical: "Redemptor Hominis", (On the Redemption and Dignity of the Human Race), published March 15. *(Mar. 4)*
Archbishop Agostino Casaroli is appointed Pro-Secretary of State and Pro-prefect of the Council for the Public Affairs of the Church. *(Apr. 28)*
Second pastoral visit of John Paul II outside Italy: to Poland.*(June 2-10)*
Historic homily of John Paul II at Victory Square in Warsaw: "It is not possible to understand the history of the Polish nation without Christ".*(June 2)*
Celebration of the first Consistory in his pontificate for the creation of 14 Cardinals, among whom were Card. Casaroli, Secretary of State. (One additional Cardinal was reserved "in pectore" – Chinese Ignatius Gong Pin-mei, whose appointment was published only in the Consistory of June 28, 1991.*(June 30)*
Third pastoral visit of John Paul II outside Italy: to Ireland, the U.N. and the United States of America. *(Sep. 29 – Oct. 8)*

John Paul II addresses the General Assembly of the U.N. in New York.*(Oct. 2)*
Post-Synodal Pastoral Exhortation "Catechesi Tradendae", published October 25, 1979. *(Oct. 16)*
First Plenary Assembly of the College of Cardinals on the themes: the structure of the Roman Curia; the Church and culture; the financial situation of the Holy See. *(Nov. 5-9)*
Fourth pastoral visit of John Paul II outside Italy: Turkey.*(Nov. 28-30)*

1980

Opening of the Special Assembly for the Netherlands of the Synod of Bishops on: "The pastoral action of the Church in Holland in the present situation". *(Jan. 14-31)*
Good Friday: John Paul II hears confessions of the faithful for the first time in St. Peter's Basilica. *(Apr. 4)*
Fifth pastoral visit of John Paul II outside Italy: to Zaire, the Republic of the Congo, Kenya, Ghana, Upper Volta, the Ivory Coast. *(May 2-12)*
Sixth pastoral visit of John Paul II outside Italy: to France. *(May 30-June 2)*
John Paul II's address to UNESCO in Paris. *(June 2)*
Visit of the President Jimmy Carter of the United States. *(June 21)*
Seventh pastoral visit outside Italy: to Brazil. *(June 30-July 12)*
For the first time John Paul II alludes to the events happening in Poland regarding Solidarnosc. *(Aug. 20)*
Fifth Ordinary General Assembly of the Synod of Bishops on the theme: "The Role of the Christian Family in the Modern World".*(Sept. 26-Oct. 25)*
Pastoral visit to Subiaco and meeting with the European Bishops.*(Sept. 28)*
Official visit of H.M. Queen Elizabeth II of Great Britain and of H.R.H. Prince Philip, Duke of Edinburgh. *(Oct. 17)*
Eighth pastoral visit outside Italy: to West Germany. *(Nov. 15-19)*
Pastoral visit to Capodichino (Naples), Potenza, Balvano, Avellino, after the earthquake. *(Nov. 25)*
Second papal encyclical "Dives in Misericordia", (On the Mercy of God), published December 2, 1980. *(Nov. 30)*
Official visit of President Cviyetin Mijatovic of the Socialist Federal Republic of Yugoslavia. *(Dec. 19)*
Apostolic Letter proclaiming Sts. Cyril and Methodius, together with St. Benedict, Patrons of Europe. *(Dec. 30)*

1981

Pope John Paul II receives in Audience a delegation of the Polish Independent Syndicate "Solidarnosc," headed by Lech Walesa. *(Jan. 15)*
John Paul II meets with Rome's Chief Rabbi Elio Toaff, during his pastoral visit to the parish of Sts. Carlo e Biagio in Catinari. *(Feb. 8)*
Ninth pastoral visit outside Italy: to Pakistan, the Philippines, Guam (USA), Japan, and Anchorage (USA). *(Feb. 16-27)*

At 5:19 p.m.Turkish terrorist Mehmet Alì Agca makes an attempt on the Pope's life, while he was circling St. Peter's Square before his Wednesday general audience; following an operation which lasted 6 hours, he was hospitalized for 77 days at Gemelli hospital. *(May 13)*

John Paul II recites the Angelus at Gemelli hospital: "Pray for the brother who shot me, whom I have sincerely forgiven." *(May 17)*

John Paul II creates the Council of Cardinals for the study of organizational and economic problems of the Holy See, following the meeting of the Sacred College from November 5-9, 1981. *(May 31)*

John Paul II returns to the Vatican after 22 days of recovery at Gemelli Hospital. *(June 3)*

John Paul II is newly hospitalized for a "cytomegalo" virus infection. *(June 20)* On August 5th he undergoes a second operation; leaves hospital definitively, returns to the Vatican on the 14th of August and from there goes to Castelgandolfo on August 16th.

First meeting of the Council of Cardinals for the study of organizational and economic problems of the Holy See. *(July 13)*

Third papal encyclical "Laborem Exercens" (On Human Work).*(Sept. 14)*

Post-Synodal Pastoral Exhortation "Familiaris Consortio" (On the Family), published on December 15, 1981. *(Nov. 22)*

Card. Joseph Ratzinger appointed prefect of the Congregation for the Doctrine of the Faith. *(Nov. 25)*

John Paul II sends delegates of the Pontifical Academy of Sciences to the presidents of the USA, USSR, Great Britain, France, and the UN, to explain their document on the eventual consequences of the use of nuclear arms in Europe and the world. *(Dec. 12)*

John Paul II invites prayers for the Polish nation, calling the situation a state of emergency. *(Dec. 13)*

1982

Apostolic Letter "Caritatis Christi", for the church in China. *(Jan 6)*

10th pastoral visit outside Italy: to Nigeria, Benin, Gabon, Equatorial Guinea. *(Feb. 12-19)*

Holy Mass in St. Peter's Basilica for the Chinese Church. *(Mar. 21)*

11th pastoral visit outside Italy: to Portugal, one year after the assassination attempt on his life in St. Peter's Square. *(May 12-15)*

Holy Mass for justice and peace, for peace between Argentina and Great Britain (the Falkland Islands/Malvinas) in St. Peter's Basilica. *(May 22)*

12th pastoral visit outside Italy: to Great Britain. *(May 28-June 2)*

Joint statement of John Paul II and the Archbishop of Canterbury, Dr. Robert Runcie, at the end of the ecumenical celebration in the Anglican Canterbury Cathedral. *(May 29)*

John Paul II meets the U.S. President Ronald Reagan for the first time; they pledge to work for world peace and justice. *(June 7)*

13th pastoral visit outside Italy: to Argentina, in relation to the war between Argentina and Great Britain, regarding the Falkland Islands and Malvinas. *(June 10-13)*

14th pastoral visit outside Italy: to Geneva, Switzerland – Speech by John Paul II at the 68 session of the International Workers Conference in Geneva. *(June 15)*

15th pastoral visit outside Italy: to San Marino and Rimini. *(Aug. 29)*

Private meeting with Yasser Arafat on the prospects for peace in the Middle East. *(Sept. 15)*

Renewed appeal for peace in Lebanon, after the murder of president-elect Bechir Gemayel. *(Sept. 15)*

Canonization of Fr. Maximilian Kolbe. Present at the canonization ceremony was Mr. Franciszek Gajownizek, the man for whom Fr. Maximilian offered his life in the concentration camp at Auschwitz. *(Oct. 10)*

Meeting with Italian President Sandro Pertini, at Castelporziano. *(Oct. 19)*

Official visit of the president of the Federal Republic of Germany, Prof. Karl Carstens. *(Oct. 28)*

16th pastoral visit outside Italy: to Spain, for the closure of the 4th Centenary of the death of St. Teresa of Avila.*(Oct. 31- Nov. 9)*

Message to the peoples of Europe from the cathedral of Santiago de Compostela. *(Nov. 9)*

Second Plenary Session of the College of Cardinals on: curial reforms; state of revisions of the Code of Canon Law; financial solvency of the Holy See; relations between the Institute of the Works of Religion (I.O.R.) and the "Banco Ambrosiano". *(Nov. 23-26)*

John Paul II announces the Holy Year of Redemption: from Lent 1983 to Easter 1984. *(Nov. 26)*

1983

Papal Bull "Aperite Portas Redemptori", announcing the Jubilee for the 1950 anniversary of the Redemption. *(Jan. 6)*

John Paul II's Pastoral Constitution "Sacrae Disciplinae Leges", for the promulgation of the new Code of Canon Law. *(Jan. 25)*

Promulgation of the new Code of Canon Law by John Paul II. *(Jan. 25)*

Second Consistory of John Paul II for the creation of 18 cardinals. *(Feb. 2)*

17th pastoral visit outside Italy: to Lisbon and Central America – Costa Rica, Nicaragua, Panama, El Salvador, Guatemala, Honduras, Belize, and Haiti. *(Mar. 2-10)*

Opening of the Holy Year of the Redemption. *(Mar. 25, 1983- April 22, 1984)*

18th pastoral visit outside Italy: to Poland. *(June 16-23)*

19th pastoral visit outside Italy: to Lourdes. *(Aug. 14)*

20th pastoral visit outside Italy: to Austria. *(Sept. 10-13)*

Sixth Ordinary General Assembly of the Synod of Bishops on: "Penance and Reconciliation in the Mission of the Church". *(Sept. 29 – Oct. 29)*

Act of entrustment and consecration of the world to Our Lady of Fatima by John Paul II, together with the cardinals and bishops participating in the Synod of Bishops. *(Oct. 16)*
Letter for the 500th anniversary of the birth of Martin Luther. *(Nov. 5)*
Publication of the "Charter of Rights of the Family." *(Nov. 24)*
Meeting with the Evangelic – Lutheran community in Rome. *(Dec. 11)*
Visit to the Rebibbia prison and meeting with Alì Agca, the Turk who made an attempt on the life of John Paul II, May 13, 1981. *(Dec. 27)*

1984

Diplomatic relations between the Holy See and the United States of America. *(Jan. 10)*
Pastoral Letter "Salvific Doloris" (On the Christian Meaning of Suffering). *(Feb. 11)*
Agreement between the Holy See and the Italian Republic on the revision of the Lateran Concordat: new Concordat signed. *(Feb. 18)*
John Paul II erects the Foundation for the Sahel, letter published March 3. (Feb.22)
In spiritual union with all the bishops of the world John Paul II repeats the act of entrustment of mankind and all peoples to Mary Most Holy, at Fatima on May 13.*(Mar. 25)*
Apostolic Exhortation "Redemptionis Donum," to all men and women religious, published on March 29. *(Mar. 25)*
Additional appointments to the Roman Curia: broad renovation of responsibilities of dicasteries and commissions. *(Apr. 9)*
Apostolic Letter "Redemptionis Anno" on the City of Jerusalem, sacred patrimony of all believers and crossroads of peace for the peoples of the Middle East. *(Apr. 20)*
Conclusion of the Holy Year of Redemption 1983/84.*(Apr. 22)*
Apostolic Letter "Les Grands Mystères" (On the problem of Lebanon). *(May 1)*
21st pastoral visit outside Italy: to Korea, Papua-New Guinea, the Solomon Islands, and Thailand. *(May 2-12)*
Official visit of the Italian President Sandro Pertini. *(May 21)*
Official visit of John Paul II to the president of Italy, Sandro Pertini.*(June 2)*
22nd pastoral visit outside Italy: to Switzerland. *(June 12-17)*
Visit of John Paul II to the massif of Adamello and meeting with President Pertini. *(July 16-17)*
Publication of the instruction of the Congregation of the Doctrine of the Faith on certain aspects of theology of liberation.*(Sept. 3)*
23rd pastoral visit outside Italy: to Canada. *(Sept. 9-20)*
24th pastoral visit outside Italy: to Zaragoza, Spain, Santo Domingo, Dominican Republic and San Juan, Puerto Rico. *(Oct. 10-13)*
Publication of the Post-Synodal Pastoral Exhortation "Reconciliatio and Poenitentia" (Reconciliation and Penance). *(Dec. 11)*

1985

25th pastoral visit outside Italy: to Venezuela, Ecuador, Peru, Trinidad-Tobago. *(Jan. 26- Feb. 6)*
Audience with the Israeli Prime Minister Simon Peres. *(Feb. 19)*
Official visit of the Foreign Minister of the USSR Andrei Gromyko. *(Feb. 27)*
Apostolic Letter "Dilecti Amici" (To the Youth of the World) on the occasion of the United Nation's International Year of Youth. *(Mar. 26)*
First International Youth Meeting in Rome. *(Mar. 30-31)*
Pastoral visit of John Paul II to Loreto and meeting with Italian Bishops. *(Apr. 11)*
26th pastoral visit outside Italy: to the Netherlands, Luxembourg, and Belgium. *(May 11-21)*
Third Consistory of John Paul II for the creation of 28 new Cardinals.*(May 25)*
Fourth papal encyclical "Slavorum Apostoli", published on July 2. *(June 2)*
Holy Mass in the Paoline Chapel of the Vatican for the Czechoslovak people, in remembrance of Sts. Cyril and Methodius. *(July 7)*
27th pastoral visit outside Italy: to Togo, the Ivory Coast, Cameroon, the Republic of Central Africa, Zaire, Kenya, Marocco. *(Aug. 8-19)*
28th pastoral visit outside Italy: to Kloten, Switzerland and Liechtenstein. *(Sept. 8)*
Official visit of President Francesco Cossiga of Italy. *(Oct. 4)*
Personal message of the Pope to Ronald Reagan and Mikail Gorbaciov for the Geneva summit. *(Nov. 17)*
Third Plenary Meeting of the College of Cardinals on the reform of the Roman Curia. *(Nov. 21-23)*
Second Extraordinary General Assembly of the Synod of Bishops on: "The Twentieth Anniversary of the Conclusion of the Second Vatican Council". *(Nov. 25-Dec. 8)*

1986

Official visit of John Paul II to the Italian President, Francesco Cossiga.*(Jan. 18)*
29th pastoral visit outside Italy: to India. *(Jan. 31- Feb. 10)*
Private audience with President Amin Gemayel of Lebanon. *(Feb. 19)*
Official visit of the Governor General of Canada, Mme. Jeanne Sauvé.*(Mar. 6)*
Pope John Paul II and the dicastery heads of the Roman Curia meet with Bishops of the Brazilian Episcopal Conference at the end of their "visita ad limina". *(Mar. 13-15)*
Publication of the instruction "Libertatis Conscientia" by the Congregation for the Doctrine of the Faith, on Christian freedom and liberation. *(Apr. 5)*
John Paul II makes a visit to Rome's main synagogue. *(Apr. 13)*
Fifth papal encyclical "Dominum et Vivificantem" (On the Holy Spirit), published on May 30. *(May 18)*
30th pastoral visit outside Italy: to Colombia and Santa Lucia. *(July 1-8)*
31st pastoral visit outside Italy: to France (East-Central region).*(Oct. 4-7)*

John Paul II attends the First World Day of Prayer for Peace which he convoked in Assisi. *(Oct. 27)*
Official visit of the President Paul Biya of the Republic of Cameroon. *(Oct. 31)*
32nd pastoral visit outside Italy: to Bangladesh, Singapore, Fiji Islands, New Zealand, Australia and Seychelles. *(Nov. 18- Dec. 1)*

1987
Audience with President of the Council of the People's Republic of Poland, General Wojciech Jaruzelski. *(Jan. 13)*
Instruction of the Congregation of the Doctrine of the Faith on respect for human life published March 2. *(Feb. 22)*
Sixth papal encyclical "Redemptoris Mater", (Mother of the Redeemer). *(Mar. 25)*
33rd pastoral visit outside Italy: to Uruguay, Chile, Argentina.*(Mar. 31- Apr. 13)*
34th pastoral visit outside Italy: to the Federal Republic of Germany.*(Apr. 30- May 4)*
Official visit of the President Ronald Reagan of the United States.*(June 6)*
On the vigil of Pentecost: Solemn opening of the Marian Year. (June 7- Aug. 15)
35th pastoral visit outside Italy: to Poland. *(June 8-14)*
Official visit of the President Kurt Waldheim of the Federal Republic of Austria. *(June 25)*
Celebration of the 7th Centenary of the evangelization of Lithuania.*(June 28)*
First visit of John Paul II to the Dolomites (Lorenzago di Cadore) in northern Italy for a period of rest. *(July 8-14)*
36th pastoral visit outside Italy: to the USA and Canada (Fort Simpson).*(Sept. 10-21)*
San Francisco, USA, the Holy Father meets with AIDS patients at "Mission Dolores Basilica" and embraces a little boy called Brendan. *(Sept. 17)*
Seventh Ordinary General Assembly of the Synod of Bishops on: "The Vocation and Mission of the Lay Faithful in the Church and in the World." *(Oct. 1-30)*
His Holiness Dimitrios, Ecumenical Patriarch of Constantinople, visits John Paul II, *(Dec. 3-7)* – Signing of common declaration.
Official visit with the President Raul Ricardo Alfonsin of the Republic of Argentina. *(Dec. 11)*
Seventh papal encyclical "Sollicitudo Rei Socialis" (On Social Concerns), published February 19, 1988. *(Dec. 30)*

1988
John Paul II's Apostolic Letter "Euntes in Mundum," for the millennium of the Baptism of Kievan Rus', published March 22. *(Jan. 25)*
John Paul II's message to the Ukrainian Catholics, "Magnum Baptismi Donum"for the millennium of the Baptism of Kievan Rus'. *(Feb. 14)*

First publication of the financial report of the Holy See (for the year 1986) and the estimated budget for the year 1988. *(Mar. 3)*
37th pastoral visit of John Paul II outside Italy: to Uruguay, Bolivia, Paraguay and Lima. *(May 7-19)*
Inauguration of the "Dono di Maria" shelter in the Vatican, entrusted to Mother Teresa's Missionary Sisters of Charity. *(May 21)*
Delegation to Moscow led by Secretary of State Cardinal Casaroli for the celebrations of the Millennium of Kievan Rus'. *(June 13)*
Official visit of the President Corazon C. Aquino of the Philippines.*(June 18)*
38th pastoral visit outside Italy: to Austria. *(June 23-27)*
Apostolic Constitution "Pastor Bonus" for the reform of the Roman Curia. *(June 28)*
Fourth Consistory of John Paul II for the creation of 24 new Cardinals.*(June 28)*
Motu Proprio "Ecclesia Dei", establishing a commission for the purpose of facilitating full ecclesial communion of priests, seminarians, religious communities or individuals until now linked to the Fraternity founded by Mons. Lefebvre, who may wish to remain united to the Successor of Peter in the Catholic Church. *(July 2)*
Solemn liturgy in the Byzantine-Ukrainian Rite in St. Peter's Basilica for the Millennium of the Baptism of Kievan Rus'. *(July 10)*
Solemn conclusion of the Marian Year in St. Peter's Basilica.*(Aug. 15)*
39th pastoral visit outside Italy: to Zimbabwe, Botswana, Lesotho, Mozambique, Swaziland. *(Sept. 10-20)*
Publication of the Apostolic Letter "Mulieris Dignitatem" (On the Dignity and Vocation of Women). *(Sept. 30)*
40th pastoral visit outside Italy: to the European Institutions of Strasbourg and to the dioceses of Strasbourg, Metz and Nancy, France.*(Oct. 8-11)*
Visit with the President Ciriaco De Mita of the Council of Ministers of the Italian Republic. *(Nov. 19)*

1989
Motu Proprio instituting the Labor Office of the Apostolic See, published the 25 January 1989. *(Jan. 1)*
Post-synod Apostolic Exhortation, "Christifideles laici" dated December 30, 1988. *(Jan. 30)*
Meeting of John Paul II and members of the Curia with the metropolitan archbishops of the United States of America on the theme: "Evangelization in the context of the culture and society of the United States with particular emphasis on the role of the bishop as teacher of the faith". *(Mar. 8-11)*
Reorganization of the pastoral government of the dioceses in Lithuania.*(Mar. 10)*
Official visit of the President Patrick J. Hillery of Ireland.*(Apr. 20)*
41st pastoral visit outside Italy: to Madagascar, La Réunion, Zambia and Malawi. *(Apr. 28-May 6)*

Official visit of the President George Bush of the United States of America. *(May 27)*

42nd pastoral trip outside Italy: Norway, Iceland, Finland, Denmark, Sweden. *(June 1-10)*

Restoration of diplomatic relations between Poland and the Holy See.*(July 17)*

Apostolic Exhortation, "Redemptoris Custos" (On St. Joseph).*(Aug. 15)*

Angelus message in which the Pope reveals his wish to personally go to Lebanon as soon as possible. *(Aug. 15)*

43rd pastoral visit outside Italy: to Santiago de Compostela for the 4th World Youth Day. *(Aug. 19-21)*

Apostolic Letter for the 50th anniversary of the beginning of the Second World War. *(Aug. 27)*

Appeal to the followers of Islam in favour of Lebanon.*(Sept. 7)*

Apostolic Letter to all Bishops of the Catholic Church on the situation in Lebanon. World Day of Prayer for Peace in Lebanon. *(Sept. 7)*

Official visit of Archbishop of Canterbury Robert Runcie, *(Sept. 29 -Oct.2)* – Signing of common Delaration.

44th pastoral visit outside Italy: to Seoul (Korea), Indonesia and Mauritius. *(Oct. 6-10)*

Meeting of the diocesan bishops of the Federal Republic of Germany with the Holy Father on the theme: "Handing the faith to the next generation and the pastoral work of catechesis". *(Nov. 13-14)*

Official visit of the President Mikhail Gorbaciov of the USSR.*(Dec. 1)*

New appointment of bishops in Czechoslovakia. *(Dec. 21)*

1990

45th pastoral visit outside Italy: to Cape Verde, Guinea Bissau, Mali, Burkina Faso, and Chad. *(Jan. 25-Feb.1)*

Exchange of official representatives at the level of the apostolic nuncio and special ambassador between the Holy See and the Soviet government. *(Mar. 15)*

46th pastoral visit outside Italy: to Czechoslovakia. *(Apr. 21-22)*

John Paul II announces a Special Assembly for Europe of the Synod of Bishops in Velehrad. *(Apr. 22)*

Official visit of the President Mario Soares of the Portugal. *(Apr. 27)*

47th pastoral visit outside Italy: to Mexico and Curaçao. *(May 6-14)*

48th pastoral visit outside Italy: to Malta. *(May 25-27)*

During his Angelus message John Paul II makes an appeal for peace in the Persian Gulf, following the invasion of Kuwait by Iraq. *(Aug. 26)*

49th pastoral visit outside Italy: to Tanzania, Burundi, Rwanda and Ivory Coast. *(Sept. 1- 10)*

Eighth General Assembly of the Synod of Bishops on the theme: "The Formation of Priests in Circumstances of the Present Day". *(Sept. 30-Oct. 28)*

Promulgation of the Code of Canons for the Eastern Churches. *(Oct. 18)*

"Ad limina" visit of Vietnamese bishops: for the first time all bishops are present. *(Nov. 24)*

John Paul II accepts the resignation of the Cardinal Secretary of State Agostino Casaroli and appoints Archbishop Angelo Sodano Pro-Secretary of State. *(Dec. 1)*

Papal appeal for peace in the Gulf, message taken from the Holy Father's Christmas "Urbi et Orbi". *(Dec. 25)*

1991

Letter to the U.S. President George Bush and to the President Sadam Hussein of Iraq, in an attempt to avert the Gulf War. *(Jan. 15)*

Eighth papal encyclical "Redemptoris missio" of December 7,1990. *(Jan. 22)*

Official visit of the President Lech Walesa of the Polish Republic.*(Feb. 5)*

Meeting at the Vatican of episcopal representatives from the countries directly implicated in the Gulf War. *(Mar. 4-5)*

Second session of the Brazilian Episcopate and representatives of the Roman Curia. *(Mar. 8-9)*

Fourth Plenary Meeting of the College of Cardinals on the theme: "The Church facing the threat against human life and the challenge of the sects."*(Apr. 4-7)*

Meeting of the presidents of Episcopal Conferences concerning the economic problems of the Holy See and the financial contribution of the bishops (Canon 1271, CCL).*(Apr. 8-9)*

Reorganization of the Latin-Rite Catholic Church in the Soviet Republic of Belarus, Russia and Kazakistan. *(Apr. 13)*

Official visit of the President of the Republic of Chile, Patricio Aylwuin Azocar. *(Apr. 22)*

Meeting of Swiss Bishops with the Holy Father and the Roman Curia. *(Apr. 29-30)*

Ninth papal encyclical "Centesimus Annus" (The Hundredth Year). *(May 1)*

Official visit of the King Karl Gustaf XVI of Sweden, and Queen Silvia. *(May 3)*

50th pastoral visit outside Italy: to Portugal. *(May 10-13)*

51st pastoral visit outside Italy: to Poland. *(June 1-9)*

Announcement of a Special Assembly for Lebanon of the Synod of Bishops. *(June 12)*

Fifth Consistory of John Paul II for the creation of 22 new Cardinals and the announcement of the 1979 appointment "in pectore" of Cardinal Ignatius Kung Pin-Mei. *(June 28)*

52nd pastoral visit outside Italy: to Czestochowa (Poland) for the 6th World Youth Day. *(Aug. 13-20)*

Holy See and Albania establish diplomatic ties. *(Sept. 7)*

Ecumenical prayer service at St. Peter's Basilica, on the occasion of the 6th Centenary of the canonization of St. Brigit of Sweden. For the first time since

the Reformation two Lutheran bishops prayed in St. Peter's Basilica with the Pope, together with the Catholic bishops of Stockholm and Helsinki.*(Oct. 5)*
53rd pastoral visit outside Italy: to Brazil. *(Oct. 12-21)*
Special Assembly for Europe of the Synod of Bishops on the theme: "So that we might be witnesses of Christ who has set us free".*(Nov. 28-Dec. 14)*
Ecumenical prayer service in St. Peter's Basilica, on the occasion of the Special Assembly for Europe of the Synod of Bishops. *(Dec. 7)*

1992

Holy See recognizes Russian Federation. *(Jan. 1)*
Holy See recognizes sovereignty of Croatia and Slovenia. *(Jan.13)*
Diplomatic relations with Croatia, Slovenia, and Ukraine. *(Feb. 8)*
Papal chirograph for the Autonoma Foundation "Popolorum Progressio", for use in Latin America on the occasion of the 5th centenary of the evangelization of Latin America. *(Feb 13)*
54th pastoral visit outside Italy: to Senegal, Gambia and Guinea. *(Feb. 19-26)*
Post-Synodal Apostolic Exhortation "Pastores Dabo Vobis", (Shepherds I give you).*(Apr. 7)*
Beatification of José Maria Escrivá de Balaguer, the founder of Opus Dei, and of Giuseppina Bakhita of Sudan. *(May 17)*
55th pastoral visit outside Italy: to Angola and Sao Tomé and Principe. *(June 4-10)*
At the Angelus John Paul II announces that he will go to Gemelli Hospital that evening for diagnostic tests. *(July 12)*
Holy Father undergoes colic resection surgery. John Paul II is released from Gemelli Polyclinic on July 26, 1992. *(July 15)*
Dramatic appeal for peace in the Balkans at the Angelus message.*(Aug. 22)*
Diplomatic relations between Holy See and Mexico. *(Sept. 21)*
56th pastoral visit outside Italy: to Santo Domingo, for the 5th centenary of the evangelization of Latin America and for the Fourth General Conference of the Latin American Episcopate. *(Oct. 9-14)*
Apostolic Constitution "Fidei Depositum," for new catechism, dated 11 October. *(Nov. 16)*
Official visit of the President Oscar Luigi Scalfaro of the Italian Republic. *(Nov. 27)*
John Paul II officially presents the Catechism of the Catholic Church to representatives from the Roman Curia and to the presidents of doctrinal and catechetical commissions of the Episcopal Conferences. *(Dec. 7)*
Bishops of Albania appointed. *(Dec. 25)*

1993

At Assisi, special prayer meeting for peace in Europe and particularly in the Balkans. *(Jan. 9- 0)*

Official visit of Giuliano Amato, President of the Council of Ministers of the Republic of Italy. *(Jan. 21)*
57th pastoral visit outside Italy: to Benin, Uganda and Khartoum.*(Feb. 3-10)*
Official visit of the President Milan Kacan of Slovenia. *(Feb. 19)*
58th pastoral visit outside Italy: to Albania. *(Apr. 25)*
Conclusion of the second diocesan synod of Rome. *(May 29)*
59th pastoral visit outside Italy: to Spain. *(June 12-17)*
Tenth papal encyclical "Veritatis Splendor", published October 5, 1993. *(Aug. 6)*
60th pastoral visit outside Italy: to Jamaica, Merida and Denver, for the celebration of the 8th World Youth Day. *(Aug. 9-16)*
61st pastoral visit outside Italy: to Lithuania, Latvia, Estonia.*(Sept. 4-10)*
Pope dislocates his right shoulder during a fall at the end of an audience in the Hall of Benediction. He spent one day at Gemelli Hospital; his shoulder is immobilized for one month. *(Nov. 11)*
Official visit of the President Carlos Saul Menem of Argentina. *(Dec. 16)*
Opening of the International Year of the Family of the Catholic Church. *(Dec. 26)*
Signing of the accord on basic principles regulating diplomatic relations between the Holy See and Israel. *(Dec. 30)*

1994

Motu Proprio "Socialium Scientiarum" establishing the Pontifical Academy of Social Sciences. *(Jan. 1)*
Letter to the Italian Bishops on the responsibilities of Catholics facing the challenge of the present historic situation. *(Jan. 6)*
Mass presided by the Holy Father Pope John Paul II in the St. Peter's Basilica for peace in the Balkans. *(Jan. 23)*
Letter of John Paul II to Families, for the International Year of the Family. *(Feb. 2)*
Motu Proprio "Vitae Mysterium" establishes the Pontifical Academy for Life. *(Feb. 11)*
Official visit of President Richard von Weizsäcker of the Federal Republic of Germany.*(Mar. 3)*
Diplomatic relations with the Hashemite Kingdom of Jordan. *(Mar. 3)*
Diplomatic relations with the Republic of South Africa. *(Mar. 5)*
Official visit of President Vaclav Havel of the Czech Republic. *(Mar. 7)*
Israeli Prime Minister Rabin visits the Pope. *(Mar. 17)*
Letter to heads of states around the world and to the Secretary General of the United Nations on the International Conference on Population and Development in Cairo, held in September 1994. *(Mar. 19)*
Vatican concert for the commemoration of the Shoah, in the presence of John Paul II and Chief Rabbi of Rome, Elio Toaff. *(Apr. 7)*
John Paul II celebrates Mass in the Sistine Chapel for the unveiling of the restored frescoes of Michelangelo. *(Apr. 8)*

Special Assembly for Africa of the Synod of Bishops on the theme: "The Church in Africa and Her Evangelizing Mission Towards the Year 2000: 'You Shall Be My Witnesses'. *(Apr. 10-May 8)*

Holy Father falls, breaks femur. Goes to Gemelli Hospital the morning of April 29. – Released from hospital on May 27th 1994. *(Apr. 28)*

Opening of the closed monastery "Mater Ecclesiae" within the Vatican walls. *(May 13)*

Apostolic Letter to the bishops: "Ordinatio Sacerdotalis" (On Reserving Priestly Ordination to Men Alone). *(May 22)*

Receives President Bill Clinton of the United States. *(June 2)*

Fifth plenary meeting of the College of Cardinals, with John Paul II participating, in preparation for the Jubilee of the Third Millennium. *(June 13-14)*

Diplomatic relations at the level of apostolic nunciature and embassy between the Holy See and the State of Israel. *(June 15)*

Holy See sends its delegation to the International Conference on Population and Development, held in Cairo. *(Sept. 5-13)*

John Paul offers Mass at Castelgandolfo for Bosnia-Herzegovina, after cancelling his planned visit to Sarajevo. *(Sept. 8)*

62nd pastoral visit outside Italy: to Zagreb, Croatia. *(Sept. 10-11)*

Ninth general assembly of the Synod of Bishops: "The Consecrated Life and Its Role in the Church and in the World". *(Oct. 2-29)*

International Meeting of Families with the Holy Father honouring the International Year of the Family. *(Oct. 8-9)*

Publication of Pope John Paul's book Crossing the Threshold of Hope.*(Oct. 20)*

Beginning of working contacts of a "permanent and official character" between the Holy See and the Palestine Liberation Organization. *(Oct. 25)*

Apostolic Letter "Tertio Millennio Adveniente" to Bishops, Clergy and Lay Faithful, for the preparation for the Jubilee Year 2000, published 14 November. *(Nov. 10)*

Sixth Consistory of John Paul II for the creation of 30 new cardinals. *(Nov. 26)*

Letter to Children in the Year of the Family. *(Dec. 13)*

1995

63rd pastoral visit outside Italy: to Manila for the celebration of the 10th World Youth Day on the theme. – Then to Port Moresby (Papua New Guinea), Sydney (Australia), and Colombo (Sri Lanka) for three beatifications. *(Jan. 11-21)*

Broadcast over Radio Veritas at Manila, John Paul II reads a message to Chinese Catholics. *(Jan. 14)*

Official visit to the Holy Father of the President of the Republic of Malta, Ugo Mifsud Bonnici. *(Feb. 4)*

The Holy See sends its delegation to the 7-day UN World Summit of Social Development in Copenhagen, Denmark. *(Mar. 6-12)*

Eleventh papal encyclical "Evangelium Vitae" (The Gospel of Life"), published March 30. *(Mar. 25)*

Apostolic Letter "Orientale Lumen" for the centenary of "Orientalium Dignitas" of Pope Leo XIII. *(May 2)*

Papal message on the occasion of the 50th anniversary of the end of the Second World War. *(May 8)*

64th pastoral visit outside Italy: Czech Republic and the canonization of Blessed Jan Sarkander and Bl. Zdislava di Lemberk. *(May 20-22)*

Twelfth papal encyclical "Ut Unim Sint" (That All May Be One), published May 30. *(May 25)*

65th pastoral visit outside Italy: to Belgium, for the beatification of Fr. Damiaan de Veuster. *(June 3-4)*

Holy Mass at St. Peter's Basilica in remembrance of the end of World War II in Europe. *(June 11)*

Visit of Ecumenical Patriarch of Constantinople Bartolomeo I *(June 27-30)*-Common declaration signed on June 29.

Letter to Women, published July 10. *(June 29)*

66th pastoral visit outside Italy: Slovak Republic, canonization of three martyrs *(June 30-July 3)* from Kosice (1916) – Marco da Krizevci, Stefano Pongracz and melchiovre Grodziecki.

Dr. Mary Ann Glendon, appointed by John Paul II as the first woman to head a Holy See delegation, addresses the 4th UN Conference on Women, in Beijing. *(Sept. 4-15)*

Visit to Loreto, on the occasion of the European Youth Pilgrimage, live link with Sarajevo. *(Sept. 9-10)*

67th pastoral visit outside Italy: to Yaoundé, Cameroon, Johannesburg/Pretoria, So. African; Nairobi, Kenya for the conclusion of the Special Assembly for Africa of the Synod of Bishops. *(Sept. 14-20)*

Post-Synodal Apostolic Exhortation "Ecclesia in Africa", signed by the Pope in the Apostolic Nunciature of Yaoundé, the first time a document is signed outside the Vatican. *(Sept. 14)*

John Paul leaves for the US, his 68th pastoral foreign visit: to NY, Newark, Brooklyn, Baltimore, *(Oct. 4-9)*; – his foreign trips now reach the 1 million kilometer mark.

Holy Father addresses UN General Assembly, commemorates UN's 50th anniversary. *(Oct. 5)*

The Holy Father receives the Bishops of Bosnia-Erzogovina, Croatia, Jugoslavia, Macedonia and Serbia. *(Oct. 17)*

Pope John Paul II participates in the commemoration ceremony on the occasion of the 30th anniversary of "Presbyterorum Ordinis" with a speech on his priesthood. *(Oct. 27)*

Commemoration ceremony of the 30th anniversary of the Costituzione Conciliare "Gaudium et Spes". *(Nov. 8)*

Apostolic Letter of John Paul II, for the Fourth Centenary of the Union of Brest. *(Nov. 16)*

One-day papal visit to Palermo, 123rd trip within Italy – for 3rd Ecclesial Convention of the Italian Church. *(Nov. 23)*

Opening Mass in St. Peter's for the Special Assembly for Lebanon of the Synod of Bishops. *(Nov. 26 – Dec. 14)*

During celebrations for the Immaculate Conception, the pope entrusts Rome with special mission for Jubilee Year 2000. *(Dec. 8)*

"Urbi et Orbi" Christmas message and blessing on Internet. *(Dec. 25)*

1996

State visit of the French President Jacques Chirac. *(Jan. 20)*

Official visit of Mexican President Ernesto Zedillo Ponce de León.*(Feb. 1)*

69th pastoral visit outside Italy: to Guatemala, Nicaragua, El Salvador and Venezuela. *(Feb. 5-12)*

Apostolic Constitution "Universi Dominici Gregis", On the Vacancy of the Apostolic See and the Election of the Roman Pontiff. *(Feb. 22)*

Post-Synodal Apostolic Exhortation "Vita Consecrata", On the Consecrated Life and Its Mission in the Church and in the World.*(Mar. 25)*

Way of the Cross at the Colosseum: meditations prepared by Card. Vinko Pulijc, Archbishop of Vrhbosna, Sarajevo. *(Apr. 5)*

70th pastoral visit outside Italy: to Tunisia. *(Apr. 14)*

Apostolic Letter commemorating the 350 years old Union of Uzhorod. *(Apr. 18)*

71st pastoral visit outside Italy: to Slovenia. *(May 17 – 19)*

The Holy See sends its delegation to Habitat II, the UN II Conference on Human Settlements: Istanbul. *(June 3 – 14)*

72nd pastoral visit outside Italy: Germany, *(June 21- 23)*.- Historical speech at the gate of Brandeburg, and the announcement of the new Synod for Europe.

Official visit by the Italian President of the Council of Ministers, Romano Prodi to the Holy Father. *(July 4)*

The celebration of the Divine Liturgy in the Byzantine-Ukraine rite, at the Vatican Basilica, on the occasion of the 400th Anniversary of the Union of Brest. *(July 7)*

73rd pastoral visit outside Italy: Hungary. *(Sept. 6 – 7)*

74th pastoral visit outside Italy: France. *(Sept.19 – 22)*

The Holy Father undergoes the surgical procedure of an appendectomy at the Polyclinic "Agostino Gemelli", stays in hospital till the 15 October. *(Oct. 8)*

The Holy Father celebrates Holy Mass at St. Peter's Basilica on the 50th anniversary of his priestly ordination with the diocese of Rome. *(Nov. 1)*

Solemn Eucharistic Concelebration in St. Peter's Basilica, Pope John Paul II celebrates mass with the Cardinals, Bishops and priests consecrated in the year 1946. *(Nov. 10)*

The Holy Father addresses the opening of the UN World Food Summit organised by FAO (UN's Food and Agricultural Organization) in Rome. *(Nov. 13)*

Presentation of the Holy Father's book titled "Gift and Mystery – on the Fiftieth Anniversary of My Priestly Ordination". *(Nov. 15)*
His Holiness Pope John Paul II receives in a private visit Dr. Fidel Castro Ruz, President of the Council of State and the Council of Ministers of the Republic of Cuba. *(Nov. 19)*
Pope John Paul II presides over the first vespers celebrated in St. Peter's Basilica on the solemn occasion of the beginning of the three year preparation for the Great Jubilee Year of 2000 – Announcement of "Holy Door" opening for December 24th, 1999. *(Nov. 30)*
Visit of the Archbishop of Canterbury and Primate of the Anglican Communion, His Grace Dr. George Leonard Carey to the Holy Father and the Church of Rome – Signing of the common Declaration by the Holy Father and the Anglican Primate.*(Dec. 3-6)*
His Holiness Pope John Paul II receives the Supreme Patriarch and Catholicos of all Armenian's, His Holiness Karekin I – Signing of the common Declaration. *(Dec. 10-14)*
Visit to Pope John Paul II by the Palestinian President and President of OLP Yasser Arafat. *(Dec. 19)*

1997
Visit by His Holiness Aram I Keshishian, Catholicos of Cilicia of the Armenians, to the Holy Father and the Churches of Rome – Signing of common Declaration. *(Jan. 23-26)*
Holy Father receives Israeli Prime Minister, Benjamin Netanyahu.*(Feb. 3)*
Official visit of Brazilian President, Fernando Henrique Cardoso.*(Feb. 14)*
Holy See and Libya establish Diplomatic Relations. *(Mar. 10)*
Opening presentation of the Holy See Internet Site. *(Mar. 24)*
Audience granted by Pope John Paul II to the President of Poland, Aleksander Kwasniewski. *(Apr. 7)*
75th pastoral visit outside Italy: to Sarajevo. *(Apr. 12-13)*
76th pastoral visit outside Italy: to the Czech Republic *(Apr. 25-27)* on the occasion of the 1,000th anniversary of the death of St. Adalbert.
Beatifications of five servants of God in St. Peter's Square including the first Gypsy Ceferino Giménez Malla, killed during the Spanish Civil War of 1936. *(May 4)*
77th pastoral visit outside of Italy: to Beirut (Lebanon) for the concluding phase of the Special Assembly for Lebanon of the Synod of Bishops. *(May 10-11)*
Pope John Paul II signs Post-Synodal Apostolic Exhortation, "A New Hope for Lebanon", at the end of a meeting with young people in Our Lady of Lebanon Basilica in Harissa. *(May 10)*
The Holy Father receives the President of Georgia, Eduard Shevardnadze. *(May 16)*
78th Pastoral Visit outside Italy; to Poland *(31 May -10 June)* – with the Canonization of Blessed Hedwig, Queen of Poland.

Two letters written by Pope John Paul II to Benjamin Netanyahu, Prime Minister of Israel and to Yassar Arafat, President of the Palestinian Authority, for the Middle East peace process *(June 16)*.

Letter to President Boris N. Yeltsin of the Russian Federation on Religious Freedom *(June 24)*.

79th Pastoral Visit outside Italy; to Paris (France) for the celebration of the XII World Youth Day *(Aug. 21)*.

Congregation for the Doctrine of Faith document entitled; "Regulations for Doctrinal Examination" *(June 29)*.

Apostolic Letter "Laetamur Magnopere", approval and promulgation, the official version in Latin of the Catechism of the Catholic Church *(Aug. 15)*.

Papal Visit to Bologna *(27-28 Sept.)* for the closure of the 23rd National Eucharistic Congress.

80th Pastoral Visit outside Italy; Rio de Janeiro *(Brazil, 2-6 Oct.)*, for the 2nd World Meeting of the Family.

Apostolic Letter "Divini Amoris Scientia" proclaims St. Theresa of the Child Jesus and of the Holy Face, Doctor of the Church *(Oct. 19)*.

In St. Peter's Square – solemn proclamation of St. Theresa of the Child Jesus and of the Holy Face, Doctor of the Church – 33rd Doctor of the Church – 3rd women after St. Theresa of Avila and St. Catherine of Siena.

Special Assembly for America of the Synod of Bishops *(16 Nov. – 12 Dec.)*. Theme of the Synod (Encounter with the Living Jesus Christ, the way to Conversion, Communion and Solidarity in America.

Holy Mass to inaugurate the 2nd year – dedicated to reflection on the Holy Spirit, in preparation for the Great Jubilee Year 2000 *(Nov. 30)*.

1998

Apostolic Constitution "Ecclesia in Urbe" – on the governing of the Vicariate of Rome *(Jan. 1)*.

Pastoral Visit within Italy to the people afflicted by the earthquake in Umbria and Marche *(Jan. 3)*. The Pope visits Annifo, Cesi and Assisi.

Visit to the Mayor of Rome, Francesco Rutelli and the town council in Capitoline Hill *(Jan. 15)*.

81st Pastoral Trip to the Republic of Cuba *(21-26 Jan.)*, and meeting with the Cuban President Fidel Castro Ruz at the *Palacio de la Revolución*.

Pastoral Visit to the house of a Roman family in the Parish of the Sacred Heart of Jesus, Prati, inaugurating the phase of the citizen's Mission and distribution of the Acts of the Apostle *(Feb. 1)*.

7th Consistory of John Paul II for the creation of 20 new Cardinals (plus two "In pectore") *(Feb. 21)*.

Audience of Madeleine Albright, Secretary of State for the United States of America *(Mar. 7)*.

82nd Pastoral Visit to Nigeria *(21 13 Mar.)* for the Beatification of Fr. Cyprian Michael Iwene Tansi.

Exchange of Ratification document of the Concordat between the Holy See and Poland *(Mar. 25)*.

Special Assembly of the Synod of Bishops for Asia *(Apr. 19)*: "Jesus Christ the Saviour and his Mission of Love and Service in Asia...: that they may have life and have it abundantly" – During the solemn opening of the Synod, the Pope announces his invitation to two Bishops from mainland China to attend – (permission to leave China was denied).

Pope's Audience with their Majesties King Alberto II and Queen Paola of Belgium *(May 15)*.

Pope John Paul's Motu Proprio "Ad Tuendam Fidem" (To Defend the Faith), with which several norms are inserted into the Code of Canon Law and Code of Canons of the Eastern Churches regarding the formulation of the profession of faith *(May 18)*.

Pastoral visit of John Paul II to Vercelli and Turin *(23-24 May)*: Veneration of the Holy Shroud.

Meeting in St. Peter's Square with the "Ecclesial Movements and New Communities" *(May 30)*.

The Holy Father's Apostolic Letter "Dies Domini," the Day of the Lord *(May 31)*.

Meeting with the Cuban Bishops, to examine the future prospects of the Visit to Cuba *(June 9)*.

Audience with the President of the National Palestiniam Authority, Yasser Arafat *(June 12)*.

83rd Pastoral Visit abroad to Austria *(19-21 June)* for the Beatification of Frs. Jakob Kern and Anton Maria Schwartz and Sr. Restituta Kafka.